SOMETHING ABOUT THE AUTHOR

something ABOUT THE AUTHOR

Facts and Pictures about Authors
and Illustrators of Books for Young People

ANNE COMMIRE

volume 29

GALE RESEARCH COMPANY
BOOK TOWER
DETROIT, MICHIGAN
48226

Editor: Anne Commire

Associate Editors: Agnes Garrett, Helga P. McCue

Assistant Editors: Dianne H. Anderson, Kathryn T. Floch, Susan A. Martin,
Joyce Nakamura, Michaelene F. Pepera, Linda Shedd, Cynthia J. Walker

Sketchwriters: William Anderson, Barbara G. Farnan,
Rachel Koenig, Eunice L. Petrini, Michael G. Williston

Researcher: Kathleen Betsko

Editorial Assistants: Carolyn Brudzynski, Lisa Bryon, Susan Pfanner, Elisa Ann Sawchuk

Production Supervisor: Carol Blanchard

Production Assistant: Cynthia G. La Ferle

Text Layout: Vivian Tannenbaum

Cover Design: Arthur Chartow

Special acknowledgment is due to the members of the *Contemporary Authors* staff
who assisted in the preparation of this volume.

Frederick G. Ruffner, *Publisher*

James M. Ethridge, *Editorial Director*

Adele Sarkissian, *Senior Editor*

Also Published by Gale

CONTEMPORARY AUTHORS

*A Bio-Bibliographical Guide to Current Writers in
Fiction, General Nonfiction, Poetry, Journalism,
Drama, Motion Pictures, Television,
and Other Fields*

(Now Covers More Than 70,000 Authors)

Library of Congress Catalog Card Number 72-27107

Copyright © 1982 by Gale Research Company. All rights reserved.

ISBN 0-8103-0081-8

ISSN 0276-816X

Table of Contents

Introduction 9   Acknowledgments 15

Forthcoming Authors 13   Illustrations Index 265

Author Index 279

Introduction

Have you ever wondered how some of your favorite characters in fiction first came to be—perhaps a lovable creature like Pinocchio or Charlotte the Spider or a terrifying monster like Frankenstein or Dracula? If so, then you've come to the right place for the answers. This volume of *Something about the Author* answers those questions and many more. *SATA* is the only ongoing reference series that features the authors and illustrators creating the books that young people are reading today. Whether you're a student, a teacher, a librarian, or simply someone who wants to know more about children's literature, you'll find the *SATA* series a storehouse of information on thousands of writers and artists.

Scope

Although *SATA* began solely as a guide to contemporary figures, the series expanded its coverage with Volume 15 to include significant contributors to children's literature from all time periods. Now earlier notables like John Newbery and L. Frank Baum can be found in *SATA* alongside current writers like M.E. Kerr and Richard Peck. A majority of the authors in the series represent English-speaking countries, particularly the United States, Canada, and the United Kingdom. However, there are also many authors from around the world whose work is available in English translation, for example: from France, Jean and Laurent De Brunhoff and Michel-Aimé Baudouy; from Germany, Erich Kästner and James Krüss; from Italy, Emanuele Luzzati and Renée Reggiani; from the Netherlands, Jaap ter Haar and Francine Van Anrooy; from Finland, Tove Jansson; from Norway, Babbis Friis-Baastad; from Japan, Toshiko Kanzawa; from Sweden, Astrid Lindgren; from the Soviet Union, Kornei Chukovsky; from Switzerland, Alois Carigiet; and from Austria, Felix Salten, to name only a few. The roster includes Newbery medalists from Hendrik Van Loon (1922) to Katherine Paterson (1981). And the writings represented cover the spectrum from picture books, humor, folk and fairy tales, animal stories, mystery and adventure, science fiction and fantasy, historical fiction, poetry and nonsense verse, to drama, biography, and nonfiction.

The illustrators that you'll find in *SATA* are an equally varied and distinguished group. They include the past masters of children's book illustration, like Kate Greenaway, Walter Crane, Jessie Willcox Smith, Arthur Rackham, and Ernest L. Shepard, as well as such contemporary notables as Maurice Sendak, Leonard Weisgard, Barbara Cooney, and Nancy Ekholm Burkert. There are Caldecott medalists from Dorothy Lathrop (1938) to Arnold Lobel (1981); cartoonists like Charles Schulz, Walt Kelly, Hank Ketcham, and Georges Remi ("Hergé"); photographers like Jill Krementz, Tana Hoban, and Bruce McMillan; and filmmakers like Walt Disney and Alfred Hitchcock.

What a *SATA* Sketch Provides

In every *SATA* sketch the editors attempt to give as complete a picture of the person's life and work as possible. In some cases that full range of information may simply be unavailable, or a biographee may choose not to reveal complete personal details. The information that the editors attempt to provide in every sketch is arranged in the following categories:

1. The "head" of the sketch gives

    —the most complete form of the name,
    —any part of the name not commonly used, included in parentheses,
    —birth and death dates, if known; a (?) indicates a discrepancy in published sources,
    —pseudonyms or name variants under which the person has had books published or is publicly known, in parentheses in the second line.

2. "Personal" section gives

    —date and place of birth and death,
    —parents' names and occupations,

—name of spouse, date of marriage, names of children,
—educational institutions attended, degrees received, and dates,
—religious and political affiliations,
—agent's name and address,
—home and/or office address.

3. "Career" section gives

—name of employer, position, and dates for each career post,
—military service,
—memberships,
—awards and honors.

4. "Writings" section gives

—title, first publisher and date of publication, and illustration information for each book written; revised editions and other significant editions for books with particularly long publishing histories; genre, when known.

5. "Adaptations" section gives

—title, major performers, producer, and date of all known reworkings of an author's material in another medium, like movies, filmstrips, television, recordings, plays, etc.

6. "Sidelights" section gives

—commentary on the life or work of the biographee either directly from the person (and often written specifically for the *SATA* sketch), or gathered from biographies, diaries, letters, interviews, or other published sources.

7. "For More Information See" section gives

—books, feature articles, films, plays, and reviews in which the biographee's life or work has been treated.

How a *SATA* Sketch Is Compiled

A *SATA* sketch progresses through a series of steps. If the biographee is living, the *SATA* editors try to gain information directly from him or her through a questionnaire. From the information that the biographee supplies, the editors prepare a sketch, filling in any essential missing details with research. The author or illustrator is then sent a copy of the sketch to check for accuracy and completeness.

If the biographee is deceased or cannot be reached by questionnaire, the *SATA* editors examine a wide variety of published sources to gather information for a sketch. Biographical sources are searched with the aid of Gale's *Biography and Genealogy Master Index*. Bibliographic sources like the *National Union Catalog*, the *Cumulative Book Index, American Book Publishing Record,* and the *British Museum Catologue* are consulted, as are book reviews, feature articles, published interviews, and material sometimes obtained from the biographee's family, publishers, agent, or other associates.

For each sketch presented in *SATA*, the editors also attempt to locate a photograph of the biographee as well as representative illustrations from his or her books. After surveying the available books which the biographee has written and/or illustrated, and then making a selection of appropriate photographs and illustrations, the editors request permission of the current copyright holders to reprint the material. In the case of older books for which the copyright may have passed through several hands, even locating the current copyright holder is often a long and involved process.

Other Information Features in *SATA*

Brief Entries, first introduced in Volume 27, are now a regular feature of *SATA*. Brief Entries present essentially the same types of information found in a full sketch, but do so in a capsule form and without illustration. The editors hope that these entries will give you useful and timely information while the more time-consuming process of attempting to compile a full-length sketch continues. In Volume 29 you'll find Brief Entries for Carol Ann Bales, John Donovan, and Jim Kenealy, among others.

Obituaries are another regular feature of *SATA*. An obituary in *SATA* is intended not only as a death notice, but also as a concise view of a person's life and work. Obituaries appear not only for persons listed in *SATA* prior to their death, but also for people who have not yet appeared in the series. In Volume 29 obituaries mark the recent deaths of Harriet Adams, Phyllis Fenner, and Sharon Lerner, for example.

Revised sketches became a regular element in the *SATA* series with Volume 25. For each succeeding volume the editors select from among the early *SATA* listees those authors and illustrators who remain of interest to today's young readers and who have been active enough to require extensive revision of their earlier sketches. The sketch for a given biographee may be revised as often as there is substantial new information to provide. In Volume 29 you'll find revised sketches for Irving Adler, Carolyn Haywood, Jesse Jackson, Millicent Selsam, Margery Sharp, Elizabeth Borton de Treviño, and E.B. White.

Highlights of This Volume

Here are some of the people in Volume 29 that you'll find particularly interesting:

JEAN FRITZ.....,the daughter of American missionaries, was born in China and grew up there among children of many nationalities. With a need to find her own roots, she began, as she puts it, "...to wander about in history, getting to know the people I [found] there...." She became so well acquainted with the people she discovered there that she is now one of the foremost writers of historical fiction for young people. Her book *Traitor: The Case of Benedict Arnold* was among the 1982 American Book Award finalists.

EDWARD GOREY......well-known for illustrating such highly-acclaimed children's books as *The Shrinking of Treehorn* and for his Tony Award-winning costume and set designs for the Broadway production of "Dracula." Perhaps Gorey best summed up the highly individualistic style of his work and his life when he admitted, "I always did have a leaning toward the bizarre....I'm not someone easily unnoticed....I've always tended to run around in tennis shoes, fur coats, and lots of jewelry."

CARLO LORENZINI......whose career took many turns—seminarian, journalist, minor government official, and volunteer fighter for Italian independence. But it was only an accidental turn in his career that made him the famous "Carlo Collodi," creator of *Pinocchio*.

MARGERY SHARP......the British author who wrote successful adult novels for thirty years before she ventured into children's books. But her first attempt was a winner—*The Rescuers*—which introduced the Prisoners Aid Society of Mice, captivated the hearts of children everywhere, and set the stage for the popular "Miss Bianca" series that followed.

MARY SHELLEY......at age nineteen, a most unlikely originator of one of our favorite "ghost" stories. And yet, if Switzerland hadn't been so rainy in the summer of 1816, we might never have had a "Frankenstein." See why in her *SATA* sketch.

BRAM STOKER......who was not long remembered for his newspaper work, nor for managing the business affairs of the noted actor Henry Irving, nor even for the seventeen books he wrote—that is, with the notable exception of one book called *Dracula*.

E.B. WHITE......who does the unexpected exceptionally well. You might not expect that a life-long working journalist with strong ties to the *New Yorker* and *Harper's* magazine would also write for children. And if he did, you might not expect that three books would make him a very important writer—unless of course those books were *Stuart Little, Charlotte's Web,* and *The Trumpet of the Swan,* which together garnered a Newbery honor citation, Lewis Carroll Shelf Award, National Book Award nomination, International Board on Books for Young People honor citation, and numerous state-wide awards.

LAURA INGALLS WILDER......whose girlhood is known to millions of fans thanks to the TV series that dramatized her "Little House on the Prairie" books. Wilder was in her sixties before she wrote her first book, and then only at the urging of her daughter Rose Wilder Lane, who also appears in this *SATA* volume. Convinced at first that her book was important only to preserve family memories, Wilder was astonished at the public interest it aroused. She finally came to realize, as her readers already had, that her books helped to preserve a part of the American past that today's young people could never know first-hand.

JOHANN DAVID VON WYSS......the eighteenth-century minister whose *Swiss Family Robinson* has earned him a permanent place in children's literature, even though he never intended it. Just for his family's entertainment, Wyss borrowed the idea from Defoe's *Robinson Crusoe* and made up his own version of the story, adding characters that were like his own four sons. Wyss never meant the manuscript he wrote to go beyond his own home; but thanks to his sons, that fireside tale has survived for more than 170 years.

We hope you find these and all the sketches in *SATA* both interesting and useful. Please write and tell us if we can make *SATA* even more helpful for you.

A Partial List of Authors and Illustrators
Who Will Appear in Forthcoming Volumes of
Something about the Author

Abels, Harriette S.
Adamson, George Worsley 1913-
Adrian, Mary
Ahlberg, Allan
Ahlberg, Janet
Alcorn, John 1935-
Allard, Harry
Allen, Agnes B. 1898-1959
Anastasio, Dina 1941-
Anderson, Brad 1924-
Andrist, Ralph K. 1914-
Armstrong, Louise
Arneson, D.J. 1935-
Ashley, Bernard 1935-
Axeman, Lois
Ayme, Marcel 1902-1967
Bang, Betsy
Barber, Richard 1941-
Barker, Carol 1938-
Barkin, Carol
Barnett, Moneta 1922-1976
Bartlett, Margaret F. 1896-
Batson, Larry 1930-
Becker, May Lamberton 1873-1958
Beim, Jerrold 1910-1957
Beim, Lorraine 1909-1951
Bernheim, Evelyne 1935-
Bernheim, Marc 1924-
Bjorklund, Lorence F. 1915(?)-
Blumberg, Rhoda 1917-
Boegehold, Betty 1913-
Boning, Richard A.
Bowden, Joan C. 1925-
Bracken, Carolyn
Bram, Elizabeth 1948-
Brewton, Sara W.
Bridgman, Elizabeth P. 1921-
Brock, C(harles) E(dmond) 1870-1938
Broekel, Ray 1923-
Broger, Achim 1944-
Bronin, Andrew 1947-
Bronson, Wilfrid 1894-
Brown, Fern G. 1918-
Brown, Roy Frederick 1921-
Bruna, Dick 1927-
Bryan, Ashley F. 1923-
Burchard, Marshall
Burgess, Gelett 1866-1951
Burke, David 1927-
Burstein, Chaya
Butler, Hal 1913-
Camps, Luis
Carey, M. V. 1925-
Carmer, Carl 1893-1976
Carroll, Ruth R. 1899-
Cauley, Lorinda B.
Charles, Donald
Chase, Catherine
Choate, Judith

Christopher, John 1922-
Clark, Leonard 1905-1981
Clyne, Patricia E.
Cohen, Joel H.
Cole, Joanna
Cooper, Elizabeth Keyser 1910-
Cosgrove, Margaret 1926-
Cox, William R. 1901-
Craik, Dinah M. 1826-1887
Crews, Donald
Curtis, Bruce 1944-
Dabcovich, Lydia
Danziger, Paula 1944-
Darley, F(elix) O(ctavius) C(arr) 1822-1888
D'Aulnoy, Marie-Catherine 1650(?)-1705
DeGoscinny, Rene
Diamond, Donna 1950-
Ditmars, Raymond 1876-1942
Dolan, Edward Francis, Jr. 1924-
Doremus, Robert 1913-
Dorson, Richard M. 1916-
Duggan, Maurice (Noel) 1922-1975
Dumas, Philippe 1940-
East, Ben
Eastman, Philip D. 1909-
Edwards, Audrey 1947-
Ehlert, Lois Jane 1934-
Eisenberg, Lisa
Elgin, Kathleen 1923-
Elwood, Roger 1943-
Erikson, Mel 1937-
Erwin, Betty K.
Etter, Les 1904-
Everett-Green, Evelyn 1856-1932
Falkner, John Meade 1858-1932
Farmer, Penelope 1939-
Fetz, Ingrid 1915-
Fischer, Hans Erich 1909-1958
Floyd, Gareth 1940-
Fox, Larry
Frame, Paul 1913-
Frascino, Edward
Fraser, Elizabeth Marr 1928-
Freschet, Berniece 1927-
Frimmer, Steven 1928-
Fujikawa, Gyo
Gackenbach, Dick
Gans, Roma 1894-
Garbutt, Bernard 1900-
Garcia-Sanchez, S.L.
Gardner, John C. 1933-
Garrison, Christian 1942-
Gault, Clare 1925-
Gault, Frank 1926-
Geer, Charles 1922-
Gelman, Rita G. 1937-
Gemme, Leila Boyle 1942-

Gerson, Corinne
Giff, Patricia R.
Glaser, Dianne 1937-
Gobbato, Imero 1923-
Goldstein, Nathan 1927-
Gordon, Shirley
Gould, Chester 1900-
Grabianski, Janusz 1929(?)-1976
Graboff, Abner 1919-
Gregor, Arthur S.
Gregorian, Joyce
Gregorowski, Christopher 1940-
Gridley, Marion E. 1906-1974
Gross, Ruth B.
Gruelle, Johnny 1880(?)-1938
Gutman, Bill
Hague, Michael
Halacy, Daniel S., Jr. 1919-
Harding, Lee 1937-
Hayman, LeRoy 1916-
Heide, Florence Parry 1919-
Heine, Helme 1941-
Heinemann, George A. 1918-
Henty, George Alfred 1832-1902
Hicks, Clifford B. 1920-
Highwater, Jamake
Hirshberg, Albert S. 1909-1973
Hood, Thomas 1779-1845
Horwitz, Elinor L.
Hudson, Kirsty 1947-
Hunt, Clara Whitehill 1871-1958
Hunt, Joyce 1927-
Hurlimann, Ruth 1939-
Ingelow, Jean 1820-1897
Isadora, Rachel
Jackson, Anita
Jacobs, Francine 1935-
Jacques, Robin 1920-
James, Elizabeth
Jameson, Cynthia
Jaspersohn, William
Jewell, Nancy 1940-
Johnson, Harper
Jordan, Jael 1949-
Kadesch, Robert R. 1922-
Kahl, Virginia 1919-
Kahn, Joan 1914-
Kalan, Robert
Kantrowitz, Mildred
Kasuya, Masahiro 1937-
Keith, Eros 1942-
Kelley, Leo P. 1928-
Kessler, Ethel
Kirn, Ann (Minette) 1910-
Klemm, Edward G., Jr. 1910-
Klemm, Roberta K. 1884-
Krahn, Fernando 1935-
Kraske, Robert
Krensky, Stephen 1953-

Lawrence, John 1933-
Leckie, Robert 1920-
LeRoy, Gen
Levoy, Myron
Levy, Elizabeth 1942-
Lewis, Naomi
Lewis, Shari 1934-
Lines, Kathleen
Lisowski, Gabriel
Livermore, Elaine
Lubin, Leonard
Lyons, Grant 1941-
Maar, Leonard 1927-
MacDonald, George 1824-1905
MacKinstry, Elizabeth A. d. 1956
Maestro, Betsy 1944-
Manes, Stephen
Marryat, Frederick 1792-1848
Martin, Rupert 1905-
Mazer, Harry 1925-
McKee, David 1935-
McKillip, Patricia A. 1948-
McLenighan, Valjean
McNaught, Harry 1897-1967
McNaughton, Colin
McPhail, David 1940-
McPharlin, Paul 1903-1948
Melcher, Frederic G. 1879-1963
Mendoza, George 1934-
Meriwether, Louise 1923(?)-
Mezey, Robert
Millstead, Thomas E.
Molesworth, Maria L. 1839(?)-1921
Molly, Anne S. 1907—
Momaday, N. Scott 1934-
Moore, Lilian
Moore, Patrick 1923-
Morgenroth, Barbara
Morse, Flo 1921-
Moss, Elaine (Dora) 1924-
Mozley, Charles 1915-
Murdocca, Sal
Murphy, Shirley Rousseau 1928-
Myers, Elisabeth P. 1918-
Oakley, Graham 1929-
Obligado, Lillian Isabel 1931-
O'Hanlon, Jacklyn
Oleksy, Walter 1930-
Olson, Gene 1922-
Oneal, Elizabeth 1934-
Orr, Frank 1936-
Orton, Helen Fuller 1872-1955
Overbeck, Cynthia
Owens, Gail 1939-
Packard, Edward 1931-
Parenteau, Shirley L. 1935-
Parker, Robert Andrew 1927-
Paterson, Diane 1946-
Perkins, Lucy Fitch 1865-1937
Perry, Patricia 1949-
Peterson, Jeanne Whitehouse 1939-
Phillips, Betty Lou
Pinkney, Jerry 1939-
Plotz, Helen 1913-

Pogany, Willy 1882-1955
Polushkin, Maria
Pontiflet, Ted 1932-
Pope, Elizabeth M. 1917-
Porter, Eleanor Hodgman 1868-1920
Poulsson, Emilie 1853-1939
Powers, Bill 1931-
Powers, Richard M. 1921-
Prather, Ray
Pursell, Margaret S.
Pursell, Thomas F.
Putnam, Peter B. 1920-
Pyle, Katharine 1863-1938
Rae, Gwynedd 1892-
Rand, Ann
Rayson, Steven 1932-
Rees, David 1936-
Reiff, Tana
Reig, June
Reynolds, Marjorie 1903-
Ribbons, Ian 1924-
Rice, Eve H. 1951-
Robinson, Nancy K.
Robinson, Veronica 1926-
Robison, Nancy 1934-
Rock, Gail
Rockwell, Anne 1934-
Rockwell, Harlow
Rockwood, Joyce 1947-
Rose, Gerald 1935-
Rosier, Lydia
Ross, Pat
Ross, Wilda 1915-
Roughsey, Dick 1921(?)-
Roy, Cal
Roy, Ron
Ruby, Lois 1942-
Rudley, Stephen 1946-
Rush, Peter 1937-
Russo, Susan 1947-
Ryan, Elizabeth 1943-
Ryder, Joanne
Sauer, Julia Lina 1891-
Schaller, George B. 1933-
Schatzki, Walter 1899-
Schermer, Judith 1941-
Schick, Joel 1945-
Schiller, Justin
Schindelman, Joseph 1923-
Schneider, Leo 1916-
Schoenherr, John C. 1935-
Schuyler, Pamela R. 1948-
Scott, Jack D. 1915-
Seabrooke, Brenda 1941-
Seaman, Augusta 1879-1950
Sewall, Helen 1881-
Sewell, Marcia 1935-
Shapiro, Milton J. 1926-
Shea, George
Shore, June Lewis
Shreve, Susan
Slater, Jim
Smith, Lucia B. 1943-
Smollin, Michael J.

Sobol, Harriet L. 1936-
Steiner, Charlotte
Steiner-Prag, Hugo 1880-1945
Stevens, Leonard A. 1920-
Stevenson, James
Stine, R. Conrad 1937-
Stine, Robert Lawrence 1943-
Stong, Phil 1899-1957
Stubbs, Joanna 1940-
Sutton, Felix 1910(?)-
Sweet, Ozzie
Taylor, Ann 1782-1866
Taylor, Jane 1783-1824
Teague, Robert 1929-
Terlouw, Jan 1931-
Thaler, Mike
Thomas, Ianthe
Thompson, Brenda 1935-
Thurman, Judith 1946-
Todd, Ruthven 1914-
Tourneur, Dina K. 1934-
Treadgold, Mary 1910-
Tripp, Wallace 1940-
Tunis, John R. 1889-1975
Van Steenwyk, Elizabeth
Varga, Judy
Vass, George 1927-
Victor, Joan Berg 1937-
Villiard, Paul 1910-1974
Waber, Bernard 1924-
Wagner, Jenny
Walker, Charles W.
Walther, Thomas A. 1950-
Warner, Lucille Shulberg
Watson, Aldren A. 1917-
Watson, Nancy D.
Watts, Franklin 1904-1978
Wayne, Bennett
Weiss, Ann E. 1943-
Wellman, Alice 1900-
Whitlock, Ralph 1914-
Wild, Jocelyn
Wild, Robin
Wilkie, Katharine E. 1904-
Wilkins, Marilyn 1926-
Willard, Nancy 1936-
Wilson, Edward A. 1886-1970
Wilson, Lionel 1934-
Wilson, Tom
Windsor, Patricia 1938-
Winn, Marie
Winter, Paula 1929-
Winterfeld, Henry 1901-
Wold, Jo Anne 1938-
Wolde, Gunilla
Wolf, Bernard
Wolitzer, Hilma 1930-
Wong, Herbert H.
Wood, Phyllis Anderson 1923-
Wormser, Richard
Wright, Betty R.
Zaidenberg, Arthur 1908(?)-
Zelinsky, Paul O.
Zimelman, Nathan

In the interest of making *Something about the Author* as responsive as possible to the needs of its readers, the editor welcomes your suggestions for additional authors and illustrators to be included in the series.

GRATEFUL ACKNOWLEDGMENT

is made to the following publishers, authors, and artists for
their kind permission to reproduce copyrighted material.

GEORGE ALLEN & UNWIN LTD. Illustration by Mary Moore from *Mr. Moon's Last Case* by Brian Patten. Text copyright © 1975 by Brian Patten. Illustrations copyright © 1975 by Mary Moore. Reprinted by permission of George Allen & Unwin Ltd.

AMERICAN HERITAGE PUBLISHING CO., INC. Photograph by Duane Michals from *Horizon* magazine, November, 1977. Copyright © 1977 by Duane Michals. Reprinted by permission of American Heritage Publishing Co., Inc.

ATHENEUM PUBLISHERS, INC. Illustration by David S. Rose from *Teddy Bear's Scrapbook* by Deborah and James Howe. Text copyright © 1980 by James Howe. Illustrations copyright © 1979, 1980 by David S. Rose. Reprinted by permission of Atheneum Publishers, Inc.

B. T. BATSFORD LTD. Illustration by Marjorie Quennell from *A History of Everyday Things in England, Vol. II, 1500-1799* by Marjorie and C. H. B. Quennell. Revised edition copyright © 1960 by Peter Quennell. Reprinted by permission of B. T. Batsford Ltd.

BELKNAP PRESS. Sidelight excerpts from *Emily Dickinson: An Interpretive Biography* by Thomas Johnson. Reprinted by permission of Belknap Press.

BERKLEY PUBLISHING CORP. Illustration by Garth Williams from *The Rescuers* by Margery Sharp. Copyright © 1959 by Margery Sharp. Illustrations copyright © 1959 by Garth Williams./ Illustration by Garth Williams from *Miss Bianca* by Margery Sharp. Copyright © 1962 by Margery Sharp. Illustrations copyright © 1962 by Garth Williams. Both reprinted by permission of Berkley Publishing Corp.

BLACKIE & SON LTD. Illustration by William Stobbs from "Saturday, Sunday, Monday" in *Fairy Tales from Everywhere,* retold by Amabel Williams-Ellis. Copyright © 1963, 1966, 1977 by Blackie & Son Ltd. and Amabel Williams-Ellis. Reprinted by permission of Blackie & Son Ltd.

CAROLRHODA BOOKS, INC. Illustrations by Patt Blumer from *The Case of the Smiley Faces* by Larry Sutton. Copyright © 1981 by Carolrhoda Books, Inc. Reprinted by permission of Carolrhoda Books, Inc.

CHILDRENS PRESS. Illustration by Frances Wosmek from *A Bowl of Sun* by Frances Wosmek. Copyright © 1976 by Regensteiner Publishing Enterprises, Inc./ Illustration by Anne Siberell from *Feast of Thanksgiving* by June Behrens. Text copyright © 1974 by June Behrens. Illustrations copyright © 1974 by Anne Siberell. Both reprinted by permission of Childrens Press.

COLLIER-MACMILLAN. Illustration by Lillian Hoban from *The New Teacher* by Miriam Cohen. Copyright © 1972 by Miriam Cohen. Reprinted by permission of Collier-Macmillan.

COWARD, McCANN & GEOGHEGAN, INC. Illustration by Lynd Ward from *Early Thunder* by Jean Fritz. Copyright © 1967 by Jean Fritz./ Illustration by Tomie de Paola from *Can't You Make Them Behave, King George?* by Jean Fritz. Text copyright © 1977 by Jean Fritz. Illustrations copyright © 1977 by Tomie de Paola./ Illustration by Margot Tomes from *And Then What Happened, Paul Revere?* by Jean Fritz. Text copyright © by Jean Fritz. Illustration copyright © 1973 by Margot Tomes./ Illustration by Heidi Palmer from *The Story of Your Eye* by Winifred Hammond. Text copyright © 1975 by Winifred Hammond. Illustration copyright © 1975 by Heidi Palmer. All reprinted by permission of Coward, McCann & Geoghegan, Inc.

THOMAS Y. CROWELL CO., PUBLISHERS. Sidelight excerpts from *My Heart Lies South* by Elizabeth Borton de Treviño./ Illustration by Ellen Raskin from *Poems of Edgar Allan Poe,* selected by Dwight Macdonald. Copyright © 1965 by Dwight Macdonald./ Jacket painting by Jennifer Eachus from *The Summer-House Loon* by Anne Fine. Copyright © 1978 by Anne Fine. Jacket artwork copyright © 1978 by Methuen Children's Books Ltd./ Illustration by Robert Kipniss from *Poems of Emily Dickinson,* selected by Helen Plotz. Copyright © 1964 by Helen Plotz. Drawings copyright © 1964 by Robert Kipniss. All reprinted by permission of Thomas Y. Crowell Co., Publishers.

CROWN PUBLISHERS, INC. Illustration by Nino Carbe from *Frankenstein* by Mary Wollstonecraft Shelley. Reprinted by permission of Crown Publishers, Inc.

JONATHAN DAVID PUBLISHERS, INC. Illustration by Jane Bearman from *Jonathan: A Bible Hero* by Jane Bearman. Reprinted by permission of Jonathan David Publishers, Inc.

THE JOHN DAY CO. Illustration by Ruth Adler from *Fire in Your Life* by Irving Adler. Copyright 1955 by Irving and Ruth Adler./ Illustration by Peggy Adler from *Petroleum: Gas, Oil and Asphalt* by Irving Adler. Copyright © 1975 by Irving Adler./ Illustration by Lee Smith from *Tomato Boy* by Mariana Prieto. Copyright © 1967 by The John Day Co. All reprinted by permission of The John Day Co.

DELL PUBLISHING CO., INC. Illustration by Garth Williams from *Stuart Little* by E. B. White. Copyright 1945 by E. B. White. Reprinted by permission of Dell Publishing Co., Inc.

J. M. DENT & SONS LTD. Illustration by Charles Folkard from *Pinocchio: The Tale of a Puppet* by C. Collodi./ Illustrations by Charles Folkard from *Swiss Family Robinson* by Johann Wyss. Copyright by J. M. Dent & Sons Ltd./ All reprinted by permission of J. M. Dent & Sons Ltd.

ANDRÉ DEUTSCH LTD. Illustration by Hilary Abrahams from *Sara's Giant and the Upside-Down House* by John Cunliffe. Text copyright © 1980 by John Cunliffe. Illustrations copyright © 1980 by Hilary Abrahams./ Illustration by Charlotte Firmin from *Alex's Bed* by Mary Dickinson. Text copyright © 1980 by Mary Dickinson. Illustrations copyright © 1980 by Charlotte Firmin./ Illustration by Terry Furchgott from *Phoebe and the Hot Water Bottles* by Terry Furchgott and Linda Dawson. Copyright © 1977 by Terry Furchgott and Linda Dawson./ Illustrations by Alexy Pendle from *The Great Dragon Competition and Other Stories* by John Cunliffe. Copyright © 1973 by John Cunliffe. All reprinted by permission of André Deutsch Ltd.

THE DIAL PRESS. Illustration by Richard Cuffari from *The Runaway Bus Mystery* by Irwin Touster and Richard Curtis. Text copyright © 1972 by Irwin Touster. Illustrations copyright © 1972 by Richard Cuffari./ Photographs by Patricia Perry and Marietta Lynch from *Mommy and Daddy Are Divorced* by Patricia Perry and Marietta Lynch. Text and photographs copyright © 1978 by Patricia Perry and Marietta Lynch./ Illustration by Steven Kellogg from *Uproar on Hollercat Hill* by Jean Marzollo. Text copyright © 1980 by Jean Marzollo. Pictures copyright © 1980 by Steven Kellogg./ Illustrations by Ann Schweninger from *On My Way to Grandpa's* by Ann Schweninger. Copyright © 1981 by Ann Schweninger. All reprinted by permission of The Dial Press.

DODD, MEAD & CO. Illustration by Edward Gorey from *The Gilded Bat* by Edward Gorey. Copyright © 1966 by Edward Gorey. Reprinted by permission of Dodd, Mead & Co.

DOUBLEDAY & CO., INC. Illustration by Julie Brinckloe from *Agouhanna* by Claude Aubry. Translated from the French by Harvey Swados. Translation and illustrations copyright © 1972 by Doubleday & Co., Inc./ Illustration by Lilo Fromm from *Pumpernick and Pimpernell* by Lilo Fromm. Copyright © 1967 by Heinrich Ellermann Verlag./ Sidelight excerpts from *The Hearthstone of My Heart* by Elizabeth Borton de Treviño. Copyright © 1977 by Elizabeth Borton de Treviño. All reprinted by permission of Doubleday & Co., Inc.

E. P. DUTTON, INC. Illustration by Kenneth Longtemps from *A Rainbow for Robin* by Marguerite Vance. Copyright © 1966 by the Estate of Marguerite Vance./ Illustration by Charles Folkard from *The Swiss Family Robinson* by Johann Wyss./ Illustration by Charles Folkard from *Pinocchio: The Tale of a Puppet* by C. Collodi./ Illustration by Susanne Suba from *A Flower from Dinah* by Marguerite Vance. Copyright © 1962 by Marguerite Vance and Susanne Suba./ Illustration by Bob Barner from *Elephant Facts* by Bob Barner. Copyright © 1979 by Bob Barner. All reprinted by permission of E. P. Dutton, Inc.

FABER & FABER LTD. Cover design by Dave Griffiths from *The Ready-Made Family* by Antonia Forest. Copyright © 1967 by Antonia Forest./ Illustration by Shirley Hughes from *Mrs. Pinny and the Blowing Day* by Helen Morgan. Copyright © 1968 by Helen Morgan. Both reprinted by permission of Faber & Faber Ltd.

FARRAR, STRAUS & GIROUX, INC. Jacket illustration by Enrico Arno from *I, Juan de Pareja* by Elizabeth Borton de Treviño. Copyright © 1965 by Elizabeth Borton de Treviño./ Illustration by Enrico Arno from *Turi's Poppa* by Elizabeth Borton de Treviño. Copyright © 1968 by Elizabeth Borton de Treviño. Both reprinted by permission of Farrar, Straus & Giroux, Inc.

FOUR WINDS PRESS. Jacket design by Michael Ng from *Maybe Next Summer* by Don Schellie. Copyright © 1980 by Don Schellie. Reprinted by permission of Four Winds Press (a division of Scholastic, Inc.).

GARDEN CITY PUBLISHING CO., INC. Illustration by T. H. Robinson from *The Swiss Family Robinson* by Johann Wyss. Reprinted by permission of Garden City Publishing Co., Inc.

GARLAND PUBLISHING, INC. Sidelight excerpts from the preface to *E. B. White: A Bibliographic Catalogue of Printed Materials in the Department of Rare Books, Cornell University Library,* compiled by Katherine Romans Hall. Copyright © 1979 by E. B. White. Reprinted by permission of Garland Publishing, Inc.

GROSSET & DUNLAP, INC. Illustration by Fritz Kredel from *The Adventures of Pinocchio* by C. Collodi. Copyright 1946 by Grosset & Dunlap, Inc./ Illustrations by Lynd Ward from *The Swiss Family Robinson* by Johann Wyss. Copyright 1949 by Grosset & Dunlap, Inc. All reprinted by permission of Grosset & Dunlap, Inc.

HARCOURT BRACE JOVANOVICH, INC. Sidelight excerpts from *George Orwell: A Life* by Bernard Crick./ Sidelight excerpts from *The Collected Essays, Journalism, and Letters of George Orwell, Vol. I,* edited by Sonia Orwell and Ian Angus./ Sidelight excerpts from *The Collected Essays, Journalism, and Letters of George Orwell, Vol. III,* edited by Sonia Orwell and Ian Angus./ Sidelight excerpts from *The Collected Essays, Journalism, and Letters of George Orwell, Vol. IV,* edited by Sonia Orwell and Ian Angus./ Illustration by Edward Gorey from *Old Possum's Book of Practical Cats* by T. S. Eliot. Copyright 1939 by T. S. Eliot. Copyright renewed © 1967 by Esme Valerie Eliot. Illustrations copyright © 1982 by Edward Gorey. All reprinted by permission of Harcourt Brace Jovanovich, Inc.

HARPER & ROW, PUBLISHERS, INC. Sidelight excerpts from *Emily Dickinson's Home* by Millicent Todd Bingham. Copyright 1955 by Millicent Todd./ Illustration by Harold James from *Tessie* by Jesse Jackson. Copyright © 1968 by Jesse Jackson./ Illustration by Doris Spiegel from *Call Me Charley* by Jesse Jackson. Copyright 1945 by Jesse Jackson./ Illustrations from *Let the Hurricane Roar* by Rose Wilder Lane. Copyright 1933 by Rose Wilder Lane./ Sidelight excerpts from *On the Way Home* by Laura Ingalls Wilder. Copyright © 1962 by Roger Lea MacBride./ Illustration by Arnold Lobel from *Let's Get Turtles* by Millicent E. Selsam. Text copyright © 1965 by Millicent E. Selsam. Pictures copyright © 1965 by Arnold Lobel./ Illustration by Tomi Ungerer from *Seeds and More Seeds* by Millicent E. Selsam. Text copyright © 1959 by Millicent E. Selsam. Pictures copyright © 1959 by Jean Thomas Ungerer./ Photograph from *Letters of E. B. White,* collected and edited by Dorothy Lobrano Guth. Copyright © 1976 by E. B. White./ Sidelight excerpts from "The Years of Wonder," in *The Points of My Compass* by E. B. White. Copyright © 1961 by E. B. White./ Illustration by Garth Williams from *Charlotte's Web* by E. B. White. Copyright 1952 by E. B. White./ Illustration by Edward Frascino from *The Trumpet of the Swan* by E. B. White. Text copyright © 1970 by E. B. White. Illustration copyright © 1970 by Edward Frascino./ Illustrations by Deborah Ray from *I Have a Sister—My Sister Is Deaf* by Jeanne Whitehouse Peterson. Text copyright © 1977 by Jeanne Whitehouse Peterson. Illustrations copyright © 1977 by Ray Studios, Inc./ Sidelight excerpts from *West from Home: Letters of Laura Ingalls Wilder to Almanzo./* Sidelight excerpts from *The First Four Years* by Laura Ingalls Wilder./ Illustration by Garth Williams from *Little Town on the Prairie* by Laura Ingalls Wilder. Text copyright 1941 by Laura Ingalls Wilder. Copyright renewed © 1969 by Charles F. Lamkin, Jr. Pictures copyright 1953 by Garth Williams./ Illustration by Garth Williams from *By the Shores of Silver Lake* by Laura Ingalls Wilder. Text copyright 1939 by Harper & Brothers. Pictures copyright 1953 by Garth Williams./ Illustration by Garth Williams from *Little House in the Big Woods* by Laura Ingalls Wilder. Text copyright 1932 by Laura Ingalls Wilder. Copyright renewed © 1959 by Roger L. MacBride. Pictures copyright 1953 by Garth Williams./ Illustration by Garth Williams from *Little House on the Prairie* by Laura Ingalls Wilder. Text copyright 1935 by Laura Ingalls Wilder. Copyright renewed © 1963 by Roger L. MacBride. Pictures copyright 1953 by Garth Williams./ Illustration by Garth Williams from *The Long Winter* by Laura Ingalls Wilder. Text copyright 1940 by Laura Ingalls Wilder. Copyright renewed © 1968 by Roger L. MacBride. Pictures copyright 1953 by Garth Williams./ Illustration by Garth Williams from *Farmer Boy* by Laura Ingalls Wilder. Text copyright 1933 by Laura Ingalls Wilder. Copyright renewed © 1961 by Roger L. MacBride. Pictures copyright 1953 by Garth Williams. All reprinted by permission of Harper & Row, Publishers, Inc.

HARVARD UNIVERSITY PRESS. Photographs from *Emily Dickinson: An Interpretive Biography* by Thomas H. Johnson. Copyright 1955 by the President and Fellows of Harvard College. Reprinted by permission of Harvard University Press.

HARVEY HOUSE, INC. Photograph by Gail Buzonas from *Women in Sports: Swimming* by Diana C. Gleasner. Copyright © 1975 by Harvey House, Inc./ Illustration by Chris Cummings from *The Little Book of Fowl Jokes* by Warren Lyfick. Copyright © 1980 by Harvey House, Inc. Both reprinted by permission of Harvey House, Inc.

HASTINGS HOUSE, PUBLISHERS, INC. Illustrations by Carol Maisto from *Seven True*

Bear Stories by Laura Geringer. Copyright © 1979 by Laura Geringer. Illustrations copyright © 1979 by Carol Maisto. Reprinted by permission of Hastings House, Publishers, Inc.

WILLIAM HEINEMANN LTD. Illustration by Satomi Ichikawa from *Under the Cherry Tree,* compiled by Cynthia Mitchell. Copyright © 1979 by Cynthia Mitchell. Illustrations copyright © 1979 by Satomi Ichikawa. Reprinted by permission of William Heinemann Ltd.

HERITAGE PRESS. Illustration by Everett Henry from *Frankenstein* by Mary Wollstone-craft Shelley. Reprinted by permission of Heritage Press.

HOLIDAY HOUSE, INC. Illustration by Edward Gorey from *The Shrinking of Treehorn* by Florence Parry Heide. Copyright © 1971 by Florence Parry Heide. Illustrations copyright © 1971 by Edward Gorey. Reprinted by permission of Holiday House, Inc.

HOLT, RINEHART & WINSTON. Illustrations by Nancy Grossman from *Evan's Corner* by Elizabeth Starr Hill. Text copyright © 1967 by Elizabeth Starr Hill. Illustrations copyright © 1967 by Nancy Grossman. Reprinted by permission of Holt, Rinehart & Winston.

THE HORN BOOK, INC. Sidelight excerpts from an article "On Writing Historical Fiction," by Jean Fritz, October, 1967, in *The Horn Book* magazine. Copyright © 1967 by The Horn Book, Inc./ Sidelight excerpts from an article "Newbery Award Acceptance," by Elizabeth Borton de Treviño, August, 1966, in *The Horn Book* magazine. Copyright © 1966 by The Horn Book, Inc./ Sidelight excerpts from an article "A Letter from Laura Ingalls Wilder," by Laura Ingalls Wilder, December, 1953, in *The Horn Book* magazine. Copyright 1953 by The Horn Book, Inc. All reprinted by permission of The Horn Book, Inc.

HOUGHTON MIFFLIN CO. Illustration by Susan Meddaugh from *Maude and Claude Go Abroad* by Susan Meddaugh. Copyright © 1980 by Susan Meddaugh. Reprinted by permission of Houghton Mifflin Co.

THE HUTCHINSON PUBLISHING GROUP LTD. Illustration by W. Heath Robinson from *Goblins,* verses by Spike Milligan. Illustration first published in *Heath Robinson's Book of Goblins,* copyright 1934 by Oliver Robinson. Text copyright © 1978 by Spike Milligan Production Ltd. Reprinted by permission of The Hutchinson Publishing Group Ltd.

ALFRED A. KNOPF, INC. Illustration by Ida Scheib from *Rocks and Minerals and the Stories They Tell* by Robert Irving. Copyright © 1956 by Irving Adler./ Illustration by Leonard Everett Fisher from *Energy and Power* by Robert Irving. Copyright © 1958 by Irving Adler. Both reprinted by permission of Alfred A. Knopf, Inc.

J. B. LIPPINCOTT CO. Jacket design by Robert Parker from *Martha Berry: Little Woman with a Big Dream* by Joyce Blackburn. Copyright © 1968 by Joyce Blackburn./ Illustrations by Edward Gorey from *You Read to Me, I'll Read to You* by John Ciardi. Copyright © 1962 by John Ciardi./ Illustration by Edward Gorey from *The Wuggly Ump* by Edward Gorey. All reprinted by permission of J. B. Lippincott Co.

LITTLE, BROWN & CO. Illustrations by George and Doris Hauman from *Poems for Youth* by Emily Dickinson. Edited by Alfred Leete Hampson. Copyright 1918, 1919, 1924, 1929, 1932, 1934 by Martha Dickinson Bianchi./ Illustration by John Schoenherr from *Incident at Hawk's Hill* by Allan W. Eckert. Copyright © 1971 by Allan W. Eckert./ Illustration by Leslie Morrill from *Bernard into Battle* by Margery Sharp. Copyright © 1978 by Margery Sharp. Illustrations copyright © 1978 by Little, Brown & Co./ Illustrations by Nancy Ekholm Burkert from *Acts of Light: Poems by Emily Dickinson.* Illustrations copyright © 1980 by Nancy Ekholm Burkert./ Photographs from *George Orwell: A Life* by Bernard Crick. Copyright © 1980 by Bernard Crick. All reprinted by permission of Little, Brown & Co.

MACDONALD EDUCATIONAL. Illustration by Kim Blundell from *The Christmas Book* by Susan Baker. Copyright © 1978 by Macdonald Educational. Reprinted by permission of Macdonald Educational.

MACMILLAN, INC. Illustration by Naiad Einsel from *The Adventures of Pinocchio* by C. Collodi. Afterword and illustrations copyright © 1963 by Macmillan, Inc./ Illustration by Attilio Mussino from *The Adventures of Pinocchio* by C. Collodi./ Illustration from *Memoirs of a London Doll, Written by Herself,* edited by Mrs. Fairstar. Copyright 1922 by Macmillan, Inc./ Illustration by Jimmie Daugherty from *King Penguin: A Legend of the South Sea Isles* by Richard Henry Horne. Copyright 1925 by Macmillan, Inc./ Scissor-cuts by Lisl Hummel from *The Good-Natured Bear: A Story for Children of All Ages* by Richard Henry Horne. Copyright 1927 by Macmillan, Inc./ Illustration from *Off with Their Heads* by Victor Wolfgang von Hagen. Copyright 1937 by Macmillan, Inc. All reprinted by permission of Macmillan, Inc.

McGRAW-HILL BOOK CO. Illustration by J. Winslow Higginbottom from *The Brothers Wrong and Wrong Again* by Louis Phillips. Text copyright © 1979 by Louis Phillips.

Illustrations copyright © 1979 by J. Winslow Higginbottom. Reprinted by permission of McGraw-Hill Book Co.

DAVID McKAY CO., INC. Illustration from *Military Customs and Traditions* by Mark Mayo Boatner III. Reprinted by permission of David McKay Co., Inc.

JULIAN MESSNER, INC. Illustration by Francis Lee Jaques from *South American Zoo* by Victor W. von Hagen. Copyright 1946, renewed © 1973 by Victor W. von Hagen. Reprinted by permission of Julian Messner, Inc.

METHUEN & CO. LTD. Photograph by Camilla Jessel from *Life at the Royal Ballet School* by Camilla Jessel. Text and photographs copyright © 1979 by Camilla Jessel. Reprinted by permission of Methuen & Co. Ltd.

WILLIAM MORROW & CO., INC. Illustrations by Judy Varga from *Once-a-Year Witch* by Judy Varga. Copyright © 1973 by Judy Varga./ Illustration by Carolyn Haywood from *Eddie and the Fire Engine* by Carolyn Haywood. Copyright 1949 by William Morrow & Co., Inc./ Illustration by Ingrid Fetz from *Eddie's Menagerie* by Carolyn Haywood. Copyright © 1978 by Carolyn Haywood./ Illustration by Carolyn Haywood from *Snowbound with Betsy* by Carolyn Haywood. Copyright © 1962 by Carolyn Haywood./ Illustration by Victoria de Larrea from *Halloween Treats* by Carolyn Haywood. Copyright © 1981 by Carolyn Haywood. All reprinted by permission of William Morrow & Co., Inc.

THE NEW AMERICAN LIBRARY, INC. Sidelight excerpts from *Narrative of the Life of Frederick Douglass, an American Slave* by Frederick Douglass. Reprinted by permission of The New American Library, Inc.

IVAN OBOLENSKY, INC. Illustration by Edward Gorey from *The Sinking Spell* by Edward Gorey. Reprinted by permission of Ivan Obolensky, Inc.

OXFORD UNIVERSITY PRESS, INC. Sidelight excerpts from *Mary Shelley: A Biography* by R. Glynn Grylls. Copyright 1938 by Oxford University Press, Inc. Reprinted by permission of Oxford University Press, Inc.

CLARKSON N. POTTER, INC. Illustration by Marcia Huyette from *The Annotated Frankenstein,* introduction and notes by Leonard Wolf. Copyright © 1977 by Leonard Wolf./ Illustration by Robert Andrew Parker from *Frankenstein* by Mary Shelley. Edited by Robert Andrew Parker./ Illustrations and photograph by Sätty from *The Annotated Dracula,* introduction, notes and bibliography by Leonard Wolf. Copyright © 1975 by Leonard Wolf. All reprinted by permission of Clarkson N. Potter, Inc.

PRENTICE-HALL, INC. Illustration by Joanne Scribner from *Bad Luck Tony* by Dennis B. Fradin. Copyright © 1978 by Dennis B. Fradin./ Illustration by Edna Miller from *Mousekin's Christmas Eve* by Edna Miller. Copyright © 1965 by Prentice-Hall, Inc./ Illustration by Polly Bolian from *Setting Up a Science Project* by Ann Stepp. Copyright © 1966 by Ann Stepp./ Illustrations by Christine Westerberg from *The Cap That Mother Made* by Christine Westerberg. All reprinted by permission of Prentice-Hall, Inc.

THE PUTNAM PUBLISHING GROUP. Illustration by Stephen Gammell from *Stonewall* by Jean Fritz. Copyright © 1979 by Jean Fritz./ Jacket illustration by Kong Studios from *Ferguson Jenkins: The Quiet Winner* by Stanley Pashko. Copyright © 1975 by Stanley Pashko./ Illustration by Marjorie Quennell from *Everyday Life in Prehistoric Times* by Marjorie & C. H. B. Quennell. Revised edition © 1959 by Marjorie Quennell./ Illustration by Margot Tomes from *Jack and the Wonder Beans* by James Still. Text copyright © 1977 by James Still. Illustrations copyright © 1977 by Margot Tomes./ Illustration by Trina Schart Hyman from *The Man Who Loved Books* by Jean Fritz. Text copyright © 1981 by Jean Fritz. Illustrations copyright © by Trina Schart Hyman./ Illustration by Jeanne Edwards from *The Swiss Family Robinson* by Johann Wyss. Edited by William H. G. Kingston. Copyright 1946 by the World Publishing Co. and © 1974 by The Putnam Publishing Group. All reprinted by permission of The Putnam Publishing Group.

HARLIN QUIST, INC. Illustrations by Józef Sumichrast from *Q Is for Crazy* by Ed Leander. Illustrations copyright © 1975 by Józef Sumichrast. Text copyright © 1977 by Ed Leander. Both reprinted by permission of Harlin Quist, Inc.

RAINTREE PUBLISHERS GROUP. Illustrations by Allen Davis from *I Love to Laugh* by Lillian Nordlicht. Copyright © 1980 by Raintree Publishers, Inc. Both reprinted by permission of Raintree Publishers Group.

RAND McNALLY & CO. Sidelight excerpts from *Counterpoint* by Roy Newquist. Copyright © 1964 by Rand McNally & Co. Reprinted by permission of Rand McNally & Co.

RANDOM HOUSE, INC. Sidelight excerpts from *Women of Wonder,* edited by Pamela

Sargent. Copyright © 1974 by Pamela Sargent. Reprinted by permission of Random House, Inc.

RUTGERS UNIVERSITY PRESS. Sidelight excerpts from *Portrait of Emily Dickinson: The Poet and Her Prose* by David Higgins. Copyright © 1967 by Rutgers, The State University of New Jersey. Reprinted by permission of Rutgers University Press.

ST. MARTIN'S PRESS, INC. Photographs from *The Man Who Wrote Dracula* by Daniel Farson. Copyright © 1975 by Daniel Farson. Both reprinted by permission of St. Martin's Press, Inc.

SCHOLASTIC, INC. Sidelight excerpts from *Books Are by People* by Lee Bennett Hopkins. Copyright © 1969 by Scholastic, Inc. Reprinted by permission of Scholastic, Inc.

CHARLES SCRIBNER'S SONS. Illustration by Martha Weston from *My Garden Companion: A Complete Guide for the Beginner* by Jamie Jobb. Copyright © 1977 by Jamie Jobb./ Illustration by Mary Moore from *Mr. Moon's Last Case* by Brian Patten. Text copyright © 1975 by Brian Patten. Illustrations copyright © 1975 by Mary Moore. Both reprinted by permission of Charles Scribner's Sons.

SHOAL CREEK PUBLISHERS, INC. Illustration by Jan Waide from *Weed* by Jan Waide. Copyright © 1980 by Jan Waide. Reprinted by permission of Shoal Creek Publishers, Inc.

SIERRA CLUB BOOKS. Illustration by Martha Weston from *My Garden Companion: A Complete Guide for the Beginner* by Jamie Jobb. Copyright © 1977 by Jamie Jobb. Reprinted by permission of Sierra Club Books.

SMITH & HAAS. Illustration by Lynd Ward from *Frankenstein* by Mary Wollstonecraft Shelley. Copyright 1934 by Lynd Ward. Reprinted by permission of Smith & Haas.

STEIN & DAY PUBLISHERS. Sidelight excerpts from *Rose Wilder Lane: Her Story* by Rose Wilder Lane and Roger Lea MacBride. Copyright © 1977 by Roger Lea MacBride, Edwin S. Friendly, Jr., and Rose Wilder Lane. Reprinted by permission of Stein & Day Publishers.

STEMMER HOUSE PUBLISHERS, INC. Illustration by Rex Schneider from *I'm Nobody! Who Are You? Poems of Emily Dickinson for Children.* Copyright © 1978 by Stemmer House Publishers, Inc. Illustrations copyright © 1978 by Rex Schneider./ Illustration by Tony Chen from *Flying Fur, Fin and Scale: Strange Animals That Swoop and Soar* by Mary Leister. Text copyright © 1977 by Mary Leister. Illustrations copyright © 1977 by Tony Chen. Both reprinted by permission of Stemmer House Publishers, Inc.

UNIVERSITY OF OKLAHOMA PRESS. Sidelight excerpts from *Mary Shelley's Journal,* edited by Frederick L. Jones. Copyright 1947 by University of Oklahoma Press./ Sidelight excerpts from *The Letters of Mary W. Shelley, Vol. I,* edited by Frederick L. Jones./ Sidelight excerpts from *The Letters of Mary W. Shelley, Vol. II,* edited by Frederick L. Jones. All reprinted by permission of University of Oklahoma Press.

VIKING PENGUIN, INC. Sidelight excerpts from *The Marble Foot* by Peter Quennell. Copyright © 1976 by Peter Quennell. Reprinted by permission of Viking Penguin, Inc.

FRANKLIN WATTS, INC. Illustration by G. Richardson Cook from *Toni's Crowd* by Ellen Rabinowich. Text copyright © 1978 by Ellen Rabinowich. Illustrations copyright © 1978 by Franklin Watts, Inc. Reprinted by permission of Franklin Watts, Inc.

WESTERN PUBLISHING CO., INC. Cover illustration by Tom Nachreiner from *Frankenstein* by Mary Shelley. Adapted by Dale Carlson. Text copyright © 1968 by Dale Carlson. Cover illustration copyright © 1978 by Western Publishing Co., Inc. Reprinted by permission of Western Publishing Co., Inc.

YOUNG SCOTT BOOKS. Illustration by Edward Gorey from *The Dong with the Luminous Nose* by Edward Lear. Illustrations copyright © 1969 by Edward Gorey. Reprinted by permission of Young Scott Books.

Illustration by Szecskó Tamas from *The Adventures of Pinocchio* by C. Collodi. Reprinted by permission of Academy of Fine Arts, Budapest, Hungary./ Sidelight excerpts from an article "On Writing Science Books for Children," October, 1965, in *The Horn Book* magazine. Copyright © 1965 by Irving Adler. Reprinted by permission of Irving Adler./ Sidelight excerpts from an article "The Education of an American," by Jean Fritz, June, 1976, in *Top of the News.* Copyright © 1976 by the American Library Association.

Sidelight excerpts from an article "According to Experts," in *Laura Ingalls Wilder Lore* by Laura Ingalls Wilder, Fall-Winter, 1980. Copyright © 1980 by William T. Anderson. Reprinted by permission of William T. Anderson./ Sidelight excerpts from an article "Stories That Had to be Told," by William T. Anderson in *American Ideals.* Copyright © 1981 by Ideals. Reprinted by permission of William T. Anderson./ Sidelight excerpts from *The Story of the Ingalls* by William T. Anderson. Copyright © 1971 by William T. Anderson. Reprinted by permission of William T. Anderson./ Sidelight excerpts from a 1966 letter from Rose Wilder Lane to William T. Anderson, taken from the personal collection of William T. Anderson. Copyright © 1971 by William T. Anderson. Reprinted by permission of William T. Anderson.

Illustration by Ron Bower from *The Ghosts* by Antonia Barber. Copyright © 1969 by Barbara Anthony. Reprinted by permission of Ron Bower./ Illustrations by Joy Batchelor and John Halas from *Animal Farm* by George Orwell. Copyright 1946 by Harcourt Brace & World, Inc. Copyright 1954 by Joy Batchelor and John Halas. All reprinted by permission of Brandt & Brandt Literary Agents, Inc./ Sidelight excerpts from *More Books by More People* by Lee Bennett Hopkins. Copyright © 1974 by Lee Bennett Hopkins. Reprinted by permission of Curtis Brown Ltd./ Sidelight excerpts from *Selected Poems and Letters of Emily Dickinson,* edited by Robert N. Linscott. Reprinted by permission of Curtis Brown Ltd./ Jacket painting by Judith Gwyn Brown from *Myself and I* by Norma Johnston. Copyright © 1981 by Norma Johnston. Jacket painting copyright © 1981 by Judith Gwyn Brown. Reprinted by permission of Judith Gwyn Brown.

Illustration by Edward Gorey from *The Epiplectic Bicycle* by Edward Gorey. Copyright © 1969 by Edward Gorey. Reprinted by permission of Candida Donadio & Associates, Inc./ Illustration by Edward Gorey from *The Gilded Bat* by Edward Gorey. Copyright © 1966 by Edward Gorey. Reprinted by permission of Candida Donadio & Associates, Inc./ Photograph courtesy of the Charles River Breeding Laboratories from *The $100,000 Rat* by Frank Stilley. Copyright © 1975 by Frank Stilley. Reprinted by permission of The Charles River Breeding Laboratories, Inc./ Sidelight excerpts from an article in *Currant* art magazine, Vol. I, No. 6, February, March, April, 1976. Reprinted by permission of *Currant.*/ Sidelight excerpts from an article "Ballet Gorey," by Tobi Tobias, January, 1974, in *Dance Magazine.* Copyright © 1974 by *Dance Magazine* and Tobi Tobias. Reprinted by permission of *Dance Magazine.*

Illustration by Alan Daniel from *Bunnicula: A Rabbit-Tale of Mystery* by Deborah and James Howe. Text copyright © 1979 by James Howe. Illustrations copyright © 1979 by Alan Daniel. Reprinted by permission of Alan Daniel./ Theater still from the New York City Opera production of "Help, Help the Globolinks." Reprinted by permission of Fred Fehl./ Illustration by Edward Gorey from *The Remembered Visit: A Story Taken from Life* by Edward Gorey. Reprinted by permission of Lanz-Donadio Agency./ Illustration by Edward Gorey from *The Gashlycrumb Tinies* by Edward Gorey. Reprinted by permission of Lanz-Donadio Agency./ Sidelight excerpts from an article "The Prose Imagination," December 15, 1966, in *Library Journal.* Copyright © 1966 by Xerox Corp. Reprinted by permission of *Library Journal.*/ Sidelight excerpts from an article "The Real Swiss Wysses," by Robert L. Wyss, December, 1954, in *Life* magazine, Vol. 37. Reprinted by permission of *Life* magazine.

Sidelight excerpts from the Laura Ingalls Wilder speech in Detroit, Michigan, 1937, taken from the collection in the Herbert Hoover Presidential Library. Copyright © 1982 by Roger L. MacBride. Reprinted by permission of Roger Lea MacBride./ Sidelight excerpts from *The Lady and the Tycoon: Letters of Rose Wilder Lane and Jasper Crane,* edited by Roger Lea MacBride. Copyright © 1973 by Roger Lea MacBride. Reprinted by permission of Roger Lea MacBride./ Sidelight excerpts from *The Hearthstone of My Heart* by Elizabeth Borton de Treviño. Copyright © 1977 by Elizabeth Borton de Treviño. Reprinted by permission of McIntosh & Otis, Inc./ Photograph by Duane Michals from *Horizon* magazine, November, 1977. Copyright by Duane Michals. Reprinted by permission of Duane Michals./ Television still from the television special "Stuart Little," presented on NBC-TV, March 6, 1966. Reprinted by permission of NBC-TV, Inc./ Television still from "Little House on the Prairie," presented on NBC-TV, part one, September 22, 1980, and part two, September 29, 1980. Reprinted by permission of NBC-TV, Inc.

Sidelight excerpts from an article "Profile: Call Me Jesse Jackson," by Ruby J. Lanier, March, 1977, in *Language Arts.* Reprinted by permission of the National Council of Teachers of English./ Photograph of Frederick Douglass from *Sojourner Truth, a Self-Made Woman* by Victoria Ortiz. Reprinted by permission of the New York Historical Society./ Sidelight excerpts from an article "Edward Gorey Inhabits an Odd World of Tiny Drawings, Fussy Cats, and 'Doomed Enterprises,'" June 3, 1978, in *People* magazine. Reprinted by permission of *People* magazine./ Sidelight excerpts from an article "And 'G' Is for Gorey Who Here Tells His Story," by Jan Hodenfield, January 10, 1973, in the *New York Post.* Copyright © 1973 by the New York Post Corp. Reprinted by permission of the *New York Post.*/ Sidelight excerpts from an article "The Faith of a Writer: Remarks by E. B. White Upon Receiving the 1971 National Medal for Literature," by E. B. White, December 6, 1971, in *Publishers Weekly.* Copyright © 1971 by Xerox Corp. Reprinted by permission of *Publishers Weekly.*

Photograph from *George Orwell: A Life* by Bernard Crick. Copyright © 1980 by Bernard Crick. Reprinted by permission of Radio Times, London./ Photograph from *My Heart Lies South* by Elizabeth Borton de Treviño. Copyright 1953 by Elizabeth Borton de Treviño. Reprinted by permission of Virginia Rice./ Sidelight excerpts from "Editor's Note," in *The Voyage of the Beagle* by Charles Darwin. Copyright © 1959 by Millicent Selsam. Copyright renewed © 1982 by Millicent Selsam. Reprinted by permission of Millicent Selsam./ Sidelight excerpts from a letter to the *Decorah Public Opinion* by Laura Ingalls Wilder, 1947, in *Treasures from Laura Wilder*. Reprinted by permission of Aubrey Sherwood./ Sidelight excerpts from an 1894 letter to the editor of *De Smet News*. Reprinted by permission of Aubrey Sherwood./ Sidelight excerpts from an article "Rose Wilder Lane," by Rose Wilder Lane, November, 1918, in *Sunset,* the Pacific monthly. Reprinted by permission of *Sunset,* the Pacific monthly.

Sidelight excerpts from *Where the Heart Is* by Elizabeth Borton de Treviño. Copyright © 1980 by Elizabeth Borton de Treviño. Reprinted by permission of Elizabeth Borton de Treviño./ Photographs from *The Story of Rose Wilder Lane* by William T. Anderson. Copyright © 1976 by William T. Anderson. Reprinted by permission of the Laura Ingalls Wilder Memorial Society./ Sidelight excerpts from *Laura's Rose: The Story of Rose Wilder Lane* by William T. Anderson. Reprinted by permission of the Laura Ingalls Wilder Memorial Society./ Sidelight excerpts from an article "Not So Easy," by Amabel Williams-Ellis, February, 1934, in *Left Review*. Copyright by Amabel Williams-Ellis. Reprinted by permission of Amabel Williams-Ellis.

Appreciation also to the Performing Arts Research Center of the New York Public Library at Lincoln Center for permission to reprint the following theater stills: "The Belle of Amherst" and "Dracula."

PHOTOGRAPH CREDITS

Claude Aubry: Jon Joosten; Joyce Knight Blackburn: Mary Ragland Photography; Mark Mayo Boatner III: R. D. Buquol; Allan W. Eckert: Henry Schofield Photographer; Jean Fritz: Marc Bernheim; Lilo Fromm: Isolde Ohlbaum; Diana Gleasner: Bill Gleasner; Nancy Grossman: M. Kroplier; Carolyn Haywood: Lotte Meitner-Graf; Mary Leister: Charles L. Smith; Alice Munro: Sheila Munro; Don Schellie: Tucson Citizen Photo; Barbara Smucker: Kitchener-Waterloo Record; James Still: Dean Cadle; Jan Waide: Jim Pitts.

something about the author

ABRAHAMS, Hilary (Ruth)   1938-

PERSONAL: Born April 18, 1938, in London, England; married Jan van de Watering (a graphic designer), September 2, 1963; children: Saskia. *Education:* St. Martin's School of Art, National Diploma in Design, 1959; Royal College of Art, Arca, 1962. *Residence:* Cambridge, England.

CAREER: Free-lance book illustrator, 1962—. Has held various teaching positions at Rochester art schools, Cambridge College of Art and community center art classes.

ILLUSTRATOR—All for children, except as indicated: Anthony Abrahams, *Polonius Penguin Comes to Town,* Dobson, 1963; Abrahams, *Polonius Penguin Learns to Swim,* Dobson, 1963, F. Watts, 1964; Noel Streatfeild, *The First Book of the Opera,* F. Watts, 1966; Abrahams, *Polonius Penguin and the Flying Doctor,* F. Watts, 1966; Jean G. Hughes, *Queen of the Desert: The Story of Lady Hester Stanhope,* Macmillan (London), 1967; John Harris, *Sam and the Kite,* Hutchinson, 1968; Harris, *Sir Sam and the Dragon,* Hutchinson, 1968.

Cyril Niven, *Danger at the Zoo,* Methuen, 1970; Lev Nikolaevich Tolstoi, *How Varinka Grew Up in a Single Night,* translated by Ivy Low Litvinov, Dobson, 1966, F. Watts, 1970; Niven, *The Runaway Lion,* Methuen, 1970; Niven, *The Vanishing Children,* Methuen, 1970; Althea, *Life in a Castle,* Colourmaster International, 1972; David Close, *School Discipline* (adult), Cambridge Aids to Learning, 1972; Althea, *All about Poppies and Bluebells and Things,* Dinosaur Publications, 1973;

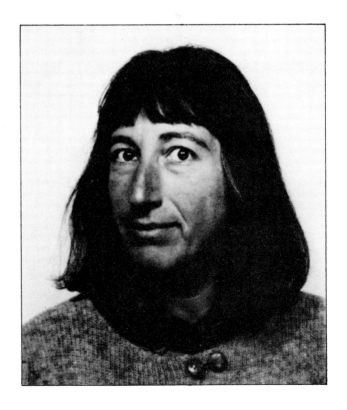

HILARY ABRAHAMS

Sara climbed into the kitchen. Most of the things were screwed to the walls. Cupboards, work-surfaces, cooker, deep-freeze and refrigerator hung above her. The toaster and electric-kettle swung from their wires. All the food had fallen out of the deep-freeze, and lay thawing on the ceiling. Sara scooped up a big handful of strawberries, and ate them. They were delicious. Piles of tins and packets lay all over the ceiling, where they had spilled out of the cupboards.

"How are we going to do the washing-up?" said Sara, looking up at the sink, with the plug dangling from its chain. Then she went to look at the lounge, where upside-down television was on show.

(From *Sara's Giant and the Upside-Down House* by John Cunliffe. Illustrated by Hilary Abrahams.)

Althea, *Bridges,* Colourmaster International, 1973; Barbara Willard, *Jubilee!,* Heinemann, 1973; Margery Sharp, *The Children Next Door,* Heinemann, 1974; William Sansom, *Skimpy,* Deutsch, 1974.

Mike Graham-Cameron, *The Farmer,* Dinosaur Publications, 1975, Merrimack Book Services, 1978; Helen Young, *Magic Balloon, Sleeping Chair,* Deutsch, 1975; Edna Jenkins, *Ar y fferm,* Macmillan, 1978; Mike Graham-Cameron, *Cage Birds,* Dinosaur Publications, 1978; Edward Ramsbottom and Joan Redmayne, *Where Is It From?,* Macmillan, 1978; Estelle Corney, *Pa's Top Hat,* Deutsch, 1980; John Cunliffe, *Sara's Giant and the Upside-Down House,* Deutsch, 1980; George Sand, *Wings of Courage,* Kestrel, 1982.

SIDELIGHTS: "I think the illustrations in a book should greatly expand the story, not be part of it (this is an ideal and doesn't always work). I love adding small things that aren't in the text but could be there. Of course, it's *really* important not to contradict the text. I try very hard not to make mistakes when I'm illustrating a book. It's something that I found very upsetting as a child and I try hard not to do it to children today.

"My drawings are sometimes considered old-fashioned, which isn't a surprise since I grew up with Ardizzone drawings in the nursery. In art school drawing was everything. Colored books were rare, so one mostly drew in pen. All very old-fashioned, perhaps, but the great thing was that we were *taught* to *illustrate* the *book*—not improve ourselves on it.

"I draw with an Oriental pen that is no longer manufactured, but I discovered the address of the manufacturer and bought several gross from them, which I guard very carefully for I fear I shall never learn to draw anything else without them.

"I love doing anything creative with my hands and sitting in the sun whenever the English weather allows it—one of the bonuses of being a free-lancer."

FOR MORE INFORMATION SEE: Lee Kingman, and others, compilers, *Illustrators of Children's Books: 1967-1976,* Horn Book, 1978.

ADAMS, Harriet S(tratemeyer) 1893(?)-1982
(Victor Appleton II, May Hollis Barton, Franklin W. Dixon, Laura Lee Hope, Carolyn Keene)

OBITUARY NOTICE—See sketch in *SATA* Volume I: Born about 1893, in Newark, N.J.; died of a heart attack March 27, 1982, in Pottersville, N.J. Full-time professional writer and senior business partner. A graduate of Wellesley College, Adams began her career in 1914 as a writer for the Stratemeyer Syndicate. The firm, founded in 1906 by her father Edward Stratemeyer, published more than 1,200 books for children and young adults. Following her father's death in 1930, Adams took over the business as senior partner with her sister, Edna C. Squier, who remained an active partner until 1942. Adams remained the head of operations there for 52 years, and in the tradition of her father before her, created hundreds of chapter-by-chapter book outlines which staff writers completed. Adams wrote an estimated 200 books during her career under the

pseudonyms Carolyn Keene for the "Nancy Drew" series; Franklin W. Dixon for the "Hardy Boys"; Victor W. Appleton II for "Tom Swift Jr." and Laura Lee Hope for "The Bobbsey Twins." *For More Information See: Saturday Review,* July 10, 1971; *New York Times Book Review,* May 4, 1975; *Detroit Free Press,* October 10, 1975; *Contemporary Authors,* Volumes 19-20, revised, Gale, 1976; *Authors in the News,* Volumes 2, Gale, 1976; *Encyclopedia of Mystery and Detection,* McGraw, 1976. *Obituaries: Publishers Weekly,* April 9, 1982; *School Library Journal,* May, 1982.

ADLER, Irving 1913-
(Robert Irving)

PERSONAL: Born 1913, in New York, N.Y., married Ruth Relis (writer, illustrator, teacher), 1935 (died, 1968); married Joyce Sparer (a teacher); children: Peggy (Mrs. Richard Robohm), Stephen. *Education:* City College of New York, B.S. (magna cum laude), 1931; Columbia University, M.A., 1938, Ph.D. in Math, 1961. *Address:* North Bennington, Vt.

At first man had only one source of power for his work, the power of his own muscles....Later, many skilled crafts developed, each with its special tools. But in every case human hands manipulated the tools.
■(From *Energy and Power* by Robert Irving. Illustrated by Leonard Everett Fisher.)

CAREER: Began teaching mathematics in 1932 while attending Columbia University, and taught in New York, N.Y., high schools until 1952; taught at Columbia University, New York, N.Y., 1957-60, and at Bennington College, Bennington, Vt., 1961. Writer and lecturer, 1952—. Consultant, Educational Policies Commission of National Education Association, 1940-41; conducted courses in in-service training program of New York City Board of Education, 1947-49. *Member:* Mathematical Association of America, American Mathematical Society, Authors League, Vermont Academy of Arts and Sciences (trustee, 1975-81; president 1978-81), Phi Beta Kappa, Kappa Delta Pi. *Awards, honors:* National Science Foundation fellowship, 1959; recipient with first wife, Ruth Adler, of award for "outstanding contributions to children's literature" from New York State Association for Supervision and Curriculum Development, 1961; cited for "outstanding science books for children" by the National Science Teachers Association and the Children's Book Council, 1972, 1975, 1980; elected to Sigma Xi, 1980.

WRITINGS—For children; all illustrated by first wife, Ruth Adler, and published by John Day, except as noted: *The Secret of Light* (illustrated by Ida Weisburd), International Publishers, 1952, published as *The Story of Light* (illustrated by Anne Lewis), Harvey House, 1971; (with Gaylord Johnson) *Discover the Stars,* Sentinel, 1954, revised edition, 1965; *Fire in Your Life,* 1955; *Time in Your Life,* 1955, revised edition, 1969; *The Stars: Decoding Their Messages,* 1956; *Tools in Your Life,* 1956; *Monkey Business: Hoaxes in the Name of Science,* 1957; *Man-Made Moons,* 1957; *Magic House of Numbers,* 1957, revised edition, 1977; *Dust,* 1958; *How Life Began,* 1957, revised edition (illustrated by R. Adler, and daughter, Peggy Adler), 1977; *The Sun and Its Family,* 1958; *Mathematics: The Story of Numbers, Symbols and Space* (illustrated by Lowell Hess), Golden Press, 1958; *The Giant Golden Book of Mathematics: Exploring the World of Numbers and Space,* Golden Press, 1960; *The Tools of Science,* 1958, published as *The Changing Tools of Science: From Yardstick to Synchrotron,* 1973; *Weather in Your Life* (illustrated with P. Adler), 1959, revised edition, 1975; *Hot and Cold* (illustrated by P. Adler), 1959, revised edition, 1975.

Temperature in Your Life (illustrated by P. Adler), Dobson, 1960; *Light in Your Life* (illustrated by Ida Weisburd), Dobson, 1961; (with P. Adler) *The Adler Book of Puzzles and Riddles, or, Sam Loyd Up to Date* (illustrated by P. Adler), 1962; *Mathematics Workbooks with Self-Teaching and Learning Exercises* (illustrated by Dick Martin), Golden Press, 1962; *Color in Your Life,* 1962; *Inside the Nucleus,* 1963; *Logic for Beginners,* 1964; *Electricity in Your Life,* 1965; *The Wonders of Physics* (illustrated by Cornelius De Witt), Golden Press, 1966; *Energy* (illustrated with Viereck), 1970; (with second wife, Joyce Adler) *Language and Man* (illustrated by Laurie Jo Lambie), 1970; *Atomic Energy* (illustrated by Viereck), 1971; *Integers: Positive and Negative* (illustrated by Lambie), 1972; (editor) *Reading in Mathematics,* Ginn, 1972; *Petroleum: Gas, Oil, and Asphalt* (illustrated by P. Adler), 1975; *The Environment* (illustrated by P. Adler) 1976; *Food* (illustrated by P. Adler), 1977; (with P. Adler), *Metric Puzzles,* F. Watts, 1977; (with P. Adler) *Math Puzzles,* F. Watts, 1978; *The Stars: Decoding Their Messages* (illustrated with P. Adler), 1980.

For children; all with Ruth Adler, and illustrated by her, unless noted; all published by John Day: *Numbers Old and New* (illustrated by P. Adler), 1960; *Things That Spin,* 1960; *Rivers,* 1961; *Shadows,* 1961, revised edition, 1968; *The Story of a Nail,* 1961; *Why? A Book of Reasons,* 1961; *Your Eyes,* 1962; *Oceans,* 1962; *Insects and Plants,* 1962; *Air,* 1962, revised

IRVING ADLER

edition, 1972; *Storms,* 1963; *Your Ears* (illustrated by P. Adler), 1963; *Why and How?,* 1963; *The Earth's Crust,* 1963; *Irrigation,* 1964; *Numerals: New Dresses for Old Numbers,* 1964; *Fibers,* 1964; *Heat,* 1964, published as *Heat and Its Uses,* 1973; *Houses,* 1964; *Machines,* 1964; *Coal,* 1965, revised edition, 1974; *Evolution,* 1965; *Atoms and Molecules,* 1966; *Taste, Touch and Smell,* 1966; *Magnets,* 1966; *Tree Products,* 1967; *Sets,* 1967; *The Calendar,* 1967; *Communication,* 1967; *Directions and Angles,* 1969; *Sets and Numbers for the Very Young* (illustrated by P. Adler), 1969.

For children; under pseudonym, Robert Irving; all published by Knopf: *Hurricanes and Twisters* (illustrated by R. Adler), 1955; *Rocks and Minerals and the Story They Tell* (illustrated by Ida Scheib), 1956; *Energy and Power* (illustrated by Leonard E. Fisher), 1958; *Sound and Ultrasonics* (illustrated by L. E. Fisher), 1959; *Electromagnetic Waves* (illustrated by L. E. Fisher), 1960; *Electronics* (illustrated by R. Adler), 1961; *Volcanoes and Earthquakes* (illustrated by R. Adler), 1962.

For adults; all published by John Day, except as noted: *What We Want from Our Schools,* 1957; *The New Mathematics,* 1958, revised and enlarged edition, 1969; *Thinking Machines* (diagrams by R. Adler), 1961, revised and enlarged edition, 1974; *Probability and Statistics for Every Man* (diagrams by R. Adler), 1963; *A New Look at Arithmetic,* 1964; *The Elementary Mathematics of the Atom,* 1965; *A New Look at Geometry,* 1966; *Groups in the New Mathematics* (illustrated with Ellen Viereck), 1968; *Mathematics and Mental Growth* (illustrated by R. Adler and E. Viereck), 1968. Also author of *The*

If you walk along a dry stream bed you find piles of pebbles in the middle. ■(From *Rocks and Minerals and the Stories They Tell* by Robert Irving. Illustrated by Ida Scheib.)

Impossible in Mathematics, National Council of Teachers of Mathematics, c.1957. Contributor of articles to periodicals and professional journals.

SIDELIGHTS: **1913.** "I was born in Harlem, the third of five children. I was eighteen when I graduated from college and started working on my Master's degree, but it was not until thirty years later that I received my Ph.D. degree. The reason was that the 1930s were the depression years and I had to go to work full-time, first to help my father and mother and then to support my own family."

Adler taught in New York City from 1932 until his dismissal in 1953, during the purges of the McCarthy era. He was reinstated in 1972 and retired in 1976.

1935. Married Ruth Relis, a writer, illustrator and teacher.

1938. Received a Masters degree from Columbia University.

1952. Began writing science books, especially for children. His wife illustrated his books and helped him with the text. "People often ask us, 'How do you pick the topics of your books?' There are many answers, but I shall mention only one of them. Sometimes we choose *a topic that we know nothing about.* An unfamiliar subject offers certain obvious advantages.

First, it gives us an opportunity to learn something new, and we always enjoy learning. Second, precisely because the subject matter is new to us, we have to study, analyze, and work over it until it is simple enough for us to understand. By that time it is simple enough for anybody to understand, and we are ready to explain it to children.

"Our primary goal is to present scientific ideas so simply that they can be followed and understood by an unsophisticated reader. In this respect science writing has much in common with the writing of fiction. In her article 'On the Art of Fiction' (published in *Willa Cather on Writing,* Knopf, 1949), Willa Cather said:

"'Art, it seems to me, should simplify. That, indeed, is very nearly the whole of the higher artistic process; finding what conventions of form and what detail one can do without and yet preserve the spirit of the whole—so that all that one has suppressed and cut away is there to the reader's consciousness as much as if it were in type on the page.'

"The science writer, too, must decide what to leave out and what to put in. He must select and organize his material so that the essential idea is developed logically and clearly and is not obscured by unnecessary detail. Of course he must be careful not to distort an idea when he simplifies it. The key to presenting a complex idea simply and accurately is to break it up into its constituent parts and then to present the parts one at a time in the proper sequence.

"Simplicity of style is especially appropriate to science writing because scientific ideas are basically simple. And scientific ideas are basically simple because nature is basically simple. For example, all the chemical complexity and variety that we find in the organic and inorganic worlds is built out of a few fundamental particles—the electron, the proton, and the neutron.

"As a matter of fact, if a scientific theory about some area of study is not simple, it usually means that we don't understand that area well. As scientific study progresses, connections are found between facts that at first seemed unrelated. When the science reaches maturity with an adequate theory, all the separate pieces fit together like the parts of a jigsaw puzzle.

"Therefore, a science book is more easily comprehended if it is based on the most advanced scientific ideas. For example chemistry is difficult and confusing if it is taught as a hodge-podge of separate reactions. It becomes simple and understandable if these reactions are shown to be consequences of the properties of the atom as postulated in modern atomic theory. Thus, there is no conflict between being simple and being up to date.

"Being up to date is the second goal we try to achieve in our writing. Because of the rapid pace at which science is advancing, this goal is not always easy to reach. Sometimes, what is up to date when you write a book is out of date by the time you receive galley proofs from the printer. For example, when the books *Your Eyes* and *Color in Your Life* were written, we stated correctly that there was no experimental evidence for the Helmholtz theory that there are three different kinds of cones in the retina of the eye, sensitive to red, green, and blue respectively. Since then, the experimental evidence has been produced by George Wald and Paul K. Brown. This fact will be noted in the next printing of these books.

"A third goal we try to achieve is accuracy. This requires checking and rechecking all the information we get, no matter how reputable its source may be. Checking is obviously necessary when two authoritative sources give contradictory in-

In October 1871,...a great fire destroyed most of the city of Chicago.... The fire began on De Koven Street on October 8th, in a barn owned by Patrick O'Leary. Mrs. O'Leary's cow kicked over a lantern, which set fire to the straw in the barn. ■(From *Fire in Your Life* by Irving Adler. Illustrated by Ruth Adler.)

formation. We have discovered that it is also necessary even when several sources agree. For example, when we were gathering information for *Insects and Plants,* we found in several reputable sources the same story of how the prickly pear cactus, which choked fields and woods in Australia for a while, was originally introduced to the island. The prickly pear is the plant on which the cochineal insect feeds, and the cochineal insect is the source of a red dye. According to the story, a governor of Australia who wanted red coats for his troops introduced the prickly pear for the culture of cochineal insects. This is a rather nice story, and we wanted to include it in our book. However, according to the Bureau of Entomology of the Australian Department of Agriculture, there is no evidence to support the story. More probable is the theory that the prickly pear was brought to Australia accidentally when used as ballast in a ship that came from Galveston.

"There were several other instances, too, when we found widely accepted stories to be false. Many books have reported the occasional appearance of human beings whose eyes reflect light as a cat's eyes do. We tried to verify these stories in correspondence with Dr. Arnold J. Kroll, the scientist who has studied and photographed the tapetum, the reflecting layer in the cat's eye. Dr. Kroll assured us that, because of the structure of the human eye, these stories could not be true.

"Sometimes, to get accurate information in the form in which we want to present it to children, we have to make our own independent calculations. . . .

"So far I have been discussing errors we have discovered in other people's books. I don't want to give the impression that we think there are no errors in our own. There have been, and there probably still are errors in some of our books.

"One of the errors that crept into my book *The New Mathematics* provides a good example of how difficult it is to make a book completely free of error. In the opening paragraph of the book I intended to give the number 1.414 as an approximate value of the square root of two. I type with two fingers, however, and a slight alteration of my typing rhythm produced the number 1.141. I proofread my manuscripts several times and of course proofread the galleys and page proofs, never detecting the error. Neither did my wife, who read the manuscript, nor did the editor and the copy editor. We all looked at 1.141 and saw 1.414 as we expected to. One week after the book was published, a reader called the error to our attention. Producing accurate books is a co-operative undertaking that involves the reader as well as the author and the editor. We hope that readers who spot errors will continue to call them to our attention so that we may eliminate them in the future printings of our books.

"A fourth goal we try to achieve is unification. Science is increasingly subdivided into specialties. The scientist necessarily studies intensively small fragments of reality. To make the scientist's discoveries meaningful to the general reader, the writer should show how these different fragments of reality are related to each other. For this reason we seek unifying topics that cut across the boundaries between specialties. We try as far as we can within the scope of any one book to relate science to technology and to relate both to significant social problems. The book *Time in Your Life* is an example of one that is based on a unifying theme.

"A fifth goal we seek is to give answers to the question, 'How do we know?' It is not enough merely to present 'facts' discovered by science. It is necessary to present as well the reasoning by which these 'facts' have been established. In this age of atomic energy and space travel, the achievements of science and technology are as fantastic as the wildest creations of the writers of science fiction. If we merely ask children to believe the fantastic facts without explaining how we know them to be facts, we will be cultivating a gullible generation incapable of distinguishing fact from fiction. This is why my book *The Stars: Decoding Their Messages* does not merely present some facts of astronomy, with the usual devices for dramatizing them, but it also outlines the techniques and the reasoning by which these facts were established.

"A sixth goal we seek is to explain unfamiliar concepts by means of familiar ideas. In my book *Dust,* for example, in order to explain why dust particles, which are denser than air, can float in the air, I had to make clear first the concept that the smaller a body is, the higher is its surface-to-volume ratio. I developed the idea without using mathematics by calling attention to a familiar experience: If you break a stone into two pieces, the volume of the stone is not changed. But the total surface of the stone is increased because two new surfaces are created at the break. If you break the stone into smaller and smaller pieces, each new break adds more surface. Finally, when the stone has been ground to a powder, it has a tremendous amount of surface, but its volume is the same as it was in the first place.

"A seventh goal is best expressed negatively as a prohibition: Don't talk down to the child. Talk to him seriously about serious subjects. The stuff of science is interesting by itself; there is no need to motivate enthusiasm artificially by providing a so-called 'human interest' setting. I squirm with embarrassment whenever I read a science book that begins with conversations between Ned and his uncle as they take a walk. I am sure that the child reader squirms, too, because he is not interested in Ned or his uncle or their inane conversation. He is interested in science, and he wishes they would hurry and get to it.

"Our eighth goal is also best expressed negatively: Do not be hobbled by word lists. If the vocabulary of a book is restricted to words that children ordinarily use, how will they ever learn to use new words? A good book should help to expand the child's vocabulary. This does not mean that we should smother the ideas in the book with five-syllable words. As a matter of fact, both in speech and in writing we prefer a simple vocabulary. Whenever a short word will do as well as a long word, we habitually use the short word. However, if a somewhat longer word is necessary to avoid circumlocution, we use the longer word and explain its meaning. Where a technical word is appropriate in a discussion, we introduce the word, define it, give its pronunciation, and use it.

"A ninth goal is to convey the idea that learning is fun. Learning is a great adventure, offering the child opportunities to experience the excitement of discovery and the pride of accomplishment. We try to infuse our writing with this spirit of adventure.

"The relationship between learning and fun is two-sided. You can have fun while you learn, and conversely, you can learn while you have fun. We make frequent use of recreational activities as a teaching device. For example, we develop some solid mathematical ideas through the games and puzzles of *Magic House of Numbers.* And we introduce important ideas about reasoning and scientific method through games, jokes, and puzzles in the book *Logic for Beginners.*

"A tenth goal that we try to achieve through our books is to convey to the child a sense of history. The child is a beneficiary of a great cultural heritage that has grown through thousands of years. We try to get the child to appreciate his role as a participant in a great historical process. His mission is to receive the culture heritage from past generations and add to it before passing it on to future generations. We hope that our books help to prepare him for carrying out this mission." [Irving Adler, "On Writing Science Books for Children," *Horn Book,* October, 1965.[1]]

1960. Moved to Vermont. ". . . I live in Vermont, one of the most beautiful of states. Besides writing I take care of my garden, of which I am extremely proud. I used to raise only vegetables but . . . I [also] raised some beautiful flowers. . . ."

1968. Wife died. Married teacher, Joyce Sparer. Adler is a prominent author of over eighty-five science books for children, which he attempts to present in a stimulating and attractive way. "The resemblance between science and art is not adequately appreciated. There is a common misconception about the work of scientists and science writers. People think of a scientist as someone who gathers *facts* like a clerk taking inventory in a hardware store. And they think the work of the science writer is like recording the inventory in a hardware catalog. To see the error in this view, let us examine briefly the work of the scientist and science writer.

"The scientist bases all his work on *observation* of some segment of reality. But his observation is not like taking inventory of objects already neatly arranged in piles on a shelf. It is more like taking inventory of things jumbled in a heap on the floor. He must first separate them, identify them, and classify them according to some pattern of organization. This pattern does not flow automatically out of the things themselves; it has to be created by the scientist.

"However, there is an important way in which scientific observation is not at all like taking inventory. The *facts* of science are not simply lying around exposed to view and waiting to be seen. They have to be looked for, and, in many cases, they first have to be produced. Scientific observation is not a mere passive viewing of phenomena. It involves active intervention in the phenomena. The scientist does not merely say, 'Let me see what is happening.' He says, 'Let me see what happens if I do this and what happens if I do that.' In short, observation is closely linked to experimentation.

"When he performs an experiment, the scientist is asking nature a question, and he creates conditions under which nature will give him a clear answer. Before he performs the experiment, the scientist must first decide what question he wants nature to answer. Choosing a good question is neither simple nor automatic; it requires knowledge, insight and imagination. Getting an answer to the question is equally difficult. Nature is often reluctant to reveal her secrets. She keeps them hidden in 'a riddle wrapped in a mystery inside an enigma.' It requires skill, insight, and inventiveness to be able to create the conditions under which nature stops talking in riddles and starts giving clear-cut answers to a question. Thus, the design of a successful experiment, from asking a significant question to obtaining a clear answer, involves acts of creative imagination.

"Observation and experiment are the foundations of science, but it is important to note that they are only the foundations, and not the whole structure. Scientific knowledge is not merely a list of results obtained from experiment and observation. As

(1) the gas for cooking; (2) the fuel oil that heats the home and (3) powers the electric generator; (4) the gasoline and oil for the car, truck and tractor; (5) the asphalt of the pavement; and (6) the rubber of the tires, all came from crude oil. ■ (From *Petroleum: Gas, Oil, and Asphalt* by Irving Adler. Illustrated by Peggy Adler.)

the British scientist J. D. Bernal has put it, 'If it were, science would soon become as unwieldy and as difficult to understand as the Nature from which it started. Before these results can be of any use, and in many cases before they can even be obtained, it is necessary to tie them together, so to speak, in bundles, to group them and to relate them to each other.' The scientist puts together and relates the results of his experiments and observations to form a *theory,* which is a mental picture of the phenomena he is studying.

"The formulation of a scientific theory is sometimes compared to solving a jigsaw puzzle. But it is a puzzle with most of the pieces missing. The scientist has to use his imagination to fill in the gaps and produce a whole picture. Actually, the jigsaw puzzle analogy is somewhat misleading, because the relationship of observed facts to scientific theory is not that of part to whole. The relationship, on the contrary, is really that of conclusion to premises in a deductive system of propositions. The scientist says in his theory that if we make certain assumptions or hypotheses, then we can deduce from them conclusions that correspond to the observed facts. What a scientist does when he formulates a theory is better expressed by the closed box analogy: Nature is like a closed box containing a mechanism which controls some observable events that occur outside the box. The scientist cannot see what is inside the box. So, instead, he *imagines* what the inside mechanism must be like in order to produce the outside effects that he observes. Thus, the formulation of a scientific theory is a creative act of the imagination. Of course a theory is a creation of a special kind, whose consequences must stand up under the rigorous tests of experience.

"The science writer has the job of transmitting to the layman an understanding of the vast, complex, and growing body of scientific knowledge. He cannot do this by merely recording scientific knowledge and then playing it back like a tape recorder. The form in which scientific knowledge is reported to the community of scientists is not the same as the form in which it may be introduced to the uninitiated. Before he can present scientific knowledge to the child or to the general reader, he must rework the material in a special way. He must first select from the great mass of scientific knowledge certain key ideas that can serve to convey to the reader an understanding of the problems, the methods, and the ever-changing conclusions of science. He must break these ideas down into their constituent parts, so that when the parts are presented in the proper sequence, each is easy to understand. He must organize this sequence, so that the reader is led step by step from simple ideas to more and more complex combinations. By the use of appropriate analogies and images, he relates new ideas to familiar ideas in the reader's experience. And finally, while doing this, he must convey to the reader some feeling of the excitement of science as an exploration of unknown regions of the universe; an appreciation of the beauty of the imaginative structure produced by scientists; and a grasp of the significance of science in man's efforts to control his environment for human purposes.

"To do these things is no routine job that can be performed in a perfunctory manner. Successful science writing is, as Max Born says, 'an artistic task.' Like the discovery of new scientific knowledge or the writing of poems, plays or novels, it requires the play of a creative imagination, which, no less than artistic constructs, illuminates the structure of reality." [Irving Adler, "The Prose Imagination," *Library Journal*, December 15, 1966.²]

Adler's works are included in the Kerlan Collection at the University of Minnesota and the de Grummond Collection at the University of Southern Mississippi.

FOR MORE INFORMATION SEE: Horn Book, October, 1965, April, 1973, April, 1974, April, 1975; *Library Journal,* December, 1966; Jean Poindexter Colby, *Writing, Illustrating, and Editing Children's Books,* Hastings House, 1967; Doris de Montreville and Donna Hill, editors, *Third Book of Junior Authors,* H. W. Wilson, 1972; *New York Times,* December 2, 1976, October 26, 1977; *Nation,* April 9, 1977.

ALBION, Lee Smith (Lee Smith)

PERSONAL: Born in Rochester, N.Y.; married an attorney in 1965; children: one son. *Education:* Attended Radcliffe College, Columbia University, Art Students League, New York, N.Y., Art Center, Los Angeles, Calif. *Residence:* Miami, Fla.

CAREER: Children's book and magazine illustrator.

ILLUSTRATOR—All for children; all under name Lee Smith: Carroll L. Fenton and E. F. Turner, *Inside You and Me: A Child's Introduction to the Human Body,* Harper, 1961; Mariana B. de Prieto, *The Wise Rooster,* John Day, 1962; James Holding, *Cato, the Kiwi Bird,* Putnam, 1963; Prieto, *Ah Ucu and Itzo: A Story of the Mayan People of Yucatan,* John Day, 1964; Prieto, *A Kite for Carlos,* John Day, 1966; Prieto, *Tomato Boy,* Harper, 1967.

Contributor of illustrations to periodicals, including *Jack and Jill, Saturday Review, Gourmet,* and *Scholastic.*

ALLEN, Jack 1899-

BRIEF ENTRY: Born March 8, 1899, in Sussex, England. Author and illustrator of books for children. Allen was in training to become a teacher when he interrupted his studies to serve in the Royal Flying Corps during World War I. Following that service he pursued his interest in drawing by studying art and

The boys fished and talked. ■(From *Tomato Boy* by Mariana Prieto. Illustrated by Lee Smith.)

later worked as a commercial artist with a printing firm and for a national newspaper. It was not until his marriage to Agnes Allen, however, that he began illustrating. In 1947 the first of many collaborative works written and illustrated by the Allens was published in 1947—*The Story of the Village* (Farber, 1947). It was followed by many other successful works for children, most of them inspired by the museums, art galleries, and archaeological sites the Allens explored during numerous travels throughout Great Britain and Europe. Their books include *The Story of Your Home* (Farber, 1949, new edition, 1972), winner of the 1949 Carnegie Medal, *The Story of Our Parliament*, (Farber, 1949, revised edition, 1971), *The Story of Michaelangelo* (Farber, 1953), and *The Story of the Book* (Farber, 1953, 2nd edition, 1967). The couple's successful collaboration ended in 1959 with the death of Mrs. Allen. *For More Information See: Fourth Book of Junior Authors and Illustrators,* H. W. Wilson, 1978.

AMBLER, C(hristopher) Gifford   1886-

BRIEF ENTRY: Born in 1886, in Bedford, Yorkshire, England. British illustrator, painter, and pottery designer. Ambler received his art training at the Leeds School of Art and upon leaving school began designing and modeling pottery for the Leeds Foreclay Company. In 1910 he moved to London and spent four years doing book illustration and design before visiting Canada and the United States in 1914. During his travels, he spent a short time in Providence, R.I., where he worked for the *Providence Journal*. Ambler saw active service in both World Wars but returned to illustrating soon after World War I, specializing in drawing dogs and horses. Among his illustrated works for children are *Storm of Dancerwood* (Hutchinson, 1944), *Black Lightning* (Viking, 1954), and *Checoba, Stallion of the Comanche* (Hutchinson, 1964). Ambler also wrote several books, including *Ten Little Foxhounds* (Hutchinson, 1950, Children's Press, 1968) and *Zoolyricks* (Hutchinson, 1950), both self-illustrated. An honorary life member of the Schipperke Club of America, he designed and executed the group's memorial medallion in 1950. *Residence:* Oxford, England. *For More Information See: Illustrators of Children's Books, 1946-56,* Horn Book, 1958.

ANTHONY, Barbara   1932-
(Antonia Barber)

PERSONAL: Born December 10, 1932, in London, England; daughter of Derek (a box office manager) and Julie (a landscape gardener; maiden name, Jeal) Wilson; married Ken Anthony (a structural engineering consultant), August 6, 1956; children: Jonathan Charles, Nicholas James, Gemma Thi-Phi-Yen. *Education:* University College, London, B.A. (with honors), 1955. *Home:* Horne's Place Oast, Appledore, Kent, England. *Agent:* Murray Pollinger, 4 Garrick St., London, England.

CAREER: Writer. *Member:* National Book League.

WRITINGS—All under pseudonym Antonia Barber; all for children: *The Affair of the Rockerbye Baby,* J. Cape, 1966, Delacorte, 1970; *The Ghosts,* Farrar, Straus, 1969, published as *The Amazing Mr. Blunden,* Penguin, 1972.

"Now turn around slowly and don't be frightened by what you see."
Lucy gripped his hand as she turned around, but in spite of his warning her heart leaped into her mouth....
■ (From *The Ghosts* by Antonia Barber. Cover illustrated by Ron Bower.)

WORK IN PROGRESS: The Rough Stuff, a children's book about the Thames sailing barges at the time of the first World War; *The Women,* a series of adult novels about the changing nature of women's lives over a period of five hundred years.

SIDELIGHTS: ''I am an example of a contemporary phenomenon: the professional woman writer who takes a few years out for the fascinating experience of raising young children. After two successful children's books: both widely published and translated; I gave up writing for a while to bring up two adopted sons, intending to return to work when they reached school age. The chance to add a baby daughter, a Vietnamese war orphan, to our family delayed me again, but now that she has joined the boys in school, I have returned to writing fulltime. The marvelous years in between have been of inestimable value to me as a writer. Having seen childhood now from the outside as well as the inside, and known what it is to be a parent as well as to have them, I have a much deeper understanding of human character and relationships.

''The question children ask me most often in their letters is, 'What made you write the book about *The Ghosts!*' Answer:

Barbara Anthony with her family.

J. W. Dunne's book *An Experiment with Time,* which I read when I was seventeen, T. S. Eliot's poem *Four Quartets,* which I read when I was twenty-two, a story about a real apparition told to me by the elderly man who saw it, when I was twenty-six, and an old house I visited for a furniture auction when I was thirty-two: only then did all the other memories come together to make a story. Moral: you never know what may be useful, if you are a writer.

HOBBIES AND OTHER INTERESTS: Reading, sailing, theater.

FOR MORE INFORMATION SEE: Times Literary Supplement, June 26, 1969.

AUBRY, Claude B.   1914-

PERSONAL: Born October 23, 1914, in Morin Heights, Quebec, Canada. *Education:* University of Montreal, B.A., 1936; McGill University, B.L.S., 1945. *Home and office:* 14 Claver St., Ottawa, Ontario K1J 6W7, Canada.

CAREER: Worked as accountant, 1936-44; Montreal Civic Library (also called Montreal Municipal Library), Montreal, Quebec, Canada, chief of personnel, 1945-49; Ottawa Public Library, Ottawa, Ontario, Canada, assistant chief librarian,

1949-53, director, 1953-79; Eastern Ontario Regional Library System, director, 1965-76. Member of the board, Montfort Hospital Corporation; member of library consultants board, *Encyclopedia Canadiana;* editorial board member, *Canadian Children's Literature;* vice-president, Canadian Film Institute, 1974-76. *Member:* Canadian Authors' Association, Canadian Library Association, Society of Canadian Writers, Ontario Library Association, Alliance Francaise, Association France-Canada. *Awards, honors:* Association Canadienne des Bibliothécaires de Langue Francaise award, for *Les Iles du roi Maha Maha II,* 1962; Book of the Year for Children medal, Canadian Library Association, 1962, for *Le Loup de Noël, 1965;* invested in the Order of Canada, 1974; appointed Officier de l'Ordre International du Bien Public, 1975; Quebec Provincial Government award, for *Le Loup de Noël.*

WRITINGS—In English translation; juvenile: *Les Iles du roi Maha Maha II* (illustrated by Edouard Perret), Pelican (Quebec), 1960, translation by Alice Kane published as *The King of the Thousand Islands: A Canadian Fairy Tale,* McClelland & Stewart (Toronto), 1963, another edition translated by Harvey Swados (illustrated by Grey Cohoe), Doubleday, 1971; *Le Loup de Noël* (illustrated by Perret), Editions Centre de psychologie et de pedagogie (Montreal), 1962, translation by Kane published as *The Christmas Wolf,* McClelland & Stewart, 1965; *Le Violon magique et autres legendes du Canada francais* (illustrated by Saul Field), Editions des Deux rives (Ottawa), 1968, translation by Kane published as *The Magic Fiddler and*

Other Legends of French Canada, Peter Martin (Toronto), 1968; *Agouhanna* (illustrated by Julie Brinckloe), translated from the French by Swados, Doubleday, 1972.

Other writings: *La Vengeance des hommes de bonne volonte,* Fides (Montreal), 1944: *Miroirs deformants,* Fides, 1945; (with Laurent G. Denis) *Rapport de l'etude des bibliotheques publiques de la region de Montreal,* Ministere des affaires culturelles, 1976; *Legendes du Canada francais,* Les Editions de l'Espoir, 1977.

WORK IN PROGRESS: Translation of *River Runners* by James Houston.

SIDELIGHTS: "Since retirement I have translated into French three English books for teenagers: *Tom Penny* by Tony German, *River Race* by Tony German and *You Can Pick Me Up at Peggy's Cove* by Brian Doyle."

CLAUDE B. AUBRY

BAKER, Susan (Catherine) 1942- (Kay Richards)

PERSONAL: Born June 30, 1942, in England; daughter of Alexander Robert (a banker and free-lance journalist) and Catherine (Evans) Ellis; married Richard John Baker (a solicitor), June 9, 1973; *Education:* University of Edinburgh, B.Sc., 1963. *Home:* 1 Elm Close, Amersham, Buckinghamshire, England. *Office:* Macdonald Educational, Holywell House, Worship St., London EC2, England.

CAREER: Author, 1973—. McDonald Educational, London, England, children's book editor. Has worked as a research physicist at electrical and metallurgical laboratories. *Member:* Austrian Alpine Club (United Kingdom section).

WRITINGS—All for young people: (Editor, with Valerie Pitt, John Daintith, Alan Isaacs) *The Hamlyn Junior Science Encyclopedia,* Hamlin, 1973; (under pseudonym Kay Richards) *Science Magic with Physics* (illustrated by Mike Whittlesea and Brian Edwards), Purnell, 1974; *Answer Book of Science,* Hamlyn, 1975; (with Nora Stein) *Animals,* Macdonald Educational, 1976; (with Stein) *Famous People,* Macdonald Educational, 1976; (with Stein) *Long Ago,* Macdonald Educational, 1976; (with Stein) *Transport,* Macdonald Educational, 1976; (editor) Richard Blythe, *Fabulous Beasts* (illustrated by Fiona French and Joanna Troughton), Macdonald Educational, 1977; *Farms,* Macdonald Educational, 1977; *The Christmas Book* (illustrated by Frank Baber, Kim Blundell, and Sara Cole), Macdonald Educational, 1978, Grosset, 1979. Editor, "Junior Reference Library" series Macdonald Educational, 1969.

WORK IN PROGRESS: "At present I am researching and developing books for pre-school children."

SIDELIGHTS: "After receiving a scientific education and training, and having enjoyed practical work in laboratories, I

"**Agouhanna will never be able to become a warrior, because he's always hanging onto his mother's skirts....**" ■ (From *Agouhanna* by Claude Aubry. Translated from the French by Harvey Swados. Illustrated by Julie Brinckloe.)

...When the long-expected gush of stuffing issued forth, one murmur of delight arose all round the board, and even Tiny Tim, excited by the two young Cratchits, beat on the table with the handle of his knife, and feebly cried Hurrah! ▪ (From *The Christmas Book* by Susan Baker. Illustrated by Kim Blundell.)

discovered that career advancement provided me with a desk job. If that was to be the case, data processing and laboratory management were not going to provide me with the right kind of job satisfaction; so, I moved into the field of scientific publishing. Having learnt the basic editorial skills, I found that I was ideally suited to working on the production of colour information books for children, which came to the fore in the early 1970s.''

awards for his etchings and illustrations, and has contributed articles and drawings to periodicals, including *New Republic, Century,* and *Scribner's Magazine. Residence:* Santa Fe, N.M. *For More Information See: New York Times Book Review,* November 2, 1919, October 6, 1935, October 17, 1937, December 28, 1947; *New York Herald Tribune Weekly Book Review,* Part 3, November 30, 1947; *Illustrators of Children's Books, 1946-1956,* Horn Book, 1958.

BALDRIDGE, Cyrus LeRoy 1889-

BRIEF ENTRY: Born May 27, 1889, in Alton, N.Y. A cartoonist and illustrator, Baldridge received his only formal art training at Frank Holme's School of Illustration in Chicago, although he later received a degree in literature from the University of Chicago. In his early years, he worked as a cowpuncher in Texas and served in France with the Army Expeditionary Forces before joining the staff of *Stars & Stripes* as a cartoonist in 1918. After leaving the army, Baldridge spent several years traveling all over the world, sketching scenes in Japan, China, Africa, India, and the Middle East. Many of the books he has written and illustrated grew directly from these trips, including *Boomba Lives in Africa* (Holiday House, 1935) and *Ali Lives in Iran* (Holiday House, 1937), written with his wife, Caroline Singer. For *The Adventures and Discoveries of Marco Polo* (John Day, 1948), Baldridge prepared his illustrations by actually tracing the route of the famous explorer. His other illustrated works, noted for their accuracy and realism, include Mary Dodge's *Hans Brinker* (Grosset, 1945). Also an author, Baldridge wrote *Americanism: What Is It?* (Farrar, Straus, 1936) for children as well as his autobiography, *Time and Chance* (John Day, 1947). He taught book design and illustration and served as president of the National Association of Commercial Arts, the Artists Guild of New York, and the University of Chicago Club. He has received several

BALES, Carol Ann 1940-

BRIEF ENTRY: Born November 9, 1940, in St. Louis, Mo. Bales is a free-lance writer and photographer who has contributed to numerous local and national publications, including *Saturday Review, Life International, Transaction,* and the *Chicago Tribune.* A graduate of the University of Missouri, Bales has written numerous books for young people. Among her books are *Kevin Cloud: Chippewa Boy in the City* (Reilly & Lee, 1972), *Chinatown Sunday: The Story of Lillian Der* (Reilly & Lee, 1973), and *Tales Of The Elders: A Memory Book of Men and Women Who Came to America as Immigrants, 1900-1930* (Follett, 1977). *Address:* Box 5, Route 1, Wentzville, Mo. 63385. *For More Information See: Contemporary Authors,* Volumes 45-48, Gale, 1974.

As I was going to St. Ives,
I met a man with seven wives,
Each wife had seven sacks,
Each sack had seven cats,
Each cat had seven kits:
Kits, cats, sacks, and wives,
How many were there going to St. Ives?
—Nursery rhyme

BARNER, Bob 1947-

PERSONAL: Born November 11, 1947, in Tuckerman, Ark.; son of Jewel and Jean (McClure) Barner. *Education:* Columbus College of Art and Design, B.F.A., 1970. *Home and office:* 65 Mount Vernon St., Boston, Mass. 02108.

CAREER: Riverside Hospital, Columbus, Ohio, art therapist, 1970-78; Art Institute of Boston, Boston, Mass., instructor in art, 1978-79; free-lance writer and artist, 1979—. *Member:* Art Directors Club of Boston. *Awards, honors:* Andy Award for Illustration from Children's International Book Fair, 1975, for *The Elephants' Visit.*

WRITINGS—Self-illustrated children's books: *The Elephants' Visit,* Little, Brown, 1975; *Elephant Facts,* Dutton, 1979.

WORK IN PROGRESS: Children's books.

SIDELIGHTS: "Most of my work is inspired by simple doodles. *Elephant Facts* came about after work on the purely fanciful *The Elephants' Visit* aroused my interest in real facts about elephants."

BATCHELOR, Joy 1914-

BRIEF ENTRY: Born May 12, 1914, in Watford, Hertfordshire, England. An animated film producer and illustrator, Batchelor, with her husband John Halas, formed Halas-Batchelor Productions which has produced numerous educational and animated film features. Included in their work is the animated motion picture version of George Orwell's *Animal Farm* which was the first feature-length cartoon production in Great Britain. Batchelor began in the film industry in 1935 after working as a graphic artist and designer. Five years later, she formed a team with Halas, a Hungarian-born animator and one-time-assistant to George Pal. During the war, Halas-Batchelor studios produced propaganda and wartime information films. Afterwards, they continued producing educational and advertising films to finance their independent animation projects. Their production company was the first in Britain to use computer animation for math and science films. Among their most notable films are "Magic Canvas" (1951), "The History of the Cinema" (1956), and "Automania 2000" (1963). Besides films, they have produced numerous commercials and several television series. Joy Batchelor and her husband have also co-illustrated an edition of Orwell's *Animal Farm* (Harcourt, 1954). *For More Information See: Dictionary of Film Makers,* University of California Press, 1972; *Oxford Companion to Film,* Oxford University Press, 1976; *International Motion Picture Almanac, 1980,* Quigley, 1980.

Wild elephants live in herds of ten to fifty or more. The leader of the herd is usually an older female.

Elephants travel in single file at a speed of about 6 miles an hour.

(From *Elephant Facts* by Bob Barner. Illustrated by the author.)

BEARMAN, Jane (Ruth) 1917-

PERSONAL: Born September 12, 1917, in Minneapolis, Minn.; daughter of Arthur Samuel (a produce broker) and Sarah Ruth (Berman) Bearman; married Saul Frances (a life scientist), November 2, 1941; children: David J., Sally Ann. *Education:* Attended Minneapolis Art Institute, 1932-37, American Academy of Art, 1934-35, and Chicago Institute of Art, 1935-36; University of Minnesota, B.A., 1937, and Montclair College. *Home and office:* 30 Spier Dr., Livingston, N.J. 07039.

CAREER: Artist. The Dayton Co., Minneapolis, Minn., advertising artist, 1937-41; Department of War Training, New York City, art director, 1941-45; author and illustrator of children's books, 1945—. Board member, Friends of Livingston Library, 1958-65. Lecturer, Seton Hall University, 1969-70. Work has been exhibited in one-woman shows, including those at Panoras Gallery, New York City, 1966, Hallmark Gallery, Kansas City, Mo., 1966-67, Brandeis University, Waltham, Mass., 1968-69, Carver Museum, Tuskeegee Institute, Ala., 1968-69, Loyola University, Chicago, Ill., 1970-71, Gallery 9, Chatham, N.J., 1976; Jewish Community Center, Minneapolis, Minn., 1978, and Temple B'nai Jeshurun, Short Hills, N.J., 1980; has participated in numerous traveling exhibitions, including Contemporary American Graphics, 1965-66, Impressions in Water Color, 1969-70, and New Jersey Printmakers, 1969-70. Travelling exhibition sponsored by U.S. State Department in Israel and Egypt, 1980-81.

MEMBER: National Association of Women Artists, Painters and Sculptors Society, Artists Equity Association, American Field Service (local president, 1960-61), New Jersey Watercolor Society. *Awards, honors:* First in graphics, Montclair Museum Annual State Exhibition, 1962; medal of honor, Painters and Sculptors Society, 1962; first place in oils, Hunterdon Annual State Exhibition, 1965; Mary Yelen prize, National Association of Women Artists, 1970, medal of honor, 1973; Bainbridge Award, 1974.

WRITINGS—For children; all self-illustrated; all published by Union of American Hebrew Congregations, except as noted: *Happy Chanuko*, 1943; *Fun on Sukos*, 1946; *Passover Party*, 1946; *Mother Goose ABC*, Saalfield, 1946; *Purim Parade*, 1947; *Shovuos Time*, 1947; *Good Shabos*, 1950; (with Mildred Weil) *Shalom!: A Holiday Book for Little Children*, Jonathan David, 1958; *David: A Bible Hero*, Jonathan David, 1965; *Jonathan: A Bible Hero*, Jonathan David, 1965; *The Eight Nights: A Chanukah Counting Book*, edited by Daniel B. Syme, 1978.

Illustrator: Lillian Freehof, *Candle Light Stories*, Bloch, 1951.

Contributor of articles to professional journals, including *National Parent-Teachers*.

SIDELIGHTS: "When I was a teenager, I taught Sunday School. I realized then that the books we used were antiquated, dull, and the illustrations were not at all interesting to the children. I thought then that some day I would try my hand at colorful picture books for preschoolers about the Jewish holidays, books the children would really relate to.

"It was gratifying when the first of the holiday series was accepted and published. The editor's comment in all six books was: 'This is the first picture book in English about this lovely holiday.'

The two young friends rose and walked slowly back to the camp. ■ (From *Jonathan: A Bible Hero* by Jane Bearman. Illustrated by the author.)

"I don't believe in talking down to children. If a book doesn't interest me as an adult, regardless of the age of the child for whom it is selected, I would never buy it. That's a pretty good rule to go by, whether one is doing the selecting or the creating. Having small children of my own, being aware of their interests, did help me when I began in this work.

"Because I am primarily an artist, most of my books have been picture books. In the Bible hero books, which are not picture books, but which I wrote and illustrated, I followed as closely as possible the words of the Soncino translation of the David and Jonathan stories."

HOBBIES AND OTHER INTERESTS: "Aside from art, my interests are music and books. My husband and I are members of a music group and a book group, both of which meet once a month."

Monday's child is fair of face,
Tuesday's child is full of grace,
Wednesday's child is full of woe,
Thursday's child has far to go,
Friday's child is loving and giving,
Saturday's child has to work for its living,
But a child that's born on the Sabbath day
Is fair and wise and good and gay.
—Nursery rhyme

BLACKBURN, Joyce Knight 1920-

PERSONAL: Born November 1, 1920, in Mount Vernon, Ind.; daughter of Leroy (a minister) and Audry (an artist; maiden name, Knight) Blackburn. *Education:* Moody Institute, Chicago, graduate; attended Northwestern University, 1943, 1950, 1957, Chicago Institute of Design, 1950. *Politics:* Jeffersonian Independent. *Religion:* Christian. *Home address:* Route 4, Box 287-A, St. Simons Island, Ga. 31522.

CAREER: Radio station WMBI, Chicago, Ill., 1941-60, broadcaster and supervisor, directing dramatic programs and presenting own series, "Listening Post," "From a City Tower," and "Music-Story Lady"; Zondervan Publishing House, Grand Rapids, Mich., editorial consultant, 1961—. Sometime actress in motion pictures (educational and feature films), slide films, and in radio series, "Unshackled," WGN, Chicago. *Member:* Authors Guild, Authors League of America, Screen Actors Guild, American Federation of Television and Radio Artists, Coastal Georgia Historical Society. *Awards, honors:* Literary achievement award for non-fiction, Georgia Writers Association, 1970; Fiction Author of the Year, Dixie Council of Authors and Journalists, 1971; National Christian School Award, 1971, for *Suki and the Wonder Star.*

WRITINGS—Juveniles: Suki and the Invisible Peacock, Zondervan, 1965; *Wilfred Grenfell: Explorer-Doctor,* Zondervan, 1966; *Suki and the Old Umbrella,* Zondervan, 1966; *Theodore Roosevelt: Naturalist-Statesman,* Zondervan, 1967; *Martha Berry: Little Woman with a Big Dream,* Lippincott, 1968; *Suki and the Magic Sand Dollar,* Word Books, 1969; *John Adams:*

JOYCE KNIGHT BLACKBURN

Farmer and Braintree, Word Books, 1970; *James Edward Oglethorpe,* Lippincott, 1970; *Suki and the Wonder Star,* Word Books, 1971.

Adult: *The Earth Is the Lord's?,* Word Books, 1972; *George Wythe,* Harper, 1975; *Roads to Reality,* Revell, 1978; *A Book of Praises,* Zondervan, 1980.

SIDELIGHTS: Blackburn's work is represented in the Special Collections Library of Emory University.

(From *Martha Berry: Little Woman with a Big Dream* by Joyce Blackburn. Jacket design by Robert Parker.)

BLAIR, Eric Arthur 1903-1950
(George Orwell)

PERSONAL: Born June 25, 1903, in Motihari, Bengal, India; died of tuberculosis January 21, 1950, in London, England; son of Richard Walmesley Blair (a customs and excise officer); married Eileen O'Shaughnessy (a teacher and journalist), June 9, 1936 (died March 29, 1945); married Sonia Brownell, October, 1949; children: Richard (adopted). *Education:* Attended Eton College, 1917-21.

CAREER: Essayist, novelist, critic, and journalist. Served as policeman with Indian Imperial Police, Burma, India, 1922-27; travelled to Paris and worked as a full-time writer, 1927-29; returned to London penniless and began working a series of ill-paid jobs, including those as a tutor, a teacher in cheap private schools, and as an assistant in a bookshop, 1929-35.

ERIC ARTHUR BLAIR

Joined the militia of the Partido Obrero de Unificacion Marxista (POUM) and fought in the Spanish Civil War, 1936-37; returned to England to work as a full-time writer, beginning 1939. At the outbreak of World War II, joined the Indian service of the British Broadcasting Co. (BBC) as an overseas broadcaster, 1941-43; columnist for the *Partisan Review,* 1941; travelled to France, Germany, and Austria as a reporter at the end of World War II. *Awards, honors:* First annual award for a distinguished body of work from the *Partisan Review,* 1949.

WRITINGS—Of interest to young adults: *Animal Farm: A Fairy Story,* Secker & Warburg, 1945, Harcourt, 1946 [other editions include those illustrated by Joy Batchelor and John Halas, Harcourt, 1954; Margaret Cusack, Franklin Library, 1978]; *1984,* Harcourt, 1949 [other editions include those edited by Irving Howe, Harcourt, 1963; and illustrated by Sian Cardy, Edito-Service S.A. (Geneva), 1974].

Other principal writings—Novels: *Down and Out in Paris and London,* Harper, 1933, reprinted, Berkley Publishing, 1969; *Burmese Days,* Harper, 1934, reprinted, Harcourt, 1974; *A Clergyman's Daughter,* Gollancz, 1935, Harcourt, 1960; *Keep the Aspidistra Flying,* Gollancz, 1936, Harcourt, 1956; *Hom-*

age to Catalonia, Secker & Warburg, 1938, Harcourt, 1952; *Coming Up for Air,* Gollancz, 1939, Harcourt, 1950.

Essays: *Inside the Whale, and Other Essays,* Gollancz, 1940, published as *Selected Essays,* Penguin, 1957; *The Lion and the Unicorn: Socialism and the English Genius,* Secker & Warburg, 1941, reprinted, AMS Press, 1976; *Dickens, Dali, & Others: Studies in Popular Culture,* Reynal & Hitchcock, 1946, reprinted, Harcourt, 1970 (published in England as *Critical Essays,* Secker & Warburg, 1946); *Shooting an Elephant, and Other Essays,* Harcourt, 1950, later published in *Collected Essays,* Secker & Warburg, 1961; *England, Your England, and Other Essays,* Secker & Warburg, 1953, later published in *Collected Essays,* Secker & Warburg, 1961; *Such, Such Were the Joys,* Harcourt, 1953.

Other writings: (Editor) *Talking to India,* Allen & Unwin, 1943; (editor with Reginald Reynolds) *British Pamphleteers,* Volume I: *From the Sixteenth Century to the French Revolution,* A. Wingate, 1948.

Collections: *A Collection of Essays,* Doubleday, 1954; *The Orwell Reader: Fiction, Essays, and Reportage,* Harcourt, 1956;

Selected Writings, edited by George Bott, Heinemann, 1958; *Decline of the English Murder, and Other Essays,* Penguin, 1965; *The Collected Essays, Journalism, and Letters of George Orwell,* edited by Sonia Orwell and Ian Angus, Harcourt, 1968, Volume I: *An Age Like This, 1920-1940,* Volume II: *My Country Right or Left, 1940-1943,* Volume III: *As I Please, 1943-1945,* Volume IV: *In Front of Your Nose, 1945-50; Animal Farm* (collection includes *Animal Farm, Burmese Days, A Clergyman's Daughter, Coming Up for Air, Keep the Aspidistra Flying, 1984),* Octopus Books, 1976.

Contributor of articles to numerous periodicals, including *New Republic, Newsweek, Time,* and *Fortnightly.*

ADAPTATIONS—Movies: ''Animal Farm'' (animated motion picture), Louis de Rochemont Associates, 1954; ''1984'' (motion picture), starring Michael Redgrave, Edmond O'Brien, and Jan Sterling, Holiday Film Productions, 1956; ''Animal Farm: A Review of the Novel of George Orwell'' (filmstrip), Current Affairs Films, 1978; ''Animal Farm'' (filmstrip), Ealing Films, 1979.

Plays: *George Orwell's ''1984''* (three-act), Dramatic Publishing Co., 1963; *Animal Farm* (two-act), S. French, 1964.

SIDELIGHTS: **June 25, 1903.** Born as Eric Arthur Blair at Motihari, Bengal, India, the second child of an Anglo-Indian family. ''My father was an official in the English administration there, and my family was one of those ordinary middle-class families of soldiers, clergymen, government officials, teachers, lawyers, doctors, etc.'' [Sonia Orwell and Ian Angus, editors, *The Collected Essays, Journalism and Letters of George Orwell,* Vol. III, Secker and Warburg, 1968.¹]

1907. Family returned to England leaving father behind to manage his post in India.

Nevertheless, some of the animals were disturbed when they heard that the pigs not only took their meals in the kitchen and used the drawing-room as a recreation room, but also slept in the beds. ■ (From *Animal Farm: A Fairy Story* by George Orwell. Illustrated by Joy Batchelor and John Halas.)

''...You do not appreciate, comrade, the mighty thing that we have done. The enemy was in occupation of this very ground that we stand upon. And now—thanks to the leadership of Comrade Napoleon—we have won every inch of it back again!'' ■ (From *Animal Farm: A Fairy Story* by George Orwell. Illustrated by Joy Batchelor and John Halas.)

''From a very early age, perhaps the age of five or six, I knew that when I grew up I should be a writer. Between the ages of about seventeen and twenty-four I tried to abandon this idea, but I did so with the consciousness that I was outraging my true nature and that sooner or later I should have to settle down and write books.

''I was the middle child of three, but there was a gap of five years on either side, and I barely saw my father before I was eight. For this and other reasons I was somewhat lonely, and I soon developed disagreeable mannerisms which made me unpopular throughout my schooldays. I had the lonely child's habit of making up stories and holding conversations with imaginary persons, and I think from the very start my literary ambitions were mixed up with the feeling of being isolated and undervalued. I knew that I had a facility with words and a power of facing unpleasant facts, and I felt that this created a sort of private world in which I could get my own back for my failure in everyday life.

''. . . I used to imagine that I was, say, Robin Hood, and picture myself as the hero of thrilling adventures, but quite soon my 'story' ceased to be narcissistic in a crude way and became more and more a mere description of what I was doing and the things I saw. For minutes at a time this kind of thing would be running through my head: 'He pushed the door open and entered the room. A yellow beam of sunlight, filtering through the muslin curtains, slanted on to the table, where a

Blair, far right. Summer, 1919.

matchbox, half open, lay beside the inkpot. With his right hand in his pocket he moved across to the window. Down in the street a tortoiseshell cat was chasing a dead leaf,' etc etc. This habit continued till I was about twenty-five, right through my non-literary years. Although I had to search, and did search, for the right words, I seemed to be making this descriptive effort almost against my will, under a kind of compulsion from outside. The 'story' must, I suppose, have reflected the styles of the various writers I admired at different ages, but so far as I remember it always had the same meticulous descriptive quality.

''Nevertheless the volume of serious . . . writing which I produced all through my childhood and boyhood would not amount to half a dozen pages. I wrote my first poem at the age of four or five, my mother taking it down to dictation. I cannot remember anything about it except that it was about a tiger and the tiger had 'chair-like teeth'—a good enough phrase, but I fancy the poem was a plagiarism of Blake's 'Tiger, Tiger.' At seven years old I was a member of the Navy League and wore a sailor suit with 'HMS *Invincible*' on my cap. Even before my public-school OTC I had been in a private school cadet corps. At eleven, when the war of 1914-18 broke out, I wrote

a patriotic poem which was printed in the local newspaper. . . . I also, about twice, attempted a short story which was a ghastly failure.

''. . . At fourteen I wrote a whole rhyming play, in imitation of Aristophanes, in about a week—and helped to edit school magazines, both printed and in manuscript. These magazines were the most pitiful burlesque stuff that you could imagine. . . .

''When I was about sixteen I suddenly discovered the joy of mere words. . . . I wanted to write enormous naturalistic novels and unhappy endings, full of detailed descriptions and arresting similes, and also full of purple passages in which words were used partly for the sake of their sound.'' [Sonia Orwell and Ian Angus, editors, *The Collected Essays, Journalism and Letters of George Orwell,* Vol. 1, Secker and Warburg, 1968.²]

1911-1916. Attended St. Cyprian's Preparatory School on a scholarship. ''. . . I had been made to understand that I was not on the same footing as most of the other boys. In effect there were three castes in the school. There was the minority with an aristocratic or millionaire background, there were the children of the ordinary suburban rich, who made up the bulk of the school, and there were a few underlings like myself, the sons of clergyman, Indian civil servants, struggling widows and the like. . . .

". . . The overcrowded, underfed, underwashed life that we led [at St. Cyprian's] *was* disgusting, as I recall it. . . . Never before or since have I seen butter or jam scraped on bread so thinly. I do not think I can be imagining the fact that we were underfed, when I remember the lengths we would go in order to steal food. On a number of occasions I remember creeping down at two or three o'clock in the morning through what seemed like miles of pitch-dark stairways and passages—barefooted, stopping to listen after each step, paralysed with about equal fear of Sambo [the Headmaster], ghosts and burglars—to steal stale bread from the pantry.

"Soon after I arrived at St. Cyprian's (not immediately, but after a week or two, just when I seemed to be settling into the routine of school life) I began wetting my bed. . . .

"In those days . . . it was looked on as a disgusting crime which the child committed on purpose and for which the proper cure was a beating. For my part I did not need to be told it was a crime. Night after night I prayed, with a fervour never previously attained in my prayers, 'Please God, do not let me wet my bed! Oh, please God, do not let me wet my bed!,' but it made remarkable little difference.

"Oh, the despair, the feeling of cruel injustice, after all my prayers and resolutions, at once again waking between the clammy sheets! There was no chance of hiding what I had done. The grim statuesque matron, Margaret by name, arrived in the dormitory specially to inspect my bed. She pulled back the clothes, then drew herself up, and the dreaded words seemed to come rolling out of her like a peal of thunder:

"'REPORT YOURSELF to the Headmaster after breakfast!'

". . . In the study the Headmaster . . . was waiting. He knew, of course, why I had been sent to him, and had already taken a bone-handled riding-crop out of the cupboard. . . . The beating did not hurt (perhaps, as it was the first time, he was not hitting me very hard), and I walked out feeling very much better." [Sonia Orwell and Ian Angus, editors, *The Collected Essays, Journalism and Letters of George Orwell*, Vol. IV, Secker and Warburg, 1968.[3]]

1917-1921. Attended Eton. ". . . The most costly and snobbish of the English Public Schools. But I had only got in there by means of a scholarship; otherwise my father could not have afforded to send me to a school of this type.

"Shortly after I left school (I wasn't quite twenty years old then) I went to Burma and joined the Indian Imperial Police. This was an armed police, a sort of 'gendarmerie' very similar to the Spanish 'Guardia Civil' or the 'Garde Mobile' in France."[1]

"Theoretically—and secretly, of course—I was all for the Burmese and all against their oppressors, the British. As for the job I was doing, I hated it more bitterly than I can perhaps make clear."[2]

"I gave [the Imperial Police] up partly because the climate had ruined my health, partly because I already had vague ideas of writing books, but mainly because I could not go on any longer

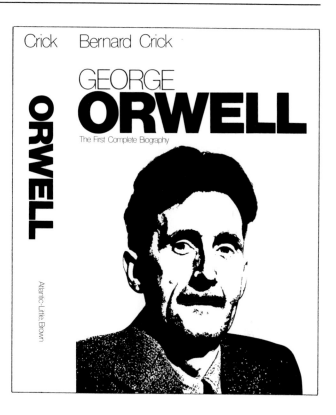

(From *George Orwell: A Life* by Bernard Crick.)

serving an imperialism which I had come to regard as very largely a racket."[1]

Submitted his resignation in **1928** and set off for Paris. ". . . To live cheaply while writing two novels—which I regret to say were never published—and also to learn French."[1]

Penniless, Orwell sought odd jobs washing dishes before returning to England. ". . . After leaving Paris towards the end of 1929 I earned my living largely by teaching and in a small way be writing. . . ."[2]

"I sometimes lived for months on end amongst the poor and half criminal elements who inhabit the worst parts of the poorer quarters, or take to the streets, begging and stealing. At that time I associated with them through lack of money, but later their way of life interested me very much for its own sake.

"Dressed as I was, I was half afraid that the police might arrest me as a vagabond, and I dared not speak to anyone, imagining that they must notice a disparity between my accent and my clothes. . . . My new clothes had put me instantly into a new world. Everyone's demeanour seemed to have changed abruptly. I helped a hawker pick up a barrow that he had upset. 'Thanks, mate,' he said with a grin. No one had called me mate before in my life—it was the clothes that had done it."[Bernard Crick, *George Orwell: A Life,* Little, Brown, 1980.[4]]

On one of his excursions to London, Orwell decided to experience prison life. "I started out on Saturday afternoon with four or five shillings. . . . I bought some tobacco and a 'Yank Mag' against my forthcoming imprisonment, and then, as soon as the pubs opened, went and had four or five pints, topping

NATIONAL UNION OF JOURNALISTS

7 John Street, Bedford Row, London, W.C.1

'Phone :   Telegrams :
HOLborn 2258   Natujay Holb, London

This is to certify that

Mr. GEORGE ORWELL

of The Tribune

is a member of the T. + P.
Branch of the National Union of Journalists.

{ Leslie R. Aldous Branch Sec.

(Address) 66, Priory Gdns.. N.6.

Member's Sig.

Orwell's union card, dated 29 December 1943.

up with a quarter bottle of whisky, which left me with twopence in hand. By the time the whisky was low in the bottle I was tolerably drunk—more drunk than I had intended, for it happened that I had eaten nothing all day. . . .

"I began staggering along the pavement in a westward direction, and for a long time did not meet any policemen, though the streets were crowded and all the people pointed and laughed at me. Finally I saw two policemen coming. I pulled the whisky bottle out of my pocket and, in their sight, drank what was left, which nearly knocked me out, so that I clutched a lamppost and fell down. The two policemen ran towards me, turned me over and took the bottle out of my hand.

"They had my arms in the grip . . . by which you can break a man's arm with one twist, but they were as gentle with me as though I had been a child. I was internally quite sober, and it amused me very much to see the cunning way in which they persuaded me along, never once disclosing the fact that we were making for the police station. This is, I suppose, the usual procedure with drunks.

"This trip was a failure, as the object of it was to get into prison, and I did not, in fact, get more than forty-eight hours in custody. . . ."[2]

1931-1935. Picked hops and taught at a small private school.

1933. First book, *Down and Out in Paris and London,* was published under his pseudonym, George Orwell—a name, he felt, which had a manly, English, country-sounding ring.

1934-1935. Part-time assistant in a London bookshop. ". . . I was able to live on what I earned by writing, and at the end of that year I moved into the country and set up a small general store. It barely paid its way, but it taught me things about the trade which would be useful if I ever made a venture in that direction again."[2]

1935. Publisher, Victor Gollancz, commissioned Orwell to gather material for *Road to Wigan Pier,* which was published two years later. "I spent many months . . . studying the conditions of the miners in the north of England."[1]

"Down below [in the mine] it was lighter than I expected, because apart from the lamps we all carried there were electric lights in the main roads. But what I had not expected, and what for me was the most important feature all through, was the lowness of the roof. I had vaguely imagined wandering about in places rather like the tunnels of the Underground; but as a matter of fact there were very few places where you could stand upright. In general the roof was about 4 ft or 4 ft 6 ins high, sometimes much lower.

"After a few hundred yards of walking doubled up and once or twice having to crawl, I began to feel the effects in a violent pain all down my thighs. One also gets a bad crick in the neck, because though stooping one has to look up for fear of knocking into the beams, but the pain in the thighs is the worst. Of course as we got nearer the coal face the roads tended to get lower. Once we crawled through a temporary tunnel which was like an enlarged rat hole, with no props, and in one place there had been a fall of stone during the night—3 or 4 tons of stuff, I should judge. It had blocked up the entire road except for a tiny aperture near the roof which we had to crawl through without touching any timber. Presently I had to stop for a minute to rest my knees, which were giving way, and then after a few hundred yards more we came to the first working.[2]

Orwell's research profoundly affected his political views. "Up to 1930 I did not on the whole look upon myself as a Socialist. In fact I had as yet no clearly defined political views. I became pro-Socialist more out of disgust with the way the poorer section of the industrial workers were oppressed and neglected than out of any theoretical admiration for a planned society."[1]

June 9, 1936. "I am getting married very shortly [to Eileen O'Shaughnessy]—it is fixed for June 9th at the parish church here. This is as it were in confidence because we are telling as few people as possible till the deed is done, lest our relatives combine against us in some way & prevent it. It is very rash of course but we have talked it over & decided I should never by economically justified in marrying so might as well be unjustified now as later. I expect we shall rub along all right— as to money I mean—but it will always be hand to mouth as I don't see myself ever writing a best-seller. . . ."[4]

". . . In almost the same week the civil war broke out in Spain. My wife and I both wanted to go to Spain and fight for the Spanish Government.

". . . We were very lucky to get out of Spain alive, and not even to have been arrested once. Many of our friends were shot, and others spent a long time in prison or simply disappeared."[1]

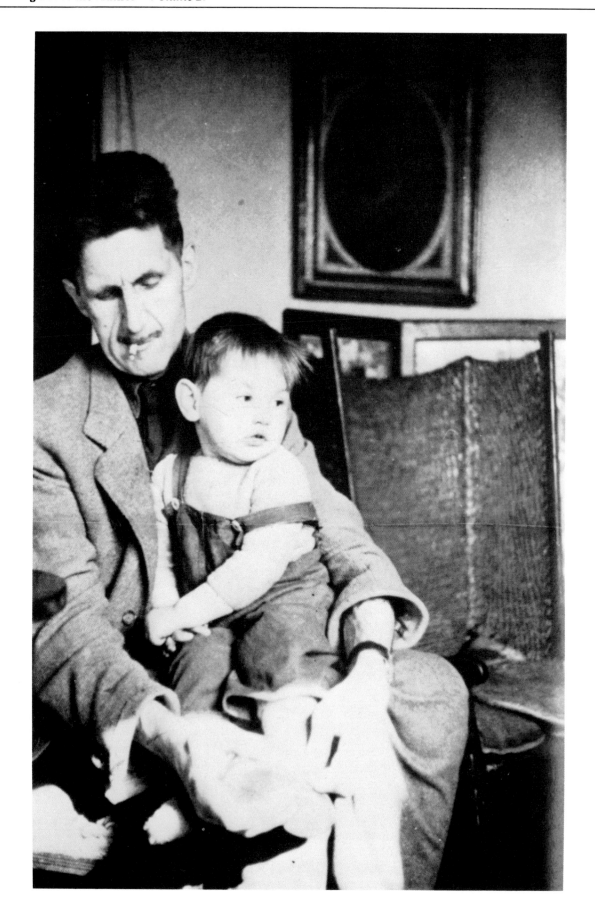

Orwell with his son Richard, Islington, Winter, 1945.

(From the animated cartoon "Animal Farm." Produced by Louis de Rochemont, 1955. Re-released by Phoenix Films, 1974.)

(From the movie "1984," starring Edmond O'Brien and Jan Sterling. A Holiday Production, released by Columbia Pictures Corp., 1955.)

"... After that awful nightmare in Spain, I had seriously thought I would never be able to write a novel again."[2]

1938. Went to Morocco to recuperate from an illness. 'I had defective bronchial tubes and a lesion on one lung which was not discovered till many years later. Hence I not only had a chronic cough, but running was a torment to me.''[3]

1939-1945. Returned to England and began writing for the *Tribune*. Wrote reviews to supplement his income. ''I had a difficult time making a living out of writing at the start, though looking back now, and knowing what a racket literary journalism is, I see that I could have managed much better if I had known the ropes.''[3]

1940. Joined Home Guard, an organization of local defense volunteers. ''I was very busy trying to earn a living and write a book amid the bombs and the general disorganisation, and any spare time I had was taken up by the Home Guard. . . .''[3]

1941. Joined BBC for war-time broadcasts. ''. . . Where I wrote enough rubbish (news commentaries and so on) to fill a shelf of books.''[3]

November, 1943. Left the Home Guard and the BBC to become the *Tribune's* literary editor.

1944. Adopted only son, Richard Horatio Blair.

1945. Left the *Tribune* to become a war correspondent. ''The only bit of war I saw apart from blitzes and the Home Guard was being a war correspondent for a little while in Germany about the time of the collapse, which was quite interesting.''[3]

Wife, Eileen, died. ''I lost my wife in March [29]. . . . It was a beastly, cruel business, however I don't think she expected to die (it happened during an operation), so perhaps it was not so bad as it might have been. I was in France at the time and only got back after she was dead.''[1]

In the middle of the summer Moses the raven suddenly reappeared on the farm, after an absence of several years.... He would perch on a stump, flap his black wings, and talk by the hour to anyone who would listen. ■ (From *Animal Farm: A Fairy Story* by George Orwell. Illustrated by Joy Batchelor and John Halas.)

August, 1945. *Animal Farm* published. "At the time when this book was finished, it was very hard indeed to get it published, and I determined then that if possible I would take all my future output to the publisher who would produce it, because I knew that anyone who would risk this book would risk anything.

". . . *Animal Farm* was the first book in which I tried, with full consciousness of what I was doing, to fuse political purpose and artistic purpose into one whole.

". . . It was invariably where I lacked a *political* purpose that I wrote lifeless books and was betrayed into purple passages, sentences without meaning, decorative adjectives and humbug generally."[3]

Orwell resumed his journalism and worked on *1984,* but his health deteriorated.

1946. Suffered another lung hemorrhage.

1949. He wrote his last articles and reviews. *1984* was published in June. In October he married Sonia Brownell while still in his hospital bed. "Writing a book is a horrible, exhausting struggle, like a long bout of some painful illness. One would never undertake such a thing if one were not driven on by some demon whom one can neither resist nor understand."[2]

January 21, 1950. Died in London of pulmonary tuberculosis and was buried in Sutton Courtney, Berkshire, England.

FOR MORE INFORMATION SEE: Laurence Brander, *George Orwell,* Longmans, Green, 1954; John A. Atkins, *George Orwell: A Literary and Biographical Study,* Ungar, 1955, revised edition, Calder & Boyars, 1971; Christopher Hollis, *Study of George Orwell: The Man and His Works,* Regnery, 1956; George Woodcock, *The Crystal Spirit: A Study of George Orwell,* Little, Brown, 1966; Ruth A. Lief, *Home to Oceania: The Prophetic Vision of George Orwell,* Ohio State University, 1969; Raymond Williams, *George Orwell,* Viking, 1971; William Abrahams and Peter Stansky, *The Unknown Orwell,* Knopf, 1972; Roberta Kalechofsky, *George Orwell,* Ungar, 1973; Raymond Williams, editor, *George Orwell: A Collection of Critical Essays,* Prentice-Hall, 1974; (for children) Alan L. Paley, *George Orwell: Writer and Critic of Modern Society,* SamHar Press, 1974; Jeffery Meyers, editor, *George Orwell, the Critical Heritage,* Routledge, 1975; C. J. Concannon, *George*

The creatures outside looked from pig to man, and from man to pig, and from pig to man again; but already it was impossible to say which was which. ■ (From *Animal Farm: A Fairy Story* by George Orwell. Illustrated by Joy Batchelor and John Halas.)

Barnhill, 1948.

Orwell, Revisionist Press, 1976; Sant S. Bal, *George Orwell: The Ethical Imagination,* Humanities, 1981; Bernard Crick, *George Orwell,* Little, Brown, 1981; Peter Lewis, *George Orwell: The Road to 1984,* Harcourt, 1982.

OBITUARIES: *New York Times,* January 22, 1950; *Illustrated London News,* January 28, 1950; *Newsweek,* January 30, 1950; *Time,* January 30, 1950; *Saturday Review of Literature,* February 4, 1950; *Publishers Weekly,* February 11, 1950; *Wilson Library Bulletin,* March, 1950.

BLAIR, Helen 1910-

BRIEF ENTRY: Born December 29, 1910, in Hibbing, Minn. Artist, illustrator, and sculptor. Blair studied art at both the Massachusetts Normal Art School and Boston Museum School of Fine Arts. Chiefly interested in sculpture, she has been associated for many years with Portraits Incorporated of New York City, as a sculptor of small portrait figures. Her work has been exhibited in one-man shows at Ardan Studios, New York City, Vose Galleries, Boston, Mass., St. Paul Art Center, St. Paul, Minn., and Martin Gallery, Phoenix, Ariz. Blair has illustrated several books for children, including Florence Means's

Great Day in the Morning (Houghton, 1946), *Assorted Sisters* (a Junior Literary Guild selection; Houghton, 1947), *House under the Hill* (Houghton, 1949), and *Hetty of the Grande Deluxe* (Houghton, 1951). *Address:* 1919 E. Claremont St., Phoenix, Ariz. 85016. *For More Information See: Who's Who in American Art,* R. R. Bowker, 1980.

BOATNER, Mark Mayo III 1921-

PERSONAL: Born June 28, 1921, in Alexandria, Va.; son of Mark Mayo, Jr. (an army engineer officer) and Amenie Nelson (Gunnell) Boatner; married Patricia Dilworth, June 15, 1957; children: Stirling (daughter), Bruce, Andrew, Nelson, Spencer, Carter. *Education:* University of Kansas, student 1938-39; U.S. Military Academy, B.S., 1943; U.S. Army War College and George Washington University, M.S., 1966. *Politics:* "None, being second-generation regular army officer." *Religion:* Episcopalian. *Home:* Penrith Plantation, Jackson, La. 70748. *Agent:* Oliver G. Swan, Collier Associates, 280 Madison Ave., New York, N.Y. 10016.

CAREER: U.S. Army, regular officer, 1943-69. Combat service in Italy, 1944-45, and Korea, 1953-54; served at Supreme Headquarters Allied Powers Europe, Paris, France, 1959-63;

commanded mechanized infantry battalion at Fort Carson, Colorado, 1963-65; duty at the Pentagon, Arlington, Va., 1966-69. *Awards, honors*—Military: Bronze Star with three oak leaf clusters, Combat Infantryman's Badge with star, and Croix de Guerre. Civilian: American Revolutionary Round Table award, 1967, for *Encyclopedia of the American Revolution.*

WRITINGS: Company Duties, Combat Forces Press, 1950; *Military Customs and Traditions,* McKay, 1956, reprinted, Greenwood Press, 1976; *Civil War Dictionary,* McKay, 1959; *Encyclopedia of the American Revolution,* McKay, 1966; *Landmarks of the American Revolution,* Stackpole, 1973. Contributor to *Encyclopaedia Britannica* and other encyclopedias, and to military journals.

WORK IN PROGRESS: Encyclopedia of World War II and continued consultant work for the History Book Club, Stamford, Conn.

SIDELIGHTS: Born and reared in the pre-World War II army, then following a military career himself, Colonel Boatner has had advantages of travel and personal association that have contributed greatly to his writing.

"A curious experience in my recent work on World War II is finding how many leaders I know from personal association. Marshal Petain, for example, I met as a boy in Paris. Twenty years later I worked with Lord Louis Mountbatten and many

MARK MAYO BOATNER III

other prominent commanders of World War II when I returned to Paris for duty in the international headquarters there.

"It helps also to have seen the historical landmarks and the terrain, not to mention mingling with the people and hearing first-hand their personal views.

"Of course, I can't inject such personal matters directly into my historical writing, but they inevitably color it somewhat and certainly enliven research.

"Since my early retirement from the Army, prompted by a desire for more time to write and for managing family property in Virginia and Louisiana, I have rediscovered the life of the country squire. It's distracting to look out the window of my second-story study and see twenty wild turkeys or a carpet of bluebirds. But the nice thing is that the time I spend watching them can be made up: I have no time clock in my study, but I do have electric lights."

BOLLEN, Roger   1941(?)-

BRIEF ENTRY: Born June 27, 1941 (some sources cite 1942), in Cleveland, Ohio. Bollen received his degree in Fine Arts at Kent State University in 1963 and began work as a commercial artist at an art studio in Cleveland. Primarily a cartoonist, Bollen is best known for his comic strip "Animal Crackers," first released by the Chicago Tribune-New York News Syndicate in 1968. The strip, which features an assortment of animals bemused by contemporary society, was at one time carried by over 125 newspapers nationwide. Bollen also created

■ (From *Military Customs and Traditions* by Mark Mayo Boatner III.)

two other comic strips, "Funny Business," for Newspaper Enterprise Associates in 1965, and "Catfish," based on the Old West and first released in 1973. Bollen has taught a special illustration course in the art department of Kent State University. *Address:* 21 Louise Dr., Chagrin Falls, Ohio 44022. *For More Information See: Authors in the News,* Volume I, Gale, 1976; *Who's Who in America,* 41st edition, Marquis, 1980.

BRIGHTWELL, L(eonard) R(obert)   1889-

BRIEF ENTRY: Born May 17, 1889, in London, England. One of the century's most prominent animal artists, Brightwell sold his first animal drawing at the age of sixteen to *Boys' Own Paper.* From that time on, he has been a free-lance illustrator, contributing drawings, mostly humorous, to many journals, including *Punch, Strand,* and *Captain.* Brightwell received his art training at the Lambert Art School and worked for both the British Museum and the London Zoological Society. His later work includes animated cartoons, both serious and comic, and restoration of extinct animal group exhibits. He became a fellow of the London Zoo in 1906 and of the New York Zoo in 1922. He also joined the Marine Biology Association and made numerous trips aboard scientific and commercial deep-sea trawlers. Brightwell is the author of many books, including *A Cartoonist Amongst Animals* (Hurst & Blackett, 1921), *The Pond People* (Wells Gardner, Darton, 1949), and *Trimmer: The Tale of a Trawler Tyke* (Muller, 1956). He has also illustrated numerous books, including *Reynard the Fox* (Evans Brothers, 1921), and *A Naturalist at the Zoo* (Duckworth, 1926). *For More Information See: Illustrators of Children's Books, 1744-1945,* Horn Book, 1947.

BUGBEE, Emma   1888(?)-1981

OBITUARY NOTICE: Born about 1888 in Shippensburg, Pa.; died October 6, 1981, in Warwick, R.I. A graduate of Barnard College, Bugbee taught Greek at a high school in Methuen, Massachusetts, prior to beginning her 55-year career as a journalist with the *New York Herald Tribune.* To her readers, Bugbee was best known for her coverage of Eleanor Roosevelt. In her profession, however, she was a leading activist against the male-dominated environment of the newspaper business. For many decades Bugbee was one of only two female reporters employed by the *New York Herald* (which later became *New York Herald Tribune),* and until the end of World War I she and her colleague Ishbel Ross were excluded from the city room. To alleviate the isolation and unfair working conditions imposed on women in the field, she became a founder of the Newspaper Women's Club of New York and led efforts to expand the role and opportunities for female journalists. She was the author of a children's book, *Peggy Goes Overseas,* published by Dodd in 1945. *For More Information See: Authors of Books for Young People,* 2nd edition, Scarecrow, 1971. *Obituaries: New York Times,* October 10, 1981; *Time,* October 26, 1981.

BUSBY, Edith   (?)-1964

OBITUARY NOTICE: Born in Terre Haute, Ind.; died, after a long illness, November 16, 1964, in New York, N.Y. Edith Busby attended both Baylor University in Waco, Tex., and the Juilliard School of Music in New York City. After working one summer as a clerk in the New York Public Library, she decided to become a librarian and spent many years there and at the Brooklyn Public Library in various positions, including children's librarian and supervisor of book ordering. At the time of her death, she was director of school and library services at Dodd, Mead & Company. Busby also taught courses in library science at Pratt Institute and Columbia University and served on the Governor's subcommittee for book selection standards in New York State libraries. She served terms as president of the Women's National Book Association and the Public Library Promotion Group and was active in the American Library Association. Among the books she wrote for children are *Behind the Scenes at the Library* and *What Does a Librarian Do?.* *For More Information See: Authors of Books for Young People,* Scarecrow Press, 1964; *Indiana Authors and Their Books, 1917-1966,* Lakeside Press, 1974. *Obituaries: New York Times,* November 17, 1964; *Publishers Weekly,* November 23, 1964.

CHAPIAN, Marie   1938-

PERSONAL: Born October 10, 1938, in Minneapolis, Minn.; daughter of Leo R. and Dorothy (a businesswoman and author; maiden name, Buck) Jordan; married Peter Chapian (an artist), February 5, 1965 (divorced, April 18, 1977); children: Christa Deirdre, Liza Dorothy. *Education:* Attended the University of Minnesota and Moody Bible Institute; Metropolitan State University, B.A., 1978. *Religion:* Christian. *Address:* Marie Chapian Ministries, P.O. Box 897, La Jolla, Calif. 92038.

CAREER: Has worked as an elementary school teacher in Minneapolis, Minn., and as an instructor at a Bible College. Creation House (publisher), Carol Stream, Ill., originator of "Mustard Seed Library" books for children, 1974; Center for Christian Psychological Services, Roseville, Minn., psychotherapist, 1978-80; Christian minister, 1980—. Lecturer and seminar leader, 1972—. Originator of television program, "Being a Loved Person." *Member:* Authors Guild, Christian Association for Psychological Studies. *Awards, honors:* Most significant book of the year, poetry category, from *Chicago Church News,* 1973, award of recognition of graphic arts excellence from Consolidated Papers, 1973, Poetry and Fiction Mark of Excellence Award from *Campus Life Magazine,* 1974, all for *Mind Things;* the San Diego Christian Writers' Guild cited Chapian for having made the most outstanding contribution to Christian literature in 1979.

WRITINGS: City Psalms (poems; illustrated by husband, Peter Chapian), Moody, 1972; *Mind Things* (poems; illustrated by P. Chapian), Creation House, 1973; *I Learn about the Fruit of the Holy Spirit* (juvenile; illustrated by P. Chapian), Creation House, 1974; *I Learn about the Gifts of the Holy Spirit* (juvenile; illustrated by P. Chapian), Creation House, 1974; *The Holy Spirit and Me* (juvenile; illustrated by P. Chapian), Creation House, 1974; "To My Friend" series, twelve books, Successful Living, 1974; *The Emancipation of Robert Sadler* (biography), Bethany Fellowship, 1976; *Of Whom the World Was Not Worthy* (biography), Bethany Fellowship, 1978; *Free to Be Thin,* Bethany Fellowship, 1979; (with Tom Netherton) *In the Morning of My Life* (biography), Tyndale, 1979; (with William Backus) *Telling Yourself the Truth,* Bethany Fellowship, 1980; *At the End of the Rainbow* (biography), Tyndale, 1981.

MARIE CHAPIAN

Contributor to numerous magazines including, *Christian Life, Campus Life, Eternity, Christian Bookseller, Moody Monthly, Saturday Evening Post, Guidepost,* and others.

WORK IN PROGRESS: ''Currently writing 'Being a Loved Person' which is also the name of my television program. It is a book of five years of research and clinical case histories of lives touched by love.'' Also completing *Where Do I Find Heaven?,* the life story of evangelist, Roger Vann.

SIDELIGHTS: Chapian travels the world as a speaker and Bible teacher. Her books with their Christian inspirational theme have been translated into Norwegian, Swedish and Chinese.

CHASE, Mary Coyle   1907-1981

OBITUARY NOTICE—See sketch in *SATA* Volume 17: Born February 25, 1907, in Denver, Colo.; died of a heart attack, October 20, 1981, in Denver. Playwright best known for her Pulitzer Prize-winning play ''Harvey,'' the story of an inebriate and his imaginary six-foot-tall rabbit. While working at newspaper and public relations jobs, Chase began to write plays. The comedy ''Harvey,'' her first critical success, opened in November, 1944, at the Forty-Eighth Street Theatre on Broad-

way and ran for 1,775 performances. A 1952 film version of the play, starring Jimmy Stewart, and several television performances of the comedy increased its popularity. ''Harvey'' has been translated into many languages and performed in many countries. Chase successfully conveyed her penchant for the fantastical in two other plays for children, ''Mrs. McThing,'' and ''Loretta Mason Potts'' (also a novel). Her other publications for children include ''Bernadine,'' a play about adolescent boys, and *The Wicked Pigeon Ladies in the Garden. For More Information See: Authors of Books for Young People,* 2nd edition, Scarecrow, 1971; *American Authors and Books, 1640 to the Present Day,* 3rd revised edition, Crown, 1972; *Contemporary Dramatists,* St. Martin's, 1973; *American Women Writers: A Critical Reference Guide from Colonial Times to Present,* Ungar, 1979-80; *Contemporary Authors,* Volumes 77-80, Gale, 1979. *Obituaries: Washington Post,* October 23, 1981; *New York Times,* October 23, 1981; *Time,* November 2, 1981; *Newsweek* November 2, 1981.

A good book is the precious life-blood of a master spirit, embalmed and treasured up on purpose to life beyond life.

—John Milton

CLARK, Leonard 1905-1981

OBITUARY NOTICE: Born August 1, 1905, in St. Peter Port, Guernsey, Channel Islands; died in 1981 in London, England. Educator, editor, poet, and author. Clark began his career as a teacher in Gloucestershire and in London in 1921. In 1936 he left teaching to become an inspector of schools with the Ministry of Education, a time he preserved in *The Inspector Remembers.* Clark was made knight of St. Sylvester in 1970, and he won first prize in 1972 from the *International Who's Who in Poetry* competition for his poem, "The Coin." He served as a consultant editor for Chatto & Windus Poetry Books for the Young, and was a lecturer and broadcaster on poetry and education of children. Clark wrote more than sixty books, including the "Robert Andrew" and "Mr. Pettigrew" series of stories for children. Among his many children's books of verse are *The Open Door: An Anthology of Verse for Children, Near and Far, Secret as Toads,* and *Four Seasons. For More Information See:* Leonard Clark, *Green Wood: A Gloucestershire Childhood* (autobiography), Parrish, 1962; Clark, *A Fool in the Forest* (autobiography), Dobson, 1965; Clark, *Grateful Caliban* (autobiography), Dobson, 1968; *Contemporary Authors,* Volumes 13-14, revised, Gale, 1974; Clark, *The Inspector Remembers: A Diary of One of Her Majesty's Inspectors of Schools, 1936-1970* (autobiography), Dobson, 1976; *Twentieth-Century Children's Writers,* St. Martin's, 1978. *Obituaries: AB Bookman's Weekly,* November 2, 1981.

COHEN, Miriam 1926-

PERSONAL: Born October 14, 1926, in Brooklyn, N.Y.; daughter of Jacob and Bessie Echelman; married Sid Grossman, 1949 (died, 1955); married Monroe D. Cohen (a professor), May 31, 1959; children: (first marriage) Adam; (second marriage) Gabriel, Jean. *Education:* Attended Newburgh Free Academy, 1943, and Antioch College, 1944-45. *Politics:* Independent progressive. *Religion:* Jewish. *Home and office:* 618 6th St., Brooklyn, N.Y. 11215.

CAREER: Writer.

WRITINGS—All for children; all illustrated by Lillian Hoban: *Will I Have a Friend?,* Macmillan, 1967; *Best Friends,* Macmillan, 1971; *The New Teacher* (Junior Literary Guild selection), Macmillan, 1972; *Tough Jim,* Macmillan, 1974; *When Will I Read?,* Greenwillow, 1977; *Bee My Valentine!,* Greenwillow, 1978; *Lost in the Museum,* Greenwillow, 1979; *First Grade Takes a Test,* Greenwillow, 1980; *No Good in Art,* Greenwillow, 1980; *Jim Meets the Thing,* Greenwillow, 1981.

ADAPTATIONS: "Will I Have a Friend?" (filmstrip with cassett), Threshold Filmstrips, 1974.

WORK IN PROGRESS: A novel on Brazil for ages nine to eleven.

It didn't really seem funny to Jim. He couldn't read either. Anna-Maria was the only one in first grade who could.

(From *The New Teacher* by Miriam Cohen. Illustrated by Lillian Hoban.)

SIDELIGHTS: Although Cohen was born in Brooklyn, she grew up in Newburgh, N.Y. She spent a year at Antioch College. "School did not interest me very much. I only wanted to read. I read walking to school, at the dinner table, walking home from the library with the six books a week allowed me. I never thought of being a writer."

Cohen's books are books with causes—she is an avid champion of the rights of children. Her first book was written twenty years ago when Cohen was the mother of an infant son. "I've always been fascinated by the idea of bringing something into being that wasn't there before, like a painting or a play or a story. It wasn't till I met Susan Carr Hirschman [then at Harper, and now children's book editor at Greenwillow] that I began to think I really might try to be a writer. I'd written a children's story (a very bad one) and I looked in the phone book for the nearest publisher. Harper was closest to my apartment in Manhattan. So I just put my first baby into his buggy with the story and pushed up the ten blocks. Susan looked at my work and said, 'This isn't it. But you *are* a writer. You must read everything that's been written for children, and then write something different, something that comes from you.'

"That gave me the courage to keep trying. It wasn't till eight years and two babies later that I had a story accepted by this same wonderful editor. The story was *Will I Have A Friend?* My [first] three books are all about the same little kids. I loved watching nursery and kindergarten life as my boys went through. *The New Teacher* was written because I was angry and sad at the meanness of a few teachers (not those my boys had; they were wonderful). But I didn't want my story to make little children anxious about school. So I made the new teacher's meanness only a fantasy rumor of how she *might* be. She isn't at all, as it turns out."

Two decades after her first manuscript Cohen is still defending the rights of small children. Her works are included in the Kerlan Collection at the University of Minnesota.

COURTIS, Stuart Appleton 1874-1969

OBITUARY NOTICE: Born May 15, 1874, in Wyandotte, Mich.; died October 19, 1969, in Cupertino, Calif. Educator, consultant on education, and author of works in his field. Courtis served in various educational capacities for Detroit public schools and Detroit Teachers College during the 1920's. He was also professor of education at both the University of Michigan and Wayne University (now Wayne State University). He created the Courtis standardizing tests and used them in school surveys in Indiana and New York City. His writings include *Why Children Succeed, The Measurement of Growth,* and *A Picture Dictionary for Children. For More Information See: Who Was Who in America, With World Notables,* Volume V: 1969-73, Marquis, 1973; *Who Was Who Among North American Authors, 1921-1939,* Gale, 1976; *Biographical Dictionary of American Educators,* Greenwood Press, 1978.

Dreams, books, are each a world; and books,
     we know,
Are a substantial world, both pure and good:
Round these, with tendrils strong as flesh and blood,
Our pastime and our happiness will grow.
                 —William Wordsworth

CURTIS, Richard (Alan) 1937- (Ray Lilly, Curtis Richards, Morton Stultifer, Melanie Ward)

PERSONAL: Born June 23, 1937, in New York, N.Y.; son of Charles (a manufacturer) and Betty Curtis; married Leslie Tonner (an author), June 21, 1981; *Education:* Attended Syracuse University and University of Wyoming. *Office:* Richard Curtis Associates, Inc., 340 E. 66th St., New York, N.Y. 10021.

CAREER: Free-lance writer and literary agent.

WRITINGS: (Compiler) *Future Tense* (short stories), Dell, 1968; *The Genial Idiots: The American Saga as Seen by Our Humorists* (juvenile), Crowell-Collier Press, 1968; (with Althea Gibson) *So Much to Live For* (juvenile biography), Putnam, 1968; *Chiang Kai-Shek* (juvenile biography), Hawthorn, 1969; (with Elizabeth Hogan) *Perils of the Peaceful Atom: The Myth of Safe Nuclear Power Plants,* Doubleday, 1969.

(Under pseudonym Morton Stultifer) *The Case for Extinction: An Answer to Conservationists* (illustrated by Robert Powell), Dial, 1970; *The Life of Malcolm X* (juvenile biography), Macrae Smith, 1971; (with Maggie Wells) *Not Exactly a Crime: Our Vice Presidents from Adams to Agnew,* Dial, 1972; (with

A mother halfway across Temple snatched up her two children and staggered the rest of the way.... ■ (From *The Runaway Bus Mystery* by Irwin Touster and Richard Curtis. Illustrated by Richard Cuffari.)

Irwin Touster) *The Perez Arson Mystery* (juvenile; illustrated by Richard Cuffari), Dial, 1972; *Ralph Nader's Crusade* (juvenile biography), Macrae Smith, 1972; (with I. Touster) *The Runaway Bus Mystery* (juvenile), Dial, 1972; *The Berrigan Brothers: The Story of Daniel and Philip Berrigan*, Hawthorn, 1974; (under pseudonym Ray Lilly) *The Sunday Alibi*, Manor, 1977; (under pseudonym Melanie Ward) *Dreams to Come*, BJ Publishing Group, 1978; (with Hogan) *Nuclear Lessons*, Stackpole, 1980; *How to Prosper in the Coming Apocalypse*, St. Martin's, 1981; *How to Be Your Own Literary Agent*, Houghton Mifflin, 1982.

Contributor of articles to periodicals, including *Esquire, Gentleman's Quarterly, Natural History, News Front,* and *American Legion,* and of crime fiction to mystery magazines, including *Ellery Queen's Mystery Magazine.*

FOR MORE INFORMATION SEE: Natural History, March, 1969.

DASENT, Sir George Webbe   1817-1896

BRIEF ENTRY: Born May 22, 1817, on the island of St. Vincent, West Indies; died June 11, 1896 in Ascot, Berkshire, England. British scholar, author, translator, and civil servant. While Dasent was in Stockholm serving as secretary to the British envoy, he was encouraged by Jacob Grimm to begin to study Scandinavian literature and folklore. Dasent subsequently translated numerous Icelandic sagas, including *Popular Tales from the Norse* (1859), *Tales from the Fjeld* (1874), and *The Story of Burnt Njal* (1861). Returning to England in 1845, Dasent was appointed assistant editor of the *London Times.* During this time, he also became a civil service commissioner, a position he held for over twenty-two years. Dasent was appointed Professor of English Literature and Modern History of King's College, London, and knighted in 1876 for his many contributions to literature. Besides translations, Dasent wrote four of his own novels, including *Annals of an Eventful Life* (1870) and *Jest and Earnest: A Collection of Essays and Reviews* (1873). *For More Information See: Biographical Dictionary and Synopsis of Books,* Werner, 1902, reprinted, Gale, 1965; *British Authors of the Nineteenth Century,* H. W. Wilson, 1936; *The Who's Who of Children's Literature,* Schocken Books, 1968.

DICKINSON, Emily (Elizabeth)   1830-1886

PERSONAL: Born December 10, 1830, in Amherst, Mass.; died May 15, 1886, in Amherst; daughter of Edward (a lawyer, later a congressman, and treasurer of Amherst College), and Emily (Norcross) Dickinson. *Education:* Graduated from Amherst Academy, 1947; attended Mt. Holyoke Female Seminary, 1847-48. *Home:* Amherst, Mass. Dickinson's birthplace was named a National Historic Landmark, 1964.

CAREER: Poet. Now recognized by many critics as one of the finest lyric poets of the English language, Dickinson was an unknown poet in her own lifetime, when only seven of her poems were published, anonymously and without her consent in local journals. Discouraged from publishing her ''unorthodox'' work, she wrote in secret for herself. After her death, her family discovered 1,775 poems, most of them written between 1858 and 1866. Dickinson led an uneventful life, influenced by a dominating father and a mysterious ''lost'' love.

Emily Dickinson, at seventeen.

Naturally shy, she kept more and more to herself until she became a recluse who never left her home after 1871. Her father died in 1874, and her mother became an invalid in the next year. Dickinson nursed her until 1882, when her mother died.

WRITINGS—Poems selected for children: *Poems for Youth* (edited by Alfred Leete Hampson; foreword by May Lamberton Becker; illustrations by George and Doris Hauman), Little, Brown, 1934; *Poems* (edited by Helen Plotz; illustrated by Robert Kipniss), Crowell, 1964; *A Letter to the World: Poems for Young Readers* (selected and introduced by Rumer Godden; decorated by Prudence Seward), Bodley Head, 1968, Macmillan, 1969; *I'm Nobody! Who Are You?: Poems of Emily Dickinson for Children* (introduced by Richard B. Sewall; illustrated by Rex Schneider), Stemmer House, 1978.

Principal collections: *Poems by Emily Dickinson,* three series, Roberts Brothers, 1890-96 (first series, 1890, and second series, 1891, edited by Mabel Loomis Todd and Thomas Wentworth Higginson; third series, 1896, edited by Todd), facsimile reprint, *Poems, 1890-1896,* Scholars' Facsimiles, 1967; *The Poems of Emily Dickinson* (centenary edition; edited by niece, Martha Dickinson Bianchi, and A. L. Hampson), Little, Brown, 1930, 2nd revised edition, 1957; *The Complete Poems of Emily Dickinson* (first collection of all 1,775 poems; edited by Thomas H. Johnson), Little, Brown, 1968; *Acts of Light: Poems by Emily Dickinson* (with an appreciation by Jane Langton; paintings by Nancy Ekholm Burkert), New York Graphic Society, 1980.

Letters: *Emily Dickinson Face to Face: The Unpublished Letters, with Reminiscences and Notes* (edited by M. D. Bianchi), Houghton, 1932, reprinted, Shoe String, 1970; *The Letters of*

(From the stage production "The Belle of Amherst," with Julie Harris recreating the world of Emily Dickinson. Premiered at the Longacre Theatre, April 28, 1976.)

Emily Dickinson, three volumes (edited by T. H. Johnson), Belknap Press of Harvard University Press, 1958.

Collections of manuscripts and letters are held in the Houghton Library of Harvard University, the Frost Library at Amherst College, the Margaret J. Pershing Collection of Emily Dickinson at Princeton University, the Galatea Collection at the Boston Public Library, the Jones Library at Amherst College, and the Todd-Bingham Archive at Yale University.

ADAPTATIONS—Films: "Emily Dickinson" (filmstrip), Encyclopaedia Britannica Films, 1954; "Magic Prison" (written by Archibald MacLeish), Encyclopaedia Britannica Educational Corp., 1969; "The Private World of Emily Dickinson" (filmstrip), Guidance Associates (Pleasantville, N.Y.), 1971; "Emily Dickinson" (filmstrip) Thomas S. Klise Co. (Peoria, Ill.), 1976; "Emily Dickinson: I'm Nobody! Who Are You?" (filmstrip), Aids of Cape Cod, 1977; "Emily Dickinson: A Certain Slant of Light" (featuring Julie Harris), Pyramid Films, 1978; "Emily Dickinson'" (with teacher's guide), Journal Films (Evanston, Ill.), 1978.

Plays based on Dickinson's life: Susan Glaspell, *Alison's House* (Pulitzer Prize winner; staged by Eva LeGallienne), S. French, 1930; Dorothy Gardner, *Eastward in Eden: The Love Story of Emily Dickinson,* Longmans, 1949; Norman Rosten, *Come Slowly, Eden: A Portrait of Emily Dickinson* (stage production starring Kim Hunter), Dramatists Play Service, 1967; William Luce, *Belle of Amherst* (stage production starring Julie Harris), Houghton, 1976.

Recordings: "Poems and Letters of Emily Dickinson" (read by Julie Harris), Caedmon, 1960; "The Mind of Emily Dickinson" (anthology of letters and poems; edited by Dillon Usill; read by Glenda Jackson), Argo, 1977.

SIDELIGHTS: **December 10, 1830.** Born in the small farming village of Amherst, Massachusetts. Dickinson was the second of three children of Edward and Emily Dickinson. Dickinson's father, a lawyer, was treasurer of Amherst college, a member of the state legislature for several terms, and a member of Congress for one term. As a father, he was stern, somewhat harsh, and remote. He had been reared on the ideals of the eighteenth century, the Puritan Ethic—hard-work, devotion under God for family and the commonwealth, reason over passion, and moderation in all things. Self-denial and self-restraint were considered virtues. Dickinson said of her father: "You know he never played." [Millicent Todd Bingham, *Emily Dickinson's Home,* Harper, 1955.[1]] She tried to follow his example. "Flowers are so enticing that I fear they are sins—like gambling or apostasy."[1]

Dickinson loved her father and was in constant awe of him. In her teenage years, she began to realize that he was probably the greatest shaping force of her nature. "I never had a mother. I suppose a mother is one to whom you hurry when you are troubled.

"I always ran Home to Awe when a child, if anything befell me. He was an awful Mother, but I liked him better than none." [Thomas Johnson, *Emily Dickinson, An Interpretive Biography,* Belknap Press, 1955.[2]]

"I have a brother and sister; my mother does not care for thought, and father, too busy with his briefs to notice what we do. He buys me many books, but begs me not to read them, because he fears they joggle the mind. They are religious, except me, and address an eclipse, every morning, whom they call their 'Father.'" [Martha Dickinson Bianchi, *The Life and Letters of Emily Dickinson,* Riverside Press, 1924.[3]]

1841. Attended Amherst Academy, which was founded by her grandfather. She studied Latin, French, history, rhetoric, botany, geology, and mental philosophy. "I am growing handsome very fast indeed! I expect to be the belle of Amherst when I reach my 17th year. I don't doubt that I shall have perfect crowds of admirers at that age. Then how I shall delight to make them await my bidding, and with what delight shall I witness their suspense while I make my final decision." [David Higgins, *Portrait of Emily Dickinson,* Rutgers University Press, 1967.[4]]

1847. Graduated from Amherst Academy after six years of irregular attendance, due to poor health.

1847-1848. Attended Mount Holyoke Female Seminary in South Hadley, Massachusetts. She wrote to a friend: "My dear Abiah,—I am really at Mount Holyoke Seminary and this is to be my home for a long year. . . . It has been nearly six weeks since I left home, and that is a longer time than I was ever away from home before now. I was very homesick for a few days, and it seemed to me I could not live here. But I am now contented and quite happy, if I can be happy when absent from my dear home and friends. You may laugh at the idea that I cannot be happy when away from home, but you must remember that I have a very dear home and that this is my first trial in the way of absence for any length of time in my life. . . .

"I came to South Hadley six weeks ago next Thursday. I was much fatigued with the ride, and had a severe cold besides, which prevented me from commencing my examinations until the next day, when I began. I finished them in three days, and found them about what I had anticipated, though the old scholars say they are more strict than they ever have been before. As you can easily imagine, I was much delighted to finish without failures, and I came to the conclusion then, that I should not be at all homesick, but the reaction left me as homesick a girl as it is not usual to see. I am now quite contented and am very occupied in reviewing the Junior studies, as I wish to enter the middle class. The school is very large, and though quite a number have left, on account of finding the examinations more difficult than they anticipated, yet there are nearly 300 now. Perhaps you know that Miss Lyon is raising her standard of scholarship a good deal, on account of the number of applicants this year, and she makes the examinations more severe than usual.

"You cannot imagine how trying they are, because if we cannot go through them all in a specified time, we are sent home. I cannot be too thankful that I got through as soon as I did, and I am sure that I never would endure the suspense which I endured during those three days again for all the treasures of the world.

"I room with my cousin Emily, who is a Senior. She is an excellent room-mate, and does all in her power to make me happy. . . . Everything is pleasant and happy here, and I think I could be no happier at any other school away from home. Things seem much more like home than I anticipated, and the teachers are all very kind and affectionate to us. They call on us frequently and urge us to return their calls, and when we do, we always receive a cordial welcome from them.

"I will tell you my order of time for the day. . . . At 6 o'clock we all rise. We breakfast at 7. Our study hours begin at 8. At

Emily, Austin, and Lavinia Dickinson.

9 we all meet in Seminary Hall for devotions. At 10¼ I recite a review of Ancient History, in connection with which we read Goldsmith and Grimshaw. At 11, I recite a lesson in Pope's *Essay on Man,* which is merely transposition. At 12 I practice calisthenics, and at 12¼ read until dinner, which is at 12½, and after dinner, from 1½ until 2, I sing in Seminary Hall. From 2¾ until 3¾ I practice upon the piano. At 3¾ I go to Sections, where we give in all our accounts for the day, including absence, tardiness, communications, breaking silent study hours, receiving company in our rooms, and ten thousand other things which I will not take time or place to mention. At 4½ we go into Seminary Hall and receive advice from Miss Lyon in the form of a lecture. We have supper at 6, and study silent hours from then until the retiring bell, which rings at 8¾, but the tardy bell does not ring until 9¾, so that we don't often obey the first warning to retire. Unless we have a good and reasonable excuse for failure upon any of the times that I mentioned above, they are recorded and a *black mark* stands against our names. As you can easily imagine, we do not like very well to get 'exceptions,' as they are called scientifically here.

"My domestic work is not difficult and consists in carrying the knives from the first tier of tables at morning and noon, and at night washing and wiping the same quantity of knives. I am quite well and hope to spend the year here, free from sickness.

"You have probably heard many reports of the food here; and if so, I can tell you that I have yet seen nothing corresponding to my ideas on that point from what I have heard. Everything is wholesome and abundant and much nicer than I should imagine could be provided for almost 300 girls. We have also a great variety upon our tables and frequent changes. One thing is certain, and that is, that Miss Lyon and all the teachers seem to consult our comfort and happiness in everything they do, and you know that is pleasant. When I left home I did not

There is no frigate like a book
To take us lands away,
Nor any coursers like a page
Of prancing poetry.

■ (From *Poems for Youth* by Emily Dickinson. Edited by Alfred Leete Hampson. Illustrated by George and Doris Hauman.)

think I should find a campanion or a dear friend in all the multitude. I expected to find rough and uncultivated manners, and, to be sure, I have found some of that stamp, but on the whole, there is an ease and grace, a desire to make one another happy, which delights and at the same time surprises me very much. I find no Abby nor Abiah nor Mary, but I love many of the girls.

"Austin [my brother] came to see me when I had been here about two weeks . . . I need not tell you how delighted I was to see them all, nor how happy it made me to hear them say that 'they were *so lonely*.' It is a sweet feeling to know that you are missed and that your memory is precious at home. This week, on Wednesday, I was at my window, when I happened to look towards the hotel and saw father and mother, walking over here as dignified as you please. I need not tell you that I danced and clapped my hands, and flew to meet them, for you can imagine how I felt. I will only ask you, do you love your parents? They wanted to surprise me, and for that reason did not let me know they were coming. I could not bear to have them go, but go they must, and so I submitted in sadness. . . ." [Robert N. Linscott, editor, *Selected Poems and Letters of Emily Dickinson*, Doubleday, 1959.[5]]

Described her visit home in another letter to Abiah: "Never did Amherst look more lovely to me, and gratitude rose in my heart to God, for granting me such a safe return to my *own dear home*. Soon the carriage stopped in front of our own house, and all were at the door to welcome the returned one, from mother, with tears in her eyes, down to pussy, who tried to look as graceful as was becoming to her dignity. . . . It was the first meeting, as it had been the first separation, and it was a joyful one to all of us.

". . . In the morning I was waked by the glorious sunshine staring full in my face. We went to church in the morning and listened to an excellent sermon from our own minister, Mr.

Colton. At noon we returned and had a nice dinner, which, you well know, cannot be dispensed with on Thanksgiving day. We had several calls in the afternoon, and had four invitations out for the evening. Of course we could not accept them all, much to my sorrow, but decided to make two visits. At about 7 o'clock father, mother, Austin, Viny, cousin Emily, and myself to bring up at the rear, went to Professor Warner's, where we spent an hour delightfully with a few friends, and then bidding them good eve, we young folks went down to Mrs. S. Mack's, accompanied by *sister Mary*. There was quite a company of young people assembled when we arrived, and after we had played many games we had, in familiar terms, a 'candy scrape.' We enjoyed the evening much, and returned not until the clock pealed out, 'Remember ten o'clock, my dear, remember ten o'clock.' After our return, father wishing to hear the piano, I, like an obedient daughter, played and sang a few tunes, much to his apparent gratification. We then retired, and the next day and the next were as happily spent as the eventful Thanksgiving day itself.

". . . Monday came so soon, and with it came a carriage to our door, and amidst tears falling thick and fast away I went again. Slowly and sadly dragged a few of the days after my return to the Seminary, and I was very homesick, but 'after a storm there comes a calm,' and so it was in my case. My sorrows were soon lost in study, and I again felt happy, if happiness there can be away from 'home, sweet home.'"[5]

If I can stop one heart from breaking,
I shall not live in vain;
If I can ease one life the aching,
Or cool one pain,
Or help one fainting robin
Unto his nest again,
I shall not live in vain.

■ (From *Poems for Youth* by Emily Dickinson. Edited by Alfred Leete Hampson. Illustrated by George and Doris Hauman.)

Dickinson left the seminary after one year because everyone was asked to join the church; something she found impossible to do. She was also very homesick and often ill.

1850. It was then the custom for young people to set aside a week in February to exchange personally written valentines. Dickinson wrote a forty-line rhyme to a young bachelor practicing law in her father's office which was published in the Amherst undergraduate magazine, *The Indicator*.

Throughout the 1850s, Dickinson took part in the social activities of the community. ''There is a good deal going on just now—the last two weeks of vacation were full to the brim of fun. Austin was reading Hume's History—and his getting through was the signal for general uproar. Campaign opened by a sleigh ride on a very magnificent plan . . . a party of ten from here met a party of the same number from Greenfield—at South-Deerfield the evening next New Year's—and had a frolic, comprising charades—walking around *indefinitely*—music—conversation—and supper—set in the most modern style; got home at two o'clock—and felt no worse for it the next morning—which we all thought was very remarkable. Tableaux at the President's followed next in the train—a Sliding party close upon it's heels—and several cozy sociables brought up the rear. To say nothing of a party *universale* at the house of Sydney Adams—and one *confidentiale* at Tempe Linnell's.''[4]

''When I am not at work, I sit by the side of mother, provide for her little wants, and try to cheer and encourage her. I ought to be glad and grateful that I *can* do anything now, but I do feel so very lonely, and so anxious to have her cured. I haven't repined but once, and you shall know all the why. At noon . . . I heard a well-known rap, and a friend I love *so* dearly

'Twas such a little, little boat
That toddled down the bay!
'Twas such a gallant, gallant sea
That beckoned it away!

■(From *Poems for Youth* by Emily Dickinson. Edited by Alfred Leete Hampson. Illustrated by George and Doris Hauman.)

Futile the winds
To a heart in port,—...

■(From *Poems of Emily Dickinson*, selected by Helen Plotz. Illustrated by Robert Kipniss.)

came and asked me to ride in the woods, the sweet, still woods,—I wanted to exceedingly. I told him I could not go, and he said he was disappointed, he wanted me very much. Then the tears came into my eyes, though I tried to choke them back, and he said I *could* and *should* go, and it seemed to me unjust. Oh, I struggled with great temptation, and it cost me much of denial; but I think in the end I conquered,—not a glorious victory, where you hear the rolling drum, but a kind of a helpless victory, where triumph would come to itself, faintest music, weary soldiers, nor a waving flag, nor a long, loud shout. I had read of Christ's temptations, and how they were like our own, only he didn't sin; I wondered if *one* was like mine, and whether it made him angry. I couldn't make up my mind; do you think he ever did?

''I went cheerfully round my work, humming a little air till mother had gone to sleep, then cried with all my might—seemed to think I was much abused—that this wicked world was unworthy such devoted and terrible suffering—and came to my various senses in great dudgeon at life, and time, and love for affliction and anguish.

''What shall we do, my darling, when trial grows more and more, when the dim, lone light expires, and it's dark, so very dark, and we wander, and know not where, and cannot get out of the forest—whose is the hand to help us, and to lead, and forever guide us; they talk of a 'Jesus of Nazareth'—will you tell me if it be he?. . .''[5]

1852. First poem published in the *Springfield Daily Republican*. She had written a valentine to another young man studying law

(From *Acts of Light: Poems by Emily Dickinson.* Illustrated by Nancy Ekholm Burkert.)

...Pluck up its stakes, and disappear—
Without the sound of Boards
Or Rip of Nail—or Carpenter—
But just the miles of stare—
That signalize a Show's Retreat—....

■ (From *Acts of Light: Poems by Emily Dickinson.* Illustrated by Nancy Ekholm Burkert.)

(From "Come Slowly, Eden: A Portrait of Emily Dickinson," starring Kim Hunter. Presented as part of the ANTA Matinee Series at the Theatre De Lys, December, 1966.)

in her father's office. Recognizing its worth, he submitted it to the newspaper.

Met Benjamin Franklin Newton, a young man employed in her father's office. "Mr. Newton became to me a gentle, yet grave Preceptor, teaching me what to read, what authors to admire, what was most grand and beautiful in nature, and that sublimer lesson, a faith in things unseen, and in a life again, nobler, and much more blessed—"[4]

1852. Father elected to Congress.

March 24, 1853. Newton died. "When a little Girl, I had a friend, who taught me Immortality—but venturing too near, himself—he never returned—Soon after, my Tutor, died—and for several years, my Lexicon— was my only companion—.

"My dying Tutor told me that he would like to live till I had been a poet, but Death was much of Mob as I could master—then—"[4]

1854. "We were three weeks in Washington, while father was there, and have been two in Philadelphia. We have had many pleasant times, and seen much that is fair, and heard much that is wonderful—many sweet ladies and noble gentlemen have taken us by the hand and smiled upon us pleasantly—and the sun shines brighter for our way thus far.

"I will not tell you what I saw—the elegance, the grandeur; you will not care to know the value of the diamonds my Lord and Lady wore, but if you haven't been to the sweet Mount Vernon, then I *will* tell you how on one soft spring day we glided down the Potomac in a painted boat, and jumped upon the shore—how hand in hand we stole along up a tangled pathway till we reached the tomb of General George Washington, how we paused beside it, and no one spoke a word, then hand in hand, walked on again, not less wise or sad for that marble story; how we went within the door—raised the latch he lifted when he last went home—thank the Ones in Light that he's since passed in through a brighter wicket! Oh, I could spend a long day, if it did not weary you, telling of Mount Vernon. . . ." [Mabel Loomis Todd, editor, *Letters of Emily Dickinson,* Roberts Brothers, 1894.[6]]

In Dickinson's time, household chores were a full-time occupation. "I have been at work, providing 'the food that perisheth,' scaring the timorous dust, and being obedient and kind. . . . Mother is still an invalid, though a partially restored one; father and Austin still clamor for food; and I, like a martyr, am feeding them."[3]

Dickinson had almost no time for herself. A chance to be alone with her books and her thoughts did not come often, and then usually only late at night while others slept.

> "Unto my books so good to turn
> Far ends of tired days;
> It half endears the abstinence,
> And pain is missed praise."[1]

Gradually she began to withdraw. Her sister, Lavinia, said: "As for Emily, she was not withdrawn or exclusive really. She was always watching for the rewarding person to come, but she was a very busy person herself. She had to think—she was the only one of us who had that to do. Father believed; and Mother loved; and Austin and Amherst; and I had the family to keep track of."[4]

1858. Began gathering her poems into packets: fifty poems that year; one hundred in 1859; sixty-five in 1860; eighty in 1861, and 366 in 1862.

April 15, 1862. Sent four poems to Thomas Wentworth Higginson, a professional author, for critique. "Mr. Higginson,— Are you too deeply occupied to say if my verse is alive?

"The mind is so near itself it cannot see distinctly, and I have none to ask.

"Should you think it breathed, and had you the leisure to tell me, I should feel quick gratitude.

"If I make the mistake, that you dared to tell me would give me sincerer honor toward you.

"I enclose my name, asking you, if you please, sir, to tell me what is true?

"That you will not betray me it is needless to ask, since honor is its own pawn."[3]

Higginson did not think her poems were fit to publish, but he was fascinated by them, and thus began a correspondence which continued until her death. Higginson once asked for her photograph. She replied: "I had no portrait, now, but am small, like the Wren, and my Hair is bold, like the Chestnut Bur, and my eyes, like the Sherry in the Glass, that the Guest leaves."[2]

August 16, 1870. Higginson paid his first visit to Dickinson. In the only existing record of a conversation with her; he said he heard: "A step like a pattering child's in entry & in glided a little plain woman with two smooth bands of reddish hair . . . in a very plain & exquisitely clean white piqué & a blue net worsted shawl. She came to me with two day lilies, which she put in a sort of childlike way into my hand & said 'These are my introduction' in a soft frightened breathless childlike voice—and added under her breath Forgive me if I am frightened; I never see strangers & hardly know what I say—but she talked soon & thenceforward continuously—& deferentially—sometimes stopping to ask me to talk instead of her—but readily recommencing. . . . Thoroughly ingenuous & simple . . . & saying many things which you would have thought foolish & I wise—& some things you would have liked. I add a few over the page. . . . 'Women talk; men are silent. That is why I dread women.' 'Truth is such a rare thing it is delightful to tell it.' 'It is oblivion or absorption when things pass from our minds?'

"If I read a book and it makes my whole body so cold no fire ever can warm me, I know *that* is poetry. If I feel physically as if the top of my head were taken off, I know *that* is poetry. These are the only ways I know it. Is there any other way?"[2]

Higginson said that he had found her "much too enigmatical a being for me to solve in an hour's interview, and an instinct told me that the slightest attempt at direct cross-examination would make her withdraw into her shell; I could only sit and watch, as one does in the woods. I was never with any one who drained my nerve power so much. Without touching her, she drew from me. I am glad not to live near her."[2]

June 16, 1874. Father died. "We were eating our supper the fifteenth of June, and Austin came in. He had a despatch in his hand, and I saw by his face we were all lost, though I didn't know how. He said that father was very sick, and he and Vinnie must go. The train had already gone. While horses were dressing, news came he was dead.

"Father does not live with us now—he lives in a new house. Though it was built in an hour it is better than this. He hasn't

(The Pulitzer Prize winning play "Alison's House," based on the life of Emily Dickinson, was written by Susan Glaspell and starred Eva LeGallienne. It opened at the Civic Repertory Theatre, December 1, 1930.)

There is no frigate like a book
To take us lands away,
Nor any coursers like a page
Of prancing poetry.
This traverse may the poorest take
Without oppress of toll—
How frugal is the chariot
That bears a human soul!

(From *I'm Nobody! Who Are You? Poems of Emily Dickinson for Children.* Illustrated by Rex Schneider.)

any garden because he moved after gardens were made, so we take him the best flowers, and if we only knew he knew, perhaps we could stop crying. . . .''[1]

From that time on, she never left her house. The following year, her mother became paralyzed and Dickinson with the help from her sister cared for her until her death seven years later. ''We dwell as when you saw us—the mighty dying of my Father made no external change—Mother and Sister are with me, and my Brother and pseudo Sister, in the nearest House—When Father lived I remained with him because he would miss me—Now, Mother is helpless—a holier demand—I do not go away, but the Grounds are ample—almost travel—to me, and the few that I knew—came—since my Father died.'' [Leonard Unger, editor, *American Writers: A Collection of Literary Biographies*, Scribner, 1974.[7]]

Biographer, Thomas H. Johnson noted: ''Her stratagems, like her poetry, once thought to be eccentric, were part of the drama of her existence. She saw only those she chose to see. She conversed in aphorisms. She dressed immaculately and only in white. To small children she was always accessible, and to them she opened her heart and her cookie jar. She secured her privacy by the stalwart aid of her sister and their faithful Irish maid. She organized her daily routines so that she could live and think and express her thoughts as she herself wished them lived and expressed. Her life, like her art, was planned with utmost economy.''[2]

1878. Fell in love with Judge Otis Lord, a former friend of her father's, who was eighteen years older than she was.

1882. Mother died. ''We were never intimate Mother and Children while she was our Mother—but Mines in the same Ground meet by tunneling and when she became our Child, the Affection came.''[2]

1883. Nephew, Gilbert, whom Dickinson took a special delight in, died at the age of eight.

March 13, 1884. Judge Lord died.

June 14, 1884. Suffered a physical and emotional collapse from which, despite improvements, she never fully recovered. ''The dyings have been too deep for me.'' [Theodora Ward, *The Capsule of the Mind*, Belknap Press, 1961.[8]]

May 15, 1886. Died in Amherst.

> ''Because I could not stop for Death—
> He kindly stopped for me—
> The Carriage held but just Ourselves—
> And Immortality.''[2]

FOR MORE INFORMATION SEE—For young people: Jean Gould, *Miss Emily* (illustrated by Ursula Koering), Houghton, 1946; Laura Benét, *Famous American Poets*, Dodd, 1950; Jane Muir, *Famous Modern American Women Writers*, Dodd, 1959; Polly Longsworth, *Emily Dickinson: Her Letter to the World*, Crowell, 1965; Aileen L. Fisher and Olive Rabe, *We Dickinsons: The Life of Emily Dickinson as Seen through the Eyes of Her Brother Austin* (decorations by Ellen Raskin), Atheneum, 1965; Edna Barth, *I'm Nobody! Who Are You?: The Story of Emily Dickinson* (illustrated by Richard Cuffari), Seabury, 1971; L. Benét, *Famous New England Authors*, Dodd, 1970; James Playsted Wood, *Emily Elizabeth Dickinson*, Nelson, 1972; L. Benét, *The Mystery of Emily Dickinson*, Dodd, 1974; Mary-Ellen Kulkin, *Her Way*, American Library Association, 1976.

Adult: Martha Dickinson Bianchi, *The Life and Letters of Emily Dickinson*, Houghton, 1924, reprinted, Biblo & Tannen, 1971; Josephine Pollitt, *Emily Dickinson: The Human Background of Her Poetry*, Harper, 1930, reprinted, Cooper Square, 1970; MacGregor Jenkins, *Emily Dickinson, Friend and Neighbor*, Little, Brown, 1930; George F. Whicher, *This Was A Poet: A Critical Biography of Emily Dickinson*, Scribner, 1938, reprinted, Shoe String, 1980; Richard V. Chase, *Emily Dickinson*, Sloane, 1951, reprinted, Greenwood, 1971; Grace Parkinson, ''Emily Dickinson and Children,'' *Horn Book*, February, 1957; Albert J. Gelpi, *Emily Dickinson: The Mind of the Poet*, Harvard University Press, 1965, Norton, 1971; John Cody, *After Great Pain: The Inner Life of Emily Dickinson*, Belknap Press of Harvard University Press, 1971; Willis J. Buckingham, editor, *Emily Dickinson: An Annotated Bibliography*, Indiana University Press, 1970; Richard B. Sewall, *The Life of Emily Dickinson*, Farrar, Straus, 1974; Paul J. Feriazzo, *Emily Dickinson*, Twayne, 1976; *Dictionary of Literary Biography*, Volume I: *The American Renaissance in New England*, edited by Joel Myerson, Gale, 1978; David Porter, *Dickinson: The Modern Idiom*, Harvard University Press, 1981.

DONOVAN, John   1928-

BRIEF ENTRY: Born in 1928. Playwright, author of young adult fiction, and executive director of the Children's Book Council. Donovan's young adult novels explore some of the most potent problems confronting teens today—alcoholism, homosexuality, divorce, loneliness, guilt, and death. Critics have noted that each of his novels is very different from the other; yet all his books share a theme of isolation and alienation. Donovan's first book to receive widespread critical acclaim, as well as a nomination for the Newbery Medal, was *I'll Get There. It Better Be Worth the Trip* (Harper, 1969). His next effort, *Wild in the World* (Harper, 1971), won the National Book Award, Children's Book Category in 1972. Among his later works are *Remove Protective Coating a Little at a Time* (Harper, 1973), *Good Old James* (Harper, 1974), and *Family* (Harper, 1976). *Office address:* Children's Book Council Inc., 67 Irving Pl., New York, N.Y. 10003. *For More Information See: Twentieth-Century Children's Writers*, St. Martin's, 1978; *Contemporary Authors*, Volumes 97-100, Gale, 1981.

DOUBTFIRE, Dianne (Abrams)   1918-

PERSONAL: Born October 18, 1918, in Leeds, New Yorkshire, England; daughter of Frederick Samuel and Etty (Heslewood) Abrams: married Stanley Doubtfire, 1946; children: Ashley Graham (son). *Education:* Studied at Harrogate School of Art, Yorkshire; Slade School of Fine Art, University of London, diploma, 1941; Institute of Education, University of London, A.T.D., 1947. *Home:* Folly Cottage, Ventnor, Isle of Wight, England. *Agent:* Curtis Brown Ltd., 1 Craven Hill, London, W.2., England.

CAREER: Free-lance writer 1952—. Adult education lecturer in creative writing for Surrey County Council and Isle of Wight County Council. *Military service:* Women's Auxiliary Air Force, 1941-46; became flight sergeant; served in the Middle East in administrative capacity, 1944-46. *Member:* International P.E.N., Society of Authors, National Book League, Writers Guild of Great Britain.

DIANNE DOUBTFIRE

WRITINGS—Juveniles: *Escape on Monday,* Macmillan, 1970; *Girl in Cotton Wool,* Scholastic, 1975; *A Girl Called Rosemary,* Scholastic, 1977; *Girl with Wings,* Scholastic, 1978; *Girl in a Gondola,* Macmillan, 1980; *This Jim,* Macmillan, 1980; *Sky Lovers,* Macmillan, 1981.

Other: *Fun with Stamps,* Hutchinson, 1957; *More Fun with Stamps,* Hutchinson, 1958; *Lust for Innocence* (novel), Morrow, 1960; *Reason for Violence* (novel), P. Davies, 1961; *Kick a Tin Can* (novel), P. Davies, 1964; *The Flesh Is Strong* (novel), P. Davies, 1966; *Behind the Screen* (novel), P. Davies, 1969; *The Craft of Novel-Writing* (non-fiction), Allison and Busby, 1978; *Creative Writing,* Hodder & Stoughton, 1983.

WORK IN PROGRESS: Adult novel.

SIDELIGHTS: "There should be no aspect of human affairs which the serious novelist cannot introduce, with taste and compassion into his books. . . . I try to work six hours a day, during which I am lucky if I complete one thousand words. When I reach a temporary deadlock (a frequent occurrence) I go for a walk, talking aloud to myself, battling the thing out. I never prepare a rigid plot in advance; the story grows as the characters develop. . . . My greatest ambition is to write a novel that really satisfies me."

Doubtfire finds great pleasure in public speaking. "There is a wide interest in the techniques of writing and I discover new angles on my work when I lecture. The preparation of new talks is a constant challenge and the discussions which follow the lectures are a source of great inspiration to me. My book, *The Craft of Novel-Writing*, was sparked off by the remarkable interest shown by audiences when I spoke on the subject. I also enjoy addressing school children. I receive a great many letters from young readers and their questions and comments show an involvement and understanding which delights my heart."

HOBBIES AND OTHER INTERESTS: Motoring, meditation, cookery, making cine films, travel.

DOUGLASS, Frederick   1817(?)-1895

PERSONAL: Original name, Frederick Augustus Washington Bailey; name legally changed, 1838; born about February, 1817, in Tuckahoe, Md.; died February 20, 1895, in Anacostia Heights, D.C.; son of an unidentified white man and Harriet Bailey (a Negro slave); married Anna Murray (a freed slave), September, 1838 (died); married Helen Pitts, 1884. *Residence:* Anacostia Heights, D.C.

CAREER: Abolitionist, journalist, orator, and author. Escaped from slavery, 1838; worked as laborer in New Bedford, Mass., for two years; made speech before Massachusetts Anti-Slavery Society, 1841, and became their agent, 1841-45; became central figure in "One Hundred Conventions" of New England Anti-Slavery Society; lectured in England and Ireland, 1845-47, following publication of autobiography; returned to United States and bought his freedom, 1847; founder, editor, and publisher, *North Star* (abolitionist journal; later renamed *Frederick Douglass's Paper*), Rochester, N.Y., 1847-60; from 1851 on, he was allied with the conservative wing of the abolitionists and lectured frequently on topics including the use of Negroes in the armed forces, industrial education for Negroes, equal rights for freedmen, and women's suffrage. Assisted in recruiting 54th and 55th Massachusetts Colored Regiments during the Civil War; appointed assistant secretary to Santo Domingo Commission, 1871; District of Columbia, marshal, 1877-81, recorder of deeds, 1881-86; United States minister-resident and consul general, Haiti, 1889-91.

WRITINGS—Of interest to young readers: *Narrative of the Life of Frederick Douglass, an American Slave*, Boston Anti-Slavery Society, 1845, reprinted with an introduction by Rayford W. Logan, Collier, 1962; *My Bondage and My Freedom*, introduction by James M'Cune Smith, Miller, Orton & Mulligan, 1955, reprinted with a new introduction by Philip S. Foner, Dover, 1969; *The Life and Times of Frederick Douglass, Written by Himself: His Early Life as a Slave, His Escape from Bondage, and His Complete History to the Present Time*, Park Publishing, 1881, a new edition edited and adapted by Genevieve S. Gray (illustrated by Scott Duncan), Grosset, 1970, a revised edition published as *From Slave to Statesman: The Life and Times of Frederick Douglass, Written by Himself*, abridged by Glenn Munson, Noble & Noble, 1972; *The Life and Times of Frederick Douglass, Written by Himself*, Pathway Press, 1941; *Frederick Douglass: Selections from His Writings*, edited by Philip S. Foner, International Publishers, 1945, reprinted, 1964; *The Mind and Heart of Frederick Douglass: Excerpts from Speeches of the Great Negro Orator*, adapted by Barbara Ritchie, Crowell, 1968.

Drawing of Frederick Douglass. ■ (From *Life and Times of Frederick Douglass* by Frederick Douglass.)

The full list of Douglass's speeches and collected works is long and varied, including treatises on women's suffrage and the rights of freed slaves. His principal writings are given below.

Collected works: *The Life and Writings of Frederick Douglass*, edited by Philip S. Foner, International Publishers, 1950-55, Volume I: *Early Years, 1817-1849*, Volume II: *Pre-Civil War Decade, 1850-1860*, Volume III: *The Civil War, 1861-1865*, Volume IV: *Reconstruction and After*, Volume V: *Supplementary Volume, 1844-1860*, 1975; *Frederick Douglass on Women's Rights*, edited by Philip S. Foner, Greenwood Press, 1976; *A Black Diplomat in Haiti: The Diplomatic Correspondence of U.S. Minister Frederick Douglass from Haiti, 1889-1891*, edited and introduced by Norma Brown, Documentary Publications, 1977; *The Frederick Douglass Papers*, edited by John W. Blassingame and others, Yale University Press, 1979.

Speeches: *The Anti-Slavery Movement*, Lee, Mann & Co., 1855; *The Constitution of the United States: Is It Pro-Slavery or Anti-Slavery?*, T. & W. Birtwhistle, 1860; *Men of Color to Arms!: A Call by Frederick Douglass*, [Rochester, N.Y.], 1863; *John Brown: An Address by Frederick Douglass at the Fourteenth Anniversary of Storer College*, Morning Star Job Printing House, 1881; *Negroes and the National War Effort*, foreward by James W. Ford, Workers Library Publishers, 1942; *Frederick Douglass: A Lecture on Our National Capital*, Smithsonian Institution Press, 1978.

SIDELIGHTS: **1817** or **1818.** Born into slavery as Frederick Augustus Washington Bailey. "I was born in Tuckahoe, near Hillsborough, and about twelve miles from Easton, in Talbot county, Maryland. I have no accurate knowledge of my age, never having seen any authentic record containing it. By far the larger part of the slaves know as little of their ages as horses know of theirs, and it is the wish of most masters within my knowledge to keep their slaves thus ignorant. I do not remember to have ever met a slave who could tell of his birthday. They seldom came nearer to it than planting-time, harvest-time, cherry-time, spring-time, or fall-time. A want of information concerning my own was a source of unhappiness to me even during childhood. The white children could tell their ages. I could not tell why I ought to be deprived of the same privilege. I was not allowed to make any inquires of my master concerning it. He deemed all such inquiries on the part of a slave improper and impertinent, and evidence of a restless spirit. . . .

"My mother was named Harriet Bailey. She was the daughter of Isaac and Betsey Bailey, both colored, and quite dark. My mother was a darker complexion than either my grandmother or grandfather.

"My father was a white man. He was admitted to be such by all I ever heard speak of my parentage. The opinion was also whispered that my master was my father; but of the correctness of this opinion, I know nothing; the means of knowing was withheld from me. My mother and I were separated when I was but an infant—before I knew her as my mother. It is a common custom, in the part of Maryland from which I ran away, to part children from their mothers at a very early age. Frequently, before the child has reached its twelfth month, its mother is taken from it, and hired out on some farm a considerable distance off, and the child is placed under the care of an old woman, too old for field labor. For what this separation is done, I do not know, unless it be to hinder the development of the child's affection toward its mother, and to blunt and destroy the natural affection of the mother for the child. This is the inevitable result.

"I never saw my mother, to know her as such, more than four or five times in my life; and each of these times was very short in duration, and at night. She was hired by a Mr. Stewart, who lived about twelve miles from my home. She made her journeys to see me in the night, travelling the whole distance on foot, after the performance of her day's work. She was a field hand, and a whipping is the penalty of not being in the field at sunrise, unless a slave has special permission from his or her master to the contrary—a permission which they seldom get, and one that gives to him that gives it the proud name of being a kind master. I do not recollect of ever seeing my mother by the light of day. She was with me in the night. She would lie down with me, and get me to sleep, but long before I waked she was gone. Very little communication ever took place between us. Death soon ended what little we could have while she lived, and with it her hardships and suffering. She died when I was about seven years old, on one of my master's farms, near Lee's Mill. I was not allowed to be present during her illness, at her death, or burial. She was gone long before I knew any thing about it. Never having enjoyed, to any considerable extent, her soothing presence, her tender and watchful care, I received the tidings of her death with much the same emotions I should have probably felt at the death of a stranger." [Frederick Douglass, *Narrative of the Life of Frederick Douglass, an American Slave,* Boston Anti-Slavery Society, 1845.[1]]

About 1825. "I was probably seven and eight years old when I left Colonel Lloyd's plantation. I left it with joy. I shall never forget the ecstasy with which I received the intelligence that my old master . . . had determined to let me go to Baltimore, to live with Mr. Hugh Auld, brother to my old master's son-in-law, Captain Thomas Auld. I received this information about

three days before my departure. They were three of the happiest days I ever enjoyed. I spent the most part of all these three days in the creek, washing off the plantation scurf, and preparing myself for my departure.

"The pride of appearance which this would indicate was not my own. I spent the time in washing, not so much because I wished to, but because [I was told that] I must get all the dead skin off my feet and knees before I could go to Baltimore; for the people in Baltimore were very cleanly, and would laugh at me if I looked dirty. Besides, [I was going to be given] a pair of trousers, which I should not put on unless I got all the dirt off me. The thought of owning a pair of trousers was great indeed! It was almost a sufficient motive, not only to make me take off what would be called by pig-drovers the mange, but the skin itself. I went at it in good earnest, working for the first time with the hope of reward.

"The ties that ordinarily bind children to their homes were all suspended in my case. I found no severe trial in my departure. My home was charmless; it was not home to me; on parting from it, I could not feel that I was leaving any thing which I could have enjoyed by staying. My mother was dead, my grandmother lived far off, so that I seldom saw her. I had two sisters and one brother, that lived in the same house with me; but the early separation of us from our mother had well nigh blotted the fact of our relationship from our memories. I looked for home elsewhere, and was confident of finding none which I should relish less than the one which I was leaving. . . . I left without a regret, and with the highest hopes of future happiness."[1]

Arrived in Baltimore: "My new mistress proved to be all she appeared when I first met her at the door,—a woman of the kindest heart and finest feelings. She had never had a slave under her control previously to myself, and prior to her marriage she had been dependent upon her own industry for a living. She was by trade a weaver; and by constant application to her business, she had been in a good degree preserved from the blighting and dehumanizing effects of slavery. I was utterly astonished at her goodness. I scarcely knew how to behave towards her. She was entirely unlike any other white woman I had ever seen. I could not approach her as I was accustomed to approach other white ladies. My early instruction was all out of place. The crouching servility, usually so acceptable a quality in a slave, did not answer when manifested toward her. Her favor was not gained by it; she seemed to be disturbed by it. She did not deem it impudent or unmannerly for a slave to look her in the face. The meanest slave was put fully at ease in her presence, and none left without feeling better for having seen her. Her face was made of heavenly smiles, and her voice of tranquil music.

"But, alas! this kind heart had but a short time to remain such. The fatal poison of irresponsible power was already in her hands, and soon commenced its infernal work. That cheerful eye, under the influence of slavery, soon became red with rage; that voice, made all of sweet accord, changed to one of harsh and horrid discord; and that angelic face gave place to that of a demon.

"Very soon after I went to live with Mr. and Mrs. Auld, she very kindly commenced to teach me the A,B,C. After I had learned this, she assisted me in learning to spell words of three or four letters. Just at this point of my progress, Mr. Auld found out what was going on, and at once forbade Mrs. Auld to instruct me further, telling her, among other things, that it was unlawful, as well as unsafe, to teach a slave to read. To use his own words, further, he said, 'If you give a nigger an inch, he will take an ell. A nigger should know nothing but to obey his master—to do as he is told to do. Learning would *spoil* the best nigger in the world. Now,' said he, 'if you teach that nigger (speaking of myself) how to read, there would be no keeping him. It would forever unfit him to be a slave. He would at once become unmanageable, and of no value to his master. As to himself, it could do him no good, but a great deal of harm. It would make him discontented and unhappy.' These words sank deep into my heart, stirred up sentiments within that lay slumbering, and called into existence an entirely new train of thought. It was a new and special revelation, explaining dark and mysterious things, with which my youthful understanding had struggled, but struggled in vain. I now understood what had been to me a most perplexing difficulty— to wit, the white man's power to enslave the black man. It was a grand achievement and I prized it highly. From that moment, I understood the pathway from slavery to freedom. It was just what I wanted, and I got it at a time when I the least expected it. Whilst I was saddened by the thought of losing the aid of my kind mistress, I was gladdened by the invaluable instruction which, by the merest accident, I had gained from my master. Though conscious of the difficulty of learning without a teacher, I set out with high hope, and a fixed purpose, at whatever cost of trouble, to learn how to read. . . .

"I had resided but a short time in Baltimore before I observed a marked difference, in the treatment of slaves, from that which I had witnessed in the country. A city slave is almost a freeman, compared with a slave on the plantation. He is much better fed and clothed, and enjoys privileges altogether unknown to the slave on the plantation. There is a vestige of decency, a sense of shame, that does much to curb and check those outbreaks of atrocious cruelty so commonly enacted upon the plantation.

"During this time, my copy-book was the board fence, brick wall, and pavement; my pen and ink was a lump of chalk. With these, I learned mainly how to write. I then commenced and continued copying the Italics in Webster's Spelling Book, until I could make them all without looking on the book. By this time, my little Master Thomas had gone to school, and learned how to write, and had written over a number of copy-books. These had been brought home, and shown to some of our near neighbors, and then laid aside. My mistress used to go to class meeting at the Wilk Street meetinghouse every Monday afternoon, and leave me to take care of the house. When left thus, I used to spend the time in writing in the spaces left in Master Thomas's copy-book, copying what he had written. I continued to do this until I could write a hand very similar to that of Master Thomas. Thus, after a long, tedious effort for years, I finally succeeded in learning how to write."[1]

1835. First attempted escape to freedom was thwarted. Douglass was imprisoned and then returned to owner.

September 3, 1838. Successful escape to freedom. "I left my chains, and succeeded in reaching New York without the slightest interruption of any kind. How I did so,—what means I adopted,—what direction I travelled, and by what mode of conveyance,—I must leave unexplained. . . .

"I have been frequently asked how I felt when I found myself in a free State. I have never been able to answer the question with any satisfaction to myself. It was a moment of the highest excitement I ever experienced. I suppose I felt as one may imagine the unarmed mariner to feel when he is rescued by a friendly man-of-war from the pursuit of a pirate. In writing to

...I was well on the way to Havre de Grace before the conductor came into the Negro car to collect tickets and examine the papers of his black passengers. ■ (From *Life and Times of Frederick Douglass* by Frederick Douglass.)

a dear friend, immediately after my arrival at New York, I said I felt like one who had escaped a den of hungry lions. This state of mind, however, very soon subsided; and I was again seized with a feeling of great insecurity and loneliness. I was yet liable to be taken back, and subjected to all the tortures of slavery. This in itself was enough to damp the ardor of my enthusiasm. But the loneliness overcame me.

"There I was in the midst of thousands, and yet a perfect stranger; without home and without friends, in the midst of thousands of my own brethren—children of a common Father, and yet I dared not to unfold to any of them my sad condition. I was afraid to speak to any one for fear of speaking to the wrong one, and thereby falling into the hands of money-loving kidnappers, whose business it was to lie in wait for the panting fugitive, as the ferocious beasts of the forest lie in wait for their prey. The motto which I adopted when I started from slavery was this—'Trust no man!'

Frederick Douglass. (Photograph courtesy of the New York Historical Society.)

"I saw in every white man an enemy, and in almost every colored man cause for distrust. It was a most painful situation; and, to understand it, one must needs experience it, or imagine himself in similar circumstances. Let him be a fugitive slave in a strange land . . . where he is every moment subjected to the terrible liability of being seized upon by his fellowmen, as the hideous crocodile seizes upon his prey!—I say, let him place himself in my situation—without home or friends—without money or credit—wanting shelter, and no one to give it—wanting bread, and no money to buy it,—and at the same time let him feel that he is pursued by merciless, men-hunters, and in total darkness as to what to do, where to go, or where to stay,—perfectly helpless both as to the means of defence and means of escape,—in the midst of plenty, yet suffering the terrible gnawings of hunger,—in the midst of houses, yet having no home,—among fellow-men, yet feeling as if in the midst of wild beasts, whose greediness to swallow up the trembling and half-famished fugitive is only equalled by that with which the monsters of the deep swallow up the helpless fish upon which they subsist,—I say, let him be placed in this most trying situation,—the situation in which I was placed,—then, and not till then, will he fully appreciate the hardships of, and know how to sympathize with, the toil-worn and whip-scarred fugitive slave."[1]

September 15, 1838. Married Anna Murray (a free woman) in New York City. "At this time, Anna, my intended wife, came on; for I wrote to her immediately after my arrival at New York, (notwithstanding my homeless, houseless, and helpless condition,) informing her of my successful flight, and wishing her to come on forthwith. In a few days after her arrival . . . the Rev. J. W. C. Pennington . . . performed the marriage ceremony, and gave us a certificate."[1]

Traveled to New Bedford to seek employment. "I found employment, the third day after my arrival, in stowing a sloop with a load of oil. It was new, dirty, and hard work for me; but I went at it with a glad heart and a willing hand. I was now my own master. It was a happy moment, the rapture of which can be understood only by those who have been slaves. It was the first work, the reward of which was to be entirely my own. There was no Master Hugh standing ready, the moment I earned the money, to rob me of it. I worked that day with a pleasure I had never before experienced. I was at work for myself and newly-married wife. It was to me the starting-point of a new existence."[1]

Took the name Frederick Douglass, which he continued to use the rest of his life. Became known as an eloquent orator who argued for the emancipation of slaves.

April 28, 1845. Wrote the *Narrative of the Life of Frederick Douglass, an American Slave,* the first of three autobiographies. The book has been reprinted numerous times, including contemporary paperback editions for students.

1847. Founded the *North Star,* a Rochester, New York newspaper, which he issued for seventeen years. "The object of *The North Star* will be to attack slavery in all its forms and aspects; advocate Universal Emancipation . . . promote the moral and intellectual improvement of the colored people; and to hasten the day of freedom to our three million enslaved fellow-countrymen.

"I shall be under no party or society, but shall advocate the slave's cause in the way which in my judgement, will be best suited to the advancement of the cause." [Nathan Irvin Huggins, *Slave and Citizen: The Life of Frederick Douglass,* edited by Oscar Handlin, Little, Brown, 1980.[2]]

A champion of all human rights, Douglass attended the first woman's rights convention at Seneca Falls, New York. "When I ran away from slavery, it was for myself; when I advocated emancipation, it was for my people; but when I stood up for the rights of women, self was out of the question, and I found a little nobility in the act."[2]

1860. Assisted in recruiting men for the 54th and 55th Massachusetts Regiment, during the Civil War. Demanded the right to enlist black men in the army. "Liberty won by white men would lose half its luster. 'Who would be free themselves must strike the blow.' I am authorized to assure you that you will receive the same wages, the same rations, the same protection, the same treatment, and the same bounty, secured to white soldiers. The chance is now given to you to end in a day the bondage of centuries, and to rise in one bound from social degradation to . . . common equality with all other varieties of men."[2]

1877-1881. Made assistant of the Santo Domingo Commission. Served as U.S. marshall of the District of Columbia.

February 20, 1889. Appointed minister to Haiti.

February 20, 1895. Died of a heart attack. "We should never forget that, whatever may be the incidental mistakes and misconduct of rulers, government is better than anarchy, and patient reform is better than violent revolution."[2]

FOR MORE INFORMATON SEE—Books of interest to young readers: Edmund Fuller, *A Star Pointed North,* Harper & Brothers, 1946; Shirley Graham, *There Was Once a Slave: The Heroic Story of Frederick Douglass,* Messner, 1947; Langston Hughes, *Famous Negro Heroes of America* (illustrated by Gerald McCann), Dodd, 1958; Arna W. Bontemps, *Frederick Douglass: Slave, Fighter, Freeman* (illustrated by Harper Johnson), Knopf, 1959; Lillie Patterson, *Frederick Douglass, Freedom Fighter* (illustrated by Gray Morrow), Garrard, 1965; Philip Sterling and Rayford Logan, *Four Took Freedom,* Four Winds Press, 1968; Frances T. Humphreville, *For All People: The Story of Frederick Douglass,* Houghton, 1969; Mildred B. Herschler, *Frederick Douglass* (illustrated by John Downs), Follett, 1969; Charles P. Graves, *Frederick Douglass* (illustrated by Joel Snyder), Putnam, 1970; Elisabeth P. Myers, *Frederick Douglass, Boy Champion of Human Rights* (illustrated by Robert Doremus), Bobbs-Merrill, 1970; Ruth Wilson, *Our Blood and Tears: Black Freedom Fighters,* Putnam, 1972; Ossie Davis, *Escape to Freedom: A Play about Young Frederick Douglass,* Viking, 1978.

Other books: Frederick May Holland, *Frederick Douglass: The Colored Orator,* Funk, 1891, reprinted, Negro Universities Press, 1970, revised edition, Funk, 1894, reprinted, Haskell House, 1969; James Monroe Gregory, *Frederick Douglass, the Orator,* Willey Co., 1907, reprinted, Crowell, 1971; Charles W. Chesnutt, *Frederick Douglass,* Small, Maynard, 1899, reprinted, Johnson Reprint, 1970; Booker T. Washington, *Frederick Douglass,* Jacobs, 1907, reprinted, Greenwood Press, 1969; Benjamin Quarles, *Frederick Douglass,* Associated Publishers, 1948, reprinted with a preface by James M. McPherson, Atheneum, 1968; Robert Patterson, editor, *Frederick Douglass: A Biography,* Citadel, 1964; Lerone Bennett, *Pioneers in Protest,* Johnson Publishing Co., 1968; Corinne K. Hoexter, *Black Crusader: Frederick Douglass,* Rand McNally, 1970; Arna W. Bontemps, *Free At Last: The Life of Frederick Douglass,* Dodd, 1971; Nathan I. Huggins, *Slave and Citizen: The Life of Frederick Douglass,* Little, Brown, 1980.

Periodicals: *New England Magazine,* March, 1901; *Independent,* April 1923; *Negro History Bulletin,* February, 1953, April, 1953, June, 1953, July, 1953, January, 1956, March, 1960, February, 1966, February, 1969; *Scholastic,* April 29, 1946; *UNESCO Courier,* February, 1962; *Time,* May 24, 1963; *Ebony,* September, 1963, June, 1964, April, 1975; *Life,* November 22, 1968; *New York Review of Books,* December 3, 1970; *Black Scholar,* December, 1973; *Christianity Today,* January 31, 1975; *Encore,* December 3, 1979; *Ms,* October, 1981.

Obituaries: *Outlook,* March 2, 1895; *Harper's Weekly,* March 2, 1895; *Review of Reviews,* April, 1895.

Movies and filmstrips: ''Frederick Douglass'' (filmstrips), Society for Visual Education, 1964; ''Frederick Douglass'' (motion picture), Robert Saudek Associates, 1965; ''Frederick Douglass, Freedom's Spokesman'' (filmstrips), Popular Science, 1967; ''Frederick Douglass: The Fight for Equal Rights'' (filmstrips), McGraw, 1968; ''Frederick Douglass'' (filmstrips), Encyclopaedia Britannica Educational Corp., 1969; ''Frederick Douglass'' (filmstrips), Troll Associates, 1969; ''Frederick Douglass'' (motion picture), Encyclopaedia Britannica Educational Corp., 1971.

DRUCKER, Malka   1945-

BRIEF ENTRY: Born March 14, 1945, in Tucson, Ariz. A graduate of the University of California, Drucker has been a full-time writer since 1975. She is the author of *Tom Seaver: Portrait of a Pitcher* (Holiday House, 1978), chosen as a Book-of-the-Month Club alternate selection. Drucker is also the author of a series of Jewish holiday books, including *Hanukkah:*

Eight Nights, Eight Lights (Holiday House, 1980), *Passover: A Season of Freedom* (Holiday House, 1981), and *Rosh Hashanah & Yom Kippur: Sweet Beginnings* (Holiday House, 1981). All of these titles are for young people. Malka Drucker has also written *The George Foster Story* (Holiday House, 1980) in conjunction with Foster. *Address:* 863 Manning Ave., Los Angeles, Calif. 90024. *For More Information See: Contemporary Authors,* Volumes 81-84, Gale, 1979.

ECKERT, Allan W.   1931-

PERSONAL: Born January 30, 1931, in Buffalo, N.Y.; son of Edward Russell and Ruth (Roth) Eckert; married Joan Dowling, May 14, 1955 (divorced May, 1975); married Gail Ann Hagemann Green, April, 1976 (divorced June, 1978); married Nancy Cross Dent, 1978; children: Joseph Matthew, Julie Anne. *Education:* Attended University of Dayton and Ohio State University. *Politics:* Uncommitted. *Religion:* Agnostic. *Home and office:* 209 Riverside Dr., P.O. Box 211, Everglades, Fla. 33929. *Agent:* Nancy Cross, P.O. Box 211, Everglades, Fla. 33929.

CAREER: Prior to 1955, worked as postman, private detective, fireman, plastics technician, cook, dishwasher, laundryman,

ALLAN W. ECKERT

Benjamin MacDonald was following a mouse. ■
(From *Incident at Hawk's Hill* by Allan W. Eckert.
Illustrated by John Schoenherr.)

salesman, chemist's assistant, trapper, commercial artist, draftsman, and at perhaps fifteen types of factory work and farming; National Cash Register Co., Dayton, Ohio, associate editor of *NRC Factory News,* 1955-56; *Dayton Journal-Herald,* Dayton, Ohio, at various times outdoor editor, nature editor, police reporter, columnist, feature writer, 1957-60; became a full-time free-lance magazine writer in 1960; free-lance book writer since 1963; Writer's Digest, Inc., Cincinnati, Ohio, consultant; Dayton Museum of Natural History, Dayton, Ohio, board of trustees, 1964-65, life member, 1965—; founder and board chairman of Lemon Bay Conservancy (Englewood, Fla.); member of board of directors of Charlotte County (Florida) Civic Association. *Military service:* U.S. Air Force, 1948-52, became staff sergeant. *Member:* Outdoor Writers Association (board member, 1962—), Society of Magazine Writers, Authors Guild. *Awards, honors:* Received four Pulitzer Prize nominations; Ohioana Book Award, 1968; Best Book award from Friends of American Writers, 1968; Newbery-Caldecott Honor Book award from American Library Association, 1972, George C. Stone Award of Merit for Children's Literature,

Claremont Colleges, Calif., 1974, Austrian Juvenile Book of the Year Award, 1977, all for *Incident at Hawk's Hill.*

WRITINGS—All published by Little, Brown, except as indicated: *The Writer's Digest Course in Article Writing,* Writer's Digest, 1962; *The Great Auk,* 1963; *The Writer's Digest Course in Short Story Writing,* Writer's Digest, 1965; *The Silent Sky: The Incredible Extinction of the Passenger Pigeon,* 1965; *A Time of Terror: The Great Dayton Flood,* 1965; *Wild Season* (nature study), 1967; *The Frontiersman* (historical narrative), 1967; *The Bayou Backwaters* (nature study), Doubleday, 1968; *The Crossbreed* (nature novel), 1968; *The Dreaming Tree* (novel), 1968; *The King Snake* (nature novel), 1968; *Blue Jacket: War Chief of the Shawnees,* 1969; *Wilderness Empire* (historical narrative), 1969; *The Conquerors* (historical narrative), 1970; *In Search of a Whale* (non-fiction), Doubleday, 1970; *Incident at Hawk's Hill* (novel; ALA Notable Book), 1971; *The Court-Martial of Daniel Boone* (historical novel), 1973; *Tecumseh!* (play), 1974; *The Owls of North America: All the Species and Subspecies Described and Illustrated* (illustrated by Karl Karalus), Doubleday, 1974, new edition, 1975; *The HAB Theory* (contemporary novel), 1976; *The Wilderness War* (historical narrative), 1978; *The Wading Birds of North America: All the Species and Subspecies Described and Illustrated* (illustrated by K. Karalus), Doubleday, 1979; *Savage Journey* (novel), 1979; *Song of the Wild* (novel), 1980; *Whattizzit?* (humor), Landfall Press, 1981.

Author of over 150 television scripts for "Wild Kingdom" and screenplays, "The Legend of Koo-Tan," 1971; "Wild Journey," 1972; "The Kentucky Pioneers," 1972; "George Rogers Clark," 1973. Contributor of over 200 articles to magazines.

WORK IN PROGRESS: Gateway to Empire; Twilight of Empire, publication date, Fall, 1985; *The Scarlet Mansion* (nonfiction); an untitled biography of Tecumseh, scheduled for publication, Fall, 1986.

SIDELIGHTS: "In those few works wherein I have written for children, I do not actually write for children—rather, I write in a manner that will please adults just as well. Thus, there is no 'writing down' to a certain age level. I strongly believe that young readers can handle almost anything, providing it is interestingly presented. As proof of this, some of the most enthusiastic letters I've received have come from youngsters who have read and thoroughly enjoyed books in my 'Winning of America' series, which are certainly not what would reasonably be called 'children's literature.' My book *Incident at Hawk's Hill* was written as an adult book, yet won three major juvenile literature awards—Newbery Honor Book, George C. Stone Award of Merit, and Austrian Book of the Year Award. I like to write *about* children, but in an adult way—and that's what young people want to read."

Eckert's books have been translated into eleven languages. Thirteen of his books have become paperback editions after initial hardcover publication. Book Club editions have appeared in the Literary Guild, Outdoor Book Club, Popular Science Book Club, Doubleday Best-in-Books Club; and three selections in *Reader's Digest Condensed Books.*

All that mankind has done, thought, gained or been: it
is lying as in magic preservation in the pages of books.
                                                —Thomas Carlyle

R.E. ESHMEYER

ESHMEYER, R(einhart) E(rnst) 1898-

PERSONAL: Born May 2, 1898, in New Knoxville, Ohio; son of Ernst (a salesman) and Fredericka (Harlamert) Eshmeyer; married Aurelia Dickman, August, 1919 (died, 1968); married Elba May Butts, 1971 (died, 1975); children: Nancy, Donna, Ruth. *Education:* Heidelberg College, B.A., 1922; graduated from Central Theological Seminary (now Eden Theological Seminary). *Politics:* "I vote for the man." *Religion:* United Church of Christ. *Home:* 224 Elizabeth St., East Lansing, Mich. 48823.

CAREER: Ordained to United Church of Christ ministry, 1924; minister in Bloomville, Ohio, 1934-41, Cleveland, Ohio, 1941-46, and Akron, Ohio, 1946-54; St. Paul United Church of Christ, Lansing, Mich., minister, 1954-63, pastor emeritus, 1963—. Board of trustees, Heidelberg College, 1945-53; teacher of oil painting, American Youth Foundation, Camp Miniwanca, 1945-76; has served on various civic and church council committees.

WRITINGS: It Crossed My Mind (poetry), self-published, 1973; *Ask Any Vegetable* (juvenile nonfiction; self-illustrated), Prentice-Hall, 1975. Contributor of articles on nature to newspapers in Cleveland, Ohio; Akron, Ohio; and Lansing, Michigan; and of a column, "Junior Sermon," to the Sunday edition of the *Lansing State Journal.*

WORK IN PROGRESS: A book of short-short nature stories for children; a book of miniature dioramas; a short novel; a book of poetry.

SIDELIGHTS: Eshmeyer has drawn on his understanding of nature and of arts and crafts in order to enrich both his personal life and his career as a clergyman. "My forty years in the active ministry were certainly well spent. At eighty-three I still attend the last church I served.

"In retirement I developed interests in photography and writing poetry and subsidized a book of my poems in 1973. Each Christmas I send out a list of twenty or more new poems to over a hundred friends.

"Away back in high school I had a special privilege of being tutored in versification. Through the years I have tried nearly

all of the meters but feel most at home in iambic tetrameter. While I see no good reason for rhyme, I do, when there's a choice, take advantage of alliteration."

HOBBIES AND OTHER INTERESTS: Model building, color photography, oil painting, and writing.

FENNER, Phyllis R(eid) 1899-1982

OBITUARY NOTICE—See sketch in *SATA* Volume 1: Born October 24, 1899, in Almond, N.Y.; died February 26, 1982, in Manchester, Vt. Librarian, author, anthologist. For 32 years Fenner served as a librarian at the Plandome Road School in Manhasset, New York, until her retirement in 1955. She was the editor of numerous anthologies for children, including *Ghost, Ghost, Ghosts, Giggle Box,* and her most recent, *Midnight Prowlers: Stories of Cats & Their Enslaved Owners.* She was also the author of *Our Library,* the story about the development of a centralized library system at the elementary school level. Fenner, a member of the American Library Association and the Woman's National Book Association, served on the editorial boards of Cadmus Books and Weekly Reader Club. *For More Information See: Contemporary Authors,* New Revised Series, Volume 2, Gale, 1981; *School Library Journal,* April, 1982.

FINE, Anne 1947-

PERSONAL: Born December 7, 1947, in Leicester, England; daughter of Brian (chief scientific experimental officer) and Mary Laker; married Kit Fine (a university professor), 1968. children: two daughters. *Education:* Attended Northampton High School for Girls, 1958-65; University of Warwick, B.A. (with honors), 1968. *Residence:* Edinburgh, Scotland. *Agent:* Gina Pollinger, 4 Garrick St., WC2E 9BH, London, England.

CAREER: Has worked as a secondary school English teacher, 1968-70; an assistant information officer, Oxford Committee for Famine Relief, and as a teacher, Saughton Jail, Edinburgh, Scotland. Free-lance writer, 1978—. Has done volunteer work for Amnesty International. *Awards, honors: Guardian/Kestrel* Award for Children's Fiction, runner-up, 1978, for *The Summer-House Loon.*

WRITINGS: The Summer-House Loon, Crowell, 1978; *The Other, Darker Ned,* Methuen, 1979; *The Stone Menagerie,* Methuen, 1980; *Round Behind the Ice-House,* Methuen, 1981; *The Granny Project,* Methuen, 1983. Contributor of short stories to periodicals.

SIDELIGHTS: "I was brought up in the country, in a family of five girls, including one set of triplets. My husband was brought up in a family of six boys, including twins. Family relationships have always interested me and it is with the close members of their families that the characters in my books are either getting, or not getting, along.

"I find I write mostly about that period during which the stability of childhood, when almost all decisions are made by others, is giving way to a wider world. A sense of the need for a sort of personal elbow-room is developing, and people outside the family seem to be showing other ways to go. Growing through to a full autonomy is, for anyone, a long and doggy

(From *The Summer-House Loon* by Anne Fine. Jacket painting by Jennifer Eachus.)

business and for some, more sabotaged than others by their nature or upbringing, it can seem impossible. I try to show that the battle through the chaos and confusions is worthwhile and can, at times, be seen as very funny.

"I work with pencil and eraser and never go near a typewriter until I have completely finished each piece of work. Since I have moved house over a dozen times because of my husband's work, I have never had a room of my own to work in, and use the kitchen table. At mealtimes, I console myself that Jane Austen had similar problems.

"From 1968 to 1970 I taught English at a girls' secondary school. I also, for a time, taught in Saughton Jail in Edinburgh. I was an assistant information officer at OXFAM (Oxford Committee for Famine Relief), where I wrote up fact sheets on Third World problems and reports on Oxfam funded programs overseas.

"Since my first daughter was born, the jobs I have done, apart from writing, have been mostly voluntary activities, including working actively for Amnesty International, translating from Spanish, and teaching English as a second language to immigrants from Mexico, Vietnam, and Russia."

FOR MORE INFORMATION SEE: The Times Literary Supplement, July 7, 1978; *Horn Book*, August, 1979.

The love of learning, the sequestered nooks,
And all the sweet serenity of books.
—Henry Wadsworth Longfellow

FIRMIN, Charlotte 1954-

PERSONAL: Born May 2, 1954, in London, England; daughter of Peter (a writer and illustrator) and Joan (a bookbinder; maiden name, Clapham) Firmin; married Robert Herbert (television designer) in 1981. *Education:* Attended Hornsey School of Art, 1972-73; Brighton Polytechnic, B.A. (with honors), 1976. *Politics:* Socialist. *Religion:* Agnostic. *Home:* 4 Vale Cottages, Chapel St., Ryarsh, Maidstone, Kent, England.

CAREER: Author and illustrator of books for young people.

WRITINGS—All for young people; self-illustrated: *Hannah's Great Decision*, Macmillan (London), 1978; *Claire's Secret Ambition*, Macmillan, 1979; *Eggbert's Balloon*, Collins, 1979; *The Eggham Pot of Gold*, Collins, 1979; *Egglantine's Party*, Collins, 1979; *The Giant Egg Plant*, Collins, 1979.

Illustrator: Annabel Farjeon, *The Cock of Round Hill*, Kaye & Ward, 1977; Terence Deary, *The Custard Kid*, A. & C. Black, 1978; H. Rice, *The Remarkable Feat of King Caboodle*, A. & C. Black, 1979; Birthe Alton, *The Magic of Ah*, Kaye & Ward, 1980; Deary, *Calamity Kate*, A. & C. Black, 1980; Mary Dickinson, *Alex's Bed*, Deutsch, 1980; Dickinson, *Alex and Roy*, Deutsch, 1981.

WORK IN PROGRESS: Further books for Andre Deutsch in the "Alex" series.

SIDELIGHTS: About her work, Firmin said: "It's all a matter of luck, observation, persistence, and optimism. And, it's no good sitting down to a typewriter when you can only think of where the next month's rent is going to come from—you just can't write good stories in this mood."

CHARLOTTE FIRMIN

"He thought about it till his eyebrows nearly met over his nose." ■ (From *Alex's Bed* by Mary Dickinson. Illustrated by Charlotte Firmin.)

FORD, Nancy K(effer) 1906-1961

OBITUARY NOTICE: Born April 1, 1906, in Camp Hill, Pa.; died May, 1961. Editor and author of writings for children. Ford began her career in 1927 as a reporter for the Harrisburg (Pennsylvania) *Evening News* and later became associate editor of *Jack & Jill* magazine where she devoted the major part of her career. She was senior editor of that children's publication at the time of her death. Among the books Ford wrote for children are the fairy stories *Baba Yaga's Secret, Baba Yaga and the Enchanted Rings,* and *Baba Yaga and the Prince*. Ford also published stories, poems, and plays in children's magazines and was a member of several folklore societies in Pennsylvania. *For More Information See: Authors of Books for Young People,* Scarecrow Press, 1964; *Who Was Who in America,* Volume IV: 1961-1968, Marquis, 1968.

Most of the basic material a writer works with is acquired before the age of fifteen.

—Willa Cather

FOREST, Antonia

PERSONAL: Born in London, England.

CAREER: Author of books for young people. *Awards, honors:* Commendation, British Library Association, 1961, for *Peter's Room.*

WRITINGS—All juvenile; all published by Faber & Faber, except as indicated: *Autumn Term* (illustrated by Marjorie Owens), 1948, reprinted, Puffin, 1977; *The Marlows and the Traitor* (illustrated by Doritie Kettlewell), 1953; *Falconer's Lure: The Story of a Summer Holiday* (illustrated by Tasha Kallin), 1957; *End of Term,* 1959, reprinted, Puffin, 1978; *Peter's Room,* 1961; *The Thursday Kidnapping,* 1963, Coward, 1965; *The Thuggery Affair,* 1965, reprinted, 1979; *The Ready-Made Family,* 1967, reprinted, 1980; *The Player's Boy,* 1970; *The Players and the Rebels,* 1971; *The Cricket Term,* 1974; *The Attic Term,* 1976; *Run Away Home,* 1982.

SIDELIGHTS: Forest was born in London, England. As an only child, she was brought up with a next door family of seven

(From *The Ready-Made Family* by Antonia Forest. Cover design by Dave Griffiths.)

ANTONIA FOREST

who became her best friends, although she admits that "this gave me a certain scepticism about the real-life joys of being one of a large family." As a child she studied ballet and won poetry society medals for verse-speaking. She also acted in school and university plays, "being better if allowed to be either comic or sinister."

There was never a time when Forest did not intend to be a professional writer, and the first of the Marlow stories was published in 1948. A lifelong interest in ships and the sea is reflected in many of her books. While writing *Run Away Home* she took "a crash course in dinghy sailing in the interests of verisimilitude." Her comment: "Exhausting, but wildly enjoyable."

Only one of her books is not about the Marlow family—*The Thursday Kidnapping*, which was commended by the Library Association.

FRADIN, Dennis Brindell   1945-

PERSONAL: Born December 20, 1945, in Chicago, Ill.; son of Myron (an accountant) and Selma (Brindell) Fradin; married Judith Bloom (a college English teacher), March 19, 1967; children: Anthony, Diana, Michael. *Education:* Northwestern University, B.A., 1967; University of Illinois, graduate study, 1968. *Religion:* Jewish. *Home:* 2121 Dobson, Evanston, Ill. 60202.

CAREER: Free-lance writer.

WRITINGS—For children; all published by Childrens Press; "Young People Stories of Our States" series; all illustrated by Richard Wahl, except as noted: *Illinois in Words and Pictures,* 1976; *Virginia . . . ,* 1976; *California . . .* (illustrated by Robert Ulm), 1977; *Ohio . . .* (illustrated by R. Ulm), 1977; *Alaska . . .* (illustrated by R. Ulm), 1977; *Wisconsin . . . ,* 1977; *South Carolina . . . ,* 1980; *Alabama . . . ,* 1980; *Arizona . . . ,* 1980; *Arkansas . . . ,* 1980; *Colorado . . . ,* 1980; *Connecticut . . .* (illustrated by R. Wahl and Len Meents), 1980; *Delaware . . . ,* 1980; *Florida . . . ,* 1980; *Hawaii . . . ,* 1980; *Idaho . . . ,* 1980; *Indiana . . . ,* 1980; *Iowa . . . ,* 1980; *Kansas . . . ,* 1980; *Maine . . . ,* 1980; *Maryland . . . ,* 1980; *Michigan . . . ,* 1980; *Minnesota . . . ,* 1980; *Mississippi . . . ,* 1980; *Missouri . . . ,* 1980; *Nebraska . . . ,* 1980; *New Jersey . . . ,* 1980; *North Carolina . . . ,* 1980; *Oklahoma . . . ,* 1980; *Oregon . . . ,* 1980; *Pennsylvania . . . ,* 1980; *Tennessee . . . ,* 1980; *Utah . . . ,* 1980; *Wyoming . . . ,* 1980; *West Virginia . . . ,* 1980; *Washington . . . ,* 1980; *Vermont . . . ,* 1980; *Texas . . . ,* 1981; *South Dakota . . . ,* 1981; *Rhode Island . . .* (maps by L. Meents), 1981; *New York . . . ,* (maps by L. Meents), 1981; *North Dakota . . . ,* 1981; *New Mexico . . . ,* 1981; *New Hampshire . . . ,* 1981; *Nevada . . . ,* 1981; *Montana . . . ,* 1981; *Louisiana . . . ,* 1981; *Kentucky . . . ,* 1981; *Georgia . . . ,* 1981; *Massachusetts . . . ,* 1981.

"Disaster!" series; all published by Childrens Press: *Disaster! Volcanoes,* 1982; *. . . Tornadoes,* 1982; *. . . Earthquakes,* 1982; *. . . Fires,* 1982; *. . . Floods,* 1982; *. . . Hurricanes,* 1982.

Others; all published by Childrens Press; except as noted: *Cara* (fiction), 1977; *Cave Painter,* 1978; *Bad Luck Tony* (illustrated by Joanne Scribner), Printice-Hall, 1978; *North Star* (illustrated by William Neebe), 1978; *The New Spear* (illustrated by Tom Dunnington), 1979; *Beyond the Mountain, Beyond the Forest* (illustrated by John Maggard), 1979.

WORK IN PROGRESS: A novel for children.

SIDELIGHTS: "From the time I was very young, I always wanted to be a writer. I wrote my first story when I was eight or so. I wrote it in longhand and my mother typed it for me. When I was in high school I had a teacher who encouraged me. He read one of my stories to his classes and said it was the best story by a freshman he'd ever seen. I also had another teacher who looked at some of my stories and told me to forget about becoming a writer. So it was at the age of about fourteen that I realized something important: some people will like what you do and some people won't, so you'd better make sure to please the main critic in your life—yourself.

"I sold a couple of stories and won a creative writing scholarship while I was in college, but it took me until my late twenties to really start selling my work. I kept sending out one story that had been rejected more then thirty times. In keeping with my idea that my opinion counted for something, I sent the story out again and again because I thought it was good. Finally, I sold it. I've been selling my work pretty regularly ever since.

"I used to read in writers' magazines about authors who had sixty books published. I figured they had to be ninety years old or thereabouts. But now, I find myself with more than sixty books published. Fifty of them belong to a series called the 'Young People's Stories of Our States,' which I did for Childrens Press.

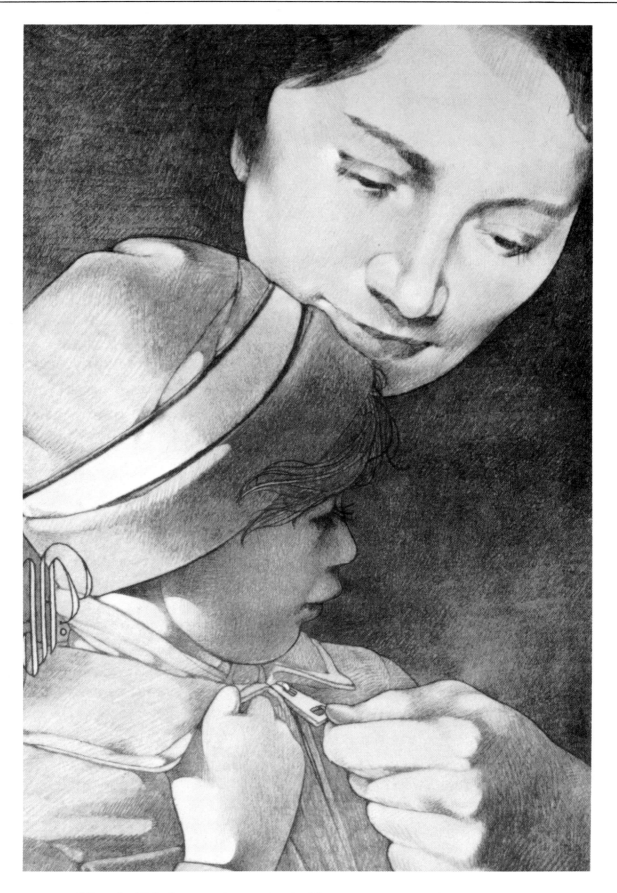

"Listen," said Mother, managing a weak smile. "Get some scraps of meat from the refrigerator for the dog. But take them far away so she won't hang around." ■ (From *Bad Luck Tony* by Dennis B. Fradin. Illustrated by Joanne Scribner.)

"Now that I'm established somewhat as a writer, I find that I can write about the topics that interest me. My interests are astronomy, baseball, games, and animals. I plan to write stories and books about those topics."

FRITZ, Jean (Guttery) 1915-

PERSONAL: Born November 16, 1915, in Hankow, China; daughter of Arthur Minton (minister) and Myrtle (Chaney), Guttery; married Michael Fritz (assistant laboratory manager, Hudson Laboratory, Columbia University), November 1, 1941; children: David, Andrea. *Education:* Wheaton College (Norton, Mass.), A.B., 1937; graduate studies at Columbia University. *Home:* 50 Bellewood Ave., Dobbs Ferry, N.Y. 10522. *Agent:* Russell & Volkening, 551 Fifth Ave., New York, N.Y. 10017.

CAREER: Writer. Silver Burdett Co., New York, N.Y., research assistant, 1937-41; children's librarian, Dobbs Ferry, N.Y., 1952-56; director of Jean Fritz Writing Workshop, Westchester County, 1961-69; *New York Times,* book reviewer, 1965—. May Hill Arbuthnot honor lecturer, 1976; faculty member, Appalachian State University, Boone, N.C., summers, 1980-82. *Awards, honors: New York Times* Outstanding Book of the Year, 1973 for *And Then What Happened, Paul Revere?,* 1974 for *Why Don't You Get a Horse, Sam Adams?,* 1975 for *Where Was Patrick Henry on the 29th of May?,* 1976 for *What's the Big Idea, Ben Franklin?; Boston Globe-Horn Book* honor book for fiction, 1976 for *Will You Sign Here, John Hancock?,* 1979 for *Stonewall;* Children's Book Guild Non-Fiction Award for "total body of creative writing," 1978;

JEAN FRITZ

Pennsylvania Author of the Year from Pennsylvania School Librarians Association, 1978; American Book Awards, finalist, 1981 for *Where Do You Think You're Going, Christopher Columbus?;* American Book Award finalist for *Traitor: The Case of Benedict Arnold,* 1982; Honorary D.Litt. from Washington and Jefferson College in Washington, Penn.

WRITINGS—All juveniles; all published by Coward, except where noted: *Fish Head,* 1954; *121 Pudding Street,* 1955; *Growing Up,* Rand McNally, 1956; *The Late Spring,* 1957; *The Cabin Faced West,* 1958; *Champion Dog, Prince Tom,* 1958; *The Animals of Doctor Schweitzer,* 1958; *How to Read a Rabbit,* 1959; *Brady* (ALA Notable Book), 1960; *Tap, Tap Lion, 1,2,3,* 1962; *San Francisco,* Rand McNally, 1962; *I, Adam* (ALA Notable Book), 1963; *Magic to Burn,* 1964; *Early Thunder* (*Horn Book* honor list), 1967; *George Washington's Breakfast,* 1969.

And Then What Happened, Paul Revere? (ALA Notable Book), 1973; *Why Don't You Get a Horse, Sam Adams?* (ALA Notable Book; *Horn Book* honor list), 1974; *Where Was Patrick Henry on the 29th of May?* (ALA Notable Book), 1975; *Who's That Stepping on Plymouth Rock?* (Junior Literary Guild selection), 1975; *Will You Sign Here, John Hancock?* (Junior Literary Guild selection), 1976; *What's the Big Idea, Ben Franklin?,* 1976; *Can't You Make Them Behave, King George?,* 1976; *Brendan the Navigator,* 1979; *Stonewall* (ALA Notable Book), Putnam, 1979; *The Man Who Loved Books,* Putnam, 1980; *Where Do You Think You're Going, Christopher Columbus?* (ALA Notable Book), Putnam, 1980; *Traitor: The Case of Benedict Arnold,* Putnam, 1981; *The Good Giants and the Bad Pukwudgies,* Putnam, 1982; *Homesick: My Own Story,* Putnam, 1982. Contributor of short stories to *Seventeen, Redbook,* and *The New Yorker.*

Then Daniel and Beckett watched Peter inch his way slowly up the hill, his lantern flickering in one hand, the toy sword dangling from the other. ■ (From *Early Thunder* by Jean Fritz. Illustrated by Lynd Ward.)

Before King George the Third was either King or the Third, he was just plain George.... ■(From *Can't You Make Them Behave, King George?* by Jean Fritz. Illustrated by Tomie de Paola.)

Paul went back to Boston, married Sarah Orne, and began filling up his house with children. ∎
(From *And Then What Happened, Paul Revere?* by Jean Fritz. Illustrated by Margot Tomes.)

Adult: *Cast for a Revolution,* Houghton, 1972.

SIDELIGHTS: **1915.** Born in Hankow, China where her parents served as missionaries. "I was brought up in China and until I was eleven years old I attended an English school. I felt very American and often thought I had to speak up for my country. At recess, for instance. The English children would sometimes tease me by making fun of America. I never let that pass even if it meant a fight. And in history class. The teacher described our Revolution as if it had just been a stupid American mistake. I didn't let that pass either." [Jean Fritz, "American Bicentennial Reading," Children's Book Council, 1975.[1]]

". . . Indeed, I think it is because I was so far away that I developed a homesickness that made me want to embrace not just a given part of America at a given time but the whole of it. No one is more patriotic than the one separated from his country; no one is as eager to find roots as the person who has been uprooted. . . ." [Jean Fritz, "On Writing Historical Fiction," *Horn Book,* October, 1967.[2]]

"In the international community where we lived, 500 miles up the Yangtse River, my friends and classmates represented many countries—German, English, Italian, Russian, as well as American; going into their homes, celebrating their holidays with them, I had a miniature exposure to a wide world. I could see the different life-styles of each country and enjoy them, yet I knew with the passionate chauvinism of an expatriated child that America was best. My friends, of course, were just as passionate about their loyalties. And I am afraid that we all felt fortunate that we were not Chinese because in those days to be Chinese might mean that you were impoverished to a degree that was hard to conceive even when the evidence was before your eyes. Every day as I walked to the British school that I attended, I passed lines of ragged, miserable, sick, filthy, often monstrously deformed beggers and I remember the confusion of emotion that never failed to sweep over me—pity, shame, repulsion, helplessness, wonder that human beings in such a condition could still be human beings, but always I ended up feeling guilty but lucky. Supremely lucky to be an American. Such a scene could never take place in

America because there were two things I knew with certainty: America was the land of opportunity and America was moral. More moral than other countries. I suppose I learned this in so many ways, spoken and implied, that is became embedded in my consciousness as, indeed, it has been part of Americans' collective consciousness for much of our two hundred years. . . ." [Jean Fritz, "The Education of an American," *Top of the News,* June, 1976.[3]]

1923. Came to America with her family for a brief furlough. During the cross-Pacific journey, their ship rescued a sinking freighter. Eight-year-old Fritz, inspired by the event, wrote a poem celebrating the rescue which was printed in the ship's paper. "I decided then and there that (1) I liked to write, and (2) I liked to be read."

". . . I appealed to poetry and mark an occasion, rich nineteenth-century poetry with which, fortunately, I was from an early age well furnished. So it was in the spring of 1928 when I returned to America after a childhood in China that I prepared myself for what seemed to me to be a peak occasion, the fairy-tale point of my own story. My long exile was over, the loneliness behind me, the trials overcome, and when on the deck of the Robert Dollar liner, the *President Taft* we came into sight of American soil—the Golden Gate no less—I was ready to live happily ever after. I was 'The Man Without a Country' (and I knew the story well) but *I* was returning home. I strode to the railing of the deck and I addressed the passengers who had assembled to watch our approach to land. 'Breathes there the man, with soul so dead,' I cried, 'who never to himself hath said,' "This is my own, my native land!" ' The passengers looked, as I reconstruct the scene, somewhat nonplussed, my parents looked decidedly embarrassed, but in the background the ship's band struck up 'California, Here I come!' Perhaps the band merely wanted to forestall further theatrics, but I felt the moment had been well served. I was satisfied."[3]

1941. Married Michael Fritz and spent "five years of a pillar-and-post existence in the army." [Lee Bennett Hopkins, *More Books by More People,* Citation, 1974.[4]]

During this time she worked as a researcher, book reviewer and editor.

1952-1956. Children's librarian in the public library of Dobbs Ferry, New York, where she started a children's room within the library. "... When I ran the children's department of our local library, I found that I not only wanted to read children's stories, I wanted to write them, too. But to be honest, most children's books, like most other books, are only a writer's way of traveling his individual river and, with luck, finding some of the sources.

"Fish Head started at our dinner table with the story an ocean-ographer friend told of an experiment at sea off Bermuda when a cat stowed away on his research vessel. This was the germ of an idea that appealed to me, probably because I was house-bound with young children at that moment and would have liked nothing better than to have escaped to sea!''[4]

As her son and daughter reached school age, Fritz began writing for them. "I remember taking my children when they were small to a family reunion in a little village in Pennsylvania called Prosperity, a village that even now seems closer to the nineteenth than to the twentieth century, a village with pat-terned lace curtains still at the windows and anti-macassars, like stepping stones, strategically dotting the front rooms. We had a picnic lunch in the churchyard at Prosperity and afterward we walked up the slope of the cemetery. At the bottom was the gravestone of my great-great-grandfather with his four wives beside him. At the top of the hill my father stopped with my children, and looking over the sunny green rolling Pennsylvania country, he pointed out the barn that as a boy he had helped to build in a barn-raising frolic involving the whole neighbor-hood. It was one of those rare moments of insight into time when, at a turn of a phrase, one leaps back into another era and one longs to tell one's children, 'Don't forget. This is important.'

"I do not know whether they have forgotten or not; I do know that the feeling I had was persistent, recurring, and probably the impetus at the back of my wanting to write historical fiction for children, of my wanting not only as a parent but as a writer to bridge the distance between past and present, of my wanting to say, 'Don't forget.'

It wasn't a large force, considering the strength of the opposition, but it was enough. ■ (From *Stonewall* by Jean Fritz. Illustrated by Stephen Gammell.)

...That night Finian became suspicious. He sent a messenger to the library....■ (From *The Man Who Loved Books* by Jean Fritz. Illustrated by Trina Schart Hyman.)

". . . There is still this need of getting into the veins of this country. . . .

"My first excursion into historical fiction was with the story of the dinner that my grandmother's grandmother, Ann Hamilton, had with George Washington. Her family had just moved over the Allegheny Mountains from Gettysburg to the western part of the state, now Washington County. One day as Ann was picking blackberries, a stranger on a white horse rode up. 'Little girl,' he said, 'can you tell me what your mother is having for dinner tonight?' 'Peas and potatoes,' she answered. 'And blackberry pie.' The stranger smiled. 'Would you tell her that General Washington would like to take dinner with her?'

"The story had been handed down in our family, and Washington's diary records the fact that he 'bated' one night at the Hamiltons. I started doing research on the period and place, almost blindly at first, picking up pieces as I went along, finding characters and threads for my plot as I became immersed in the period. County histories were one of the best sources for the book, and as I went over the records, I discovered not only that the families had lived far apart but that among those families there had been, as far as I could determine, no girls Ann Hamilton's age. Boys and babies there

were, girls older and younger, but no one for Ann; and I, who had grown up lonely, far from what I considered home, knew how lonely Ann must have been, how rebellious she must have felt. As an adult, I also knew that at the time I had not appreciated the unique opportunities of my own childhood situation, and so I set about trying, as a writer for children does, not only to re-create the temper of childhood but to bring to it some of the wisdom that comes with maturity. I was both Ann Hamilton and someone trying to show Ann Hamilton the challenge of her own times."[2]

"I have never felt that one lifetime is long enough to meet all the people you would like to meet and to have all the experiences you would like to have. So I wander about in history, getting to know the people I find there—not just the obvious things about them that are in the textbooks, but the out-of-the-way things as well. For instance: The swimming stunts Benjamin Franklin did. The kind of doodling Paul Revere resorted to when he was bored. Why Samuel Adams was so stubborn about refusing to ride a horse."

Late 1950s. ". . . I suspect *The Cabin Faced West* is emotionally closest to my own experience. After I had written it, I realized the story, although presumably about my great-great-grandmother, a lonely little girl in pioneer Pennsylvania, was really about me as a lonely girl in an equally foreign environment.

"With it I discovered the joys of research. It was like exploring, only you could sit down. And you were always on the edge of a surprise. Digging into American history also seemed to satisfy a need that I had . . . of finding my roots, of trying to come to terms with just what it has meant historically to be an American.

"I am not one of those people who can mine for ideas. I simply stumble across them or do without. Once I have an idea, however, I worry about it, lie awake with it, walk the floor with it, and make countless false starts before I can successfully launch it. I work an eight-hour day—not from discipline but because I can't put the story down. I work slowly, writing in pencil and typing it up at the end of each day's work; however, it is often not more than one or two typed pages. Rewrite? Of course I do. By the law of averages one would think there would be a certain percentage of sentences that would turn out right the first time. None of mine seem to, though. My children have been my most severe critics and have often been the ones who gave my books their titles."[4]

"I think young people of almost any age or ability read biography for the same reason that adults do—or would if they could find what they want. We all seek insight into the human condition, and it is helpful to find familiar threads running through the lives of others, however famous. We need to know more people in all circumstances and times so we can pursue our private, never-to-be-fulfilled quest to find out what life is all about. In actual experience we are able to see so few lives in the round and to follow them closely from beginning to end. I, for one, need to possess a certain number of relatively whole lives in the long span of history. . . .

"The Founding Fathers are often spoken of as if they were a breed apart, a race sent for a special mission, their like not to be seen again. Big they certainly were, but I'm not sure that it's healthy to elevate our leaders from respect and affection to reverence.

"Surely children will be better off examining historic figures in rounded and realistic terms; nor need we apologize for their shortcomings." [Jean Fritz, "George Washington, My Father and Walt Disney," *Horn Book,* April, 1976.[5]]

Fritz admits that "I have now lived long enough in the 18th century so that I can walk through a graveyard in Boston and recognize most of the names, famous or not. I feel that I am among friends. One of my favorite people is John Hancock. I always smile when I think of John, who in so many ways was like a small boy, wanting attention, liking to show off, ready for a party or a parade, and so eager for everyone to like him. We owe John Hancock a great deal; still, he is not the serious figure who appears in our traditional history books. Perhaps he is best appreciated from the distance of two hundred years. In any case, I want not only to remember him as he really was, I want the stories about him to survive. So many of them are funny!"

Fritz's works are included in the Kerlan Collection at the University of Minnesota, and the Children's Literature Collection at the University of Toledo.

FOR MORE INFORMATION SEE: Best Sellers, October 1, 1967; *Book World,* October 1, 1967, December 3, 1967; *New York Times Book Review,* October 22, 1967; *Commonweal,*

November 10, 1967; *Young Readers' Review,* December, 1967; Elizabeth Hostetler, *Jean Fritz: A Critical Biography,* University of Toledo, 1982.

FROMM, Lilo   1928-

PERSONAL: Born December 27, 1928, in Berlin, Germany; daughter of Hugo (a merchant) and Ida (Koslowski) Fromm. *Education:* Studied at colleges of art in Freiburg, Munich, and Hamburg. *Home:* Brunnhildestrasse 3, D-1000 Berlin 4A, Germany.

CAREER: Worked as advertising artist and illustrator for newspapers, 1951-56; free-lance painter, illustrator, and author, 1956—. *Awards, honors:* German Children's Book Prize and Bratislava Gold Medal, both 1967 for *Der Goldene Vogel.*

WRITINGS—All self-illustrated: (With Tilde Michels) *Karlines Ente,* G. Lentz (Munich), 1960, H. Ellermann, 1975, translation published as *Karline's Duck,* Oxford University Press, 1961; *No Zoo Without Mumba,* translated from German by Anne Marie Jauss, Norton, 1962; *Gusti Sucht die Eisenbahn,* George Lentz Verlag, 1962; *Pumpernick and Pimpernell,* H. Ellermann (Munich), 1967, translation by Sophie Wilkins pub-

LILO FROMM

Then they began to hit each other and pull each other's hair, bellowing so loudly that the mouse woke up. ▪ (From *Pumpernick and Pimpernell* by Lilo Fromm. Illustrated by the author.)

lished as *Pumpernick and Pimpernell*, Doubleday, 1970; *Die Geschichte der Geschichten*, H. Ellermann, 1971; *My Name ist Meise*, H. Ellermann, 1974; *Hopp-Hopp-Hopp-Pferdchen Lauf Galopp*, Liederbuch, 1978; *Hinterm Berge Abezee*, H. Ellermann, 1979; *Himpelchen und Pimpelchen*, H. Ellermann, 1979; *Mi-Ma-Mäuschen*, H. Ellermann, 1980; *Klein Häschen*, H. Ellermann, 1982. Also author of *Geburtstag* (title means "The Birthday"), 1969, and *Wenn Du Einen Drachen Hast*, 1973.

Illustrator of more than forty books, including Christa Duchow, *Oberpotz und Hoppelhans*, Obpacher Buch und Kunstverlag, 1962; Jakob Ludwig Karl Grimm, *Der Goldene Vogel*, H. Ellermann, 1966, translation published as *The Golden Bird*, Doubleday, 1970; Wilma Mönckeberg, *Die Märchentruhe*, H. Ellermann, 1968; Grimm, *Sechse Kommen Durch die Ganze Welt*, H. Ellermann, 1969, translation by Katya Sheppard published as *Six Campanions Find Their Fortune*, Macdonald & Co., 1970, Doubleday, 1971; Grimm, *Der Eisenhans*, H. Ellermann, 1970; Gerlinde Schneider, *Mein Onkel Harry*, H. Ellermann, 1971, translation by Elizabeth Shub published as *Uncle Harry*, Macmillan, 1972; Grimm, *Das blaue Licht*, H. Ellermann, 1975; Grimm, *Das Meerhäschen*, H. Ellermann, 1979; W. Mönckeberg, *Das Goldene Schloss*, H. Ellermann, 1981.

Creator of story book of pictures only: *Muffel and Plums I*, H. Ellermann, 1972, American edition published as *Muffel and Plums*, Macmillan, 1972; *Muffel and Plums II*, H. Ellermann, 1973; *Muffel and Plums III*, H. Ellermann, 1976.

SIDELIGHTS: "I was an active child—bicycling, swimming, rollerskating, ice skating, skiing, and dabbling with chemical experimentations in the form of stinkbombs. I also played wild games with my two brothers and fought with them constantly. We practiced mountain climbing on the roof of our house.

"Vacations were spent away from parents on the farm of our relatives. There we rode horses bareback, milked cows. . . ." And Fromm admits that, during their wild flights of imagination, she and her brothers fantasized trips to Mars and built rivers by diverting the water of a small bay on which they fought sea battles.

Besides an active and playful childhood Fromm remembers finding much comfort in spending lone hours in her room with her drawing, writing and sewing outfits for her dolls. At the age of ten she recalls, "a girl friend and I constructed marionettes, a theater, and wrote plays. We produced many plays for the grown-ups and received flowers and candy for the performances. This lasted for three years and took all of my interests.

"I've enjoyed drawing and painting for as long as I can remember. As a matter of fact as a child I kept a diary filled with nothing but drawings. At the age of ten, under the watchful eye of my art teacher, I wrote and illustrated my first book. . . .

"The book was displayed at my school and received much attention. From that time on, without knowing exactly how to get started, I decided to become an illustrator."

Fromm's career choice did not surprise her parents. As a matter of fact they encouraged her studies especially when she almost abandoned her schooling because of her painful struggles with mathematics.

It was during her studies in Munich that she happened to live in an apartment building with a children's book publisher. "Impressed with my drawings, he gave me a text to illustrate." The book became so successful that Fromm approached another publisher. Subsequently both publishers went out of business. "During that time I became acquainted with Dr. Ellermann [Ellermann Publisher of Munich]. He looked through all of my paintings and suggested that I pick a tale from Grimm and illustrate it as freely as I desired. The result was *The Golden Bird* for which I won the German Children's Book Prize and the gold medal from Bratislava. Thereafter I was awarded many assignments for illustrations."

When asked why she preferred to illustrate fairy tales and children's verse, Fromm replied, "because these books contain so many pictures. Many of the modern children's stories seem to flow right out of someone's head and do not lend themselves to many illustrations, or they are heavily moralistic which I don't like.

"In 1972 I tried something completely different: I drew pictures without words. The origin of this goes back several years. While I was spending my first summer in the south of France, I amused myself with the invention of two characters. I started to draw stories which I included in letters I wrote to my friends. This was the beginning of *Muffel and Plums*. . . ."

FOR MORE INFORMATION SEE: Kirkus Reviews, July 15, 1970, January 1, 1973; *New York Times Book Reveiw,* April 1, 1973; *Christian Science Monitor,* May 2, 1973; *New Statesman,* November 9, 1973.

FURCHGOTT, Terry 1948-

PERSONAL: Born July 29, 1948, in New York, N.Y.; daughter of Robert Francis (a pharmacologist) and Lenore (a social service worker; maiden name, Mandelbaum); companion: Glenn Leichman (a psychologist); children: Damon Leo Leichman. *Education:* Radcliffe College, B.A. (with honors), 1970; further study at Camden Arts Centre, London, England, 1972-75. *Residence:* Seattle, Wash.

CAREER: Author, illustrator, painter. *Member:* Fremont Artist-Mothers' Cooperative (founding member).

WRITINGS—For children; self-illustrated: (With Linda Dawson) *Phoebe and the Hot Water Bottles,* Deutsch, 1977; *The*

She gave them baths.... ■ (From *Phoebe and the Hot Water Bottles* by Terry Furchgott and Linda Dawson. Illustrated by Terry Furchgott.)

Great Garden Adventure, Deutsch, 1979; *Nanda in India,* Deutsch, 1982.

SIDELIGHTS: "I started doing book illustration and posters in high school, and continued in college while studying art history. Following graduation, I studied painting in London and turned to children's book illustration as a way to earn money.

"I wrote my first book with the help of a kindergarten teacher-friend. The story was inspired by the cozy qualities of hot water bottles and by the corner chemist's shop. *The Great Garden Adventure* was a more conscious attempt to write a feminist-oriented picture book about the joys of gardening. *Nanda* is based on my two years of travel in Asia, which ended with the birth of my son. Today I live in Seattle where I am a full time painter, illustrator, and mother.

Some books are to be tasted, others to be swallowed, and some few to be chewed and digested: that is, some books are to be read only in parts, others to be read, but not curiously, and some few to be read wholly, and with diligence and attention.

—Francis Bacon

GERINGER, Laura   1948-

PERSONAL: Born February 23, 1948, in New York, N.Y.; daughter of Benjamin and Ann Geringer. *Education:* Bernard College, B.A., 1968; Yale University, M.F.A., 1975.

CAREER: Author. Worked as an editor of children's books for Harper & Row Publishers, Inc., New York, N.Y. *Member:*

Women's National Book Association, New York Critics Circle.

WRITINGS: Seven True Bear Stories (juvenile), Hastings, 1978. Contributor of book reviews to such periodicals as *Saturday Review, Newsweek,* and *Library Journal.*

WORK IN PROGRESS: A novel.

Peeking around the far corner of the house, was a bear. ■(From *Seven True Bear Stories* by Laura Geringer. Illustrated by Carol Maisto.)

LAURA GERINGER

GLEASNER, Diana (Cottle)   1936-

PERSONAL: Born April 26, 1936, in New Jersey; daughter of Delmer Leroy (a research chemist) and Elizabeth (Stanton) Cottle; married G. William Gleasner (a free-lance photographer), July 12, 1958; children: Stephen William, Suzanne Lynn. *Education:* Ohio Wesleyan University, B.A. (cum laude), 1958; University of Buffalo, M.A., 1964. *Home and office:* 132 Holly Ct., Denver, N.C. 28037.

CAREER: High school teacher of English and physical education in Kenmore, N.Y., 1958-64; free-lance photojournalist, 1964—. Instructor at State University of New York at Buffalo, 1973-76. *Member:* American Society of Journalists and Authors, Outdoor Writers of America, Authors Guild, Society of American Travel Writers.

WRITINGS—Of interest to young people: *The Plaid Mouse,* Daughters of St. Paul, 1966; *Pete Polar Bear's Trip Down the Erie Canal,* University of Buffalo Press, 1969; *Women in Sports,* Harvey House, 1976; *Women in Track and Field,* Harvey House, 1977; *Breakthrough: Women in Writing* (photographs by Bill Gleasner), Walker, 1980; *Illustrated Dictionary of Surfing, Swimming, and Diving,* Harvey House, 1980; *Rock Climbing*

(photographs by B. Gleasner), McKay, 1981; *Windsurfing* (photographs by B. Gleasner), Harvey House, 1982; *Inventions That Changed Our Lives: Dynamite,* Walker, 1982; *Inventions That Changed Our Lives: The Movies,* Walker, 1982; *Breakthrough: Women in Science,* Walker, 1983.

Other: (With B. Gleasner) *Hawaiian Gardens,* Oriental, 1977; *Kauai Traveler's Guide* (photographs by B. Gleasner), Oriental 1977; *Oahu Traveler's Guide* (photographs by B. Gleasner), Oriental, 1977; *Big Island Traveler's Guide* (photographs by B. Gleasner), Oriental, 1978; *Maui Traveler's Guide* (photographs by B. Gleasner) Oriental, 1978; *Sea Islands of the South* (photographs by B. Gleasner) Eastwoods Press, 1980. Contributor of more than three hundred articles to magazines, including *Better Homes and Gardens, Field and Stream, Good Housekeeping, Travel, Argosy, Rotarian, Boating, Camping, Journal,* and *Science Digest.* Author of monthly travel column for *The Charlotte Observer* (Charlotte, N.C.).

SIDELIGHTS: "My husband and I are a full time free-lance team. He handles the photography and I do the writing. I can't imagine a better life. Our careers allow us to express our creative urges while pursuing our enthusiasm for travel, sports, people and outdoor recreation."

...Gail...has the coordination, buoyancy, grace, and timing needed to be a top-flight synchronized star. ■ (From *Women in Sports: Swimming* by Diana C. Gleasner. Photograph by Gail Buzonas.)

DIANA GLEASNER

GOREY, Edward St. John 1925-
(Eduard Blutig, Mrs. Regera Dowdy, Raddory Gewe, Hyacinthe Phypps, Edward Pig, Ogdred Weary)

PERSONAL: Born February 22, 1925, in Chicago, Ill.; son of Edward Leo (a journalist) and Helen Dunham (Garvey) Gorey. *Education:* Harvard University, B.A., 1950; attended the Art Institute of Chicago. *Home:* 36 East 38th St., New York, N.Y. 10016; and Barnstable, Cape Cod, Mass.

CAREER: Self-taught artist, illustrator, designer, and author. Worked in Boston at a variety of odd jobs, including bookstore clerk and book-jacket designer, 1950-53; Doubleday Publishing Co., New York, N.Y., staff artist, 1953; established Fantod Press, 1962; set and costume designer of the Broadway play "Dracula," 1977. *Military service:* U.S. Army, 1944-46; served as a company clerk at the Dugway Proving Ground, Utah. *Awards, honors:* Several books included among the New York Times Choice of Best Illustrated Books of the Year, including *The Monster Den,* 1966, *The Dong with the Luminous Nose,* 1969, and *The Shrinking of Treehorn,* 1971, which was also chosen as one of the American Institute of Graphic Arts fifty books of the year, 1971; books chosen for Children's Book Showcase include *Lions and Lobsters and Foxes and Frogs, Sam and Emma,* and *The Shrinking of Treehorn,* 1972, and *Red Riding Hood,* 1973; Art Books for Children Citation from the Brooklyn Museum, 1975, for *Red Riding Hood;* Antoinette Perry ("Tony") Award, 1978, for costume and set designs of the Broadway show "Dracula."

EDWARD GOREY, 1977

(Gorey designed the stage sets for the Broadway production "Dracula," which opened at the
Martin Beck Theatre, October 20, 1977. Raul Julia [above] assumed the lead in 1979.)

WRITINGS—Of interest to young people; all self-illustrated, except as noted: *The Bug Book*, Looking Glass Library, 1959; (editor) *The Haunted Looking Glass*, Looking Glass Library, 1959; *The Wuggly Ump*, Lippincott, 1963; (with Victoria Chess) *Fletcher and Zenobia*, Meredith, 1967; (with Peter F. Neumeyer) *Why We Have Day and Night*, Young Scott Books, 1970; *Fletcher and Zenobia Save the Circus* (illustrated by Chess), Dodd, 1971; *Dracula: A Toy Theatre for All Ages: The Sets and Costumes of the Broadway Production of the Play*, Scribner, 1979; (with Larry Evans) *Gorey Games*, Troubador Press, 1979.

Gorey's work often varies between verse and prose, and his audience ranges from preschool to adult. Listed below are all of his principal works which appeal to a variety of audiences.

Other writings; all self-illustrated: *The Unstrung Harp; or, Mr. Earbrass Writes a Novel*, Duell, Sloan & Pearce, 1953; *The Listing Attic*, Duell, Sloan & Pearce, 1954 (published in Germany as *Balaclava: 60 Limericks*, Diogenes, 1972), published with *The Unstrung Harp*, Abelard-Schuman, 1975; *The Doubtful Guest*, Doubleday, 1957, reprinted, Dodd, 1978; *The Object-Lesson*, Doubleday, 1958; *The Fatal Lozenge: An Alphabet*, Obolensky, 1960; (under pseudonym Ogdred Weary) *The Curious Sofa*, Obolensky, 1961, reprinted, Dodd, 1980; *The Hapless Child*, Obolensky, 1961, reprinted, Dodd, 1980; (under pseudonym Ogdred Weary) *The Beastly Baby*, Fantod, 1962; *The Willowdale Handcar: or, The Return of the Black Doll*, Bobbs-Merrill, 1962; *The Vinegar Works (including The Gashlycrumb Tinies, The Insect God,* and *The West Wing)*, Simon & Schuster, 1963; *The Remembered Visit: A Story Taken from Life*, Simon & Schuster, 1965; *The Sinking Spell*, Obolensky, 1965; (under the pseudonym Edward Bluting) *The Evil Garden*, Fantod, 1966; *The Gilded Bat*, Simon & Schuster, 1966; *The Inanimate Tragedy*, Fantod, 1966; (under the pseudonym Mrs. Regera Dowdy) *The Pious Infant*, Fantod, 1966; (under the pseudonym Hyacinthe Phypps) *The Recently Deflowered Girl*, Diogenes, 1966; *The Utter Zoo*, Meredith, 1967; *Other Statue*, Simon & Schuster, 1968; *The Blue Aspic*, Dutton, 1969; *The Epiplectic Bicycle*, Dodd, 1969.

**O look, there's something way up high:
A creature floating in the sky.**

■ (From *The Sinking Spell* by Edward Gorey. Illustrated by the author.)

The Disrespectful Summons, Fantod, 1971; *The Sopping Thursday*, Capricorn Press, 1971; (under the pseudonym Edward Pig) *The Untitled Book*, Fantod, 1971; *The Abandoned Sock*, Fantod, 1972; *Amphigorey* (collection), Putnam, 1972; *The Awdrey-Gore Legacy*, Dodd, 1972; *The Chinese Obelisks*, Diogenes, 1972; *The Osbick Bird*, Diogenes, 1972; *The Black Doll, a Silent Film*, Gotham Book Mart, 1973; *Category: Fifty Drawings by Edward Gorey*, Gotham Book Mart, 1973; *The Lavender Leotard: Or, Going a Lot to the New York City Ballet*, Gotham Book Mart, 1973; *The Lost Lions*, Fantod, 1973; *The Glorious Nosebleed: Fifth Alphabet*, Dodd, 1974; *Amphigorey Too* (collection), Putnam, 1975; (under the pseudonym Raddory Gewe) *The Eleventh Episode*, Diogenes, 1975; *L'Heure bleue*, Fantod, 1975; *An Ominous Gathering*, seven volumes, Diogenes, 1975; *The Broken Spoke*, Dodd, 1976; *Gorey x 3: Drawings by Edward Gorey*, Addison-Wesley, 1976; *The Loathsome Couple*, Dodd, 1977; *The Fantod Works*, ten volumes, Diogenes, 1978; *The Green Beads*, Albondocani Press, 1978; *Gorey Endings*, Workman Publishing, 1979; *Gorey Posters*, Abrams, 1979; *Dancing Cats and Neglected Murderesses*, Workman Publishing, 1980.

A is for AMY who fell down the stairs

(From *The Gashlycrumb Tinies* by Edward Gorey. Illustrated by the author.)

Gorey has also written under an estimated twenty additional pseudonyms.

Gorey in front of his thirty-foot high stage set for "Dracula." (Photograph courtesy of Jack Mitchell.)

The Rum Tum Tugger is a Curious Cat:
If you offer him pheasant he would rather
        have grouse.
If you put him in a house he would
        much prefer a flat . . .

■ (From *Old Possum's Book of Practical Cats* by T.S. Eliot. Illustrated by Edward Gorey.)

Illustrator; all for young people; except as noted: Merrill Moore, *Case Record from a Sonnetorium* (adult), Twayne, 1954, also published as *Merrill More and the American Sonnet*, Pegasus, 1954; Rex Warner, *Men and Gods*, Farrar, Straus, 1959; John Ciardi, *Man Who Sang the Sillies*, Lippincott, 1961; Ciardi, *You Read to Me, I'll Read to You*, Lippincott, 1962; Rhoda Levine, *Three Ladies Beside the Sea*, Atheneum, 1963; Ciardi, *You Know Who*, Lippincott, 1964; Frank Jacobs, *Alvin Steadfast on Vernacular Island*, Dial, 1965; Ciardi, *The King Who Saved Himself from Being Saved*, Lippincott, 1965; Eric Potter, *Monster Festival*, Vanguard Press, 1965; Polly Redford, *Christmas Bower*, Dutton, 1966; Felicia Lamport, *Cultural Slag* (adult), Houghton, 1966; Ciardi, *Monster Den; or, Look What Happened at My House and to It*, Lippincott, 1966; Jan Wahl, *Cobweb Castle*, Holt, 1968; Henry Mazzeo, editor, *Hauntings: Tales of the Supernatural*, Doubleday, 1968; Levine, *He Was There from the Day We Moved In*, Quist, 1968; Edward Lear, *The Jumblies*, W. R. Scott, 1968; Ennis Rees, *More of Brer Rabbit's Tricks*, W. R. Scott, 1968; Muriel Spark,

Very Fine Clock, Knopf, 1968; Felice Holman, *At the Top of My Voice, and Other Poems*, Norton, 1969; Rees, *Brer Rabbit and His Tricks*, W. R. Scott, 1969; Peter F. Neumeyer, *Donald & the . . .*, Addisonian, 1969; Lear, *The Dong with the Luminous Nose*, W. R. Scott, 1969; Doris Orgel, *Merry Rose, and Christmas Tree June*, Knopf, 1969.

Edward Fenton, *Penny Candy*, Holt, 1970; Ciardi, *Someone Could Win a Polar Bear*, Lippincott, 1970; Rees, *Lions and Lobsters and Foxes and Frogs*, Addison-Wesley, 1971; H. J. Townsend, *Miss Clafooty and the Demon*, Lothrop, 1971; Donald Nelson, *Sam and Emma*, Parents Magazine Press, 1971; Florence P. Heide, *The Shrinking of Treehorn*, Holiday House, 1971; Beatrice De Regniers, *Red Riding Hood*, Atheneum, 1972; John Bellairs, *The House with a Clock in Its Walls*, Dial, 1973; De Regniers, *The Enchanted Forest*, Atheneum, 1974; Howard Moss, *Instant Lives* (adult), Saturday Review Press, 1974; Edmund Wilson, *The Rats of Rutland Grange*, Gotham Book Mart, 1974; Grimm Brothers, retold by Edith H. Tarcov, *Rumpelstiltskin*, School Book Services, 1974; Terence Winch, *Nuns: Poems* (adult), Wyrd Press, 1976; Heide, *Treehorn's Treasure*, Holiday House, 1981.

ADAPTATIONS—Plays: Stephen Currens, "Gorey Stories," produced on Broadway at Booth Theatre, October 30, 1978.

Recordings: "Gorey by Grimes," read by Tammy Grimes, Caedmon Records, 1980.

SIDELIGHTS: **February 22, 1925.** Born an only child to parents who divorced when Gorey was eleven, only to remarry sixteen years later. "Yes, that does strike me as a trifle bizarre. My father worked for a Hearst newspaper, but I never saw

And then with a hiss as loud as a jet
The water came down like strings of
wet.
Did I say strings? It was more like
rocks!
It filled my shoes! It wet my socks!

■ (From *You Read to Me, I'll Read to You* by John Ciardi. Illustrated by Edward Gorey.)

**And since that day he wanders still
By lake and forest, marsh and hill....**

■ (From *The Dong with the Luminous Nose* by Edward Lear. Illustrated by Edward Gorey.)

(From *The Epiplectic Bicycle* by Edward Gorey. Illustrated by the author.)

much of him until he left home.'' [Paul Gardner, ''A Pain in the Neck,'' *New York,* September 19, 1977.[1]]

''I agree with people who say what happened after five is irrelevant but I don't remember what happened before then. I always did have a leaning toward the bizarre, I guess. I was the kind of kid who thought it funny to throw an epileptic fit on the bus and that kind of thing. But I haven't the slightest idea why my work has taken the tack it has. I just do what occurs to me—if it occurs to me strong enough.

''I started drawing when I was a year and a half old—little trains that looked like sausages. I don't know when I started to write. . . .'' [Jan Hodenfield, ''And 'G' Is for Gorey Who Here Tells His Story,'' *New York Post,* January 10, 1973.[2]]

Educated at Francis W. Parker, a private Chicago school. ''. . . I skipped some grades in school. My father was Catholic; my mother was Episcopal. They tried to raise me as a Catholic and I went to Catholic school for a year. But then I got measles, mumps or something. I suspect it was psychosomatic. I used to throw up in church regularly. Looking back on my childhood, I seem to have had no motivations whatever.'' [''Edward Gorey Inhabits an Odd World of Tiny Drawings, Fussy Cats and 'Doomed Enterprises,''' *People,* July 3, 1978.[3]]

June, 1944-February, 1946. Served in non-combatant duty in the U.S. Army as a company clerk. ''There was this one company: it had all of three people. One man was in jail, one was in the hospital and one was AWOL for the entire time I was there. But every morning I had to type out this idiot report on the company's progress.''[3]

Majored in French at Harvard. ''I figured nothing in the curriculum would advance my career, so why not take French.''[1] Obtained his B.A. in 1950. That same year Gorey moved to Boston for three years where he lived a hand to mouth existance. ''I never had to live on peanut butter and bananas, but close.''[3]

"If you want to pretend you're shrinking, that's all right," said Treehorn's mother, **"as long as you don't do it at the table."** ■ (From *The Shrinking of Treehorn* by Florence Parry Heide. Illustrated by Edward Gorey.)

1953. Moved to New York City, spending the summers at Cape Cod in a family circle which includes two cousins, an aunt and nine cats. "Five of the cats are mine. I keep them segregated. Mine don't go out."

"All I have to do at the family house is cook dinner and finish the book."[1]

". . . If I'm not working on something of my own I get very nervous and hung up. The rest of my life is a shambles, but I do try and continue to produce my own work. Because you get nagged by an idea until you do something about it."[Tobi Tobias, "Ballet Gorey," *Dance* Magazine, January, 1974.[4]]

Winters in New York have a different routine. "I-usually-get-up-about-8:00. And if I can possibly find a reason for not getting to work, I do. On a good day I'll sit here and work for six to eight hours. The ballet at night. Or a movie."

"I'm a real movie nut. Not that there's anything to see any more. I'm one of those people who feels the movies have been going downhill steadily since 1918. And that things really got bad when sound came in. But there were periods when I must have seen a thousand movies a year."

"I used to go to the New York City Opera a great deal. But unfortunately they've gotten much more like the Met. I have bouts of concert-going now and then. But this last year I bought a new phonograph and I've been buying records like mad. I'll

Sing twiddle-ear, sing twaddle-or,
The Wuggly Ump is at the door.

(From *The Wuggly Ump* by Edward Gorey. Illustrated by the author.)

Maudie was only five when she was discovered gazing at a dead bird by Madame Trepidovska. ■
(From *The Gilded Bat* by Edward Gorey. Illustrated by the author.)

just sit here and play ten or twelve albums and that takes care of my concert-going, so to speak. I do some art galleries; that, also, in spasms.''[4]

That year *The Unstrung Heart* was published. ''I wanted to print it under a pseudonym—just an instinct actually. But I couldn't give a good reason. I think now I was right at the time. I'm not someone easily unnoticed. I've always tended to run around in tennis shoes, fur coats, lots of jewelry. I just can't go out of the house with naked fingers.''[2]

His first book was the result of a meeting ''with the two gentlemen who ran Duell, Sloan and Pearce. They saw some drawings of mine. They suggested I do a book. Somehow or other I came up with *The Unstrung Heart*.''[2]

1950s. Began illustrating. ''Deadlines are so irksome. I drew *The Curious Sofa* over one weekend. I was satirizing *The Story of O*. One printer actually refused to put it into type. Even today I hear that some gentlefolk are scandalized. But the details of Lady Celia's house party happened in the reader's mind.''[1]

''A lot of things I've done, I've intended for children. I don't know many children. And I don't know if I really remember what it was like being a child, or not. I use children a lot, because they're so vulnerable.''[4]

''. . . *Alice in Wonderland* is one of the earliest books I read and one of the books I know best. . . . My influences have been elsewhere. The whole genre of nineteenth century book illustration—steel and wood engravings—holds a fascination for me. There's something in that technique that obviously appealed to me strongly. I'd pour over these books and of course everybody in them was in period costume. I do think period costume is more interesting to draw. My stuff is seldom very accurate Victorian or Edwardian of course. And at times I have little deviations into the Twenties. I have, occasionally, drawn contemporary stuff, but I wouldn't do it in my own work, simply because my ideas don't lend themselves to contemporary life.

''Then there's been a strong, direct influence from a certain kind of artist—Uccello, della Francesca, de la Tour, Vermeer, Balthus, Francis Bacon—who captures what you might call the frozen moment.

"Literary influences? Well, the people I like—Jane Austen (my idol), Lady Muraski—*The Tale of Genji*. I'm very fond of Japanese and Chinese literature. I like to work in that way, leaving things out, being very oblique in what you're saying, being very brief. Ronald Firbank. Then later, Beckett, Borges. I don't know if you'd call these influences. You simply feel affinities for other works of art."[4]

"Unfortunately, I'm bad for talking about my work because I never read it after it has come out. The longer I go on and the more books I've written the more and more unfamiliar I become with the whole thing. Even when I was putting together my two anthologies I didn't really look at them.

"I suppose I have had a reasonable career, though I look on it as a total mess. . . . I just don't get that much satisfaction. I look at a shelf of my books—which is fairly wide by now— and think, 'Oh, is this what my life represents?' I suppose I'm lucky. I do what I want to do. Most people don't." ["Interview: Edward Gorey," *Mademoiselle*, August, 1976.[5]]

A passionate lover of ballet, Gorey attends every performance of the New York City Ballet. "Well, I started going to ballet back in 1937 or '38, in Chicago, when I was about twelve or thirteen. What first impelled me to go—no one in my family ever saw any ballet; oh, they might have gone to see Pavlova once, but they certainly weren't dance fans—was the decor. I was interested in art and I wanted to see the sets and costumes.

". . . I'd never seen the New York City Ballet before [1953]. I went to see them maybe three times that first winter. And the next year I went seven or eight times. And the year after that, a few more. And finally, by around '57 or '58, it had reached the point where it was just easier to buy tickets for every performance. By then I was absolutely hooked on Balanchine to the point where, I'm afraid, everybody else bores me. Rather.

"I feel absolutely and unequivocally that Balanchine is *the* great genius in the arts today. I've tried to figure it out, to myself, why what he does works so well. Whatever he does, no matter how often he changes it, or fiddles around with it, always the steps seem absolutely inevitable for the music at that given moment.

"I'm not a great one for attending rehearsals, although I suppose, now, if I really wanted to, I could hang around the company twenty-four hours a day. But occasionally, when

The summer she was eleven, Drusilla went abroad with her parents. ■(From *The Remembered Visit: A Story Taken from Life* by Edward Gorey. Illustrated by the author.)

George did *Requiem Canticles,* for example, I saw as many rehearsals as I could, because there was only going to be that one performance. I can't tell a thing from one performance of a Balanchine ballet. I usually dislike them the first time.

"Balanchine is my life now. Just the fact of Balanchine's being here dictates so much of my existence. I'm sure I would have left New York years ago if it weren't for the New York City Ballet.

"My nightmare is picking up the newspaper some day and finding out George has dropped down dead. Then, do I watch the company go into a slow decline or do I say, 'That's it. I saw it. It's past.' and just go away?"[4]

"I'm sort of depressed all the time in a mildly jolly way. My life is a total shambles at the present and I don't see that it's going to get any better. It'll probably get worse. After all, I'm older, I'm not as resilient as I was. But on the other hand, in a sense it's so awful why worry about it? I think you get what you want in this life. Or half the time I think you don't get it, and half the time you do. Anyhow, it doesn't make much difference either way. It's all the same. I'll keep working, but obviously death will cut me off. . . ."[3]

"What I'm really interested in is everyday life. It's dreadfully hazardous. I never could understand why people always feel they have to climb up Mount Everest when you know it's quite dangerous getting out of bed." ["Gothics by Gorey," *Newsweek,* October 31, 1977.[6]]

That night he had a sore throat, which by morning had turned into a fatal illness.

(From *The Pious Infant* by Mrs. Regera Dowdy. Illustrated by the author.)

FOR MORE INFORMATION SEE: New Yorker, December 26, 1959; *New York Times Book Review,* May 7, 1961; *Illustrators of Children's Books, 1957-1966,* Horn Book, 1968; *American Book Collector,* May, 1971; *Graphis 28,* 1972-73; *New York Times,* October 29, 1972, December 31, 1972, November 13, 1973; *Newsweek,* October 30, 1972, October 31, 1977; *New York Post,* January 10, 1973; *Dance,* January, 1974; *Esquire,* June, 1974; *New Times,* March 19, 1976; *Mademoiselle,* August, 1976; *Current Biography Yearbook, 1976,* H. W. Wilson, 1977; *Horizon,* November, 1977; *Fourth Book of Junior Authors and Illustrators,* H. W. Wilson, 1978; *People,* July 3, 1978; *Maatstaf,* February, 1979.

**Chang McTang McQuarter Cat
Is one part this and one part that.
One part is yowl, one part is purr.**

■ (From *You Read to Me, I'll Read to You* by John Ciardi. Illustrated by Edward Gorey.)

Piping down the valleys wild,
Piping songs of pleasant glee,
On a cloud I saw a child,
And he laughing said to me:

"Pipe a song about a Lamb."
So I piped with merry cheer;
"Piper, pipe that song again."
So I piped; he wept to hear.

—William Blake

GROSSMAN, Nancy   1940-

PERSONAL: Born April 28, 1940, in New York, N.Y. *Education:* Pratt Institute, Brooklyn, N.Y., B.F.A., 1962.

CAREER: Illustrator; artist. *Exhibitions*—One-woman shows: Krasner Gallery, New York, N.Y., 1964, 1965, 1967; Cordier & Ekstrom, 1969, 1971, 1973, 1975, 1976; Church Fine Arts Gallery, University of Nevada at Reno, 1978; Barbara Gladstone Gallery, New York, N.Y., 1980, 1982; Health Gallery, Atlanta, Ga., 1981.

Group shows: Whitney Museum of American Art, New York, N.Y., 1968, 1969, 1973, 1980; The Museum of Contemporary Crafts of the American Crafts Council, New York, N.Y., 1971; Fogg Art Museum, Harvard University, Cambridge, Mass., 1972; Andrew Crispo Gallery, New York, N.Y., 1973; Indianapolis Museum of Art, Indianapolis, Ind., 1974; Contemporary Arts Center, Cincinnati, Ohio, 1974; American Academy of Arts and Letters, National Institute of Arts and Letters, New York, N.Y., 1974; Philadelphia Museum of Art, Philadelphia, Pa., 1974; Philadelphia Civic Center, Philadelphia, Pa., 1974; Cordier & Ekstrom, New York, N.Y., 1974, 1975, 1976, 1977; Rutgers University, New Brunswick, N.J., 1975; State University of New York, Potsdam, N.Y., 1976; Soho Center for Visual Arts, New York, N.Y., 1976; Brooklyn Museum, Brooklyn, N.Y., 1977; Alex J. Rosenberg Gallery, New York, N.Y., 1978; John Michael Art Center, Sheboygan, Wis., 1979; Heckscher Museum, Huntington, N.Y., 1979; Montclair Art Museum, Montclair, N.Y., 1979; Grey Art Gallery, New York University, New York, N.Y., 1980; Newhouse Galleries, Snug Harbor Cultural Center, Staten Island, N.Y., 1980. Travelling exhibition throughout Yugoslavia, Poland, Hungary and Rumania, 1978-81. *Awards, honors:* John Simon Guggenheim Memorial Foundation fellowship, 1965; Inaugural Contemporary Achievement award, Pratt Institute, 1966; National Institute of Arts and Letters award, American Academy of Arts and Letters, 1974.

ILLUSTRATOR: Meindert De Jong, *Far Out the Long Canal,* Harper, 1964; Betty Baum, *Patricia Crosses Town,* Knopf, 1965; Rebecca Caudill, *Did You Carry the Flag Today, Charley?* (ALA Notable Book, *Horn Book* honor list), Holt, 1966; Fritz Peters, *All the Year Round,* Lion, 1966; Harriet V. Davies, *Aboard the Lizzie Ross,* Norton, 1966; Gene Inyart, *Jenny,* Watts, 1966; Elizabeth S. Hill, *Evan's Corner* (ALA Notable Book), Holt, 1967; Judith Hemschemeyer, *Trudie and the Milch Cow,* Random House, 1967; Harry Levy, *Not Over Ten Inches High,* McGraw, 1968; *Especially Sisters,* Dutton, 1967; Gunilla Norris, *A Feast of Light,* Knopf, 1967; Marion Renick, *Ricky in the World of Sport,* Seabury, 1967; Anita Feagles, *Queen Sara and the Messy Fairies,* Addison-Wesley, 1968; Charlotte Pomerantz, *Ask the Windy Sea,* Addison-Wesley, 1968; Peter Desbarats, *Gabrielle and Selena,* Harcourt, 1968; Jane Little, *Danger at Sneaker Hill,* Pocket Books, 1975. Also illustrator of *Big Nick* for Norton.

FOR MORE INFORMATION SEE: Lee Kingman and others, compilers, *Illustrators of Children's Books, 1957-1966,* Horn Book, 1968; Margery Fisher, *Who's Who in Children's Books,* Holt, 1975; Martha E. Ward and Dorothy M. Marquardt, *Illustrators of Books for Young People,* Scarecrow, 1975; *Contemporary Artists,* St. Martin's, 1977.

Evan walked home from school slowly. He stopped in front of a pet shop.

In the window, a canary sang to him from its golden cage.

Canary bird has its own cage, Evan thought. *I want a place of my own.*

(From *Evan's Corner* by Elizabeth Starr Hill. Illustrated by Nancy Grossman.)

NANCY GROSSMAN

WINIFRED G. HAMMOND

HAMMOND, Winifred G(raham)   1899-

PERSONAL: Born June 22, 1899, in Covington, Ind.; daughter of James W. and Eva (Armour) Graham; married Wesley Hammond. *Education:* Indiana University, A.B.; University of California, A.M. *Residence:* Berkeley, Calif.

CAREER: Author of science books for young people. Has worked as a high school science and mathematics teacher.

WRITINGS—All for children; all published by Coward, McCann: *Elephant Cargo* (illustrated by Charles Geer), 1959; *Rice: Food for a Hungry World,* 1961; *Plants, Food, and People,* 1964; *The Riddle of Seeds,* 1966; *Sugar from Farm to Market,* 1967; *Cotton from Farm to Market,* 1968; *Wheat from Farm to Market,* 1970; *The Riddle of Teeth,* 1971; *Corn from Farm to Market,* 1972; *The Story of Your Eye* (illustrated by Heidi Palmer), 1975.

Project to construct a model of the iris of the eyes. ∎
(From *The Story of Your Eye* by Winifred Hammond. Illustrated by Heidi Palmer.)

HAYWOOD, Carolyn   1898-

PERSONAL: Born January 3, 1898, in Philadelphia, Pa.; daughter of Charles and Mary Emma (Cook) Haywood. *Education:* Attended Pennsylvania Academy of the Fine Arts. *Home:* 210 Lynnebrook Lane, Philadelphia, Pa. 19118.

CAREER: Author of children's books; portrait painter, specializing in children's portraits; illustrator, and mural painter, lecturer on writing for children. *Member:* Pennsylvania Academy of the Fine Arts (fellow), Philadelphia Art Alliance, Philadelphia Cosmopolitan Club, Philadelphia Water Color Club. *Awards, honors:* Boys' Clubs of America Junior Book Award for *Eddie and His Big Deals*, 1956.

WRITINGS—All published by Harcourt; all self-illustrated: *"B" Is for Betsy*, 1939; *Two and Two Are Four*, 1940; *Betsy and Billy*, 1941; *Primrose Day*, 1942; *Back to School with Betsy*, 1943; *Here's a Penny*, 1944; *Betsy and the Boys*, 1945; *Penny and Peter*, 1946.

All published by Morrow; all self-illustrated, except where noted: *Little Eddie*, 1947; *Penny Goes to Camp*, 1948; *Eddie and the Fire Engine*, 1949; *Betsy's Little Star*, 1950; *Eddie and Gardenia*, 1951; *The Mixed Up Twins*, 1952; *Eddie's Pay Dirt*, 1953; *Betsy and the Circus*, 1954; *Eddie and His Big*

CAROLYN HAYWOOD

Deals, 1955; *Betsy's Busy Summer*, 1956; *Eddie Makes Music*, 1957; *Betsy's Winterhouse*, 1958; *Eddie and Louella*, 1959; *Annie Pat and Eddie*, 1960; *Snowbound with Betsy*, 1962; *Here Comes the Bus*, 1963; *Eddie's Green Thumb*, 1964; *Robert Rows the River*, 1965; *Eddie, the Dog Holder*, 1966; *Betsy and Mr. Kilpatrick*, 1967; *Ever Ready Eddie*, 1968; *Taffy and Melissa Molasses*, 1969; *Merry Christmas from Betsy*, 1970; *Eddie's Happenings*, 1971; *A Christmas Fantasy* (illustrated by Victor Ambrus and Glenys Ambrus), 1972; *Away Went the Balloons*, 1973; *"C" Is for Cupcake*, 1974; *Eddie's Valuable Property*, 1975; *A Valentine Fantasy*, 1976; *Betsy's Play School* (illustrated by James Griffin), 1977; *Eddie's Menagerie* (illustrated by Ingrid Fetz), 1978; *The King's Monster* (illustrated by V. Ambrus), 1980; *Halloween Treats*, Morrow, 1981. Contributor to *Jack and Jill*.

SIDELIGHTS: "There were only two children in my family, myself and a younger brother. In later years, he became a silversmith; he died in 1958. As a young girl I spent most of my spare time drawing and painting with the ambition of becoming an artist. After graduating from the Philadelphia High School for Girls and the Philadelphia Normal School, I taught for a year. . . ." [Lee Bennett Hopkins, *More Books by More People*, Citation, 1974.[1]]

Eddie was examining each penny under his magnifying glass when Boddles came in. ■ (From *Halloween Treats* by Carolyn Haywood. Illustrated by Victoria de Larrea.)

"I came to write my first book when I showed some illustrations to Elizabeth Hamilton who was at the time, editor of children's books at Harcourt, Brace, Jovanovich. She suggested that I write a story and I wrote *"B" Is for Betsy*. The stories were intended for children from five to twelve. I derive my material from being a good listener and a lot from my experiences in traveling. Most of my books have been translated into the three Scandinavian languages, two are in French, one in German and one in Japanese."

"Hold on to my hand, Neddie," said Betsy. "Pick up the bird with your other hand." ■ (From *Snowbound with Betsy* by Carolyn Haywood. Illustrated by the author.)

". . . Many of my own experiences while a child have found their way into my books. I travel fairly widely and make notes and sketches. Travel has given me background material for a number of books, especially *Robert Rows the River,* which is set in England, and *Eddie and Gardenia,* which is in Texas, to name just two.

"Of all the delightful features about make-believe children, the most convenient one is that their author can control not only their growing up but their growing down. The world of books is indeed an *Alice in Wonderland* world where there are bottles marked 'Drink me' and cakes marked 'Eat me' with the inevitable Alice results.

"The children in my books are not real children, but I do use children to pose for the illustrations. There have been many little Eddies, but only one by that name—Eddie Wilson. He posed for illustrations in *Eddie and the Fire Engine.* The character is actually a composite of typical little boys."[1]

Haywood was born and raised in Philadelphia, where she still lives. She calls herself the "grand-pupil" of the great American illustrator, Howard Pyle, having studied with three of his famous students, Elizabeth Shippen Elliott, Violet Oakley, and Jessie Willcox Smith. Besides writing and illustrating numerous books for children, she is also a portrait painter and has specialized in portraits of children. Many of the models for her book illustrations are the neighborhood children who come to her studio and pose for the drawings.

"Although [I am] best known for [my] children's books, [I have] also been an illustrator and artist for many years. [I am] a graduate of the Philadelphia High School for Girls and of the Normal School, where [I] studied to be a teacher, and [I] studied at the Pennsylvania Academy of Fine Arts, winning the Cresson European Scholarship for distinguished work.

"While still a student [I] assisted in the studio of Violet Oakley who was at that time working on the mural paintings for the State Capitol at Harrisburg, Pennsylvania. Later [I] did several mural paintings on [my] own, for Philadelphia banks and for a public school.

"In 1967 [I] was made a Distinguished Daughter of Pennsylvania by the Governor for [my] contribution to children's literature and for [my] skill as an artist in illuminating and lettering, having, over a period of thirty years, illuminated and hand lettered a *Book of Honor* containing brief biographies of important Pennsylvania women."

Haywood's work is represented in the Pennsylvania Academy of Fine Arts' permanent collection.

HOBBIES AND OTHER INTERESTS: Reading, travel, people.

FOR MORE INFORMATION SEE: Horn Book Magazine, Volume XXIII, January-December, 1947, Volume XXIV, January-December, 1948, December, 1962, December, 1963, February, 1965; *Publishers Weekly,* April 16, 1973, February 23, 1976; *Christian Science Monitor,* May 2, 1973; Lee Bennett Hopkins, *More Books by More People,* Citation, 1974.

Just then Rudy called down, "Hey, Eddie! Are you ready? We're going to begin." ■ (From *Eddie and the Fire Engine* by Carolyn Haywood. Illustrated by the author.)

The day before the bus trip, Mr. Cornball gave his hat to Eddie and Eddie went over to Roland's house with it. "Here's the hat," said Eddie, and he slapped it on Roland's head.

Roland's head disappeared inside the hat. The visor came down over his eyes and nose. "I can't see! I can't see!" Roland cried. ■ (From *Eddie's Menagerie* by Carolyn Haywood. Illustrated by Ingrid Fetz.)

HIGGINBOTTOM, J(effrey) Winslow 1945-

PERSONAL: Born March 24, 1945, in Worcester, Mass.; son of Russell W. (an engineer) and Barbara (Dedicke) Higginbottom. *Education:* Syracuse University, B.A., 1967; Yale University, M.A., 1972. *Home:* 35 West 84th St., New York, N.Y. 10024. *Office:* Leroy Adventures, 317 East 64th St., New York, N.Y. 10021.

CAREER: Illustrator; designer. Great Adventure Park, Jackson, N.J., senior designer, 1972-74; Maxwell International, New York, N.Y., senior designer, 1972-81; Tavern on the Green, New York, N.Y., senior designer, 1974-76; Leroy Adventures, New York, N.Y., senior designer, 1981—.

ILLUSTRATOR: Ann McGovern, *Squeals and Squiggles and Ghostly Giggles,* Four Winds Press, 1973; Barbara Brenner, *Hemi: A Mule,* Harper, 1973; Winifred R. Casey, *Hiram Makes Friends,* Four Winds Press, 1974; B. Brenner, *Baltimore Orioles,* Harper, 1974; Janet Wahl, *The Screeching Door; or, What Happened at the Elephant Hotel,* Four Winds Press, 1975; Louis Phillips, *The Brothers Wrong and Wrong Again,* McGraw, 1979; Gen Leroy, *Lucky Stiff!,* McGraw, 1981; G. Leroy, *Billy's Shoes,* McGraw, 1981.

SIDELIGHTS: "I basically work in very detailed black and white line in either pencil or ink—lively humorous style. My

When Wrong saw the dragon's claw reaching toward him, he did the wrong thing. He held out his foot for a footshake. ■ (From *The Brothers Wrong and Wrong Again* by Louis Phillips. Illustrated by J. Winslow Higginbottom.)

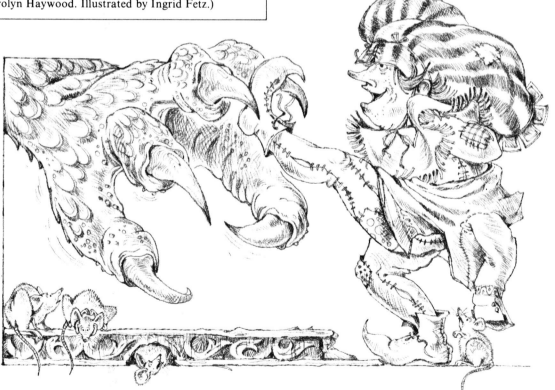

(Higginbottom designed several attractions at "Great Adventure" amusement park. Above is the Magic House.)

J. WINSLOW HIGGINBOTTOM

training as a scenic and costume designer has been a distinct advantage in several of my books, particularly in *Brothers Wrong and Wrong Again.''*

HORNE, Richard Henry   1803-1884 (Mrs. Fairstar, Sir Lucius O'Trigger, Salem ben Uzair, Ephraim Watts)

PERSONAL: Middle name is given as Hengist in some sources; born January 1, 1803, in Edmonton, England; died March 13, 1884, in Margate, England; buried at Margate; married Catherine Foggo, June 17, 1847. *Education:* Studied at the Royal Military College of Sandhurst for two years.

CAREER: Adventurer, author, and social critic. Youth spent seeking danger and adventure; following extensive travel in the United States and Canada, Horne returned to England and a literary career; *Monthly Repository of Theology and General Literature,* editor, July, 1836-June, 1837; emigrated to Australia where he served as Commander of the Gold Escort, 1852, Commissioner of Crown Lands, 1853-54, and Territorial Magistrate, 1855; adopted middle name ''Hengist'' while in Australia; returned to England, 1869. *Military service:* Served in the Mexican Navy during the war for independence with Spain. *Awards, honors:* Civil List Pension, 1874.

WRITINGS—Novels and stories: *The Good-Natured Bear: A Story for Children of All Ages,* J. Cundall, 1846, Ticknor & Co., 1854, reissued, Macmillan, 1927; (under pseudonym Mrs. Fairstar; for children) *Memoirs of a London Doll, Written by Herself,* J. Cundall, 1846, Ticknor, Reed, 1852, reprinted, Macmillan, 1967; (for children) *King Penguin: A Legend of the South Sea Isles,* [London], 1848 [another edition illustrated by James Daugherty, Macmillan, 1925]; *The Poor Artist; or, Seven Eye-Sights and One Object,* J. Van Voorst, 1850; *The Dreamer and the Worker: A Story of the Present Time,* [London], 1851; (under pseudonym Salem ben Uzair) *Sithron: The Star-Stricken,* G. Redway, 1883; (editor, under pseudonym, Mrs. Fairstar) *The Doll and Her Friends; or, Memoirs of the Lady Serapbina* (illustrated by Frank M. Gregory), Brentano's 1893.

RICHARD HENRY HORNE

Plays: *Cosmo de Medici: An Historical Tragedy* (five-act), [London], 1837; *The Death of Marlowe: A Tragedy* (one-act), [London], 1837, reprinted, AMS Press, 1970; *Gregory VII: A Tragedy* (five-act), [London], 1840; *Judas Iscariot: A Miracle Play* (two-act), C. Mitchel, 1848; *The South-Sea Sisters: A Lyric Masque,* [Melbourne, Australia], 1866; *Laura Dibalzo; or, The Patriot Martyrs* (five-act tragedy), Newman & Co., 1880.

Poetry: *The Poems of Geoffrey Chaucer Modernized,* [London], 1841; *Orion: An Epic Poem, in Three Books,* J. Miller, 1843, Roberts Brothers, 1872; *Prometheus, the Fire-Bringer,* Edmonstone & Douglas, 1864.

Miscellaneous works: *Exposition of the False Medium and Barriers Excluding Men of Genius from the Public,* E. Wilson, 1833; *Spirit of Peers and People: A National Tragi-Comedy,* E. Wilson, 1834; (author of introduction) William Hazlitt, *Characteristics in the Manner of Rochefoucault's Maxims,* second edition, [London], 1837; (under pseudonym Ephraim Watts) *The Life of Van Amburgh the Brute Tamer,* [London], 1838; (author of introduction) August Wilhelm von Schlegel, *A Course of Lectures on Dramatic Art and Literature,* second edition, [London], 1840; *Ballad Romances,* C. Ollier, 1846; *Australian Facts and Prospects,* Smith, Elder, 1859; (under pseudonym Sir Lucius O'Trigger) *History of Duelling,* [London], 1880; *Bible Tragedies,* Newman & Co., 1881.

Editor: *The History of Napoleon,* R. Tyas, 1841; *A New Spirit of the Age,* Harper, 1844, reprinted, Smith, Elder, 1971; William Shakespeare, *The Complete Works of Shakespeare,* two volumes, London Printing & Publishing Co., 1857-59; Ludovic

Sarah took me up, and turned me from side to side. Then she looked at my hems, then at my seams.... ■
(From *The Doll and Her Friends; or, Memoirs of the Lady Serapbina,* edited by Mrs. Fairstar. Illustrated by Frank M. Gregory.)

How frightened I was, as I looked down! The height was dreadful! ■ (From *Memoirs of a London Doll, Written by Herself,* edited by Mrs. Fairstar.)

Marie, *Notes and Comments on the Two Prize Essays by M. Belperroud and M. Pettavel,* [Melbourne], 1860.

SIDELIGHTS: **January 1, 1803.** Born in Edmonton, a village near London, England. "I have been told in after years that I was a good child amusing myself by myself and giving as little trouble as possible." [Ann Blainey, *The Farthing Poet,* Longmans, Green, 1968.[1]]

Attended Dr. John Clark's school at Enfield and two years at the Royal Military College, Sandhurst. "I first took to scribbling, and resolved upon literary success."[1]

Possessed by an adventurous spirit, Horne joined the Mexican Navy and then traveled through North America.

1828. First poem published. Horne lived amidst London literary life as a prolific writer contributing to many magazines on a variety of subjects. "Everything I write seems (and is too,) a mere transcription from the brain and heart, so that I am often in doubt whether I am creating or recollecting a series of facts; and on the contrary I sometimes question the more romantic events of my own life, and ask whether I really broke my ribs *under* the Falls of Niagara, whether I staid all night alone among the ruins of Caernarvon Castle, whether I wrestled with

and threw an Indian in the market place of Quebec, who waylaid and endeavoured to stab me some days after, &c, or whether I am inventing the whole? . . . With me romance is real, and reality romance. This is why I am *so* easily humbugged!. . ." [Cyril Pearl, *Always Morning, The Life of Richard Henry "Orion" Horne,* F. W. Cheshire, 1960. [2]]

1843. Horne's most famous work, *Orion* published, for which he was known as "The Farthing Poet." ". . . Anybody who ought to have the poem can buy it for a farthing. The proof that he 'ought,' which I have directed the Publisher to require, is that the applicant should have a good face and proper accent. A man with a horse-nose and boar's mouth who asked for 'Horion' would certainly not obtain it. And very rightly *not,* I think. The book is refused, in numbers, to the 'trade' and to 'unlikely' messengers; and no friend can obtain two copies for his halfpenny. Other things I have 'ordained' as check to rapacity. . . . For as the poem is published at less than the price of waste paper I had to protect myself from people sending five shillings and a sack, with an eye to trucks and pie-bottom. But, as I said, any proper person can have a copy for a farthing."[1]

June 17, 1847. Married Catherine Foggo.

Devoted his life to literature, but only Horne's children's tales have remained in print. ". . . It has always appeared to me a most important undertaking. It is, in fact, beginning the serious business of education *at the root.*

(From *King Penguin: A Legend of the South Sea Isles* by Richard Henry Horne. Illustrated by Jimmie Daugherty.)

(From *The Good-Natured Bear: A Story for Children of All Ages* by Richard Henry Horne. Scissor-cuts by Lisl Hummel.)

"... The highest private appreciation of my poetry by the noblest intellects of the time would forbid me to despond, even if I did not find self-sustaining energies, but the fact of the public neglect for twenty years drives me to Australia. ... I shall be a miner or a shepherd ... I do not go to seek for great wealth, but only an independence, so that I may indulge in the luxury of printing what I can best write. I shall occasionally make an exploring expedition. ...

"... The moment a pen is in my hand ... I forget troubles and difficulties of all kinds affecting myself."[2]

In his later years Horne remained physically fit and continued to write. "... I can still swim well ... my voice is good, my girth round the chest 42 inches, and 'fighting weight' 11 stone 5 lbs, but being out of training, I fear I am not less than 12 stone.

"Most of my evenings in London are passed in loneliness as my bad eyesight renders it dangerous for me to be out at night. ..."[2]

March 13, 1884. Died at Margate, England at the age of eighty-one.

FOR MORE INFORMATION SEE: Stanley J. Kunitz and Howard Haycraft, editors, *The Junor Book of Authors,* H. W. Wilson, 1934; Cyril Pearl, *Always Morning: The Life of Richard Henry "Orion" Horne,* Cheshire, 1960; Ann Blainey, *Far-*

thing Poet: A Biography of Richard Hengist Horne, Longmans, 1968; Martha Hale Shackford, *E. B. Browning, R. H. Horne: Two Studies,* Folcroft, 1974.

HOWE, Deborah   1946-1978

PERSONAL: Born August 12, 1946, in Boston, Mass.; died June 3, 1978, in New York, N.Y.; daughter of Lester (a radio announcer) and Mildred Smith; married James Howe (a writer), September 28, 1969. *Education:* Boston University, B.F.A., 1968.

CAREER: Actress, New York, N.Y., 1969-78. *Awards, honors:* Dorothy Canfield Fisher Award, 1981, Golden Sower Award from the Department of Elementary Education at the University of Nebraska, 1981, South Carolina Children's Book Award from South Carolina Association of School Librarians, 1981, Sequoyah Children's Book Award from the Oklahoma Library Association, 1981-82, Iowa Children's Book Award, 1982, all for *Bunnicula: A Rabbit-Tale of Mystery.*

"...This was actually taken in the Himalayas. I had set out to find the Abominable Snowman." ■ (From *Teddy Bear's Scrapbook* by Deborah and James Howe. Illustrated by David S. Rose.)

WRITINGS—For children: (With husband, James Howe) *Bunnicula: A Rabbit-Tale of Mystery* (illustrated by Alan Daniel; Junior Literary Guild selection, ALA Notable Book), Atheneum, 1979; (with J. Howe) *Teddy Bear's Scrapbook* (illustrated by David S. Rose; Junior Literary Guild selection; ALA Notable Book), Atheneum, 1980.

ADAPTATIONS: "Bunnicula" (movie for television), produced by Ruby-Spears Productions, was telecast on ABC-TV, January 9, 1982 and April 17, 1982; "Bunnicula" (recording), narrated by Lou Jacobi, Caedmon Records, 1982.

SIDELIGHTS: It was during Howe's illness with cancer that *Bunnicula* was completed. Although the idea of a "vampire bunny" was her husband's, it was her idea to write a book about him. About their first collaboration, James Howe recalled: "We sat around our kitchen table one night throwing ideas out to each other. It was in this session we decided his victims would be vegetables, not people. It was a truly collaborative process. One of us would talk out loud while the other wrote frantically. As we inspired each other's thinking, the ideas and words overlapped until there were sentences, phrases even, that were truly the creation of two people. . . . Since writing *Bunnicula*, we collaborated on another book. . . ."

Teddy Bear's Scrapbook, their second book, was published in 1980.

HOWE, James   1946-

PERSONAL: Born August 2, 1946, in Oneida, N.Y.; son of Lee Arthur (a clergyman) and Lonnelle (a teacher; maiden name, Crossley) Howe; married Deborah Smith (a writer and actress), September 28, 1969 (died June 3, 1978); married

JAMES HOWE

"Just read this to me so I'll be sure I'm doing it right."

"...pound a sharp stake into the vampire's heart...."

He dragged the steak across the floor and laid it across the inert bunny. Then with his paws, he began to hit the steak....

"Am I anywhere near his heart?" he asked. ■ (From *Bunnicula: A Rabbit-Tale of Mystery* by Deborah and James Howe. Illustrated by Alan Daniel.)

Betsy Imershein (a theater producer), April 5, 1981. *Education:* Boston University, B.F.A., 1968; Hunter College, M.A., 1977. *Residence:* New York, N.Y. *Agent:* Lucy Kroll Agency, 390 West End Ave., New York, N.Y. 10024.

CAREER: Free-lance actor and director, 1971-75; Lucy Kroll Agency, New York, N.Y., literary agent, 1976-81. On the advisory boards of Hospice of St. Vincent's Hospital, 1979-81, and the Ethnic Heritage Program, Henry Street Settlement, 1980—; on the board of trustees of The Village Temple, 1980—. *Member:* Authors Guild. *Awards, honors:* Dorothy Canfield Fisher Award, 1981, Golden Sower Award from Department of Elementary Education, University of Nebraska, 1981, South Carolina Children's Book Award from South Carolina Association of Librarians, 1981, Sequoyah Children's Book Award from Oklahoma Library Association, 1981-82, Iowa Children's Book Award, 1982, all for *Bunnicula: A Rabbit-Tale of Mystery*; *Boston Globe-Horn Book* Honor Book in non-fiction, 1981, ALA Notable Book, 1981, named "Outstanding Science Trade Books for Children in 1981" list, *School Library Journal* Best Books of the Year list, 1981, nominated for The American Book Award in Children's Books, non-fiction, 1982, all for *The Hospital Book*. *Wartime service:* Civilian Public Service, 1968-70.

WRITINGS—For children: (With first wife, Deborah Howe) *Bunnicula: A Rabbit-Tale of Mystery* (illustrated by Alan Daniel; Junior Literary Guild selection; ALA Notable Book), Atheneum, 1979; (with D. Howe) *Teddy Bear's Scrapbook* (illustrated by David S. Rose; Junior Literary Guild selection; ALA Notable Book), Atheneum, 1980; *The Hospital Book* (illustrated by Mal Warshaw), Crown, 1981; *Howliday Inn,* Atheneum, 1982; *Annie Joins the Circus,* Random House, 1982; *A Night Without Stars,* Atheneum, 1983.

ADAPTATIONS: "Bunnicula" (movie for television), produced by Ruby-Spears Productions, was telecast on ABC-TV, January 9, 1982 and April 17, 1982; "Bunnicula" (recording), narrated by Lou Jacobi, Caedmon Records, 1982.

SIDELIGHTS: "I don't believe I was born to write. Writing, at least writing professionally, is a recent development. But the creative itch *has* been with me for as long as I can remember. And it has always been strong enough that it demanded to be scratched.

"This 'scratching' has taken various forms. When I was ten, I decided I wanted to be an actor. I had two great loves in my life then: hamsters and Laurence Olivier. I couldn't see building a career around hamsters, so Olivier became my more serious inspiration. Throughout high school, I devoured whatever plays I could read or, when I was lucky enough, could see in actual performance. As I didn't live within commuting distance of Broadway, I had to settle for the occasional road tours of 'Hamlet' or 'Camelot.' When I graduated from high school, I packed up my set of Yale Shakespeare and headed for Boston University, where I majored in acting.

"Four years later, fully prepared for a career in the theater, I moved to New York City and promptly began working for the next two years as a social worker. This diversion was largely necessitated by the existence of the U.S. Army and the Vietnam War. Knowing that my own value system would not allow me to participate in either, I opted for status as a conscientious objector. The two years of social work were alternative service to the draft.

"No sooner had I put in my time than I returned to the theater—first as an actor and model (appearing in magazine ads and commercials and hawking everything from stereo components to lemonade to hand lotion), then as a director. I enjoyed directing more than acting because it allowed for a different kind of control of the creative process. I found I was able to invest more of myself in my art than had been possible as an actor. But in time, I felt frustrated. Directing was not enough. I produced several plays Off-Off-Broadway, ran a couple theaters, worked as a literary and theatrical agent. And then I began to write.

"Now, in all honesty, that last statement is not entirely true. I have always written. When I was seven, I wrote a play based on the popular 'Blondie' comic strip entitled 'Dagwood's Awful Day.' This was performed by myself and other neighborhood thespians on a front porch one hot summer day (as I recall, my lemonade-hawking career began here, too, during the intermission). And I wrote short stories and self-published newspapers, my favorite being a newsletter for an organization I founded when I was nine called the Vampire Legion.

"But 'serious' writing did not begin until several years ago, when I took a playwriting seminar in graduate school. There, I wrote two plays. One, a streamlined adaptation of a Gothic novel, *The Monk,* provided me with an invaluable lesson in economy and craft. It was during this time in my life that *Bunnicula* was written. My late wife, Deborah, suggested that

we collaborate on a children's book based on a character I had created several years earlier in an uncontrolled fit of whimsy, Count Bunnicula. And so we did.

"*Bunnicula* led to *Teddy Bear's Scrapbook,* which in turn led to my new career as an author of children's books. Deborah, who was an actress, died of cancer in 1978, shortly after we finished writing the two books. I have gone on to write several others and have found in writing a kind of creative control that is deeply fulfilling. Now, I am happily scratching my itch with the likes of vampire bunnies, chocolate-loving dogs and hyperventilating cats.

"I work and live in Manhattan with my wife, Betsy, who shares with me a love of bicycling, artichokes and life."

JACKSON, Jesse 1908-

PERSONAL: Born January 1, 1908, in Columbus, Ohio; son of Jesse (a trucker) and Mable (Rogers) Jackson; married Ann Newman (a social worker), September 19, 1938; children: Judith Ann. *Education:* Ohio State University, student, 1927-29. *Politics:* Independent. *Religion:* Baptist. *Home:* 80 La Salle St., New York, N.Y. 10027. *Agent:* Anita Diamant, Writers' Workshop, Inc., 51 East 42nd St., New York, N.Y. 10017.

"Move on, Sambo," George said and turned to Tom.

"My name is Charles. Charles Moss."...

■ (From *Call Me Charley* by Jesse Jackson. Illustrated by Doris Spiegel.)

CAREER: Has held various jobs, including newspaperman, probation officer, postal clerk, unskilled laborer, waiter, and proofreader. National Bureau of Economic Research, 1951-68. Writer for children. Lecturer, Elementary Education & Educational Departments, Appalachian State University, Boone, N.C. *Member:* Authors Guild of the Authors League of America. *Awards, honors:* Carter G. Goodson Award by the National Council of Social Studies, 1976, for *Make a Joyful Noise Unto the Lord! The Life of Mahalia Jackson, Queen of Gospel Singers.*

WRITINGS—Juveniles: *Call Me Charley* (illustrated by Doris Spiegel), Harper, 1945; *Anchor Man,* Harper, 1947; *Room for Randy,* Friendship, 1957; *Charley Starts from Scratch,* Harper, 1958; *Tessie* (illustrated by Harold James), Harper, 1968; *Tessie Keeps Her Cool,* Harper, 1970; *The Sickest Don't Always Die the Quickest,* Doubleday, 1971; (with Elaine Landau) *Black in America: A Fight for Freedom,* Messner, 1971; *The Fourteenth Cadillac,* Doubleday, 1972; *Make a Joyful Noise Unto the Lord! The Life of Mahalia Jackson, Queen of Gospel Singers,* Crowell, 1974. Contributor of articles and reviews to *Crisis,* and other periodicals.

SIDELIGHTS: ''My father was a great person in that he believed that idleness was the Devil's workshop. He'd tell me so many times, 'Son, I've found a job for you.' He worked my ass off. Here I was going to school, carrying newspapers, delivering the laundry for my mother, and he gets me this extra job of mopping floors in a factory. There was not time for me to get in trouble.'' [Ruby J. Lanier, ''Profile: Call Me Jesse Jackson,'' *Language Arts,* National Council of Teachers of English, March, 1977.[1]]

Jackson's mother worked as a domestic. The family lived in Columbus, Ohio in a small, attractive four-room house with an outdoor toilet. The yard, made quite beautiful with flowers tended by Jesse's father, provided ample space for the dog, the cat, chickens, guinea-fowl, and a few ducks. All this changed

Jesse Jackson with young friends.

Tessie went down on her hands and knees as the lights came on. Kids started to move chairs back to the wall so there was space for her to look. ■ (From *Tessie* by Jesse Jackson. Illustrated by Harold James.)

after the flood of the Scioto River in 1913. The family survived the flood but lost the household goods, the animals, and the beautiful flowers. Jackson, his parents, and his nine-year-old sister moved to the east side of town into a black ghetto. After that "all seemed downhill" to Jackson. "We moved in with my father's Uncle Chester who was not really a relative. He was a colorful old guy. He had been in the Civil War. He was a Civil War pensioner and besides this pension he had a thriving trade of voodoo and conjuring—giving people cure-alls for impotence and tansy tea for aborting. My mother didn't like that heathen trade so we had to move. Also he smoked a pipe and liked to come into the kitchen when my mother was cook-

ing. The pipe was so strong and evil smelling my mother said it ruined her food—made her cakes fall. She just didn't like the atmosphere."[1]

After graduation from high school, Jackson attended Ohio State University School of Journalism for three years, but quit to work on the *Ohio State Press*. After the newspaper folded, Jackson and a friend started their own newspaper, which they worked on for two years.

While working as a probation officer for the Juvenile Court in Columbus, Jackson decided to write books for young people.

"I came to work one morning, opened the door of my office and there sat three scared-looking young boys, three of the biggest cops I'd ever seen, an assistant to the District Attorney, and a court stenographer. The three boys had killed a restaurant owner in a robbery that netted them five dollars and life terms in the Ohio pen. Investigation of their case brought out that all three boys had dropped out of school because they were ashamed to tell their teachers they could not read. Their ages ran from fourteen to sixteen when this occurred. How to write something non-readers would want to read became an obsession of mine and still is."[1]

Actually, it was several years until Jackson saw his first book published, *Call Me Charley.* "A very small advance was asked for in using the title, *Call Me Charley* for this was in 1945, nine years before the Brown decision. Prior to this time most blacks were lost like peas in a pod under such titles as George, Sam, Sambo, Coon, Nigger. . . . So with this *Call Me Charley* it was my aim to single out one black boy, to have him fight for at least the respect of being called Charles Moss. Charley had a game plan and the game plan began with recognize me as an individual and then we will go on from there and I'll try to get into the boys' club and try to win admission to the swimming pool and try to get a part in the school play."

"We know these things exist. We know that black children have such experiences. We just do not write about them. We just do not talk about them. It was part of the invisible nature of the black at that time."[1]

Following *Call Me Charley* came two more books about the hero, Charley Moss—*Anchor Man* and *Charley Starts from Scratch.* *Room for Randy* was the result of a request from Friendship Press, the publishing organ of the National Council of Churches of Christ, who asked Jackson to write a book about the Protestant Church and integration.

Stonewall Jackson is the hero of two of Jackson's later books—*The Sickest Don't Always Die the Quickest* and *The Fourteenth Cadillac.* "Before doing *The Sickest Don't Always Die the Quickest* and *The Fourteenth Cadillac* I had worked closely with white editors who were anxious that my books reflect the viewpoint of a white writer writing for white readers. The difference in style between these two and my earlier works was that I told *The Sickest* . . . and *The Fourteenth Cadillac* purely from the viewpoint of a black in a black setting under the supervision of a white editor who happened to have been born in England and had less of the hangup about white being right than Americans. Miss Patricia Connelly is the name of that kind editor. . . . The difference was Miss Connelly seemed to be unafraid of violating the unwritten law in the juvenile field that all books for children must first satisfy the aunts, uncles and parents who set the tone for what children read."[1]

Four decades later, Jackson's first hero, Charley, continues to be read and enjoyed by young people. *Call Me Charley* has been in continuous print since 1945 and has had over a million readers. Today its author receives numerous requests from schools, colleges, clubs, and educators' groups for lectures. He is presently affiliated with Appalachian State University in Boone, North Carolina.

FOR MORE INFORMATION SEE: Charlotte Huck and Doris Young, *Children's Literature in the Elementary School,* Holt, 1961; May Hill Arbuthnot, *Children and Books,* 3rd edition, Scott, Foresman, 1964; *The Children's Bookshelf,* Child Study Association of America, Bantam, 1965; *Horn Book,* August, 1968, December, 1974; *New York Times Book Review,* February 14, 1971; Ruby J. Lanier, "Profiles: Call Me Jesse Jackson," *Language Arts,* National Council of Teachers of English, March, 1977.

JESSEL, Camilla (Ruth)　1937-

PERSONAL: Born December 7, 1937, in Bearsted, Kent, England; daughter of Richard Frederick (a naval officer) and Winifred May (Levy) Jessel; married Andrzej Panufnik (a composer of symphonic music), November 27, 1963; children: Roxanna Anna, Jeremy James. *Education:* Attended Benenden, Kent, England, 1951 and Sorbonne, Paris, France, 1959. *Home:* Riverside House, Twickenham, Middlesex TW1 3DJ, England. *Agent:* David Higham Associates Ltd., 5-8 Lower John St., London W1R 4HA, England.

CAREER: Free-lance photographer and writer. Committee member of United Kingdom Child Care Committee of Save the Children (vice-chairman, 1969-81); Richmond Pre-School Playgroup Association (patron). *Photographic exhibitions:* Royal Festival Hall, 1963; Arts Theatre Club, 1969; Photographer's Gallery, 1981. *Member:* Royal Photographic Society, Performing Rights Society, Society of Authors. *Awards, honors:* Research grant, Nuffield Foundation, 1972; fellow, Royal Photographic Society, 1980.

WRITINGS—All self-illustrated with photos; all published by Methuen, except where noted: *Manuela Lives in Portugal,* 1967, Hastings House, 1969; *Paul in Hospital,* 1972; *Mark's*

CAMILLA JESSEL

This book is about the grinding hard work of training for ballet. ■(From *Life at the Royal Ballet School* by Camilla Jessel. Photographs by the author.)

Wheelchair Adventures, 1975, 1978; *Life at the Royal Ballet School,* 1979, 1980; *The Puppy Book,* 1980; *The Joy of Birth,* 1982; *Learner Bird,* Dial, 1983.

"Chatterbook" series; all self-illustrated with photos; all published by Methuen, 1981: *The New Baby, Moving House, Going to the Doctor, Away for the Night.*

Also author of lyrics for two cantatas by her husband, Andrzej Panufnik: *Thames Pageant* (for children), 1969, and *Winter Solstice,* 1972, both published by Boosey & Hawkes.

Illustrator of photos: Dorothy Shuttlesworth, *Tower of London,* Hastings House, 1970; Susan Harvey, *Play in Hospital,* Faber, 1972; *Complete Method for the Harp,* Boosey & Hawkes, 1972; Penelope Leach, *Your Baby & Child,* Knopf, 1978; Sheila Kitzinger, *Pregnancy & Childbirth,* Knopf, 1980; David Moore, *Multi-Cultural Britain,* Save the Children, 1980.

WORK IN PROGRESS: Book about music for children. Four titles in the "Chatterbook" series.

SIDELIGHTS: "My medium is photography and words.

"My motivation is my interest in children, and the wish to combat need wherever I see it. I wish to use photography to combat prejudice against the disabled, or racial prejudice; to use photography for educational purposes, education of children, and of adults in the ways in which they can be of more use to children. I am also interested in the sheer enjoyment of photography and the constant attempt to heighten my own aesthetic standards.

"I started by working with children, then was pushed into photography by a press officer of Save the Children who liked the amateur shots I'd done of SCF work. Lots of hard work and lucky breaks! I worked free-lance, particularly illustrated articles for *Times Educational Supplement.* First book was commissioned by Methuen on strength of two photos in *The Guardian.* Taking colour slides for a lecture on psychology or play of children in hospital, I got the idea of doing a photographic book to overcome children's fears of hospital *(Paul in Hospital).* I then received a Nuffield Research Grant to do a study for a similar style of book about disabled children *(Mark's Wheelchair Adventures).* I continued over the years to work with disadvantaged children, but also worked on numerous other books on varied subjects, including *Life at the Royal Ballet School.*

"At age sixteen-seventeen, I lived for eighteen months with my parents in an Indian community. At twenty I came to America with $60, and held twenty-six temporary secretarial jobs in six cities in one year. I lived for one year in Paris studying French literature and civilisation. I have travelled extensively since as a photographer (throughout Africa and Europe), and as the wife of a conductor and composer, including South America, but not throughout Eastern Europe because my husband is a political exile.

"I have brought up a family and acted as a manager for my international composer husband, and enjoy cooking, dressmaking, etc. as well as having a career. I believe it's possible to be both liberated and a dedicated wife and mother."

Jessel's books have been translated into German, Danish, Swedish, Finnish and Norwegian.

HOBBIES AND OTHER INTERESTS: Music, theatre, art, ballet, literature, international politics.

FOR MORE INFORMATION SEE: The Guardian, August 24, 1979; *Daily Telegraph,* August 24, 1979.

JOBB, Jamie 1945-
(Osh Kabibble)

PERSONAL: Surname is pronounced Jobe; born November 29, 1945, in Gallipolis, Ohio; son of James T. (in sales) and Hortense (Dillard) Jobb; children: Bo, Sach Magee. *Education:* Miami-Dade Junior College—North, A.A., 1966; University of Florida, B.S., 1968. *Politics:* "Gardening." *Religion:* "Nature." *Home:* 2950 Walnut Blvd., Walnut Creek, Calif. 94596.

Some people talk to their garden and house plants. The plants don't talk back. ■ (From *My Garden Companion: A Complete Guide for the Beginner* by Jamie Jobb. Illustrated by Martha Weston.

CAREER: Miami Herald, Miami, Fla., sports writer and correspondent, 1965-69; *Gainesville Sun,* Gainesville, Fla., feature and entertainment writer and editor, 1969-70; Park South Teacher Center, San Francisco, Calif., editor of newsletter, 1971; Amazing Life Games (educational publisher), Sausalito, Calif., writer and editor, 1971-74; free-lance writer, 1974—. President of Diverse Unsung Miracle Plants for Healthy Evolution Among People (DUMP HEAP), 1978-79. Resident manager of Howe Homestead Park, 1980—, Permaculture designer, 1981—. *Member:* International Association of Lesser Known Food Plants and Trees, Friends of the Earth, Seed Saver's Exchange, Northern Nut Growers Association, North American Fruit Explorers, Walnut Creek Action for Beauty.

WRITINGS—Of interest to young people: *My Garden Companion: A Complete Guide for the Beginner,* Sierra Club-Scribner, 1977; *The Night Sky Book,* Little, Brown, 1977; *The Complete Book of Community Gardening,* Morrow, 1979. Also writer of television criticism for newspapers under pseudonym Osh Kabibble. Editor of *DUMP HEAP Journal* and *The Permaculture Observer.*

WORK IN PROGRESS: Books for garden innovators and people interested in uncommon plants, especially wild ones, for Diverse Unsung Miracle Plants for Healthy Evolution Among People, and for Permaculture.

SIDELIGHTS: "As a journalist, I am trying to concentrate on stories that help people realize where they fit into their communities and how they can make positive contributions for the growth of all life around them. As a gardener I am learning to see what nature will grow for me and my family."

FOR MORE INFORMATION SEE: Publishers Weekly, February 28, 1977; *Horn Book,* August, 1977, April, 1978.

JOHNSTON, Norma
(Nicole St. John, Catherine E. Chambers, Elizabeth Bolton, Lavinia Harris, Pamela Dryden)

PERSONAL: Born in Ridgewood, N.J.; daughter of Eugene Chambers (an engineer) and Marjorie (a teacher; maiden name, Pierce) Johnston. *Education:* Montclair State College, B.A.; graduate studies at Montclair State College and Ithaca College. *Politics:* None. *Religion:* Reformed Church in America. *Residence:* Wyckoff, N.J. *Agent:* McIntosh & Otis, Inc., 475 5th Ave., New York, N.Y. 10017 and A. M. Heath & Co. Ltd., 40-42 William IV St., London WC2N 4DD, England. *Office address:* St. John Enterprises, Box 67, Wyckoff, N.J. 07481.

CAREER: Writer and editor, 1961—; Glen Rock, N.J., public schools teacher of English, 1970-72; St. John Enterprises, Wyckoff, N.J., president, editor, 1980—. Has also worked in fashion and retailing, and has done free-lance editing for Prentice-Hall and others. Founder, president, director, Geneva Players, Inc. (religious drama group). *Member:* Authors League of America; Authors Guild.

WRITINGS—For young adult readers: *The Wishing Star,* Funk, 1963; *The Wider Heart,* Funk, 1964; *Ready or Not,* Funk, 1965; *The Bridge Between,* Funk, 1966; *The Keeping Days,* Atheneum, 1973; *Glory in the Flower,* Atheneum, 1974; *Of Time and of Seasons,* Atheneum, 1975; *Strangers Dark and Gold,* Atheneum, 1975; *A Striving after Wind* (sequel to *Of*

Time and of Seasons), Atheneum, 1976; *A Mustard Seed of Magic,* Atheneum, 1977; *The Sanctuary Tree,* Atheneum, 1977; *If You Love Me, Let Me Go,* Atheneum, 1978; *The Swallow's Song,* Atheneum, 1978; *The Crucible Year,* Atheneum, 1979; *Pride of Lions: The Story of the House of Atreus (Horn Book* honor list), Atheneum, 1979; *A Nice Girl Like You,* Atheneum, 1980; *Myself and I,* Atheneum, 1981; *The Days of the Dragon's Seed,* Atheneum, 1982; *Gabriel's Girl,* Atheneum, 1982; *Time Warp Summer,* Atheneum, 1982.

Under pseudonym Nicole St. John: *The Medici Ring,* Random House, 1975; *Wychwood,* Random House, 1976; *Guinever's Gift,* Random House, 1977.

WORK IN PROGRESS: (As Catherine E. Chambers) *Pioneer Living* series; (as Elizabeth Bolton) *Easy-to-Read Mystery* series; (as Norma Johnston) *Change of Heart;* (as Lavinia Harris) *Tower of the Swans;* (as Pamela Dryden) *A Masque of Hearts.*

SIDELIGHTS: "Why do I write? Because I have things that I must say—in person, over a pot of tea before the fire, on a stage, in print—and I can no more hold back from saying them than I can cease to breathe. Because all my life I have learned through vicarious empathy of literature, and I believe, with Tennessee Williams, that as a writer of fiction 'I gave you truth, in the pleasant disguise of illusion.'

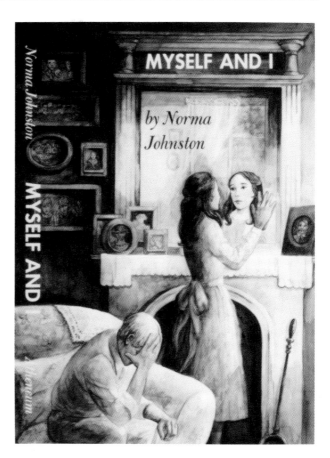

(From *Myself and I* by Norma Johnston. Jacket painting by Judith Gwyn Brown.)

"Why do I write? Because I must pass on what I've been given—by people I've known, those I've loved, those I've hated, those I've feared; by plays I have played in and plays I have directed; by sermons I've heard on Sunday mornings, and others spoken haltingly in the dark of night; by books that I have read, which became a part of me forever. Because I have sat and watched and listened to people I have loved groping or weeping or fighting or tearing themselves apart in a search for explanations and for patterns and wanted to shout *'Listen!* Will you listen! I've been there, this is what I found, this is what helped me. Please let me pass it on!' But they won't listen, any more than I would, with their ears; they may, as I did, however, listen with their hearts through empathy with a character in a book. And so I write of the keeping days in which we find moments of truth; of the rites of passage in which we know we have gone irrevocably from innocence into knowledge; of the verities I believe to be unchanged in a changing world.

"The outer manners and mores may change from generation to generation, but the basic facts of our humanity—love and hate, faith and doubt, weakness and strength, confidence and fear, community and alienation—do not. I write in the past, because the future can learn of the past. Because people in the past have gone through the same inner and outer struggles that we do now; there is nothing new under the sun. There are lessons to be learned in the things that they did wrong, and messages for us in the truths they found. I write in the past because often truth does reach us better through the guise of illusion; the past has a glamour that often makes the hard pill

NORMA JOHNSTON

easier to swallow. And I write of our own American past because there is an enduring strength and source of nurture in our own taproots that we are very much in danger of forgetting. We have ceased to look on all our forebears as perfect saints and that is good, but in recognizing their follies, their stupidities and their downright cruelties we must not overlook their very real accomplishments and the *American* ethnic strengths, which yet have much to give.

"I am supposed to be writing a 'biographical sketch,' but I cannot do it; to step outside oneself and report in that way is to immediately become artificial—or to put on a mask. My books are me. My characters are not me, but their beliefs are, and so I very much fear are many of the lessons they have to learn. The setting of the *Keeping Days* books is the neighborhood and era of my grandparents' youth; the town of *Of Time and of Seasons* is my own town; I, myself, am descended from the Jersey Dutch, and all their strengths and weaknesses are in my blood.

"It is usually easy to write one's life as a chronological résumé of fact; it is not for me, because all my life I have lived in many different overlapping worlds. Only child, ahead of myself in school; too young there, while a 'little old lady' at home; member of one crowd at church and another crowd in high school. Wrote my first book at twelve, which no one but an English teacher ever read; wrote my second at sixteen, which after a decade of revisions became my first one published. Teenage teacher of art and dramatics, disastrously; assistant to a buyer in a department store; part-time actress; secret writer. Buyer for mother's specialty shop; student at the American Theatre Wing; owner of own dress shop; published writer. Producer of summer theater; assistant in a New York fashion publication office; assistant to editor of a religious publishing house. Church youth advisor. Middle-aged 'retread' college student. Teacher in junior high (about which the less said, the better, but out of which came books and lasting friendships). Director of Geneva Players, an ecumenical religious drama group that uses the stage as a second pulpit to disturb the status quo and draw people into a closer understanding of themselves, their neighbors, and their God. That last statement is a pretty good summation of why I write, as well.

"Who am I? A Victorian. A cat curled by the fire (but I'm allergic to cats). An herb garden. The color red. Old houses with low-ceilinged rooms, with a teakettle on the hearth and a fire burning bright. Long dresses, and crosses worn on chains. Candlelight. Shakespeare, mythology, John Donne. England in the summers (I draw my strength from England, though my ancestors were Dutch). My church. My theater. We played the game 'Who Am I?' at Geneva's nurture-and-discussion group one night, and somebody described me as 'a total environment.'

"A few years ago I had to write an 'autobiography' for a freshman college English class and, being almost twice the age of the other students and intimidated by the teacher, I sought to hide behind a mask—and ended, as always, in finding that when we put on the mask of a character honestly, we drop our own. My paper started out 'Once upon a time there was an insufferable brat,' and ended, 'Call her a romanticist, but she still believes, in spite of everything, that man has at heart the potential for good as well as evil; that life is no mere accident or dirty joke but has reason and purpose. To her, that's realism. Perhaps commitment's out of style these days. This artist is past the point of no return—and she's very glad she is!'

"I think that says it all."

Johnston is influenced by such writers as: Dorothy L. Sayers, Maud Hart Lovelace, Clemence Dane, Patricia Wentworth, Madeleine L'Engle, Agnes deMille, Ngaio Marsh, and Janet Lambert.

HOBBIES AND OTHER INTERESTS: Youth counseling, religion, mythology, psychology, British and American history, travel, gourmet cooking, theatre, ballet, herb and flower gardening, 17th-century metaphysical poetry.

KARASZ, Ilonka 1896-1981

OBITUARY NOTICE: Born in 1896, in Budapest, Hungary; died May 26, 1981, in Warwick, N.Y. An artist and designer, Karasz came to the United States in 1913 after completing her education at the Royal School of Arts and Crafts in Budapest. She is best known for her cover designs which appeared in the *New Yorker* from 1924 to 1973. Karasz was also the founder-director of Design Group, Inc., an organization composed of craftsmen, artists, and designers. An expert in decorative arts, Karasz supplied designs to various manufacturers for the production of fabrics, rugs, silverware, china, and furniture. She was also well known as an illustrator of children's books, particularly for her book *The Twelve Days of Christmas,* which in 1949 was selected by the American Institute of Graphic Arts as one of their "Fifty Books of the Year." Other illustrated works include Clement Wood's *The Outline of Man's Knowledge,* W. Maxwell's *The Heavenly Tenants,* and *The Christmas Calendar: The Days before Christmas.* For More Information See: *Time,* November 8, 1948; *Illustrators of Children's Books, 1946-56,* Horn Book, 1958. *Obituaries: New York Times,* May 30, 1981.

KENEALY, James P. 1927-
(Jim Kenealy)

BRIEF ENTRY: Born June 4, 1927, in Dorchester, Mass. Kenealy is the author of numerous outdoor books for young people. Besides being the owner of a marine and environmental consulting firm, Kenealy is outdoor editor at WQBK-AM in Albany, N.Y. He is the author of the outdoor column in *Knickerbocker News* as well as the contributor of articles to other state and national magazines. Among Kenealy's books are *Boating from Bow to Stern* (Dodd, 1967), *Better Fishing for Boys* (Dodd, 1969), and *Better Camping for Boys* (Dodd, 1973). *Address:* R.D. 1, Rensselaer, N.Y. 12144. *For More Information See: Contemporary Authors,* Volumes 93-96, Gale, 1980.

LANE, Rose Wilder 1886-1968

PERSONAL: Born December 5, 1886, in De Smet, S.D.; died October 30, 1968, in Danbury, Conn.; daughter of Almanzo James (a farmer) and Laura Elizabeth (a writer; maiden name, Ingalls) Wilder; married (Claire) Gillette Lane, March 24, 1909 (divorced, 1918). *Education:* Attended public school in South Dakota, Missouri and Louisiana. *Politics:* Libertarian. *Residence:* Danbury, Conn., Mansfield, Mo., and Harlingen, Texas.

CAREER: Writer. Western Union Telegraph Co., telegrapher, c.1904-10; real estate agent in California, 1910-13; *San Fran-*

cisco Bulletin, San Francisco, Calif., reporter and feature writer, 1914-18; worked as publicist for American Red Cross in Europe and the Near East, 1918-21; National Economic Council, editor of *Review of Books,* 1945-50; *Women's Day,* correspondent in Vietman, 1965. *Member:* Missouri Writers Guild, Justamere Club of Mansfield. *Awards, honors:* O. Henry Prize, 1922, for "Innocence"; inducted into the South Dakota Cowboy and Western Hall of Fame, 1981.

WRITINGS—Fiction: *Diverging Roads,* Century Co., 1919; *He Was a Man,* Harper & Brothers, 1925; *Hill-Billy,* Harper & Brothers, 1926; *Cindy: A Romance of the Ozarks,* Harper & Brothers, 1928; *Let the Hurricane Roar,* Longmans, Green, 1933, Pelican, 1982, continuously reprinted, published as *Young Pioneers,* McGraw, 1976; *Old Home Town* (short stories), Longmans, Green, 1935; *Free Land,* Longmans, Green, 1938; *Home Over Saturday,* Laura Ingalls Wilder Memorial Society (De Smet, S.D.), 1974.

Nonfiction: *Henry Ford's Own Story: How a Farmer Boy Rose to the Power That Goes with Many Millions, Yet Never Lost Touch with Humanity,* E. O. Jones, 1917; *The Making of Herbert Hoover,* Century Co., 1920; *The Peaks of Shala: Being a Record of Certain Wanderings Among the Hill-Tribes of Albania,* Chapman & Dodd, 1922, Harper & Brothers, 1923; *Give Me Liberty,* Longmans, Green, 1936, revised edition, Caxton, 1954; *The Discovery of Freedom: Man's Struggle Against Authority,* John Day, 1943, reprinted, Arno, 1972; *Woman's Day Book of American Needlework,* Simon & Schuster, 1963. Co-author (with Frederick O'Brien) of *White Shadows in the South Seas* and translator from the French of *The Dancer of Shamahka,* 1923.

Other writings: (Author of prologue and epilogue; editor and author of setting) Laura Ingalls Wilder, *On the Way Home: The Diary of a Trip from South Dakota to Mansfield, Missouri, in 1894,* Harper, 1962; *The Lady and the Tycoon: Letters of Rose Wilder Lane and Jasper Crane,* Caxton, 1973; (with Roger Lea MacBride) *Rose Wilder Lane: Her Story,* Stein & Day, 1977. Also editor of *Art Smith's Story: The Autobiography of the Boy Aviator,* published serially in *San Francisco Bulletin,* c.1915. Ghost writer for many American authors.

Contributor of short stories and articles to periodicals, including *Saturday Evening Post, Ladies' Home Journal, Redbook, Travel, Cosmopolitan, American Mercury, Good Housekeeping, Country Gentleman, Harper's, McCall's, Woman's Day, Sunset, Esquire,* and *Independent.* Also contributor of travel letters and articles to newspapers.

ADAPTATIONS: "Young Pioneers," ABC-TV movie, 1976; "Young Pioneers Christmas," ABC-TV movie, 1977.

SIDELIGHTS: **December 5, 1886.** "I was born . . . on the snow-buried prairies of South Dakota, in cold December weather. My sagacity was apparent even earlier, for I chose the most wonderful of parents.

"They were both of the sturdy American pioneer stock that broke the way for the white race westward across the continent. My mother's father was a hunter and trapper; my mother heard in her childhood the long, blood-chilling screams of panthers in the forest around the logcabin, and saw brown bears in the woods, and knew the Indians. My father's father 'slashed and burned' three hundred acres of good hard-wood timber before he drove the plow through the virgin soil of his Minnesota

Lane, as a young woman.

farm, and my father, as a little boy, saw him shoulder his gun and march away with the men who drove back the Indian raiders.

"My mother loves courage and beauty and books; my father loves nature, birds and trees and curious stones, and both of them love the land, the stubborn, grudging, beautiful earth that wears out human lives year by year. They gave me something of all these loves, and whenever I do something that I really can't help sitting down and admiring, I always come plump up against the fact that I never would have done it if I hadn't been wise enough to pick out these particular parents." [Rose Wilder Lane, "Rose Wilder Lane," *Sunset, the Pacific Monthly,* November, 1918.[1]]

1893. "We lived . . . in our own house in De Smet, away from Main Street, where only a footpath went through the short brown grasses. It was a big rented house and empty. Upstairs and down it was dark and full of stealthy little sounds at night, but then the lamp was lighted in the kitchen, where we lived. Our cookstove and table and chairs were there; the bed was in an empty room and at bedtime my trundle bed was brought into the warmth from the cookstove. We were camping, my mother said; wasn't it fun? I knew she wanted me to say yes, so I did. To me, everything was simply what it was.

"I was going to school while my father and mother worked. Reading, writing, spelling, arithmetic, penmanship filled days almost unbearably happy with achievements satisfying Miss Barrows's strict standards. 'Procrastination is the thief of time,'

Farther west, the country was not yet settled and the land was said to be rich and level, and without forests. So they went west. ■ (From *Let the Hurricane Roar* by Rose Wilder Lane.)

I wrote twenty times in my penmanship book, without error or blot; and 'Evil communications corrupt good manners,' and 'Sweet are the uses of adversity,' every t and d exactly twice as tall as a vowel and every l exactly three times as tall; every t crossed; every i dotted.

"I was seven years old and in the Second Reader at school but I had read the Third Reader and the Fourth, and *Robinson Crusoe* and *Gulliver's Travels*. The *Chicago Inter-Ocean* came every week and after the grown-ups had read it, I did. I did not understand all of it, but I read it." [Laura Ingalls Wilder, *On the Way Home,* edited by Rose Wilder Lane, Harper, 1962.[2]]

1894. Family migrated to the Ozark Mountains and settled in Mansfield, Missouri. "We reached the Missouri at Yankton, in a string of covered wagons. The ferryman took them, one by one, across the wide yellow river. I sat between my parents in the wagon on the river bank, anxiously hoping to get across before dark . . . . Looking around the edge of the wagon cover, I saw the whole earth billowing behind us to the sky. There was something savage and terrifying in that howling yellow swallowing the sky. The color came, I now suppose, from the sunset.

"'Well, that's our last sight of Dakota,' my mother said." [William T. Anderson, *Laura's Rose: The Story of Rose Wilder Lane,* Laura Ingalls Wilder Memorial Society (De Smet, S.D.), 1976.[3]]

"My mother made daily notes of our journey in a little five-cent Memorandum book, writing with pencil on both sides of the pages, of course. Nobody then wasted paper.

". . . I remember walking to school through the snowy woods in my shoes and stockings, hearing the thuds of my father's ax sounding fainter as I went; and coming home with the sunset red behind me to hear the whirr-whirr of the crosscuts saw growing sharper in the frosty air. The ax was too heavy for

my mother; my father would not trust her with its sharpness, but she could safely handle one end of the crosscut saw.

"Winter evenings were cozy in the cabin. The horses were warm in the little barn, the hens in the new wooden coop. Snow banked against the log walls and long icicles hung from the eaves. A good fire of hickory logs burned in the fireplace. In its heat, over a newspaper spread on the hearth, my father worked oil into the harness-straps between his oily-black hands. I sat on the floor, carefully building a house of corncobs, and my mother sat by the table, knitting needles flashing while she knitted warm woolen socks for my father and read to us from a book propped under the kerosene lamp. She read us Tennyson's poems and Scott's poems; those books were ours. And she read us Prescott's *Conquest of Mexico,* and *Conquest of Peru,* and *The Green Mountain Boys,* and *John Halifax, Gentleman.* She read us *The Leatherstocking Tales* and another true book, the biggest of all: *Ancient, Medieval and Modern History.* I borrowed those from the shelf of lending-books in the Fourth Reader room at school. The teacher let me borrow them, though I wasn't in Fourth Reader yet."[2]

Family settled on their farm, Rocky Ridge, in Mansfield, where she attended the local school. "The professor used to sit before us, tipped back in his chair, watching us study, ready to catch us if we whispered. He did not have any desk; he kept his chewing tobacco in his pocket. In one hand he held a long cane—it was intended to represent authority but he usually used it to scratch his back."[3]

1903. Attended high school in Crowley, Louisiana, where she stayed at the home of her aunt. After graduation, went to work for Western Union in Kansas City. Lane had learned telegraphy in the Mansfield railroad depot.

1908. Moved to San Francisco, where she became the first female real estate salesperson in California.

Afterward Caroline remembered the day at the town site as though it had happened to someone else. ■ (From *Let the Hurricane Roar* by Rose Wilder Lane.)

March 24, 1909. Married (Claire) Gillette Lane.

Lane in a letter to her mother, detailed the financial problems she and Gillette suffered throughout the duration of their marriage. "Gillette got $18 today, and we nearly threw a fit—the first real money we've seen for ages and ages, except that you sent. So the rent is no more hanging over us like a piece of black crepe—it's funny—here we've been running carefreely around with people who have to hire secretaries to count their money, Gillette has been casually talking millions with men who are as powerful in London as here, and dining at Tait's with champagne at $12 a bottle, and I went to a lecture in the white and gold room of the St. Francis today at which the cards were $5, and it was an invitaton affair besides—and afterward ran into Techau for a bite and saw the check for the four of us—$11—and all the time inside the gnawing mad wish for $20 for the rent man, and the wonder if the gas would be cut off tonight! It was only temporary, of course—that's one of the maddening things about it—and things must loosen up soon and everything will be fine again—." [Rose Wilder Lane and Roger Lea MacBride, *Rose Wilder Lane: Her Story,* Stein & Day, 1977.[4]]

When the real estate business folded during World War I, Lane turned to free-lance writing for the San Francisco *Bulletin,* until she was asked to join the staff. As her career grew and expanded, her marriage faltered. In 1918 she was divorced.

1918-1921. Traveled with the American Red Cross and Near East Relief to the Balkans, Russia and Near East to write articles on post war conditions. "I wrote . . . about those victims of war, that should have wrung dollars from the stoniest American pocketbook."[3]

Settled in Albania for a brief period of time. Of the life style, she noted: ". . . No dusting, for there was no furniture; no making of beds, for there were no beds; no curtains to keep fresh, for there was no windows; no trouble with clothes, for

centuries saw no change in fashions; no work except hand weaving and embroidery and the washing of linen in a brook. No haste, no worry, no struggle to invent new needs that one must struggle to satisfy. All that simplicity and leisure our ancestors traded for a rug on the floor, a trinket-covered dressing table, for knives and forks and kitchen ranges, fountain pens and high white collars and fashion books. It seemed to us, on that morning, a trade in which we had been cheated.

"And even now I wonder, sometimes, about the value of the centuries that have given us civilizaton." [Rose Wilder Lane, *Peaks of Shala,* Harper & Brothers, 1923.[5]]

1922. Won the O'Henry Prize for "Innocence," the best short story of the year.

1925. Returned to her parents' home in Mansfield to live.

1926-1928. Lived in Albania with her friend, Helen Boylston.

1928. Returned to the U.S., where she wrote for a number of magazines. "I like people—clerks and farmers and highwaymen and tramps and elevator girls and poets and lawyers—all sorts of people. I would like better to write about them if only I could get them down on paper exactly as they really are, and I keep trying and trying to do it. It seems to me that the only reason for writing is the showing of a different angle of life to readers who might not have had the opportunity to see it for themselves. That is what I want a book to give me, and that is what I would like my books to give others."[1]

1930. Lived in Mansfield, Missouri, free-lance articles for magazines. Encouraged her mother to write her famous "Little House" books.

(From *Let the Hurricane Roar* by Rose Wilder Lane.)

1933. *Let the Hurricane Roar* published. *"Let the Hurricane Roar* is a reply to pessimists. It was written from my feeling that living is never easy, that all human history is a record of achievement in disaster (so that disaster is no cause for despair), and that our great asset is the valor of the American spirit—the undefeated spirit of millions of obscure men and women who are as valiant today as the pioneers were in the past." [From a letter to Mrs. Garst from Rose Wilder Lane, taken from *Laura Ingalls Wilder Lore,* Volume 7, Fall-Winter, 1981.[6]]

About the book, which was republished as *Young Pioneers* and adapted as a movie for ABC-TV in 1976, William Anderson, editor of *Laura Ingalls Wilder Lore,* said: "Interestingly, although *Let the Hurricane Roar* was written for an adult market, it is now regarded by many critics as probably the *first* of the 'junior novels' ever written, i.e. the first book that was regarded as an in-between from the children's lit. stage and adult fiction."

1938. Bought a farm in Danbury, Connecticut, where she resided for more than twenty-five years. ". . . Being a farmer's daughter—I bought this little place with a canny eye to its slope, which is south with protecting hill-shoulder east and west and my woodlots higher in the north, so my scrap of land is ten degrees warmer in winter and cooler in summer than even my nearby neighbors' places. In summer the cool breezes

flow downward across it. And hurricanes until now—my fingers are crossed—have leaped over it.

"I have canned 109 quarts of tomatoes from my garden and have a bushel to can today; this is a triumph because blight has literally destroyed nearly all tomatoes in this region. I have canned ninety-nine and a half quarts of beautiful chicken, young fat hens; and ninety-six of Gravenstein apple sauce. My corn crop was perfect; hybrid seed, mostly variants of Golden Bantam, bore abundantly, three and four ears to the stalk, all uniform and not one single cornworm or cornborer in the whole yield. Beans were harrassed by groundhogs and did not do so well, the poor Kentucky Wonders had to climb beyond groundhog reach before they could keep a leaf or set a pod; still it was a fair yield, now all in cans, and cabbages, carrots, beets, cauliflower, flourished beautifully. Eggs are scarce on the market here, being substituted for non-existent meat (not a scrap of meat in all Danbury) but I have three five-gallon jarsful of eggs in water-glass. Also I have a baby beef and a hog now nearing 300-pound weight, both boarding out so that I do not know them personally and will meet them only as pork and beef this winter. The Thorovian life isn't as simple as it seems in Walden Pond but it does have its values." [Roger Lea MacBridge, editor, *The Lady and the Tycoon: Letters of Rose Wilder Lane and Jasper Crane,* Caxton, 1973.[7]]

1944. Announced that she would quit writing in order to avoid paying taxes as a protest against the New Deal. "I stopped

ROSE WILDER LANE

Rose Wilder Lane, in later life.

writing fiction because I don't want to contribute to the New Deal. Income tax was the last straw. I don't see why I should work to support the Writer's War Board, the OWI and all such New Deal piffle while men are dying and there's work to be done at home. They've tried price fixing since before the big flood and it's never worked. The only effect is that it cuts down production and encourages black markets.

"The thing to do if you believe practices are wrong is to resist them. The American people did it with Prohibition. The colonists did it when King George III tried to overtax them. The New Deal is going back to King George's economy and scarcity. We've got to resist. I feel very, very hard times are coming, but I also feel the people will pull through. I'm not pessimistic about that. The vote will have no effect until we have a politican who'll stand up and tell the truth.''[3]

1956. Visited her ailing mother, Laura Ingalls Wilder who died on February 10, 1957. "I am indeed frantically busy. . . . I am houseworking, nursing, cooking, and figuring out diabetic diet at high speed all day long. The Springfield doctor is in charge by telephone. We hope to be able to take my mother to Springfield . . . for blood-sugar test and further examination. I wish she would stay with me in Danbury but of course I understand her attachment to her home. My own difficulty is that I have no opportunity to read or write except during the nights when she is sleeping.''[7]

1961-1962. Returned to writing for publication with a needlework series for *Woman's Day*.

1965. Always motivated by political commitments, Lane was the oldest war correspondent in Vietnam. She contributed an article about the war from a woman's point of view to *Woman's Day*. Upon her return from Vietnam, Lane settled in her winter home in Harlingen, Texas to spend her time remodeling and gardening.

The Laura Ingalls Wilder Home Association was established to include the life's works of her famous mother and was later expanded to incorporate Lane's works as well. ". . . The Laura Ingalls Wilder Home Association. This is a group of Mansfield [Missouri] people who are preserving my mother's home as a memorial library and museum. I gave them the furniture and a great deal of interesting Americana belonging to her, much of it mentioned in her books. If it is managed as well as most things in Mansfield are, for persons interested in Americana and especially interested in my mother's books, the house should be an interesting place to visit. Many schools are visiting it now, en masse, I am told. It is just one of those things, part of the reviving interest in American history that is going on all over this country now. I know that my mother's books are a real contribution to American values for children; so many parents have written me that they make all the difference in their bringing up their children to be real Americans, in spite of other influences. Preserving the house and things in it has some effect in increasing the influence of the books. . . .''[7]

1966. "In my ninth decade it's a crown of something—not sorrow—to remember—not happier—days but days irrevocably gone.

"When I was five years old, sitting one day in my grandmother's parlor in De Smet on a footstool beside her rocking chair, and helping her sew carpet rags, after a long meditative silence I said dreamily, 'I wish I had been there when Christ was crucified.' My sincerely, deeply pious grandmother was (I now realize) deeply touched by this tender, young piety; I

can recall the tone of her voice saying softly, 'Why, dear?' I replied, 'So I could have cursed him and been the Wandering Jew.'

"I'm sure I recall the incident because of the inexplicable effect, upon my grandmother, of these candidly innocent words. It was like an earthquake, a silent one. She said nothing. Somehow the air sort of crashed, terrifically.

"But for most of my life it seemed ideal to be that mythical Wanderer. Imagine having been thirty-five years old—the perfect age; vigorously young yet somewhat recovering from being a total fool—since the year One, when Rome's Golden Age was beginning and Hellenic not yet wholly ended. Imagine being able to remember 1900 years, to be able to speak all languages, and to anticipate seeing all the rest of human history to the final destruction of this planet.

"Only lately I've decided against that youthful ambition. Here I'm not yet ninety, and far from knowing all languages, I don't even know my own. Words I've relied upon all my life are quicksand under my feet. Just think of 'square' for example. And hep, hip, hippie change so rapidly that they escape a grasp. And as for understanding people—Once I thought I had begun to, but now I give up. . . .''[3]

October 30, 1968. Died in Danbury, Connecticut. "The longest lives are short; our work lasts longer.''[3]

HOBBIES AND OTHER INTERESTS: Traveling, building, gardening, needlework.

FOR MORE INFORMATION SEE: Springfield Republican, February 13, 1917; Rose Wilder Lane, "Rose Wilder Lane," *Sunset, the Pacific Monthly,* November, 1918; *New York Times,* April 13, 1919, March 22, 1925, February 26, 1933; *Boston Transcript,* October 30, 1920, June 9, 1923, March 28, 1925, April 14, 1926; *New York World,* June 3, 1923; *New York Tribune,* March 22, 1925; *Literary Review,* March 28, 1925; *New York Herald Tribune Books,* April 14, 1925; *Saturday Review of Literature,* April 10, 1926, March 4, 1933, May 7, 1938; *Bookman,* March, 1933; *Weekly Book Review,* March 14, 1943; Laura Ingalls Wilder, *On the Way Home,* Harper, 1962; Roger Lea MacBride, editor, *The Lady and the Tycoon: Letters of Rose Wilder Lane and Jasper Crane,* Caxton, 1973; William B. Anderson, *Laura's Rose: The Story of Rose Wilder Lane,* Laura Ingalls Wilder Memorial Society (De Smet, S.D.), 1976; *Rose Wilder Lane: Her Story,* Stein & Day, 1977; *Language Arts,* April, 1981; W. Anderson, editor, *Laura Ingalls Wilder Lore,* Volume 7, Fall-Winter, 1981.

OBITUARIES: New York Times, November 1, 1968; *Publishers Weekly,* December 2, 1968.

LARSON, Norita D. 1944-

PERSONAL: Born April 26, 1944, in St. Paul, Minn.; daughter of Otto L. (a salesman) and Doris (Fischer) Dittberner; married Leland L. Larson (a hospital planner), August 13, 1966; children: Eric, Jessica, Emily. *Education:* College of St. Catherine, B.A. *Politics:* Democrat. *Home:* 955 Lombard Ave., St. Paul, Minn. 55105.

CAREER: Writer, poet, teacher. Board member, The Loft (school for literature and the arts). *Member:* Onionskin.

NORITA D. LARSON

WRITINGS: Walt Disney: An American Original (juvenile), Creative Education, 1974; (with Paula Taylor) *Walter Cronkite* (juvenile), Creative Education, 1975; *Langston Hughes, Poet of Harlem,* Creative Educaton, 1981. Contributor of poetry to journals, including *Lake Street Review, Studio One,* and *Great River Review.*

LAWRENCE, Isabelle (Wentworth)

BRIEF ENTRY: Born in Cambridge, Mass.; daughter of George and Belle (Richmond) Lawrence. Educator, writer, and lecturer. Lawrence received an M.A. from Radcliffe College in 1921. She taught history in Chestnut Hill, Massachusetts, from 1920 to 1932 and at the Latin School in Chicago, Illinois, from 1933 to 1969. As a drama and literary critic, Lawrence contributed articles to the *Boston Evening Transcript* from 1915 to 1936, and since 1953 has written many reviews for the *New York Times* and the *Chicago Tribune.* An author who specializes in historical fiction for children, Lawrence has written eight books, including *The Gift of the Golden Cup* (Bobbs-Merrill, 1946), *A Spy in Williamsburg* (Junior Literary Guild selection; Rand McNally, 1955), and *West to Danger* (Bobbs-Merrill, 1964). Lawrence served as president of the Chicago Children's Reading Round Table in 1963 and was the recipient of their award in 1968. She also received the Freedom Foundation of Valley Forge award in 1960 for her demonstrated "citizenship and American way of life, over and above the call of duty." *Residence:* Chicago, Ill. *For More Information See: Chicago School Journal,* May, 1951; *Authors of Books for Young People,* Scarecrow, 1967; *Who's Who of American Women,* 8th edition, Marquis, 1973.

LEISTER, Mary   1917-

PERSONAL: Surname is pronounced *Lye*-ster; born October 4, 1917, in Brackenridge, Pa.; daughter of W. Clare and Mar-

tha (Nolf) McFarland; married Robert E. Leister (an electronics engineer), June 4, 1942. *Education:* Attended Johns Hopkins University. *Residence:* Sykesville, Md.

CAREER: Writer and lecturer. Has worked as a stenographer and volunteer elementary school teacher. Currently teaches continuing education courses at Roland Park Country School, Baltimore, Md., evening division. *Member:* International Wildlife Association, National Wildlife Association, National Audubon Society, Natural History Association, Environmental Defense Fund, Maryland Ornithological Society.

WRITINGS—Juvenile, except where noted: *The Silent Concert,* Bobbs-Merrill, 1970; *Wildlings* (adult nonfiction), Stemmer House, 1976; *Flying Fur, Fin, and Scale: Strange Animals That Swoop and Soar,* Stemmer House, 1977; *Wee Green Witch,* Stemmer House, 1978; *Seasons of Heron Pond* (adult nonfiction), Stemmer House, 1981. Author of nature columns in *Baltimore Sunday Sun,* 1972—, and "Read Aloud Nature Story," in *Humpty Dumpty,* 1976-79. Contributor of stories, articles, and poems to nature and children's magazines, including *Ranger Rick, Boys' Life, Jack and Jill, National Wildlife,* and *American Forests.*

WORK IN PROGRESS: Fiction and nonfiction for children and adults and articles for newspapers and magazines.

SIDELIGHTS: "All of my writing is of the natural world. Whether I write an imaginative story of a tiny witch or a fact-filled essay about an actual bullfrog, its heart and its source lie somewhere out there beyond the open windows of my study. I wrote *Wee Green Witch* because I needed a new story to tell to my kindergarten and first-grade friends, but the story sprang from my fascination with the great, knobby, brown mushrooms that grew at the edge of the woods in a mossy corner of my lawn. And while *Flying Fur, Fin, and Scale* is about all sorts of animals, real ones—flying snakes and flying frogs and flying lizards—that fly without feathers, it all began because I found

MARY LEISTER

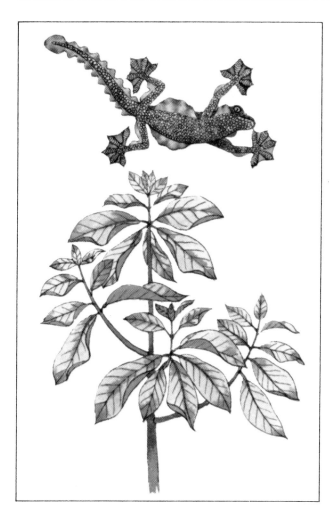

The flying lizards with the fanciful name of flying dragons are delightfully nimble.... ■ (From *Flying Fur, Fin and Scale: Strange Animals That Swoop and Soar* by Mary Leister. Illustrated by Tony Chen.)

a pile of feathers lying under the pasture fence where a red fox had eaten a mockingbird.

"I cannot remember a time when the wild, green world of plants and animals was not a valuable part of my life. Even before I could walk, my father perched me on his shoulder and took me with him on his Sunday rambles over our isolated Pennsylvania countryside. When the time came that I could manage my own feet, I still walked with my father—and my five brothers and sisters as they came along—but, I also did my own exploring in dooryard and garden, and, as I grew older, extended my solitary-but-never-lonely walks out onto the hills, down the hollows, and into the marshes and woodlands and fields.

"I learned to sit quietly, half hidden among wild plants, on the edge of a pond or a stream or in the middle of a field and to simmer down until, all around me, the little wild animals and the birds and the butterflies went on with their daily lives as though I were not there, and the green things grew and blossomed and went to seed in their fashion.

"Thus, I came to know these plants and animals, to love them, and to recognize the intertwining strands of all our lives, and

to sense the mingling within us all of a life force so great and so intricate it leaves me breathless; to feel that even the stones at my feet are, in their deep, slow, and silent way, somehow alive; and to think it quite likely that fairy folk with rainbow wings live close among the grass roots, sleep in the apple blossoms, and dance in the dappled moonlight under the trees in my dooryard.

"I cannot remember the magical moment when I first began to read, when printed words throbbed with life upon the pages of a book; when new people, new places, new knowledge sprang fully garbed into the open cradles of my wonderment, and I found myself as hungry for books as ever I've been for milk and bread.

"But I do remember the day I decided to become a writer. I was eight years old and I had just finished reading *Little Men* by Louisa May Alcott. I wish I could say that from that day forth I worked with single-minded determination to make that decision come true, but I'm afraid I did no serious writing during my years in school nor in the ensuing city-girl years of working in telephone offices, business offices, personnel offices. . . .

"And after I married, I spent more years being a homemaker and gardener, traveling all over the United States on business trips with my electronics engineer husband, spending our vacation times camping and hiking in New England and in the Smokies in the east, and, in the west, all down the Rocky Mountain and Great Basin areas from Idaho and Montana on the north to the southwestern deserts of Arizona, New Mexico and Texas on the south.

"It was not until the mid-1960s that I came up short against the fact that if I were going to become a writer I had better be about it. I began, first, writing greeting card verse, then stories, verses, and articles for children's magazines and for adult gardening, nature and outdoors publications. In 1970 my first children's book was published, and in 1972 I began the still-continuing series of nature essays for the *Baltimore Sunday Sun*—on which my reputation as both a naturalist and writer is based—and I became, at last, a real writer.

"Writing is, for me, the rich fulfillment of all my living, and it brings in its train so many extra treasures—the beautiful letters from children and adults who have enjoyed what I have written, the mounting requests for my lectures, the many new friends I make, the delightful adventures I have, and the opening, each day, of so many doors and so many new worlds before me."

HOBBIES AND OTHER INTERESTS: Camping, hiking, traveling, reading, gardening, dogs, cats, public speaking, good conversation.

FOR MORE INFORMATION SEE: Baltimore Sunday Sun, June 20, 1976; *Valley News Dispatch,* July 27, 1976; *New York Times,* August 7, 1976; *National Wildlife Federation Conservation News,* September 15, 1976; *Detroit Free Press,* October 24, 1976.

A good book is the precious life-blood of a master spirit, embalmed and treasured up on purpose to life beyond life.

—John Milton

LeMAIR, H(enriette) Willebeek   1889-1966 (Saida)

BRIEF ENTRY: Born April 23, 1889, in Rotterdam, Netherlands; died March 5, 1966, in The Hague, Netherlands. Born to a wealthy family of artists, LeMair was encouraged to study anatomy by her mentor, Maurice Boutet de Monvel. The French renowned illustrator, de Monvel, was also responsible for her decision to study art at the Rotterdam Academy from 1909 to 1911. In her late teens she travelled to the Middle East, where some of her finest work was accomplished. Deeply impressed by the religious beliefs expressed in the region's art, she came under the influence of the Murshid Inayat Khan, who preached a religion of universal brotherhood and love. LeMair's artwork adorned numerous children's books, including R. H. Elkin's *Old Dutch Nursery Rhymes* (McKay, 1917), A. A. Milne's *A Gallery of Children* (McKay, 1925), which she illustrated under the pseudonym Saida, and Robert Louis Stevenson's *A Child's Garden of Verses* (Harrap, 1931). She remains best known, however, for her *Christmas Carols for Young Children,* which was reprinted by Fine Books in 1976. Her work also includes children's breakfast sets designed for Gouda pottery, a children's recreation room in a Hague hospital, and a children's chapel in one of Holland's Catholic cathedrals. An exhibition of her books and drawings was held at Bethnal Green Museum in London, England, in 1975. *For More Information See: International Studio,* September, 1914; *Illustrators of Children's Books, 1744-1945,* Horn Book, 1947; *Dictionary of British Book Illustrators and Caricaturists, 1800-1914,* Simon Houfe, 1978.

LERNER, Sharon Ruth   1938-1982

OBITUARY NOTICE—See sketch in *SATA* Volume 11: Born November 9, 1938, in Chicago, Ill.; died of cancer, March 8, 1982. Publisher, author, and illustrator. Upon graduating from the University of Minnesota in 1961, Lerner began her publishing career with Lerner Publications as vice-president and art director. In 1969, she and her husband, Harry J. Lerner, president of Lerner Publications, founded Carolrhoda Books, Inc., publishers of juvenile picture story books, fiction and nonfiction, of which she was president. During the course of her career, Lerner was author and illustrator of eighteen children's books, as well as editor of numerous others. Her works include *Places of Musical Fame, I Picked a Flower, Orange Is a Color,* and *Jewelry Making,* all published by Lerner. She was an accomplished artist in the areas of watercolor and collage, and her jewelry was marketed across the country. *For More Information See: Foremost Women in Communications,* Bowker, 1970; *Who's Who of American Women,* 19th edition, Marquis, 1977; *Contemporary Authors,* New Revision Series, Volume 3, Gale, 1981. *Obituaries: Publishers Weekly,* April 2, 1982.

Most of the basic material a writer works with is acquired before the age of fifteen.

—Willa Cather

Thanks to my friends for their care in my breeding, Who taught me betimes to love working and reading.

—Isaac Watts

LERRIGO, Marion Olive   1898-1968

OBITUARY NOTICE: Born October 27, 1898, in Topeka, Kan.; died September 29, 1968, in North Adams, Mass. Author of books on health education. A Ph.D. graduate of Columbia University, Lerrigo served on numerous health education committees throughout the course of her career, including the White House Conference on Child Health in 1930. She was also a member of the Joint Committee on Health Problems in Education of the National Education Association and American Medical Association for which she co-authored a series of sex education books designed to inform adolescents of the physical and emotional changes that they encounter. Digressing from her usual topic of writing, in 1947 she co-authored (with Toru Matsumoto) *A Brother Is a Stranger,* the biographical story of a Japanese exile. Her other publications include *Caring for Your Disabled Child,* which she co-authored with Dr. Benjamin Spock, *Children Can Help Themselves,* and *A Doctor Talks to Nine-to-Twelve Year Olds. For More Information See: Who Was Who in America,* Volume V, 1969-1973, Marquis, 1973. *Obituaries: New York Times,* September 30, 1969.

LEWIS, Alice Hudson   1895(?)-1971

OBITUARY NOTICE: Born about 1895; died October 24, 1971, in Philadelphia, Pa. Missionary, editor, writer. Following her marriage in 1920 to the Reverend Charles H. Lewis, Alice Hudson Lewis went to China as a missionary under the auspices of the Presbyterian Board of Foreign Missions. She returned to the United States in 1938 and continued to serve with the Presbyterian Board for another 13 years. Lewis lectured throughout the country to women and youth in churches and summer camps. She was a writer and editor for the Presbyterian Board's Office of Interpretation and wrote children's books for the Friendship Press. In 1951, Lewis became the managing editor of the *Y.W.C.A. Magazine.* Lewis was employed on the staff of the Broadcasting and Film Commission of the National Council of the Churches of Christ in the U.S.A. from 1956 until her retirement in 1965. Her books for young people include *Day after Tomorrow* and *Always an Answer. For More Information See: Authors of Books for Young People,* Scarecrow, 1964. *Obituaries: New York Times,* October 28, 1971.

My bed is like a little boat;
   Nurse helps me in when I embark;
She girds me in my sailor's coat
   And starts me in the dark.

At night, I go on board and say
   Good-night to all my friends on shore;
I shut my eyes and sail away
   And see and hear no more.

—Robert Louis Stevenson

Multiplication is vexation,
Division is as bad;
The Rule of Three perplexes me,
And practice drives me mad.

—Anonymous

L'HOMMEDIEU, Dorothy K(easley) 1885-1961

OBITUARY NOTICE: Born in 1885; died March 16, 1961. Dorothy L'Hommedieu was a country dweller with a great love for animals, especially dogs. From 1920 to 1937 she and her husband owned and operated Sand Springs Kennels in New Vernon, N.Y., where they raised cocker spaniels. It was not until 1937 when they sold the kennels that she began writing her stories for children, most of which relate the adventures of various breeds of dogs. Among the books she wrote are *Leo, the Little St. Bernard, Togo, the Little Husky, Tyke, the Little Mutt,* and *Little Black Chaing,* all published by Farrar, Straus. *For More Information See: Authors of Books for Young People,* Scarecrow, 1964. *Obituaries: New York Times,* March 17, 1961; *Publishers Weekly,* April 24, 1961.

LONG, Laura Mooney 1892-1967

OBITUARY NOTICE: Born August 4, 1892, in Columbus, Ind.; died March 28, 1967, in Indianapolis, Ind. Historian and author of children's books. Telling entertaining stories to her own two children eventually led Long to write stories for young people. Among the many books she wrote are *Hannah Courageous, Singing Sisters,* and *Square Sails and Spice Island.* She also wrote several biographies for young people, including those of David Farragut, George Dewey, and Douglas MacArthur. She was the author of a weekly newspaper column, "Horse and Buggy Days." for the *Columbus Republic* for over ten years. *For More Information See: Indiana Authors and Their Books, 1917-1966,* Lakeside Press, 1974.

LORENZINI, Carlo 1826-1890
(Carlo Collodi)

PERSONAL: Born November 24, 1826, in Florence, Italy; died October 26, 1890, in Florence, Italy; son of a cook and domestic servant. *Education:* Attended schools in Florence, Italy.

...**Pinocchio, weeping bitterly, threw himself at the showman's feet....** ■ (From *Pinocchio: The Tale of a Puppet* by C. Collodi. Illustrated by Charles Folkard.)

CARLO LORENZINI

CAREER: Author and journalist. Entered a seminary to study for the priesthood shortly after leaving school; departed from his religious training and turned to a journalism career, 1846; started his own newspaper *Il Lampione,* 1849; founded a theatrical journal, *La Scarrammucia,* 1853; became a government official, 1860; began to write stories for children, 1875. *Military service:* Joined the Tuscan volunteers in the revolutionary campaigns of 1848; served with a cavalry regiment at the outbreak of the Italian-Austrian War, 1859.

WRITINGS—Under pseudonym Carlo Collodi: *Le Avventure di Pinocchio* ("The Adventures of Pinocchio"), [Italy], 1883 [numerous and variously titled English translations include *The Story of a Puppet: or, The Adventures of Pinocchio* (translated by Mary Alice Murray), Unwin, 1892, revised edition, Dutton, 1951, new edition (illustrated by Mariano Leone), Grosset, 1965; *Pinocchio: The Adventures of a Little Wooden Boy* (translated by Joseph Walker, pseudonym of Eau Claire), Crowell, 1909, new edition (illustrated by William Dempster), Childrens Press, 1968; *The Adventures of Pinocchio* (translated by Carol Della Chiesa; illustrated by Attilio Mussino), Macmillan, 1925, reissued, 1969, 1978; *Pinocchio* (translated by Jane Fior), Carousel Books, 1975; other editions illustrated by Charles Cope-

(From the animated movie "Pinocchio." Copyright 1940 by Walt Disney Productions.)

An enormous basin of water was poured down on him. ▪ (From *The Adventures of Pinocchio* by C. Collodi. Illustrated by Fritz Kredel.)

CHAPTER 8

Geppetto makes Pinocchio a new pair of feet, and sells his coat to buy him an A-B-C book.

(From *The Adventures of Pinocchio* by C. Collodi. Illustrated by Attilio Mussino.)

(From the TV special "Pinocchio," starring Danny Kaye and Sandy Duncan. Presented on CBS-TV, March 27, 1976.)

(From the "Hallmark Hall of Fame" television production of "Pinocchio," starring Peter Noone, 1968.)

land, Ginn, 1904; Charles Folkard, Dutton, 1914, revised edition, Dent, 1951; Fritz Kredel, Grosset, 1916, reissued 1946; Kurt Wiese, Nelson, 1928; Mary Liddell, Doubleday, 1930; Maud and Miska Petersham, Garden City Publishing, 1932; Helen Sewell, Appleton-Century, 1935; Pelagie Doane and Christopher Rule, S. Gabriel, 1937; Henry Muheim, Saalfield, 1939; Louise Beaujon, Books Inc., 1939; Tony Sarg, Platt, 1940; Richard Floethe, World Publishing, 1946, reissued, E. M. Hale, 1962; Lois Lenski, Random House, 1946; Anne Heyneman, Lippincott, 1948; Charles Mozley, F. Watts, 1959, large type edition, 1968; adaptations include editions edited by Dorothy Walter Baruch, Heath, 1940; Campbell Grant, Simon & Schuster, 1948; Brian Way, Dobson, 1954; Evelyn Andreas, Wonder Books, 1954; Eva Rouke, World Publishing, 1965; Michael D. Abrams, Lancelot Press, 1968; and *Pinocchio and His Puppet Show Adventure,* Random House, 1973]: *Beppo: or, The Little Rose-Colored Monkey* (translated from the Italian by Walter Samuel Cramp), Small, Maynard, 1907.

Author of the educational books *Giannettino* (based on Parravicini's *Giannetto),* 1876; *Minuzzolo: Il Viaggio per l'Italia de Giannettino* (''Giannettino's Trip through Italy''); *La Geografica di Giannettino* (''Giannettino's Geography''); and *La Grammatica de Giannettino* (''Giannettino's Grammar''). Also author of several books of fiction and nonfiction, 1850-59, including *Macchiette* (''Odd Figures in a Landscape''), *Note Gaie* (''Gay Notes''), *Occhi e Nasi* (''Eyes and Noses''), *Divagazioni Critico-Umoristiche* (''Satirical Digressions''), and *Storie Allegre* (''Light Stories''). Italian translator of the fairy tales of Charles Perrault, 1875.

ADAPTATIONS—Movies and filmstrips: ''Pinocchio'' (motion pictures), Walt Disney Productions, 1940, Buena Vista Films, 1962, Canadian Broadcasting Corp., 1972; ''Pinocchio'' (filmstrips), Key Productions, 1952, Encyclopaedia Britannica Films, 1957, Eye Gate House (with teacher's guide), 1961, H. M. Stone Productions (with teacher's guide), 1972, Walt Disney Productions (both sound and silent versions, each with teacher's guide), 1973, Current Affairs (with teacher's guide), 1976; ''Monstro the Whale'' (motion picture; excerpts from 1940 Disney movie), Walt Disney Home Movies, 1968.

Plays: Remo Bufano, *Pinocchio For the Stage,* Knopf, 1929; George T. Latshaw, *Pinocchio,* Coach House Press, 1959; Majorie Adelberg, *Pinocchio* (produced in Vancouver B.C., Canada, by Holiday Theatre, 1966), New Play Centre, 1965.

Other: Frank Yasha, *Pinocchio: A Musical Legend* (music by E. von Ottenfield and A. Loredo), Mark Music, 1939; ''Pinocchio'' (television special), starring Peter Noone, first shown on the Hallmark Hall of Fame, 1968; ''Pinocchio'' (television special), starring Sandy Duncan and Danny Kaye, CBS-TV, 1976.

SIDELIGHTS: **November 24, 1826.** Born in Florence, Italy; son of a professional cook and a domestic servant. Chiseled on a stone slab in a hidden-away street of Florence is the inscription, ''In this house in 1826, Carlo Lorenzini Collodi, Father of Pinocchio, was born.'' [Piero Bargellini, *Tre Toscani: Collodi, Fucini, Vamba,* (Italy), 1952.[1]]

Lorenzini adopted the name of Collodi from the Castello Collodi in Valdineme, a place which caught his fancy. Described as a gawky youth with two bent knees showing below his black coat and a head which one could lift and replace at will, Collodi spent his early years in a seminary.

1848. Joined the Tuscan volunteers to fight for Italian Independence.

The author spent the ten years between the two Wars of Independence writing for *Il Lampione* (''The Lamp Post'') and *La Scarrammucia* (''The Skirmish''). This period of Collodi's life was filled with guilt and remorse as a run-away seminarian.

1859. Again joined the military to fight for the independence of his beloved Italy during the outbreak of the Italian-Austrian War.

An unrepenting journalist, Collodi wrote: ''Poets are born, but one does not have to be born a journalist. The truth is, once a journalist, always a journalist. Journalism is like the shirt of Nesso; once donned and fastened, there is no getting out of it.'' [Piero Bargellini, ''Pinocchio: Prince of the Puppets,'' translated by Ida Schroeder, *Commonweal,* November 21, 1952.[2]]

Furthermore, journalism brought with it another passion, that of the theater. ''In this world the two things most easy of accomplishment are—sins of desire and comedies. Who in Italy is so illiterate that he does not know how to write a comedy? Who is the gallant among us who can close his eyes in the shadow of death without the remorse of having committed a mortal sin in four or five acts.''[2]

1861. Worked as theatrical censor.

It was quite by accident that Collodi came to write for children. A modest editor of the day, Felix Paggi, asked Collodi to translate Perrault's ''Three Fairy Tales'' from the French. Because of their immediate popularity, Collodi was invited to create something of his own.

1875. Wrote to a friend. ''Now I shall devote myself to writing only for children. Grown ups are too hard to satisfy; they are not for me.''[2]

Never married, Collodi is universally accepted as the progenitor of numerous literary sons. His first son was Giannettino (based on Parravicini's Giannetto). ''Imagine a handsome youth, healthy and slim of person, with a pair of blue eyes betraying a trace of rascal, and with a thick crop of red hair; a lock falling to the middle of the forehead.''[1]

1881. Collodi sent to Guido Biagi, editor of *The Journal for Children* the following note: ''I am sending you this children's story. Do with it as you see fit; but if you print it, pay me well so I may be spurred on to continue it.''[2] And so, Pinocchio was born when bachelor Collodi was about fifty-five years old. The boy puppet entered the life of the solitary, melancholy Collodi, much as he entered the life of bachelor, ''Geppetto''— the name itself derived from a wealthy family member.

Two cycles are evident in Pinocchio's development—''flight'' from the father and a ''return'' to the father. It is not a light amusing book, but a story which carries the profound morality that truth is hard and wisdom is bitter. Pinocchio has been described as a political commentary, an interpretation of history, a document of man's search for his soul, and a sign of the shape of things to come.

1892. *Pinocchio* was translated into English and published in the United States.

October 26, 1890. Collodi died suddenly in Florence, Italy.

(From *The Adventures of Pinocchio* by C. Collodi. Illustrated by Szecskó Tamas.)

(From *The Adventures of Pinocchio* by C. Collodi. Illustrated by Naiad Einsel.)

Benetto Croce, a famous philosopher, attributed the following qualities to the creation of Collodi's Pinocchio; ''The wood out of which Pinocchio is carved is humanity itself.'' [May Lamberton Becker, Introduction to *Pinocchio: The Adventures of a Little Wooden Boy,* by Carlo Collodi, World Publishing, 1946.³]

Pinocchio has traveled all over the world and has been translated into almost every living language, as well as into the most solemn of dead languages—Latin.

The centenary celebration in honor of *Pinocchio* spans three years and includes numerous exhibitions and festivals. An exhibit of the 250 original drawings of twenty-three illustrators of *Pinocchio* from 1881 to 1981 was held in Florence, Italy in 1981-82. Another exhibit in Florence, ''Collodi, the Journalist and the Writer,'' was held at the public library in 1981.

A gigantic merry-go-round was erected in Pinocchio's Park at Collodi to celebrate with a children's festival held in Collodi (the village from which Lorenzini derived his pen name) and in Pescia. A festival of puppets and marionettes took place in Florence and ''Pinocchio: Puppets and Marionettes,'' featuring puppets and marionettes dating from 1890 were displayed in Venice.

FOR MORE INFORMATION SEE: (For children) Elizabeth Rider Montgomery, *Story Behind Great Books,* McBride, 1946; (for children) Stanley J. Kunitz and Howard Haycraft, editors, *Junior Book of Authors,* revised edition, H. W. Wilson, 1951; S. J. Kunitz and Vineta Colby, editors, *European Authors: 1000-1900,* H. W. Wilson, 1967; Brian Doyle, editor, *Who's Who of Children's Literature,* Schocken Books, 1968; *Horn Book,* April, 1982.

LYNCH, Marietta 1947-

PERSONAL: Born December 21, 1947. *Education:* Vassar College, A.B. (cum laude), 1969; Wheelock College, M.Ed., 1973. *Home:* 240 Atlantic Rd., Gloucester, Mass. 01930.

CAREER: Belmont Hill School, Belmont, Mass., teacher, 1966-69; David Ellis School, Roxbury, Mass., teacher, 1969-72; North Shore Nursery School, Beverly, Mass., teacher, 1973-76, director, 1976—; North Shore Education Center, education director, Beverly, 1977. Trustee, North Shore Middle School; trustee, Ravenswood Park. Free-lance photographer.

WRITINGS: (With Patricia Perry) *Mommy and Daddy Are Divorced* (juvenile), Dial, 1978.

Joey and I made the see-saw go up and down. ▪(From *Mommy and Daddy Are Divorced* by Patricia Perry and Marietta Lynch. Photograph by the authors.)

MARIETTA LYNCH and PATRICIA PERRY

MACDONALD, Dwight 1906-

PERSONAL: Born March 24, 1906, in New York, N.Y.; son of Dwight (a lawyer) and Alice (Hedges) Macdonald; married Nancy Rodman, about 1935 (divorced); married Gloria Lanier, 1952; children: (first marriage) Michael Cary Dwight, Nicholas Gardner. *Education:* Phillips Exeter Academy, student, 1920-24; Yale University, B.A., 1928. *Politics:* Conservative Anarchist. *Religion:* None. *Home:* 56 East 87th St., New York, N.Y. 10028 and Spring Close Lane, East Hampton, N.Y. 11937.

CAREER: Fortune Magazine, New York, N.Y., staff writer, 1929-36; *Partisan Review,* New York, N.Y., editor, 1938-43; *Politics,* New York, N.Y., editor and publisher, 1944-49; *New Yorker,* New York, N.Y., staff writer, 1951-65; *Esquire,* New York, N.Y., film critic, 1960-66, political columnist, 1966-70. Visiting professor, University of Texas, 1966, University of California at Santa Cruz, 1969, University of Wisconsin, Milwaukee, 1970, University of Massachusetts, Amherst, 1971. Founder and chairman, Spanish Refugee Aid, 1953—. *Member:* American Academy of Arts and Sciences (fellow), American Institute of Arts and Letters (fellow). *Awards, honors:* Litt.D., Wesleyan University, 1964.

WRITINGS—Of interest to young people: (Compiler) *The Poems of Edgar Allan Poe* (illustrated by Ellen Raskin), Crowell, 1965; *Dwight Macdonald on Movies,* Prentice-Hall, 1969. Contributor to many perodicals, including *Encounter, Film Heritage, Symposium, Harper's, New York Review of Books, Esquire, New Yorker, New International,* and *Nation.* For a complete bibliography, see *Contemporary Authors,* Volumes 29-32, Gale, 1972.

SIDELIGHTS: Respected as a critic both in the U.S., and abroad, Macdonald has undergone a variety of political stances since his journalistic career began in 1929. He once remarked: "The speed with which I evolved from a liberal into a radical and from a tepid Communist sympathizer into an ardent anti-Stalinist still amazes me."

HOBBIES AND OTHER INTERESTS: Reading, talking.

FOR MORE INFORMATION SEE: New Yorker, February 21, 1948, May 20, 1956, September 28,1957, September 16, 1961; *New York Times,* February 22, 1948, September 22, 1956, August 26, 1969, March 12, 1970; *New Republic,* March 1, 1948; *Nation,* March 6, 1948, April 29, 1961; *Saturday Review,* March 6, 1948; November 16, 1957, December 15, 1962; *New York Herald Tribune Book Review,* March 17, 1948; *Canadian Forum,* June, 1948; *Atlantic,* July, 1956, November, 1957, February, 1961; *Christian Science Monitor,* September 13, 1957; *Chicago Sunday Tribune,* September 15, 1957; *New York Times Book Review,* December 21, 1960, July 16, 1969, September 21, 1969; *Time,* January 13, 1961; *New York Herald Tribune Lively Arts,* February 5, 1961; *New Statesman,* November 24, 1961; *Times Literary Supplement,* November 24, 1961; *Spectator,* December 22, 1961; *Commonweal,* December 28, 1962, October 17, 1969; *Harper's,* January, 1963; *Yale Review,* March, 1963; *New York Review of Books,* August 1, 1968; *Esquire,* August, 1969; *Book World,* August 17, 1969; *Newsday,* September 13, 1969; *New Leader,* September 15, 1969.

DWIGHT MACDONALD

(From *Poems of Edgar Allan Poe,* selected by Dwight Macdonald. Illustrated by Ellen Raskin.)

MARZOLLO, Jean 1942-

PERSONAL: Born June 24, 1942, in Manchester, Conn.; daughter of Richard (a town manager) and Ruth (a teacher; maiden name, Smith) Martin; married Claudio Marzollo (a sculptor), March, 1969; children: Daniel, David. *Education:* University of Connecticut, B.A., 1964; Harvard University, M.A.T., 1965. *Residence:* Cold Spring, N.Y. *Agent:* Sheldon Fogelman, 10 East 40th St., New York, N.Y. 10016.

CAREER: Teacher in Arlington, Mass., 1965-66; Harvard University, Cambridge, Mass., assistant director of Project Upward Bound, 1967; General Learning Corp., New York City, 1967-69; National Commissional Resources for Youth, New York City, director of publications, 1970-71; Scholastic Magazines, Inc., Englewood Cliffs, N.J., editor of *Let's Find Out* (magazine for kindergarten children), 1971—.

WRITINGS: (With Janice Lloyd) *Learning Through Play,* Harper, 1972; *Nine Months, One Day, One Year,* Harper, 1975; *Supertot,* Harper, 1978; *Close Your Eyes* (juvenile; illustrated by Susan Jeffers; Junior Literary Guild selection), Dial, 1978; *Amy Goes Fishing* (juvenile; illustrated by Ann Schweinger),

Dial, 1980; *Uproar on Holler Cat Hill* (juvenile; illustrated by Steven Kellogg), Dial, 1980; *Halfway Down Paddy Lane* (juvenile), Dial, 1981; *Superkids,* Harper, 1981; (with Claudio Marzollo) *Jed's Junior Space Patrol* (juvenile), Dial, 1982; (with C. Marzollo) *Robin of Bray* (juvenile), Dial, 1982; (with C. Marzollo) *Red Sun Girl,* Dial, 1983.

WORK IN PROGRESS: A second novel.

SIDELIGHTS: ''I am interested in children, and I like to write books that support families. Whether I'm writing a picture book, an easy-to-read book, a novel, or a book for parents, I find writing an intriguing challenge. It's a job, a hobby, and a game—all in one.

''After college, I went into teaching and then into educational publishing, both fields of great interest to me. It wasn't until the birth of my children that I began to feel the pull of poetry and fancy as I had felt it once before in my own childhood. I then began to write children's books and later when I gained enough confidence, novels.''

About the inspiration for her book, *Close Your Eyes,* Marzollo writes: ''The first verse of *Close Your Eyes* came to me all of

Poppa's drumming,
Children play....

■ (From *Uproar on Hollercat Hill* by Jean Marzollo. Illustrated by Steven Kellogg.)

JEAN MARZOLLO

a sudden one evening while I was nursing my first child. I was sitting in a great big old overstuffed chair and feeling very relaxed. I looked at my son and wondered what was going on inside his head. He looked so innocent and eager and fresh, and I kept thinking about all the kinds of experiences he might have someday, and how each new mind recreates the world.

"So much for inspiration. That was fun, but the rest was hard work. I had help from my editor, Phyllis Fogelman, and my friend, Rosemary Wells. Both kept saying the same thing to me as they read over my drafts of the whole poem: 'Keep it simple. Don't say anything that isn't natural.' . . . Once the poem was finalized, I was thrilled to find out that Susan Jeffers would illustrate it. Her delicate, imaginative, and beautiful books are like the ones I loved most as a child."

HOBBIES AND OTHER INTERESTS: Gardening, swimming, reading.

FOR MORE INFORMATION SEE: Wilson Library Bulletin, December, 1980.

MAYER, Albert Ignatius, Jr.   1906-1960

OBITUARY NOTICE: Born May 25, 1906, in Cincinnati, Ohio; died June 4, 1960; buried at Cemetery of Spring Grove, Cincinnati. In 1927 Mayer graduated from the University of Michigan, where he played varsity football. He worked in business insurance in Ohio and joined the Cincinnati firm of Theodore

Mayer & Brothers in 1927, where he was senior partner from 1947 until the time of his death. He was also a partner in Edgemon, Fast & Mayer Brothers, a firm which acted as agents in land acquisition for the Ohio Turnpike. Active in numerous community and political organizations, Mayer served as Republican minority whip in the Ohio House of Representatives in 1936 and was a delegate from his state to the Republican National Convention in 1956. He was also active in the 1940 campaign of Robert A. Taft for the Republican presidential nomination and was a member and former president of the American Association for the United Nations. An author as well, Mayer wrote several books for young people, including *Falconer's Son, Olympiad,* and *Defense of the Castle,* a tale of Germany in the tenth century. *For More Information See: The National Cyclopaedia,* Volume 47, James T. White, 1965; *Who Was Who in America,* Volume IV, 1961-1968, Marquis, 1968.

McCAIN, Murray (David, Jr.)   1926-1981

OBITUARY NOTICE—See sketch in *SATA* Volume 7: Born December 28, 1926, in Newport, N.C.; died of cancer, November 19, 1981, in New York, N.Y. Formerly an editor with Bantam Books, Criterion, and Appleton-Century, McCain is best known for his children's books, which include *Writing, Books!,* and *The Boy Who Walked Off the Page.* In his later years, McCain was a free-lance editor and co-authored adult books, including *If I Made It, So Can You,* with Virginia Graham. *For More Information See: Contemporary Authors,* Volumes 1-4, revised, Gale, 1967. *Obituaries: Publishers Weekly,* January 1, 1982.

McCULLOCH, Derek (Ivor Breashur) 1897-1967 (Uncle Mac)

OBITUARY NOTICE: Born November 18, 1897, in Plymouth, Devonshire, England; died June 1, 1967. McCulloch enlisted in the British Army at the age of seventeen but was discharged following a serious injury in which he lost an eye, a leg, and a lung. He joined the staff of the British Broadcasting Corporation (BBC) in 1926 and became well known as the gentle "Uncle Mac" of the popular "Children's Hour" program. He was appointed the program director of the broadcast in 1938, a position he held until 1950. McCulloch also produced thousands of broadcasts and was associated particularly with the "Toytown" series in which he portrayed the character of "Larry the Lamb." Among the many books he wrote and edited for children are *Cornish Adventure, Every Child's Pilgrim's Progress, Uncle Mac's Children's Hour Story Book,* and *The Son of the Ruler.* He edited many editions of the BBC *Children's Hour Annual* and was children's editor of the *News Chronicle.* McCulloch was awarded the Order of the British Empire in 1939. *For More Information See: Who's Who of Children's Literature,* Schocken, 1968. *Obituaries: Britannica Book of the Year, 1968.*

McDONALD, Jill (Masefield)   1927-1982

OBITUARY NOTICE—See sketch in *SATA* Volume 13: Born October 30, 1927, in Wellington, New Zealand; died January 2, 1982, in London, England. Although trained as an architect, McDonald became interested in illustration during the late 1950s and served as art director of the *New Zealand School Journal* from 1957 to 1965. She moved to England in the mid-1960s and was enlisted by Penguin Books to help revamp their children's book division, Puffin Books. There, McDonald created the ''Puffin Club,'' a feature in the children's magazine *Puffin Post* in which a character named Odway the Dog posed philosophical questions for young readers to answer. Also a freelance author, McDonald wrote and illustrated children's books, including *Counting On an Elephant* and *Maggy Scraggle Loves the Beautiful Ice-Cream Man*. Her other illustrated works include John Water's *The Royal Potwasher,* Carolyn Sloan's *The Penguin and the Vacuum Cleaner,* and John Cunliffe's *Farmer Barnes and the Goats. For More Information See: Contemporary Authors,* Volumes 65-68, Gale, 1977; *Illustrators of Children's Books, 1967-76,* Horn Book, 1978. *Obituaries: London Times,* January 8, 1982.

Unfortunately,
on the third day at sea,
Claude ran off alone to the stern.
And as they were sailing,
he climbed up the railing
And balanced there feeding a tern.

■ (From *Maude and Claude Go Abroad* by Susan Meddaugh. Illustrated by the author.)

MEDDAUGH, Susan 1944-

PERSONAL: Surname is pronounced Med-aw; born October 4, 1944, in Montclair, N.J.; daughter of John Stuart (a naval captain) and Justine (Leach) Meddaugh. *Education:* Wheaton College, Norton, Mass., B.A., 1966. *Home and office:* 46 Monument Square, Charlestown, Mass. 02129.

CAREER: Houghton Mifflin, Co., Boston, Mass., trade division of the children's book department, designer and art director, 1968-78; writer and illustrator of children's books, 1978—.

WRITINGS—All juvenile; all self-illustrated: *Too Short Fred,* Houghton, 1978; *Maude and Claude Go Abroad,* Houghton, 1980; *Beast,* Houghton, 1981; *Too Many Monsters,* Houghton, 1982.

Illustrator: Anne Epstein, *Good Stones,* Houghton, 1977; Carol-Lynn Waugh, *My Friend Bear,* Atlantic/Little, 1982; Jean and Claudio Marzollo, *Red Sun Girl,* Dial, 1983.

SIDELIGHTS: "I cannot comfortably speculate on my motivation and theories of writing children's books. I seem to make it up as I go along, using rationalization via hindsight.

"I do love the whole process of putting a book together, from idea to finished art. I enjoy telling stories to myself through words and pictures. It's what I did when I was ten years old and it still appeals to me. Maybe in another twenty years I'll know if I'm doing something that appeals to a larger audience; maybe by then I'll have some good theories. Maybe not."

MENOTTI, Gian Carlo 1911-

PERSONAL: Born July 7, 1911, in Cadegliano, Italy; came to the United States in 1928; son of Alfonso (a coffee importer) and Ines (Pellini) Menotti; children: Chip (adopted). *Education:* Attended Verdi Conservatory of Music, 1923-38; graduated from Curtis Institute of Music, 1933. *Home:* Yester House, East Lothian, Scotland; and, 27 East 62nd St., New York, N.Y. 10021.

CAREER: Composer, librettist, and playwright. Curtis Institute of Music, Philadelphia, Pa., part-time teacher of composition, 1948-55; Metro-Goldwyn-Mayer, Hollywood, Calif., script-writer, c.1948; director of film version of *The Medium,* 1951; Festival of Two Worlds, Spoleto, Italy, co-founder, 1958, general manager and artistic director, 1958-68, president, 1968—. Director and producer of operas, including *Carmen, Don Giovanni,* and *La Boheme. Member:* American Society of Composers, Authors, and Publishers, National Institute of Arts and Letters, Academy of St. Cecilia of Rome. *Awards, honors:* Carl R. Luber Musical Award for "Variations on a Theme of Robert Schumann," 1931; B. M., Curtis Institute of Music, 1945; Guggenheim fellowship, 1946 and 1947; Pulitzer Prize in music, 1950, and New York Drama Critics' Circle Award, 1950, both for *The Consul;* Pulitzer Prize in music, 1955, and New York Drama Critics' Circle Award, 1955, both for *The Saint of Bleecker Street; Help, Help, the Globolinks* was a *New York Times* Choice of Best Illustrated Children's Books of the Year, 1970; the film version of *The Medium* was the recipient of an award at the Cannes International Film Festival.

WRITINGS—Operas for children: *Amahl and the Night Visitors* (one-act; written as a television opera, broadcast by NBC-TV,

GIAN CARLO MENOTTI, 1950

December 24, 1951), Schirmer, 1952, narrative version of the libretto illustrated by Roger Duvoisin, Whittlesey House, 1952, McGraw, 1962; *Help, Help, the Globolinks* (first produced in Santa Fe, N.M., August, 1969; produced at New York Center, December 22, 1969), narrative version published as *Gian Carlo Menotti's Help, Help, the Globolinks* (illustrated by Milton Glaser; adapted by Leigh Dean), McGraw, 1970.

For adults: *Amelia Goes to the Ball* (one-act; first produced in Philadelphia at Academy of Music, April 1, 1937; produced in New York City at Metropolitan Opera House, March 3, 1938), Ricordi, 1938; *The Old Maid and the Thief* (written as a radio opera, broadcast by NBC-Radio, April 22, 1939; first state production in Philadelphia, February 11, 1941), Ricordi, 1942; *The Medium* (two-act; first produced in New York City at Columbia University Brander Matthews Theater, May 8, 1946; produced on Broadway at Ethel Barrymore Theater, May 1, 1947), Schirmer, 1947; *The Telephone* (one-act; first produced in New York City at the Heckscher Playhouse, February 20, 1947; produced on Broadway at Ethel Barrymore Theater, May 1, 1947), Schirmer, 1947.

The Consul (three-act; first produced in Philadelphia at the Shubert Theater, February 22, 1950; produced on Broadway at Ethel Barrymore Theater, March 15, 1950), Schirmer, 1950; *The Saint of Bleecker Street* (three-act; first produced on Broadway at Broadway Theater, December 27, 1954); *The Unicorn, the Gorgon and the Manticore* (madrigal; first produced in Washington, D.C. at Library of Congress, October 21, 1956; produced at New York City Center, January 15, 1957), Ricordi, 1956; *Maria Golovin* (three-act; first produced in Brussels at the American Pavilion, Brussels World's Fair, August 20, 1958; produced on Broadway at Martin Beck Theater, November 5, 1958), Ricordi, 1958; *The Last Savage* (three-act; first produced as "Dernier Sauvage" in Paris at the Opera-Comique, October 22, 1963; produced at Metropolitan Opera

(From the New York City Opera production of "Help, Help the Globolinks." Presented at New York City Center Theater, December, 1969.)

(From the opera "Amahl and the Night Visitors" televised December 25, 1966. This work has been presented during numerous Christmas seasons on NBC-TV, beginning December 24, 1951.)

Menotti (left) with Ezra Pound.

House, January 23, 1964), Colombo, 1964, narrative version of the libretto illustrated by Beni Montresor, New York Graphic Society, 1964.

Unpublished operas: "The Island God," first produced at Metropolitan Opera House, February 20, 1942; "Labyrinth," written as television opera, broadcast by NBC-TV, March 3, 1963; "Martin's Lie," first produced in Bristol, England, at the Bristol Cathedral, June 3, 1964; "The Most Important Man," first produced on Broadway at New York State Theater, March 12, 1971; "Tamu-Tamu," first produced in Chicago at Studebaker Theater, September 5, 1973; "The Hero," first produced in Philadelphia by Philadelphia Opera Co., June 1, 1976; "The Egg," first produced in Washington, D.C. at the Cathedral, June 17, 1976; "The Trial of the Gypsy," first produced on Broadway at Lincoln Center, 1978.

Libretti: Samuel Barber, *Vanessa* (four-act; first produced on Broadway at Metropolitan Opera House, January 15, 1958), Schirmer, revised edition, 1964; S. Barber, "A Hand of Bridge," first produced in Spoleto, Italy, at Festival of Two Worlds, June 17, 1959; Lukas Foss, "Introductions and Goodbyes," first produced in 1959.

Plays: "A Copy of Madame Aupic," first produced in Paris, 1959; "The Leper," first produced in Tallahassee, Fla., at Florida State University, April 20, 1970.

Musical compositions: (For children) *Poemetti,* Ricordi, 1937; *Sebastian* (ballet), Ricordi, 1947; *Piano Concerto in F,* Ricordi, 1948; *Apocalypse,* Schirmer, c.1951; *Ricercare and Toccata on a Theme from "The Old Maid and the Thief,"* Ricordi, 1953; *Violin Concerto in A Minor,* Schirmer, 1954; *The Death of the Bishop of Brindisi* (cantata), Schirmer, c.1963.

Composer of the operas "The Last Superman" and "Arrival," as yet neither published nor produced.

Also composer of "Variations on a Theme of Robert Schumann," c.1931; "Pastorale," 1933; "Concerto in A Minor for Piano and Orchestra," 1945; "Errand into the Maze" (ballet), 1947; "The Hero," c.1952; "Concerto for Violin and Orchestra," 1955; "Canti della Lontananza" (song cycle), 1967: "Tripolo Concerto a Tre," 1970; "Suite for Two Celli and Piano," 1973; "The Halcyon" (symphony), 1976; "Landscapes and Remembrances" (contata), 1976; "Trio for a House Warming Party."

SIDELIGHTS: Menotti was the sixth of ten children born to a coffee importer and his wife. The family formed a chamber group and Menotti was taught to play the violin, cello, and piano at an early age. A prodigy, Menotti began composing music at six, wrote an opera, "The Death of Pierrot," at eleven, and at thirteen he wrote another opera, "The Little Mermaid," based on the Hans Christian Andersen tale. The Menottis had their own box at the famous opera house, La Scala, and young Menotti went often to hear opera classics directed by Arturo Toscanini.

Menotti was not a serious music student until 1928 when his mother brought him to the United States to study at Philadelphia's Curtis Institute. His professor of composition at Curtis was Rosario Scalero, who stressed the study and imitation of the masters. She disliked opera, however, and when Menotti wrote his first opera, he intended it to be his last. The opera was commissioned by the Ballet Society.

Perhaps one of the most widely-known of Menotti's operas is *Amahl and the Night Visitors,* commissioned by NBC-TV. It is the story of a crippled boy who is healed after giving his crutches to the three Wise Men as a gift for the new-born Jesus. First presented on television on Christmas Eve in 1951, the opera was rebroadcast by NBC annually on December 24th for thirteen years.

FOR MORE INFORMATION SEE: New Yorker, May 4, 1963; *Holiday,* June, 1963; Samuel Chotzinoff, *A Little Nightmusic,* Harper, 1964; *Opera News,* February 8, 1964, May, 1977; David Ewen, editor, *Composers Since 1900,* Wilson, 1969; (for children) Melvin Berger, *Masters of Modern Music,* Lothrop, 1970; *Time,* March 22, 1971; Lyndal Grieb, *The Operas of Gian Carlo Menotti, 1937-1972,* Scarecrow, 1974; *New York Times,* April 14, 1974; John Gruen, *Menotti: A Biography,* Macmillan, 1978.

MILES, (Mary) Patricia 1930-

PERSONAL: Born September 8, 1930, in Lancashire, England; daughter of Robert (a businessman) and Bridget (a teacher and writer; maiden name, Clancy) Storey; married Francis George Miles (a company executive), October 17, 1953; children: Patrick, Siobhan, Hugh. *Education:* Somerville College, Oxford, B.A. (honors), 1953, M.A., 1956. *Politics:* "No real insight: constantly fluctuating." *Home:* Windrush, Rabley Heath, Welwyn, Hertfordshire AL6 9UF, England. *Agent:* (England) Curtis Brown, 1 Craven Hill, London, England; (U.S.) Curtis Brown Associates, Inc., 575 Madison Ave., New York, N.Y. 10022.

CAREER: Oxford University Press, London, England, reader of Latin and Greek books, 1953-54; Latin teacher in girls' schools in Kent, England, 1958-60, and 1963-65; Nobel Comprehensive School, Stevenage, England, teacher of French,

PATRICIA MILES

My father worked all his life in it, doggedly, though with distaste. My mother came from a small farm in Tipperary. . . . I myself was the archetypal provincial scholarship girl, cramming a four-year Greek course into six months in the effort to get into Oxford, which I did.

"How to reconcile all this determined striving with the free-wheeling inventiveness which is a good part of writing! The truth is, I'm a dreamer; I always was. The practicality and endeavour have been superimposed, for which I'm profoundly grateful—to realize any dream you've got to wake up.

"My dream is to provide satisfying entertainment. More precisely: to make the past come alive for children, with humor if possible, and to use language with vigor.

"I don't have a defined philosophy, though I do feel strongly that the ordinary business of living makes demands which many people meet gallantly: life is full of unsung heroes. My own life is easy enough at present; I teach occasionally and sometimes work as a guide in a stately home—we live twenty-odd miles from London in an ancient stretch of countryside.

"In 1978-79 my husband and I were unexpectedly removed from this slightly old-fashioned way of life (by his company) and spent a glorious year in Tokyo, Japan. Also visited Hong Kong, Bangkok and Hawaii, and took the opportunity to travel home via Mexico, San Francisco, Washington and New York. Felt very much at home in the U.S. and hope to return.

"And finally—as I always like reading about other people's writing methods—mine are to try to work three hours each morning, though family life often cuts into this. When a book is nearing completion, it is of course much easier to work longer hours. The first draft is hard to do: you have some bits you know about and like from the start, but also gaps; and while you're getting this down and perhaps doing necessary bits of research, you are also thinking quite seriously from time to time what your theme is and why anyone should bother to read it. After that it's a question of re-writing—many times in places, e.g. page 1—but that's the part I really enjoy. Who do I write for? Hopefully anyone, at any age, with a sense of fun and imagination."

HOBBIES AND OTHER INTERESTS: Travel in France and Italy, gardening.

English, and Latin, 1967-76; writer, 1976—. *Awards, honors: The Gods in Winter* was chosen for the Hans Christian Andersen list, 1980.

WRITINGS—Of interest to young people: *Nobody's Child,* Dutton, 1975; *If I Survive,* Hamish Hamilton, 1976; *The Gods in Winter* (humor/fantasy), Hamish Hamilton, 1978, Dutton, 1978, 1981; *A Disturbing Influence,* Hamish Hamilton, 1978, Lothrop, 1979; *Louther Hall,* Hamish Hamilton, 1981. Has written for British Broadcasting Corp. Contributor of articles and stories to newspapers and magazines.

WORK IN PROGRESS: The Mind Pirates humorous science fiction for eleven and twelve-year olds; *Rooms in a Great House;* "and other things."

SIDELIGHTS: "My background is half English, half Irish, and wholly ambitious. My grandfather leapt fully grown from the murk of Manchester with a copy of *Self-Help* in his hand and founded a food business to which he fettered all his family.

MILLER, Edna (Anita)   1920-

PERSONAL: Born March 8, 1920, in Weehawken, N.J.; daughter of Curt (an engineer) and Jean (Johansen) Freyschmidt; married Theodore R. Miller (a cartographer), July 18, 1946, (divorced, 1971); children: Theodore R., Jr. *Education:* Attended Traphagen School of Fashion and Design, 1938-40. *Religion:* Protestant. *Residence:* North Hero, Vt. 05474.

CAREER: Sportswear Originators, New York, N.Y., designer of sportswear, 1940-50. Trustee, North Hero Public Library, 1974—.

WRITINGS—For children; all self-illustrated; all published by Prentice-Hall, unless otherwise indicated: *Mousekin's Golden House,* 1964; *Mousekin's Christmas Eve,* 1965; *Mousekin Finds a Friend,* 1967; *Mousekin's Family,* 1969; *Mousekin's Woodland Sleepers,* 1970; *Duck Duck,* Holiday House, 1971; *Mou-*

He jumped aside with a start. ■(From *Mousekin's Christmas Eve* by Edna Miller. Illustrated by the author.)

EDNA MILLER

sekin's ABC's, 1972; *Mousekin's Woodland Birthday,* 1974; *Mousekin Takes a Trip,* 1976, Spanish edition, translated by Louis M. Ugalde, as *Mousekin De Viaje,* 1976; *Pebbles, a Pack Rat,* 1976; *Mousekin's Close Call,* 1978; *Jumping Bean,* 1979.

Illustrator: Michael Rheta Martin, *Graphic Guide to World History,* Holt, 1959; Phyllis Powell Sarasy, *Winter Sleepers,* Prentice-Hall, 1962; Agnes McCarthy, *Creatures of the Deep,* Prentice-Hall, 1963; Natalie Friendly, *Wildlife Teams,* Prentice-Hall, 1963; Gladys Sakon, *Secrets in Animal Names,* Prentice-Hall, 1964; Dorothy Wisbeski, *Picaro, a Pet Otter,* Hawthorn, 1971.

WORK IN PROGRESS: A new Mousekin book.

SIDELIGHTS: "I was born in New Jersey but grew up in New York City. I lived with my parents and older sister in an apartment overlooking Central Park and next to the American Museum of Natural History. As a child I developed a great love of animals mainly because, as an apartment dweller, I was not permitted to have what I wanted most—a dog. There were tidier substitutes, however: two thoroughbred turtles, a white mouse, a rabbit, and a small alligator. At the zoo in Central Park I made childish sketches of my favorite animals. The Museum of Natural History was my second home.

"For ten years I worked as a designer for a leading sportswear manufacturer. During this period I married Ted Miller, an architect and cartographer. In the Ramapo hills north of New York City we built a house overlooking untouched woodland with enough animals to satisfy the most ardent naturalist. We divided our time between the city and the country, and travelled extensively in Europe, North Africa, Mexico, and the United States. When our son Teddy was born we made the Ramapos our year-round home, and I turned to illustrating as a second career. I did illustrations for high school textbooks and assisted my husband in his work as a historical cartographer.

"As our son grew I found it little effort to invent stories of the creatures who shared the land with us. When Teddy entered school I began illustrating children's books. The idea for my first book, *Mousekin's Golden House,* came to me shortly after Halloween when I had put the family pumpkin outside. One evening I noticed a small white-footed mouse exploring the jack-o'-lantern for the few seeds it contained. I watched with great amusement as it scrambled in one entrance and out another. As the weeks passed the pumpkin rolled to the base of a tree, and I watched its expression change, day by day, from blank joviality to sweet serenity as it closed its eyes and pressed its smiling mouth shut in the cold wind. I thought what a fine house it would make for a white-footed mouse who forever discards one home and searches for another.

"Mousekin has found many homes and has had many adventures since my first story of this charming creature. I have found a new home in Vermont, on an island on Lake Champlain. There are white-footed mice in the woodland for future stories of Mousekin. And I have a new audience in our grandchildren. I hope they shall learn, as I did, that nature writes its own stories—there need only be an interested observer."

MILLER, Helen Topping   1884-1960

OBITUARY NOTICE: Born December 8, 1884, in Fenton, Mich.; died Feburary 4, 1960; buried in Morristown, Tenn. The daughter of a literary mother, Helen Miller began writing at an early age and contributed stories to *St. Nicholas Magazine* at the age of fifteen. A prolific novelist, she wrote and published over thirty books, mostly historical novels combining historical fact with romance. Among her adult novels are *Sharon, Rebellion Road,* (begun by her brother before his death in an automobile accident), and *Dark Sails.* Two of her books were published posthumously—*Nightshade* and *Christmas at Sagamore Hill.* Among Miller's books for children are those in her very successful "Christmas at . . ." series, stories about Christmas in the days of famous Americans, including Thomas Jefferson, George and Martha Washington, and Robert E. Lee. She also contributed serials, novelettes, and over 300 short stories to periodicals, including *Saturday Evening Post, Good Housekeeping,* and *McCall's.* She was a member of the Daughters of the American Revolution and the Authors' League of America. *For More Information See: American Novelists of Today,* Greenwood Press, 1951; *Who Was Who in America,* Volume IV, 1961-1968, Marquis, 1968. *Obituaries: New York Times,* February 5, 1960; *Publishers Weekly,* February 15, 1960; *Time,* February 15, 1960; *Britannica Book of the Year, 1961.*

Books should to one of these four ends conduce,
For wisdom, piety, delight, or use.

—John Denham

(From *Goblins*, verses by Spike Milligan. Illustrated by W. Heath Robinson.)

(The "Goon Show," originated by Spike Milligan, also starred Peter Sellers and Harry Secombe. It was presented on BBC Radio from May, 1951, to January, 1960.)

MILLIGAN, Terence Alan   1918-
(Spike Milligan)

PERSONAL: Born April 16, 1918, in India; son of Leo Alphonso (an Army officer) and Florence Winifred (Kettleband) Milligan; married Margaret Patricia Ridgeway (deceased); children: one son, three daughters. *Religion:* Catholic. *Office:* Spike Milligan Productions Ltd., 9 Orme Court, London, W.2, England.

CAREER: Free-lance writer, actor, composer, mainly for radio and television. Originator of "Goon Show," which ran for ten years in England; writer for award winning television show, "Fred." Artist. *Awards, honors:* TV Writer of the Year award, 1956.

WRITINGS—All under name Spike Milligan: *Silly Verse for Kids,* Dobson, 1959; (self-illustrated) *A Dustbin of Milligan,* Dobson, 1961; *The Little Pot Boiler: A Book Based Freely on His Seasonal Overdraft,* Dobson, 1963; *Puckoon* (novel), M. Joseph, 1963; *A Book of Bits; or, A Bit of a Book,* Dobson, 1965; (with Carol Barker) *The Bald Twit Lion,* Dobson, 1968; (self-illustrated) *A Book of Milliganimals,* Dobson, 1968; *The Bedside Milligan; or Read Your Way to Insomnia,* Margaret & Jack Hobbs, 1969; *Values* (poems), Offcut Press, 1969.

(With John Antrobus) *The Beginning Room* (play; first produced on West End at Mermaid Theatre, January, 1963), Margaret & Jack Hobbs, 1970; *Adolf Hitler: My Part in His Downfall,* M. Joseph, 1971; *Milligan's Ark,* edited by Milligan and Jack Hobbs, Margaret & Jack Hobbs, 1971; (with M. and J. Hobbs) *Badjelly the Witch,* M. Joseph, 1971; *Small Dreams of a Scorpion,* Margaret & Jack Hobbs, 1972; *The Goon Show Scripts,* St. Martin's, 1973; *Dip the Puppy,* Merrimack Book Services, 1973; *More Goon Show Scripts,* Woburn Press, 1973; (contributor) *Cricket's Choice,* Open Court, 1974; *Rommel? Gunner Who?,* M. Joseph, 1974; *The Book of Goons,* Sidgwick & Jackson, 1974; *Monty—His Part in My Victory,* M. Joseph, 1976; *McGonagall, the Truth at Last,* Margaret & Jack Hobbs, 1976; *Mussolini—His Part in My Downfall,* M. Joseph, 1978; *Goblins,* Hutchinson, 1978; *"Q" Annual,* Margaret & Jack Hobbs, 1979; *Open Heart University,* Margaret & Jack Hobbs, 1979.

Get in the "Q" Annual, Margaret & Jack Hobbs, 1980; *Unspun Socks from a Chicken's Laundry,* Margaret & Jack Hobbs, 1981.

ADAPTATIONS—Films: *The Bedsitting Room* was filmed in 1969; *Adolf Hitler: My Part in His Downfall* was filmed in 1972.

Recordings: "The Snow Goose," adapted from the book by Paul Gallico, narrator and part composer, RCA Records, 1976; "Adolf Hitler, My Part in His Downfall," Columbia Records, 1981.

WORK IN PROGRESS: Sir Nobonk and the Dragon, 101 Best and Only Limericks, The Indefinite Articles Culled from His Newspaper Writings and Scunthorpe, Joseph, I'm Having a Baby (book and lyrics), and work for television.

HOBBIES AND OTHER INTERESTS: Restoration of antiques, oil painting, watercolors, gardening, eating, drinking, talking, wine, and jazz.

FOR MORE INFORMATION SEE: Listener, August 8, 1968; *Bookseller,* May 15, 1971; *Observer Review,* June 20, 1971.

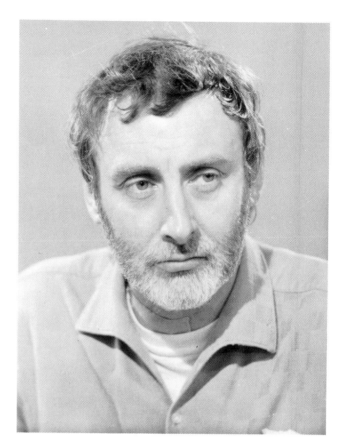

TERENCE ALAN MILLIGAN

MITCHELL, Cynthia   1922-

PERSONAL: Born August 10, 1922, in Sharlston, Yorkshire, England; daughter of Claude (a colliery accountant) and Lillian (a teacher; maiden name, Berry) Moverlay; married Dennis Hardie Mitchell (a secondary school teacher of math and physics), March 22, 1951; children: Jeanette Louise, Caroline Jane. *Education:* Balls Parks College of Education, teaching certificate, 1949. *Religion:* Religious Society of Friends. *Home:* 32 Barnsley Rd., Ackworth, West Yorkshire WF7 7NB, England. *Office:* The Howard School, Low Ackworth, Pontefract, Yorkshire, England.

CAREER: Wakefield Food Office, Wakefield, Yorkshire, England, civil servant, 1939-45; primary and secondary school teacher in Yorkshire and Hertfordshire, 1945-52; Wakefield Metropolitan Education Authority, Wakefield, Yorkshire, deputy head and pre-school teacher, 1964—. Secretary, local freedom from hunger campaign, 1961-63. *Member:* National Association of Teachers (British), Campaign for Nuclear Disarmament.

WRITINGS: Time for School: A Practical Guide for Parents of Young Children, Penguin, 1973; *Halloweena Hecatee and Other Rhymes to Skip To* (juvenile; illustrated by Eileen Browne), Heinemann, 1978, Crowell, 1979; *Playtime* (juvenile; illustrated by Satomi Ichikawa), Heinemann, 1978, Collins & World, 1979; *Hop-Along Happily and Other Rhymes for the Playground* (juvenile; illustrated by E. Browne), Heinemann, 1979; (compiler) *Under the Cherry Tree* (juvenile; illustrated by S. Ichikawa), Collins & World, 1979; *Granny in the Kitchen,* Heinemann, 1983; *The Big and Beastly Alphabet,* Heinemann,

Have you heard of the man
    Who stood on his head,
And put his clothes
    Into his bed,
And folded himself
    On a chair instead?

■ (From *Under the Cherry Tree,* compiled by Cynthia Mitchell. Illustrated by Satomi Ichikawa.)

1983. Contributor of articles to periodicals, including *Books for Your Children, The Education Guardian, The Best of "Where" on Pre-Schooling, Poetry Corner, Frank and Polly Muir's Big Dipper,* and *The Second Armada Book of Limericks.*

SIDELIGHTS: "I had never written anything for publication before *Time for School,* which was the result of years of discussing children's progress with parents, and being constantly told, in effect, 'We have access to a lot of advice about the health care of babies and young children, but the only thing we ever seem to be told about preparing them is to tie their shoelaces." Tying laces is an extremely difficult skill for the average pre-schooler to acquire, and there is so much more of far greater value that young children need to experience. So I decided to write, in non-jargon language for the benefit of the local parents, about the more profitable activities they might encourage and why, envisaging a school leaflet for distribution at the local playgroup. The 'Leaflet' finished up, three years later, as a two-hundred-forty-six-page Penguin paperback. So I became an author by accident, discovering a need that I had the experience to meet, as, of course, have thousands of other infant teachers.

"Contact with publishers and 'book people' led to the publication of the children's books. Not able to find enough vigorous, worthwhile, vocabulary-extending rhyme to bridge the gap between nursery rhymes and more sophisticated poetry, I had written some verse of my own for class use, mainly activity

rhymes that harness the young child's ready responses to rhyme and rhythm to practice control of bodily movement. Children need to extend their used vocabulary in a way that doesn't present poetry as something to be received passively because grownups think it's good for them, like medicine or a haircut. It seems to me that too often when children come to school they quickly lose their spontaneous delight in chanting nursery rhymes and begin to think of poems as small doses of description to be swallowed in relation to a topic. For instance: 'We're doing hibernation, so here's a poem about a hedgehog. . . .'

"Poetry should stimulate a feel for language; poetry should be a way of pithily expressing thought and emotion; poetry should be a means of stretching the imagination to help it work in a wide variety of subjects. These essentials to continuing enjoyment are missed by young children unless they continue to experience delight in the feel of the words, the emotions, and the new ideas opened up. My class hears poems about hedgehogs, of course, but they also hop, skip, clap, and jump to rhymes, as to music, just for the fun of wrapping the words around their tongues and the sparkle that chanting to movement brings to their eyes.

"My day-by-day classroom work is a continuing research into how young children learn, and how they respond to varied efforts to teach them specific skills. I am particularly interested in teaching reading, in increasing vocabulary, in encouraging articulate response, and in settling children happily in school." Mitchell is an advocate of nuclear disarmament and environmental protection, and enjoys gardening, reading (especially the science fiction of Ursula LeGuin and J. R. Tolkien), travel, and "conversation that explores ideas."

MOORE, Lamont 1909-

BRIEF ENTRY: Born in 1909. Art educator and author. Beginning his career at the Newark Museum in New Jersey, Moore later served as director of education at the National Gallery of Art in Washington, D.C. and as director of the Yale University Art Gallery. During World War II, Moore was an officer in the Monuments and Fine Arts Section of the Military Government. The French government awarded him membership in the Legion of Honor. Moore has written several books that introduce young readers to art, including *The First Book of Painting: An Introduction to the Appreciation of Pictures* (F. Watts, 1960), *The First Book of Architecture* (F. Watts, 1961), and *The Sculptured Image: The Art of Sculpture as Seen in Monuments to Gods, Men, and Ideas* (F. Watts, 1967). *For More Information See: Christian Science Monitor,* November 2, 1967.

CYNTHIA MITCHELL

Who has seen the wind?
  Neither I nor you;
But when the leaves lie trembling,
  The wind is passing through.

Who has seen the wind?
  Neither you nor I:
But when the trees bow down their heads,
  The wind is passing by.

—Christina G. Rossetti

MORGAN, Helen (Gertrude Louise) 1921-
(Louise Morgan, Helen Tudor Morgan)

PERSONAL: Born April 11, 1921, in Ilford, Essex, England; daughter of Herbert (a builder) and Sarah Ann (Hotchkiss) Axford; married Tudor Meredydd Morgan, May 15, 1954; children: Sian Margaret, Megan Nansi, Bronwen Delydd Elizabeth. *Education:* Attended Royal Normal College and Academy of Music for the Blind, 1938-42. *Residence:* Carmarthen, Wales. *Office:* c/o Barclays Bank, the Pantiles, Tunbridge Wells, Kent, England.

CAREER: Children's author. *Member:* Society of Authors.

WRITINGS—Children's books: *The Little Old Lady,* Faber, 1961; *Tales of Tigg's Farm,* Faber, 1963; *Meet Mary Kate,* Faber, 1963; *A Mouthful of Magic,* Harrap, 1963; *Two in the Garden,* Brockhampton Press, 1964; *The Tailor, the Sailor and the Small Black Cat,* Thomas Nelson, 1964; *Two in the House,* Brockhampton Press, 1965; *A Dream of Dragons,* Faber, 1965; *Two on the Farm,* Brockhampton Press, 1966; *Satchkin Patchkin,* Faber, 1966, Macrae, 1970; *Two by the Sea,* Brockhampton Press, 1967; *Mary Kate and the Jumble Bear,* Faber, 1967; *Mrs. Pinny and the Blowing Day,* Faber, 1968; *Mrs. Pinny and the Sudden Snow,* Faber, 1969; *Mary Kate and the School Bus,* Faber, 1970, published as *Mary Kate,* Thomas Nelson, 1972; *Mother Farthing's Luck,* Faber, 1971;

Mrs. Pinny and the Salty Sea Day, Faber, 1972; *The Sketchbook Crime,* Wearon, 1980. Contributor to magazines.

WORK IN PROGRESS: A novel, *Seascape,* and a collection of short stories.

SIDELIGHTS: ''I began to lose my sight when I was twelve years old. I had always made up stories and written poetry and by the time I was thirteen I had written my first book—a school adventure story. At fifteen I wrote my first novel—a romance. Both books were burned by my father. He thought I was wasting my time 'scribbling' when I should have been getting on with my school work. I wasn't much good at anything except English, cookery and art.

''When I was seventeen my father died and my mother finally admitted my disability and let me go away to a school for the blind where I learned Braille and was trained as a shorthand typist.

''I wrote my first children's stories for my daughter, Sian—I had to tell my children stories rather than read to them. My first book, *The Little Old Lady* was really a very little book—I had no idea how long or how short a book ought to be, nor where to send it. I sent it to Faber and they accepted it straight away, so, of course, I went on writing children's books.

From Market Square to Marrow Lane and by Broadway into Sheep Street went the pram and Mrs. Pinny. ■(From *Mrs. Pinny and the Blowing Day* by Helen Morgan. Illustrated by Shirley Hughes.)

"I started to write for women's magazines (as Louise Morgan) after winning a prize in a short story competition in *Women's Own* in 1976. I work on the typewriter and send off the manuscript, mistakes and scribbles included, to be tidily typed while I get on with something else. I write every morning from about 9:30 till 1:30. I live on a hill about three miles outside Carmarthen, with no near neighbours and a garden full of trees and birds. I can't work with any kind of noise or distraction going on.

"I enjoy pottering about in the garden, sitting in the sun doing nothing, cooking, making jams and chutneys, listening to music. I collect odd bits of china and all manner of 'rubbish' which I simply can't bear to throw away in case it might come in useful one day. For example, I still have all my children's toys and my grandson is wearing T-shirts and sweaters once worn by my youngest daughter."

MORRIS, William 1913-

PERSONAL: Born April 13, 1913, in Boston, Mass.; son of Charles Hyndman (an attorney) and Elizabeth Margaret (Hanna) Morris; married Jane Frazer, August 7, 1939 (marriage ended); married Mary Elizabeth Davis (a writer), February 8, 1947; children: Ann Elizabeth (Mrs. Paul Downie), Susan McLeod, John Boyd, William Frazer, Mary Elizabeth, Evan Nathanael. *Education:* Harvard University, A.B., 1935. *Politics:* Independent Democrat. *Religion:* Episcopalian. *Home:* 355 Sound Beach Ave., Old Greenwich, Conn. 06870.

CAREER: Newman School, Lakewood, N.J., instructor in English and Latin, 1935-37; G. & C. Merriam Co., Springfield, Mass., college department staff, 1937-43; Grosset & Dunlap, Inc., New York, N.Y., managing editor, 1945-47, executive editor, 1947-53, editor-in-chief, 1953-60; Grolier, Inc., New York, N.Y., executive editor, *International Encyclopedia,* 1960-62, *Grolier Universal Encyclopedia,* 1962-64; American Heritage Publishing Co., New York, N.Y., editor-in-chief, *American Heritage Dictionary,* 1964. Consulting editor for *Funk & Wagnalls New Standard Dictionary,* international edition, 1954-58, and *New College Standard Dictionary,* 1958-60. *Military service:* U.S. Maritime Service, 1943-45; served in various combat areas as communications officer; became lieutenant junior grade.

MEMBER: National Council of Teachers of English, Modern Language Association of America, American Library Association, Society for General Semantics; Dutch Treat Club (president), Society of Salurians, Overseas Press Club, Coffee House, and Harvard Club (all New York); Old Greenwich Boat Club.

WRITINGS: (Editor) *Words: The New Dictionary,* Grosset, 1947, revised edition with Charles P. Chadsey and Harold Wentworth published as *The Grosset Webster Dictionary,* 1953, new edition, 1966; (editor) *Concise Biographical Dictionary,* Grosset, 1949; (editor with wife, Mary Morris) *The Concise Dictionary of Famous Men and Women,* revised edition, Grosset, 1951; *It's Easy to Increase Your Vocabulary* (juvenile), Harper, 1957, revised edition, Penguin, 1975; (with M. Morris) *The Word Game Book,* Harper, 1959, revised edition, Penguin, 1975; (with M. Morris) *Dictionary of Word and Phrase Origins,* Harper, Volume I, 1962, Volume II, 1967, Volume III, 1971; *The William Morris Self-Enrichment Vocabulary Program,* Grolier, 1965; *Your Heritage of Words* (juvenile), Dell, 1970; (editor and author of introduction) *Young People's Thesaurus* (juvenile), Grosset, 1973; (editor) *Xerox Intermediate Diction-*

WILLIAM MORRIS

ary (juvenile), 1973; (editor) *The Weekly Reader Beginning Dictionary* (juvenile), Grosset and Ginn, 1974; (with M. Morris) *Harper Dictionary of Contemporary Usage,* Harper, 1975; (with M. Morris) *Morris Dictionary of Word and Phrase Origins,* Harper, 1977.

Editor of "Berlitz Self-Teacher Language Books," 1949-53. Writer of column, "William Morris on Words," for Bell-McClure Syndicate, 1954-68; author, with M. Morris, of column, "Words, Wit and Wisdom," for United Feature Syndicate, 1968—. Contributor to magazines, including *Saturday Review, Esquire, Changing Times,* and *Today's Living.*

MORRISON, Dorothy Nafus

PERSONAL: Born in Nashua, Iowa; daughter of Roy A. (a merchant) and Edwinna (a teacher of Latin and German; maiden name, Bolton) Nafus; married Carl V. Morrison (a psychiatrist); children: James, Anne (Mrs. John Feighner), David, John. *Education:* State University of Iowa, B.A. *Residence:* Beaverton, Ore.

CAREER: Teacher of stringed instruments in public schools in Beaverton, Ore., 1954-66; writer, 1965—.

*WRITINGS—*For children: *The Mystery of the Last Concert,* Westminster, 1971; (with husband, Carl V. Morrison) *Can I Help How I Feel?* (nonfiction), Atheneum, 1976; *Ladies Were Not Expected: Abigail Scott Duniway and Women's Rights,* Atheneum, 1977; *The Eagle and the Fort: The Story of John McLoughlin,* Atheneum, 1979; *Chief Sarah: Sarah Winnemucca's Fight for Indian Rights,* Atheneum, 1980.

DOROTHY NAFUS MORRISON

WORK IN PROGRESS: Biography of Jessie Benton Fremont for Atheneum.

SIDELIGHTS: "When I first came to the West Coast, I fell in love with the area, and when I started research for *The Eagle and the Fort,* I was thrilled with its history. Since I like children, and like people, and like the West, and enjoy history, it seems fortunate that I can combine them all by writing biographies of historical characters that relate to this area. They're simon-pure—no imaginary conversations beside the campfire. The truth is far more exciting than anything which could be invented."

MUNRO, Alice   1931-

PERSONAL: Born July 10, 1931, in Wingham, Ontario, Canada; daughter of Robert Eric (a farmer) and Ann (Chamney) Laidlaw; married James Munro (a bookseller), December 29, 1951 (divorced, 1976); married Gerald Fremlin (a geographer), 1976; children: Sheila, Jenny, Andrea. *Education:* University of Western Ontario, student, 1949-51. *Politics:* New Democratic Party. *Religion:* Unitarian Universalist. *Residence:* Clinton, Ontario, Canada.

CAREER: Writer. *Awards, honors:* Governor General's Literary Award, 1969, for *Dance of the Happy Shades,* 1978, for *Who Do You Think You Are?*

ALICE MUNRO

WRITINGS: Dance of the Happy Shades (short stories), Ryerson, 1968; *Lives of Girls and Women,* McGraw, 1971; *Something I've Been Meaning to Tell You,* McGraw, 1974; *Who Do You Think You Are?* Macmillan, 1978, published in the U.S. as *The Begger Maid,* Knopf, 1979. Two stories included in *Canadian Short Stories, Second Series,* Oxford University Press, 1968. Stories are represented in many anthologies.

FOR MORE INFORMATION SEE: Canadian Forum, February, 1969.

NELSON, Cordner (Bruce)   1918-

BRIEF ENTRY: Born August 6, 1918, in San Diego, Calif. Nelson is a biographer and novelist whose books depict the world of track and field sports. He served as editor of *Track & Field News* from 1948 to 1970, covering hundreds of track meets and seven Olympic games. Nelson left his editorial position in 1971 with the title, "founding editor," and in 1975 was inducted into the United States Track and Field Hall of Fame. For young people, he wrote several books, including a biography, *The Jim Ryun Story* (Tafnews, 1967). Nelson's nonfiction works include *Track and Field: The Great Ones* (Pelham Books, 1979), *How to Train* (1981), and *Distance Running* (1981). He also published a novel entitled *The Miler* (S. G. Phillips, 1969), the story of a young man's struggle to become an Olympic champion runner. *Address:* P.O. Box 6476, Carmel, Calif. 93921. *For More Information See: Kirkus Reviews,* September 15, 1969; *Library Journal,* December 15, 1969; *Contemporary Authors,* Volumes 29-32, revised, Gale, 1978; *Who's Who in the West,* 17th edition, Marquis, 1980; *The Writer's Directory, 1982-84,* Gale, 1981.

Instead, he walked away. Slowly at first.
Then faster and faster. Maybe they would
think he had some important work to
do at school.

If there was one thing Louie hated —
one thing he couldn't stand — that thing
was being laughed *at*. That was a very
different thing from just plain laughing.

"Besides," he thought to himself, "who
wants to be known as Louie the Laugher? I
want to be known as Louie. Louie. *Me*."

(From *I Love to Laugh* by Lillian Nordlicht. Illustrated by Allen Davis.)

LILLIAN NORDLICHT

NORDLICHT, Lillian

PERSONAL: Born in New York, N.Y.; daughter of Jack and
Rose Keiman; married Myron Nordlicht; children: Scott, Jon-
athan, Robert. *Education:* Attended Queen's College and Bank
Street College of Education. *Residence:* La Jolla, Calif.

CAREER: Free-lance writer. *Member:* National League of
American Pen Women, Society of Children's Book Writers.
Awards, honors: Awarded second prize for light verse in Na-
tional League of American Pen Women competition, 1979.

WRITINGS—All for young people: *A Medal for Mike* (illustrated by Sylvia Stone), Scholastic Book Services, 1979; (adaptor) Jack London, *The Call of the Wild* (illustrated by Juan
Barberis), Raintree, 1980; *I Love to Laugh* (illustrated by Allen
Davis), Raintree, 1980; (adaptor) Jules Verne, *20,000 Leagues
under the Sea* (illustrated by Steve Butz), Raintree, 1980. Contributor of stories to school textbooks and anthologies, and to
periodicals such as *Highlights for Children*.

*WORK IN PROGRESS: Suigene and Chinese Chamber of Com-
merce.*

Life being very short, and the quiet hours of it few, we
ought to waste none of them in reading valueless
books.

—John Ruskin

THOMAS C. O'BRIEN

O'BRIEN, Thomas C(lement) 1938-

PERSONAL: Born July 10, 1938, in New York, N.Y.; son of Thomas C. (an accountant) and Dorothy (Beers) O'Brien; married Gail Marshall (a researcher), July 1, 1961; children: Thomas C. III., Ellen Marie, Virginia Ann. *Education:* Iona College, B.S., 1959; Columbia University Teachers College, M.A., 1960; New York University, Ph.D., 1967. *Home:* 7050 Washington Ave., University City, Mo. 63130. *Office:* Southern Illinois University, Edwardsville, Ill. 62026.

CAREER: Iona College, New Rochelle, N.Y., instructor in mathematics, 1960-61; Macmillan Company (publishers), New York, N.Y., senior editor of school mathematics department, 1961-63; Educational Research Council, Greater Cleveland Mathematics Program, Cleveland, Ohio, research associate and co-author of program materials, 1963-68; Boston University, Boston, Mass., assistant professor, 1968-70; Southern Illinois University, Edwardsville, Ill., associate professor, 1970-75, professor, 1975—. Consultant and instructor at various seminars and conferences, including Froebel Institute, Jean Piaget Society, National Council of Teachers of Mathematics, American Educational Research Association, 1° Congresso Brasiliero Piagetiano Educacao Pela Intelligencia, National Institute of Education, National Assessment of Educational Progress, and Association of Teachers of Mathematics, beginning 1971; founder, Teachers' Center Projects, Southern Illinois University, 1972; American representative to International Day on Mathematics Education, Netherlands, 1976. *Member:* American Educational Research Association, Association of Teachers of Mathematics, National Council of Teachers of Mathematics. *Awards, honors:* Senior Research Fellowship in Science from North Atlantic Treaty Organization, 1978; A. A. Loftus award from Iona College, 1979.

WRITINGS—Of interest to young people: Odds and Evens (illustrated by Allan Eitzen), Crowell, 1971; "Solve It!" series,

five books, Educational Teaching Aids, 1977; *Wollygoggles and Other Creatures,* Cuisenaire Co., 1980; *Puzzle Tables,* Cuisenaire Co., 1980; "Mathematical Brain Teasers" series, five books, Educational Teaching Aids, 1980.

O'Brien is also author of such computer programs as: "Intuit the Iguana," "Discover the Duck," "Find the Flamingo," "Uncover the Underwear," "Detect the Donkey," 'Locate the Loon," "Detect the Dragon," "Roundup the Rhinos," "Katch the Kittens," "Locate the Llamas," "Sight the Snails," and many others.

Contributor of numerous articles to periodicals, including *The Arithmetic Teacher, School Science and Mathematics, Elementary School Journal, Childhood Education, American Education Research Journal, Child Development,* and *Journal of Research in Mathematics Education.* Editor, *Seedbed* (quarterly teaching journal), 1979—.

ADAPTATIONS—Filmstrips: "Odds and Evens" (filmstrip with cassette; filmstrip with record), Harper, 1971.

WORK IN PROGRESS: Research on children's concepts of numbers; manuscript for children's problem solving; microcomputer programs for children.

SIDELIGHTS: "My work and research are done from the Piagetian constructivist point of view. That is, the child (or the adult) is not a passive receptor of knowledge but an active constructor of reality tending toward coherence, stability, economy, and generalizability." O'Brien feels American education must adopt this point of view in order to better serve students. "(Today's) children will spend most of their lives in the twenty-first century yet present approaches provide them with a nineteenth century education."

OGILVIE, Elisabeth 1917-

BRIEF ENTRY: Born May 20, 1917, in Boston, Mass. Since her decision as a young girl to become a writer, Elisabeth Ogilvie has become a noted author of novels and of fiction for both adults and young people. She was the 1946 recipient of the North-East Woman's Press Association Award for fiction, and her book, *Blueberry Summer* (McGraw, 1956), was a Junior Literary Guild selection. Ogilvie's many books for children include *The Ceiling of Amber* (McGraw, 1964), *The Pigeon Pair* (McGraw, 1967), *Come Aboard and Bring Your Dory* (McGraw, 1969), and *Strawberries in the Sea* (McGraw, 1973). Her novels for adults include *The Dawning of the Day* (McGraw, 1954), *The Face of Innocence* (McGraw, 1970), *Where the Lost Aprils Are* (McGraw, 1974), and *The Dreaming Swimmer* (McGraw, 1976). *Address:* Cushing, Me. 04563. *For More Information See: Christian Science Monitor,* May 10, 1956; *New York Times Book Review,* Part 2, May 7, 1967; *Authors of Books for Young People,* 2nd edition, Scarecrow Press, 1971; *Who's Who of American Women,* 10th edition, Marquis, 1978.

Read not to contradict and confute, nor yet to believe and take for granted, nor to find talk and discourse, but to weigh and consider.

—Francis Bacon

PACE, Mildred Mastin 1907-

BRIEF ENTRY: Born June 8, 1907, in St. Louis, Mo. Pace has spent most of her life in New York City, working as a free-lance radio writer for NBC (National Broadcasting Company), and from 1942 to 1950 as a writer in the publicity department of the J. Walter Thompson advertising agency. Since 1940, she has been an author of children's books. Her biography, *Clara Barton* (Scribner, 1941), won the 1941 New York Herald Tribune Spring Festival Prize, and her book, *Old Bones the Wonder Horse* (McGraw, 1955), won the Dorothy Canfield Fisher Award in 1957. Pace's other books include *Home is Where the Heart Is* (Whittlesey House, 1954) and *My Japan 1930-1951* (McGraw, 1970), written with Hiroko Nakamoto. Her latest book for young people, *Wrapped for Eternity* (McGraw, 1974), is the non-fiction account of Egyptian mummies, from ancient times to modern archaeological discoveries. *Residence:* Garrison-on-Hudson, N.Y. *For More Information See: Contemporary Authors,* Volumes 5-8, revised, Gale, 1969; *New York Times Book Review,* May 26, 1974; *School Library Journal,* September, 1978; *Authors of Books for Young People,* 2nd edition supplement, Scarecrow Press, 1979.

PASHKO, Stanley 1913-
(Steve Norman, Tony Robbins)

PERSONAL: Born February 19, 1913 in New Haven, Conn.; son of Steven and Madeline Pashkowski; married wife, Pearl (a high school teacher), September 19, 1943; children: Toni Pashko Hammarlund. *Education:* Attended high school in Dickson City, Pa. *Politics:* Liberal. *Religion:* Unitarian-Universalist. *Home:* 75 Rollingmead, Princeton, N.J. 08540.

CAREER: Modern Age Books, reading editor, 1937-42; *Boys' Life,* New Brunswick, N.J., senior editor, 1943-50, 1956-77; *Journal of Lifetime Living,* Miami, Fla., associate editor, 1952-53; Cook Publications, New York City, associate editor, 1954-55; Direct Book Service, New York City, director, 1955; free-lance writer, 1977—. *Awards, honors:* Award from Junior Literary Guild, 1946, for *American Boy's Omnibus.*

WRITINGS—Of interest to young people, except as noted; all published by Greenberg, except as noted: *American Boy's Omnibus,* 1945; *How to Make the Varsity,* 1946; *Boy Showman,* 1946; *Black Sheep Patrol,* Roy, 1946; *The Book of Indoor Games,* 1947; (with wife, Pearl Pashko) *American Girl's Omnibus,* 1949; *Boy's Book of Body Building,* 1949; *A Boy and His Dog,* 1950; *Ross Duncan at Bataan* (novel), Messner, 1950; *Boy's Complete Book of Camping,* 1951; *How to Make Your Team,* Putnam, 1969; *Ferguson Jenkins: The Quiet Winner,* Putnam, 1975.

Author of a summer radio show, 1951. Author of comic book scripts. Compiler of twenty anthologies. Contributor of stories to magazines (sometimes under pseudonyms Steve Norman and Tony Robbins).

WORK IN PROGRESS: Research for books on Castro and lotteries; research on primitive hunting.

SIDELIGHTS: "In 1929 when I finished high school, I got a job in a silk mill on the night shift. The great depression impressed me with the need for knowing skills which I could sell. I had been crippled as a small child, but was active phys-

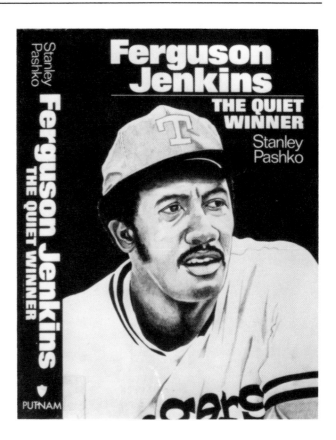

(From *Ferguson Jenkins: The Quiet Winner* by Stanley Pashko. Jacket illustration by Kong Studios.)

ically. I knew I had to turn from manual labor so I learned shorthand, typing, welding, labor organizing and was an office manager for a very brief period.

"I wanted to be a writer of books for boys from the time I was in the sixth grade and tried writing occasionally, but it wasn't until I lost my silk mill job, that I worked seriously at writing, turning out about a million words in the next four years. I finally sold my first detective story in 1934.

"As a free-lancer and a staff writer on magazines I was sent to Greece, Russia, Japan and Mexico on story assignments, and did some other traveling on my own.

"I got most of my education in the 30s and 40s in the big New York Public Library and by being a reading editor. As an editor, I am proudest of having published the work of more than a dozen new writers who have never sold before.

"Editors *do* read the slush pile."

Books are the treasured wealth of the world and the fit inheritance of generations and nations . . . . Their authors are a natural and irresistible aristocracy in every society, and, more than kings or emperors, exert an influence on mankind.

—Henry David Thoreau

The manager of the Odeon watched the children entering the cinema. ■(From *Mr. Moon's Last Case* by Brian Patten. Illustrated by Mary Moore.)

PATTEN, Brian 1946-

PERSONAL: Born February 7, 1946, in Liverpool, England; son of Ireen Stella Bevan. *Education:* Attended secondary school in Sefton Park, Liverpool, England. *Residence:* London, England.

CAREER: Worked at occasional odd jobs—as a journalist, gardener, and newspaper vendor—"but mostly stayed alive [by] wandering up and down [the] country reading poems, which I'm still doing"; currently a full-time writer. *Awards, honors:* Eric Gregory Award for poetry, 1967; Pernod Poetry Award, 1967; Arts Council grant, 1969; special award from the Mystery Writers of America, 1977, for *Mr. Moon's Last Case.*

WRITINGS—Juvenile: The Elephant and the Flower: Almost-Fables, Allen & Unwin, 1970; *Manchild,* Covent Garden Press, 1973; *Two Stories* (short stories), Covent Garden Press, 1973; *Jumping Mouse* (adaptation of American Indian folktale), Allen & Unwin, 1973; (editor with Pat Krett) *The House That Jack Built: Poems for Shelter,* Allen & Unwin, 1973; "The Pig and the Junk Hill" (play), first produced in Liverpool at Everyman Theatre, 1975; *Mr. Moon's Last Case,* Allen & Unwin, 1975, Scribner, 1977; *The Sly Cormorant and the Fishes* (adaptation of Aesop Fables), Kestral Books, 1978; *Gangsters, Ghosts, and Dragon Flies,* Allen & Unwin, 1981.

Poetry: *Portraits,* privately printed, 1962; (with Roger McGough and Adrian Henri) *The Mersey Sound: Penguin Modern Poets 10,* Penguin, 1967; *Little Johnny's Confession,* Allen & Unwin, 1967, Hill & Wang, 1968; *The Home Coming,* Turret Books, 1969; *Notes to the Hurrying Man: Poems, Winter '66—Summer '68,* Hill & Wang, 1969; *The Irrelevant Song,* Sceptre Press, 1970; *At Four O'Clock in the Morning,* Sceptre Press, 1971; *The Irrelevant Song and Other Poems,* Allen & Unwin,

1971; *The Eminent Professors and the Nature of Poetry as Enacted Out by Members of the Poetry Seminar One Rainy Evening,* Poem-of-the-Month Club (London), 1972; *The Unreliable Nightingale,* Rota, 1973; *Vanishing Trick,* Allen & Unwin, 1976; *Grave Gossip,* Allen & Unwin, 1979; *Love Poems,* Allen & Unwin, 1981; *Clare's Countryside,* Heinemann, 1981.

Poetry anthologized in *The Liverpool Scene,* edited by E. L. Smith, Rapp & Carroll, 1967 and in *The Oxford Book of 20th Century English Verse,* edited by Phillip Larkin, 1977. Former editor of *Underdog* (an English underground poetry magazine).

ADAPTATIONS—Recordings: "Selections from Little Johnny's Confession and Notes to the Hurrying Man and New Poems," Caedmon, 1969; "Vanishing Trick," Tangent, 1976; "The Sly Cormorant," Argo Records, 1978.

SIDELIGHTS: In 1969, the British Broadcasting Corporation made an hour-long feature for television on Brian Patten and Brian Jones. Patten's more recent television ventures have included a series of programs for BBC on the subject of contemporary literature.

Patten writes: "I am interested in fantasy, but always set the fantastic against realistic backgrounds, so that the everyday world is put into different perspective. I feel that this combination helps to develop the imagination. It is also a way of commenting on our hopes and fears. 'Reality' is not constant. Each child and adult creates his own version of it, depending on his needs."

FOR MORE INFORMATION SEE: Books and Bookmen, May, 1967, November, 1967, June, 1969; *Observer,* June 18, 1967; *Times Literary Supplement,* July 13, 1967; *London Magazine,* August, 1968, December, 1969; *Poetry,* autumn, 1968, May, 1971; *New Statesman,* April 25, 1969.

PENDLE, Alexy 1943-

PERSONAL: Born April 26, 1943, in Buenos Aires, Argentina; daughter of George (an author; businessman) and Olwen (Hanney) Pendle; married Larry Burnett (a builder), July 4, 1975; children: Alexander. *Education:* London County Council Central School of Arts and Crafts, England, national diploma, 1962; University of London Institute of Education, England, art teachers certificate, 1965. *Home:* 1821 Quince Ave., Boulder, Colo. 80302.

CAREER: Illustrator. Bilton Grange School, Rugby, England, art teacher, 1966-67.

WRITINGS—Self-illustrated: *The Cat Who Could Fly,* Muller, 1970.

Illustrator: Joanna Rupp, *The Rushes to the Rescue,* Epworth, 1969; Geraldine Symons, *The Workhouse Child,* Macmillan (London), 1969, (U.S.), 1971; Frances E. Crompton, *The Children of Hermitage,* Macmillan, 1970; G. Symons, *Miss Rivers & Miss Bridges,* Macmillan (London), 1971, (U.S.), 1972; John Cunliffe, *Riddles and Rhymes and Rigmaroles,* Deutsch, 1971; Dorothy Edwards, *Peter Nick-Nock and the Cuckoo Clock,* Transworld, 1971; Henry Fielding, *Tom Jones,* simplified for young readers by Michael West, Longman, 1972; G. Symons, *Mademoiselle,* Macmillan, 1973; Carol James, *The Hunting of the Unicorn,* Deutsch, 1973; J. Cunliffe, *The Great Dragon Competition and Other Stories,* Deutsch, 1973; Freya Littledale, *Ghosts and Spirits of Many Lands,* Deutsch, 1973; Horace Avron Cartledge, editor, *Stories of Fantasy and Science Fiction,* Longman, 1974; Nina Bawden, *The Peppermint Pig,* Gollancz, 1975; J. Cunliffe, *Giant Brog and the Motorway,* Deutsch, 1975; Elisabeth Kyle, *The Yellow Coach,* Heinemann, 1976; F. Littledale (editor), *Strange Tales from Many Lands,* Deutsch, 1978.

WORK IN PROGRESS: Writing and illustrating a book of rhymes.

SIDELIGHTS: Pendle's childhood was spent quietly and contentedly with her parents and two elder brothers in a small seaside town on the east coast of England. As a rather solitary

(From *The Great Dragon Competition and Other Stories* by John Cunliffe. Illustrated by Alexy Pendle.)

ALEXY PENDLE

child, who enjoyed fantasy and fairy tales, particularly those with a happy ending and plenty of detailed illustrations, she spent many hours of voracious reading. At the age of thirteen she went to boarding school where she was unhappy for four years. She moved to a flat in London and entered art school, where she felt that she had found her metier.

She spent nearly two years teaching art at a boys' private school near Rugby. While there she drew for pleasure and relaxation and, possibly, was influenced by her pupils' preference for the macabre.

In 1968 she returned to London and received her first commission. She then wrote and illustrated *The Cat Who Could Fly,* found herself an agent, and moved back to her parent's home where she lived and worked for six years. She draws with a lithograph nib and usually uses colored inks. In 1973, she met an American whom she married. They lived in the Middle East for eight months and are now settled in Boulder, Colorado.

She will always be grateful to Marni Hodgkin, the children's editor of Macmillan, London, who gave her her first commission when others refused to gamble on a newcomer; to her agent who has successfully insulated her against the buffets of the commercial world; and to her parents who have always provided refuge with love, encouragement and understanding.

FOR MORE INFORMATION SEE: Lee Kingman, and others, compilers, *Illustrators of Children's Books, 1967-1976,* Horn Book, 1978.

PERREARD, Suzanne Louise Butler 1919- (Suzanne Butler)

BRIEF ENTRY: Born May 30, 1919, in London, England. A teacher, novelist, and author of juvenile fiction, Perreard has lived in England, France, Canada, and Switzerland. Educated in private schools in Europe and Canada, she later taught at The Study, a private school for girls in Montreal, Quebec. In 1949 Perreard became secretary of the Association of Canadian Clubs National Office in Ottawa, Ontario, a position she held until 1953. After moving to Geneva, Switzerland, she opened and operated a nursery school there. Perreard, writing under her maiden name, Suzanne Butler, has written books for both adults and young people. Among her titles for young people are *Starlight in Tourrone* (Little, Brown, 1965), illustrated by Rita Fava Fegiz, and *The Chalet at Saint-Marc* (Little, Brown, 1968), illustrated by Kenneth Longtemps. Many of Perreard's stories take place during the late 18th and early 19th centuries and explore the cultural differences between Europeans and North Americans. Among Perreard's adult novels are her first book, *My Pride, My Folly* (Little, Brown, 1953), *Vale of Tyranny* (Little, Brown, 1954), and *Portrait of Peter West* (Little, Brown, 1958). *Residence:* Switzerland. *For More Information See: New York Times Book Review,* July 11, 1954; *New York Herald Tribune Book Review,* August 8, 1954; *Creative Canada: A Biographical Dictionary of Twentieth-Century Creative and Performing Arts,* Volume 2, University of Toronto Press, 1972.

PLAINE, Alfred R. 1898(?)-1981

OBITUARY NOTICE: Born about 1898; died after a long illness, December 19, 1981, in New York, N.Y. Publisher. Plaine co-founded the Almat Publishing Corporation in 1949 and published paperback fiction and nonfiction for young readers under such imprints as Little Paperback Classics and Hi-Lo Books. *Obituaries: Publishers Weekly,* January 29, 1982.

PLUMB, Charles P. 1900(?)-1982

OBITUARY NOTICE: Born about 1900; died of complications from a heart condition, January 19, 1982, in Ashland, Ore; buried in Port Charlotte, Fla. Cartoonist and author best known as the creator of the comic strip ''Ella Cinders.'' Published in both newspapers and comic books from 1924 to 1951, it was the first comic strip to be made into a full-length motion picture. Plumb also wrote three books, *Tin Can Island, The Tattooed Gun Hand,* and *The Murderous Move. Obituaries: Chicago Tribune,* January 22, 1982.

QUENNELL, Marjorie (Courtney) 1884-1972

PERSONAL: Born in 1884, in Bromley Common, Kent, England; died August 2, 1972; daughter of Allen Courtney; married Charles Henry Bourne Quennell (an architect and author; died, 1935), 1904; children: Peter (the writer), another son (killed in World War II), and one daughter. *Education:* Attended private schools and the Crystal Palace Art School, the Beckenham Technical Art School, and the Westminster Art School. *Home:* Lewes, Sussex, England.

CAREER: Author and artist. Curator of Geffrye Museum, London, 1935-41. Visited America, 1939, to study museums and education. *Member:* Honorary Associate of the Royal Institute of British Architects.

WRITINGS—With husband, Charles Henry Bourne Quennell; all self-illustrated: *A History of Everyday Things in England,* four volumes, B. T. Batsford, 1918-34, Scribner, 1922-35; *Everyday Life in the Old Stone Age,* B. T. Batsford, 1921, Putnam, 1922; *Everyday Life in the New Stone, Bronze, and Early Iron Ages,* B. T. Batsford, 1922, Putnam, 1923; *Everyday Life in Roman Britain,* B. T. Batsford, 1924, Putnam, 1925; *Everyday Life in Prehistoric Times* (originally published in two separate editions as *Everyday Life in the Old Stone Age* and *Everyday Life in the New Stone, Bronze, and Early Iron Ages),* B. T. Batsford, 1924, reissued, Transworld Publishers, 1971; *Everyday Life in Anglo-Saxon, Viking, and Norman Times,* B. T. Batsford, 1926, Putnam, 1927; *Everyday Things in Homeric Greece,* B. T. Batsford, 1929, Putnam, 1930; *Everyday Things in Archaic Greece,* Putnam, 1931, revised, B. T. Batsford, 1960; *Everyday Things in Classical Greece,* Putnam, 1933; *The Good New Days,* B. T. Batsford, 1935; *Everyday Things in Ancient Greece* (originally published in three separate editions as *Everyday Things in Homeric Greece, Everyday Things in Archaic Greece,* and *Everyday Things in Classical Greece),* Putnam, 1954; *Everyday Life in Roman and Anglo-Saxon Times,* including *Viking and Norman Times* (a revision of *Everyday Life in Roman Britain* and *Everyday Life in Anglo-Saxon, Viking, and Norman Times),* B. T. Batsford, 1950, Putnam, 1959.

Other: *London Craftsman: A Guide to Museums having Relics of Old Trades,* [London], 1939; (illustrator) Gertrude Hartman and L. S. Saunders, *Builders of the Old World,* Little, Brown, 1948.

SIDELIGHTS: **1884.** Born in Bromley Common, Kent, England, Quennell was educated in private schools and later attended several art schools. According to son, Peter: "My mother was receptive and imaginative. . . . She had grown up amid a cheerful, affectionate family. . . ." [Peter Quennell, *The Marble Foot: An Autobiography, 1905-1938,* Viking, 1976.[1]]

Married Charles Quennell in 1904 with whom she jointly wrote and illustrated the "Everyday" series describing the cultural background of history. "We hold that History is not just dates, but a long tale of man's life, labour, and achievements. . . ." [Marjorie and C.H.B. Quennell, *Everyday Life in the Old Stone Age,* Putnam, 1922.[2]]

". . . We have endeavoured to show man at work, feeding, clothing, and housing himself. We have tried to indicate the difficulties he has had to overcome, and how he has harnessed the powers of Nature to assist him. . . ." [Marjorie and C.H.B. Quennell, *Everyday Life in Anglo-Saxon, Viking and Norman Times,* Putnam, 1927.[3]]

". . . We have . . . attempted to . . . set the scene, and secure the atmosphere of his time. . . ." [Marjorie and C.H.B. Quennell, *Everyday Life in Homeric Greece,* Putnam, 1930.[4]]

Of their joint venture, Peter recalled ". . . the twin desks that he and my mother used, sitting side by side between the fireplace and the large half-curtained garden window. They had comparatively little space; other pieces of furniture surrounded them; for their work-room was also our living room; and three

The assembly before the hunt. ▪(From *A History of Everyday Things in England, Volume II, 1500-1799* by Marjorie and C.H.B. Quennell. Illustrated by Marjorie Quennell.)

children and a couple of somnolent dogs were usually assembled round the hearth. Provided they played no riotous games, my father preferred to work with his offspring grouped about him. . . . He worked steadily, his gold-rimmed spectacles glinting and his long hand swiftly moving, while his pictures of a seventeenth-century manor-house or an eighteenth-century windmill—he was now preparing Volume II of 'the Books'—took clear and energetic shape upon a sheet of Bristol-board.

"Next, it was my mother's turn. Having inked in the architectural background with a devoted attention to perspective—. . . he left a series of neat blank spaces in the foreground of his drawings. These spaces would hold my mother's figures . . . and, placing the sheet on my mother's desk, he briskly indicated the kind of personages that she should devise to fill them. . . . Once she had completed her task, my father brought up the background to join the outlines of the figures, and added the artists' joint initials, M. & C.H.B. Q. cunningly laced together in a decorative monogram. He designed it, as a symbol of their happy partnership, with particularly loving care.

". . . My mother . . . had joined him in the labours that were to last until his death. Designated 'the Books'—they required no other title—they came to form the pivot around which our lives revolved. . . . My parents' first book enjoyed an immediate success. The sale of the whole series, launched in October 1918, has since amounted to well over a million copies."[1]

After her husband's death in 1935, Quennell moved to London and was curator of the Geffrye Museum until 1941. In 1939 she traveled to the United States to study museums and education. She did some illustrating, but painted mainly for recreation. She died August 2, 1972, at the age of eighty-eight.

A pole lathe. ■ (From *Everyday Life in Prehistoric Times* by Marjorie and C.H.B. Quennell. Illustrated by Marjorie Quennell.)

HOBBIES AND OTHER INTERESTS: Painting.

FOR MORE INFORMATION SEE: Muriel Fuller, editor, *More Junior Authors*, H. W. Wilson, 1963; *Longman Companion to Twentieth Century Literature*, Longman Group Ltd., 1970; Peter Quennell, *The Marble Foot: An Autobiography, 1905-1938*, Viking, 1976; *Contemporary Authors*, Volumes 73-76, Gale, 1978; *The Lincoln Library of Language Arts*, 3rd edition, Frontier Press, 1978.

MARJORIE COURTNEY QUENNELL

The lion and the unicorn
Were fighting for the crown;
The lion beat the unicorn
All round about the town.
Some gave them white bread,
And some gave them brown;
Some gave them plum cake,
And sent them out of town.

—Nursery rhyme

ELLEN RABINOWICH

RABINOWICH, Ellen   1946-

PERSONAL: Born October 21, 1946, in Brooklyn, N.Y.; daughter of Paul (a psychologist) and Miriam (a piano teacher; maiden name, Feldman) Rabinowich; married G. Richardson Cook (a film producer), July 15, 1975. *Education:* University of Wisconsin, B.A., 1969. *Home:* 2830 Lambert Dr., Los Angeles, Calif. 90068.

CAREER: Plenum Publishing Corp., New York City, copywriter, 1969-70; Courier Production Co., New York City, coproducer, 1975; Mallory Factor Assoc., New York City, account executive, writer, producer, 1975-77; Martin Erlichman Productions, Los Angeles, Calif., story editor, 1980—. *Member:* Society of Children's Book Writers, Women in Film. *Awards, honors:* The Children's Book Council named *Seals, Sea Lions, and Walruses* an outstanding science book for children in 1980.

WRITINGS—All for children: *Queen Minna,* Macmillan, 1973; *Kangaroos, Koalas, and Other Marsupials,* Watts, 1978; *Horses and Foals,* Watts, 1979; *The Loch Ness Monster* (illustrated by Sally Law), Watts, 1979; *Rock Fever* (illustrated by Mauro Marinelli), Watts, 1979; *Toni's Crowd* (illustrated by Richard Cook), Watts, 1979; *Seals, Sea Lions, and Walruses,* Watts, 1980; *Rock Fever, Number 4,* Bantam, 1981; *Underneath I'm Different,* Delacorte, 1983.

Contributor of articles on health and beauty, television personalities, and film to various periodicals; writer of press and promotional materials for the New York State Council on the Arts, the Association for Retarded Children, and the Association of Independent Filmmakers.

WORK IN PROGRESS: Research for a film project about two stepbrothers.

SIDELIGHTS: "Certain people are much more concerned with a certain phase of their lives than others. I'm more connected to the time I was a teenager than my college days." This affinity for adolescence is evident throughout Rabinowich's fiction, which is geared to attract the interest of a low reading level group. Her novels deal with the typical problems of middle class teenagers: peer pressure, drugs and alcohol, divorced parents, and so on, yet are written in simple language and are heavily illustrated with photographs.

About *Toni's Crowd,* which is aimed at teenagers with severe reading difficulties, she said: "I felt it was important for Sandi to break away from Toni's crowd not just because they were shoplifting, but because she saw what kind of people they were and thought it was time for her to start making her own decisions. People like to connect with a group in order to feel better about themselves."

FOR MORE INFORMATION SEE: New York Times, December 10, 1978.

Stuffed animals filled Toni's room. They were everywhere. On the bed. Tables. Chairs. Toni lounged on the bed, polishing her fingernails. ▪ (From *Toni's Crowd* by Ellen Rabinowich. Photographs by G.R. Cook.)

RASKIN, Joseph 1897-1982

OBITUARY NOTICE—See sketch in *SATA* Volume 12: Born April 14, 1897, in Russia (now U.S.S.R.); died January 26, 1982, in Manhattan, N.Y. Artist and author. Raskin's paintings and etchings have been widely exhibited in galleries in the United States, France, Germany, and Israel. Raskin and his wife, Edith Raskin, wrote several books for young adults about early American life, including *Indian Tales, Tales Our Settlers Told, Tales of Justice in Early America,* and *Indentured Servants. For More Information See: Library Journal,* May 15, 1969; *Contemporary Authors,* Volumes 33-36, revised, Gale, 1978. *Obituaries: New York Times,* January 28, 1982; *AB Bookman's Weekly,* February 15, 1982.

RAYMOND, James Crossley 1917-1981

OBITUARY NOTICE: Born February 25, 1917, in Riverside, Conn.; died of cancer, October 14, 1981, in Boynton Beach, Fla. Cartoon illustrator known for drawing the cartoon strip "Blondie." For more than forty years Raymond drew the immensely popular cartoon, which still runs in more than eighteen hundred newspapers in fifty-five countries. *Obituaries: New York Times,* October 15, 1981; *Chicago Tribune,* October 16, 1981; *Time,* October, 26, 1981.

REED, Philip G. 1908-

BRIEF ENTRY: Born January 17, 1908, in Park Ridge, Ill. The son of a printer, Reed became interested in printing and illustration at an early age and studied graphic design at the Art Institute of Chicago. In 1930 he established his first printing company, the Broadside Press, which was later moved to Katonah, N.Y. Reed moved back to the Chicago area in 1939 and, with his brother John, established the Printing Office of Philip Reed. The firm's name was later changed to Monastery Hill Press and was associated with the A. & R. Roe publishing company from 1955 to 1973. Throughout his printing career, Reed has attracted clients interested in fine quality work, and with his detailed color woodprints has designed and illustrated many books for children. His *Mother Goose and Nursery Rhymes* (Atheneum, 1963) was a 1964 Caldecott Honor Book. Other illustrated works which have been cited for excellence include *The Seven Voyages of Sindbad the Sailor* (Atheneum, 1962) and James Thurber's *Many Moons* (A. & R. Roe, 1958). Reed has won several awards from the Chicago Society of Typographic Arts and nine of his works have been included among the American Institute of Graphic Arts "Fifty Books of the Year." His prints were part of the Moscow American National Exhibition and can be seen in many museums and libraries throughout the world, including the Library of Congress, Art Institute of Chicago, and the Victoria and Albert Museum in London, England. *Home:* 2901 Cleveland Ave., St. Joseph, Mich. 49085. *For More Information See: American Artist,* May, 1948; *Library Journal,* March 15, 1964; *Illustrators of Children's Books, 1957-1966,* Horn Book, 1968; *Third Book of Junior Authors,* H. W. Wilson, 1972; *Who's Who in the Midwest,* 17th edition, Marquis, 1980.

REEVES, Lawrence F. 1926-
(Warren Lyfick, R. Seever)

PERSONAL: Born June 2, 1926, in Massachusetts; son of Ralph F. (a printer) and Lillian (a nurse; maiden name, Bran-

don) Reeves; married Thetis Powers (a publisher), March 1, 1972; children: Kristin and Michael (twins). *Education:* Syracuse University, B.A., 1951, M.S.L.S., 1952. *Politics:* Liberal ("discouraged"). *Religion:* None. *Home:* Creamery Rd., Stanfordville, N.Y. *Office:* Harvey House Publishers, 20 Waterside Plaza, New York, N.Y. 10010.

CAREER: Dedham (Massachusetts) Public Library, director, 1954-56; Harper & Brothers, New York City, sales representative, 1956-59; Golden Press, New York City, sales manager, 1959-65; Grosset & Dunlap, Inc., New York City, vice-president, 1965-73; Harvey House Publishers, New York City, president, 1973—. *Member:* American Library Association, Syracuse University Library Associates (member of board of trustees), Society of Children's Book Writers. *Military service:* U.S. Navy, 1944-46.

WRITINGS—For children: (Compiler; under pseudonym Warren Lyfick) *The Little Book of Limericks* (illustrated by Chris Cummings), Harvey House, 1978; (under pseudonym R. Seever) *Mopeds,* Harvey House, 1979; (compiler; under pseudonym Warren Lyfick) *The Punny Pages* (illustrated by Cummings), Riverhouse, 1979; (under pseudonym Warren Lyfick) *Animal Tales* (illustrated by Joe Kohl), Riverhouse, 1980; (under pseudonym Warren Lyfick) *Little Book of Fowl Jokes* (illustrated by Cummings), Harvey House, 1980; *The Boston Col-*

LAWRENCE F. REEVES

Two ducks were walking through the park in a snowstorm. The duck on the right was limping.
Why? He had a stone in his boot. ■(From *The Little Book of Fowl Jokes* by Warren Lyfick.
Illustrated by Chris Cummings.)

oring Book, Harvey House, 1981; *Graphic Arts and Mopeds,* Messner, 1983.

WORK IN PROGRESS: A book of fish stories, to be published under the pseudonym Warren Lyfick.

SIDELIGHTS: "I don't sleep well so I scribble some. Joke books are fun to do if you have a good illustrator and a good card index. I'm not doing anything serious or deep, only things I like.

"I'm a children's book publisher and often have trouble finding someone to do a book, so I'll do it myself. My wife hates joke books—she has to listen to all the old groaners!"

REID, Dorothy M(arion) (?)-1974

BRIEF ENTRY: Born in Edinburgh, Scotland; died March, 1974, in Victoria, New Brunswick, Canada. Librarian and folklorist of the North American Indians. Orphaned as a young child, Reid was brought to Canada by an aunt after World War I. She was educated in Weyburn, Saskatchewan, and eventually became a teacher. Reid and her husband, Jack, lived in small Canadian towns where she gathered much of her knowledge of Indian legends and folklore. In 1956 Reid became a librarian for Fort William, Ontario, and served as the head of the children's department in the local library from 1957 to 1967. During that period she also hosted a popular weekly children's story hour on radio called "The Magic Carpet." Reid gained nation-wide recognition in Canada when her book, *Tales of Nanabozho* (Walck, 1963), was chosen book of the year for

1965 by the Canadian Library Association. She served as a judge for the Canadian Centennial Commission's competition for children's books and was a member of the first advisory committee for the journal *In Review: Canadian Books for Children*. In 1967 Reid was awarded Canada's Centennial Medal. *Residence:* Victoria, New Brunswick, Canada. *For More Information See: Profiles,* Canadian Library Association, 1975.

RICHELSON, Geraldine   1922-
(Ed Leander)

PERSONAL: Born August 20, 1922, in New York, N.Y.; daughter of Michael (a lawyer) and Frieda (Wolf) Popper: married Sigmund Richelson, July 10, 1943 (died, July 25, 1961); children: Andrew, Eric. *Education:* Hunter College, B.A., 1943. *Home:* 205 West End Ave., New York, N.Y. 10023. *Agent:* Carol Mann, Pacific St., Brooklyn, N.Y.

CAREER: Writer.

WRITINGS—All for children, unless otherwise indicated: *What Is a Child?* (illustrated by John E. Johnson), Harlin Quist, 1966; *What Is a Grownup?* (illustrated by Johnson), Harlin Quist, 1967; *From Bad to Worse* (illustrated by Claude Lapointe), Harlin Quist, 1973; *What Is a Baby?* (illustrated by Johnson), Harlin Quist, 1973; (under pseudonym Ed Leander) *Here's Looking at You!* (illustrated by Monique Gaudriault and others), Dial, 1973; (under pseudonym Ed Leander) *Crazy Days* (illustrated by Keleck; based on the French verse by Alain Diot), Harlin Quist, 1975; *The Good of It All* (illustrated by

Peep at Penelope, Peaceful and Pretty

Dressed all in Pink for her stroll through the city.

Proud as can be are her Dad and her Mum

While she lies there Peacefully sucking her thumb.

(From *Q Is for Crazy* by Ed Leander. Illustrated by Jözef Sumichrast.)

Lapointe), Harlin, Quist, 1975; (adapter) *The Piano Man* (illustrated by Henri Galeron; based on the French fantasy by Alain Diot), Harlin Quist, 1975; (under pseudonym Ed Leander) *What's the Big Idea?,* Harlin Quist, 1975; *Q Is for Crazy* (illustrated by Jözef Sumichrast), Harlin Quist, 1977; (adapter) *The Star Wars Storybook* (based on the film by George Lucas), Random House, 1978; (with Herbert J. Freudenberger) *Burn-Out: The High Cost of High Achievement* (adult nonfiction), Anchor Press, 1980; *Come Out, Come Out, Whoever You Are!*, Harlin Quist, 1980.

ROBERTS, Charles G(eorge) D(ouglas) 1860-1943

BRIEF ENTRY: Born January 10, 1860, in Douglas, New Brunswick; died November 26, 1943. Canadian poet, professor, and editor. Roberts was one of the first three Canadians ever to be knighted (1935) and received the honor primarily because of his fame as one of the country's best-loved poets. In his more than 25 stories for children, Roberts depicted the world of nature without the fanciful sentimentality often associated with nature books for children. Among Roberts' books for young people are *Red Fox* (Page, 1905), often called his masterpiece, as well as *The Watchers of the Trails* (Page, 1902), *Babes of the Wild* (Cassell, 1912), *The Secret Trails* (Macmillan, 1916), *Eyes of the Wilderness* (Macmillan, 1933), and *King of Beasts and Other Stories* (Ryerson, 1967). For adults, Roberts edited several collections of poetry and wrote numerous volumes of fiction, short stories, and verse, including *The Heart of the Ancient Wood* (fiction; Silver Burdett, 1900) and *The Vagrant of Time* (poetry; Ryerson, 1927). Roberts also taught English and economics at King's College, Windsor, Nova Scotia, from 1888 to 1895 and was a fellow of the Royal Society of Literature. *For More Information See: Who Was Who in America,* Volume 3, Marquis, 1966; William J. Keith, *Charles G. D. Roberts,* Copp, 1969; *Time,* June 12, 1972; *Christian Science Monitor,* December 4, 1972; *Twentieth-Century Children's Writers,* St. Martin's, 1978.

ROBINSON, Maurice R.   1895-1982

OBITUARY NOTICE: Born December 24, 1895, in Wilkinsburg, Pa.; died February 7, 1982, in Pelham, N.Y. Founder of Scholastic, Inc. Following his graduation from Dartmouth College in 1920, Robinson founded the *Western Pennsylvania Scholastic,* a weekly newspaper for high school students. In 1922 he changed the publication's title to *Scholastic* and served as president of Scholastic Magazine, Inc. until 1963. From 1963 to 1975 Robinson was chairman of the board and the company's chief executive officer. He stayed with Scholastic, Inc. as chairman of the board from 1975 until his death. In 1927 Robinson organized for high schools the Scholastic Awards Program in Art, Photography and Writing. A former president of the American Textbook Publishers Association, Robinson was a member of the six-person publishing delegation to the Soviet Union sponsored by the U.S. State Department and was a member of the State Department's Government Advisory Committee on International Book Programs from 1962 to 1964. Robinson received the 1969 Pennsylvania award for excellence in education and the 1970 Henry Johnson Fisher award. Scholastic, Inc. publishes thirty-four educational and professional periodicals, three magazines, five paperback book clubs and a line of texts and trade books. *Obituaries: Publishers Weekly,* February 19, 1982.

ROSS, Alex(ander)   1909-

BRIEF ENTRY: Born October 28, 1909, in Dumferline, Scotland; brought to the United States in 1912; naturalized U.S. citizen, 1921. Ross attended the Carnegie Institute of Technology and received an honorary M.A. from Boston College in 1953. He spent most of his career as a profile artist, working in Pittsburgh from 1934 to 1940. From 1942 to 1965 he was official cover artist for *Good Housekeeping* magazine and has been a free-lance portraitist since 1958. Ross has illustrated children's books, including Mary O'Neil's *Saints: Adventures in Courage* (Doubleday, 1963) and John Wright's *With Rifle and Plow: Stories of the Western Pennsylvania Frontier* (Kennikat Press, 1970). His paintings have been exhibited in numerous one-man shows, including those held at Eric Gallery, New York, N.Y., Demer's Gallery, Hilton Head, S.C., Thompson Gallery, Phoenix, Ariz., and Naples Art Gallery, Naples, Fla. Among the many awards Ross has earned for his work are the award of excellence from the Society of Illustrators Show, 1964, the Marthe T. McKinnon and the Ford Times

awards from the American Water Color Society, and the Adolf and Clara Borig Award from the National Academy of Design, 1972. Ross's work can be seen at the United States Air Force Academy and is represented in numerous private collections. *Home:* Hawthorn Trail, Ridgefield, Conn. 06877. *For More Information See: American Artist,* July, 1972; *Who's Who in America,* 41st edition, Marquis, 1980.

SARGENT, Pamela

PERSONAL: Born in Ithaca, N.Y. *Education:* State University of New York at Binghamton, B.A., 1968, M.A., 1970. *Residence:* Johnson City, N.Y. *Agent:* Joseph Elder Agency, 150 West 87th St., #6D, New York, N.Y. 10024.

CAREER: Honigsbaum's, Albany, N.Y., sales clerk and model, 1964-65; Endicott Coil Co., Inc., Binghamton, N.Y., solderer on assembly line, 1965; Towne Distributors, Binghamton, N.Y., sales clerk, 1965; State University of New York at Binghamton, typist in cataloging department of library, 1965-66, teaching assistant in philosophy, 1969-71; Webster Paper Co., Albany, N.Y., office worker, 1969; *Bulletin of the Science Fiction Writers of America,* managing editor, 1970-73, assistant editor, 1973-75, market report editor, 1973-76. Writer, 1969—. *Member:* Fiction Writers of America, Authors Guild, Amnesty International U.S.A.

WRITINGS: (Editor and contributor) *Women of Wonder: Science Fiction Stories by Women about Women,* Vintage Books, 1975; *Cloned Lives* (science fiction novel), Fawcett, 1976; (editor) *Bio-Futures,* Vintage Books, 1976; (editor) *More Women of Wonder,* Vintage Books, 1976; (editor) *The New Women of Wonder,* Vintage Books, 1978; *The Sudden Star* (novel), Fawcett, 1979; *Watchstar* (novel), Pocket Books, 1980; *The Golden Space* (novel), Simon & Schuster, 1982; *The Alien Upstairs* (novel), Doubleday, 1983; *Earthseed* (novel), Harper, in press. Author of a collection of short stories, *Starshadows,* Ace Books, 1977.

Stories for children have been anthologized in *The Missing World and Other Stories,* edited by Roger Elwood, Lerner, 1974; *The Killer Plants and Other Stories,* edited by Elwood, Lerner, 1974; *Night of the Sphinx and Other Stories,* Lerner, 1974.

Stories for adults have been anthologized in *Protostars,* edited by David Gerrold, Ballantine, 1971; *New Worlds Quarterly Three,* edited by Michael Moorcock, Berkley Books, 1972; *Universe Two,* edited by Terry Carr, Ace, 1972; *Wandering Stars* (Science Fiction Book Club selection), edited by Jack Dann, Harper, 1972; *Ten Tomorrows,* edited by Elwood, Fawcett, 1973; *And Walk Now Gently Through the Fire* (Science Fiction Book Club selection), edited by Elwood, Chilton, 1973; *Eros in Orbit,* edited by Joseph Elder, Trident, 1973; *Two Views of Wonder,* edited by Thomas N. Scortia and Chelsea Quinn Yarbro, Ballantine, 1973; *Universe Four* (Science Fiction Book Club selection), edited by Carr, Random House, 1974; *Continuum Three,* edited by Elwood, Putnam, 1974; *Fellowship of the Stars* (Science Fiction Book Club selection), edited by Carr, Simon & Schuster, 1974; *Dystopian Visions,* edited by R. Elwood, Prentice-Hall, 1975; *Orbit 20,* edited by Damon Knight, Harper, 1978; *Immortal,* edited by Jack Dann, Harper, 1978; *Contemporary Mythology* (non-fiction article), edited by Patricia Warrick and others, Harper, 1978; *Twentieth Century Science Fiction Writers* (non-fiction articles), edited by C. C. Smith, in press; (author of afterword) *The Fifth Head of Cerberus,* Ace Books, 1976; *Fantasy Annual V,* edited by

Terry Carr, Pocket Books; and *The Road to Science Fiction,* edited by James Gunn, Volume 4.

WORK IN PROGRESS: Two novels, *Venus of Dreams* and *Migratory Rooms;* several short stories.

SIDELIGHTS: Sargent is known for her science fiction stories and articles and is the editor of several books of science fiction stories written by women. "In the past, women, both as writers and as characters in sf [science fiction] novels and stories, were part of science fiction only sporadically. During the past twenty years, more women have entered the field. . . . There are signs that both female and male writers are beginning to work with new material and are questioning the assumptions which have dominated the field. Science fiction as a whole, however, still reflects the society around it.

"Most science fiction has been written by men, and they still form a majority of the writers today. About 10 to 15 percent of the writers are women. The vast majority of the readers are male and a fair number of them are young men or boys who stop reading sf regularly when they grow older. It is difficult to get exact figures on this, but publications for science fiction readers have at various times reported that most of their subscribers are men; a readership of 90 percent male and 10 percent female is not unusual.

"This is not at all surprising when one considers the relationship of science fiction to scientific and technical extrapolation, and the fact that science and technology are generally assumed to be masculine domains. Women have often been discouraged from entering scientific studies. . . .

"We can perhaps understand why the writers of science fiction took for granted certain presuppositions, as did almost everyone else in the society around them. Women, and racial minorities as well, suffered under these assumptions. If science was the province of males, it was also the province of white males. It is more common now to find black people and other minorities represented as characters in sf stories, although the number of black sf writers can be counted on the fingers of one hand. Women characters have been around longer but usually in unimportant roles. . . .

"Science fiction novels for young adults and children can also offer role models for younger readers. This has happened often enough in the past for boys. . . . There is no reason why this cannot be true for girls as well. . . .

"It should be noted that much of the truly innovative work in science fiction still remains to be done. There are, however, signs that the field is changing. Part of this is due to the growing numbers of women entering the field as writers, and to the changing views of some of the male writers. . . .

"But real changes in the genre are also dependent on the readers. Much of science fiction is a popular literature, and much of it is likely to remain so. It must satisfy and entertain its readership. This does not mean, however, that it must be simple-minded or cater only to those desiring good escapist reading. (It also does not mean that serious works are not entertaining. Some of the best and most serious sf is also the most entertaining.) If more women begin to take an interest in sf and the scientific and futurological ideas involved, publishers will have an interest in publishing and writers in writing novels exploring such ideas from different perspectives. If, however, publishers and writers can do better with the old stereotypes and have little reason to believe that readers want anything else, women will remain minor characters, and familiar roles and prejudices will be a major part of the literature. Only dedicated writers and publishers willing to take a risk would then provide more thoughtful works.

"It is up to us, both as writers and as readers, to begin exploring the unfamiliar, to acquaint ourselves with scientific and futurological concerns, and to give serious thought to what we are and what we would like to become." [Pamela Sargent, Introduction to *Women of Wonder: Science Fiction Stories by Women about Women,* Vintage Books, 1975.]

Many of Sargent's writings have been translated into foreign languages, including Dutch, German, Spanish, Japanese, and French.

SCHELLIE, Don 1932-

PERSONAL: Born March 8, 1932, in Chicago, Ill.; son of Leslie D. Schellie (a postal clerk) and Elsie (Osterberg) Schellie Nelson; married Coralee Rice (a school librarian), August 15, 1953; children: Leslie Ann, Kendall Sue, Kristina Lee. *Education:* Attended University of Arizona, 1955-56; University of Illinois, B.S., 1957. *Politics:* Independent. *Religion:* Protestant. *Home:* 5641 North Bonita Dr., Tucson, Ariz. 85704. *Agent:* John Cushman, JCA Literary Agency, 242 West 27th St., New York, N.Y. 10001. *Office address:* Tucson Citizen, P.O. Box 26767, Tucson, Ariz. 85726.

DON SCHELLIE

(From *Maybe Next Summer* by Don Schellie. Jacket design by Michael Ng.)

CAREER: News-Gazette, Champaign, Ill., reporter, 1954-55, 1956-57; *Douglas Daily Dispatch*, Douglas, Ariz., reporter, 1957-58; *Tucson Citizen*, Tucson, Ariz., reporter, 1958-60, columnist, 1960—. *Military service*: U.S. Air Force, 1951-54. *Member*: Western Writers of America, Authors Guild, Arizona Historical Society, Arizona State Press Club, National Society of Newspaper Columnists.

WRITINGS—Fiction for young readers: *Me, Cholay and Co.— Apache Warriors*, Four Winds Press, 1973; *Kidnapping Mr. Tubbs*, Four Winds Press, 1978; *Maybe Next Summer*, Four Winds Press, 1980; *Shadow and the Gunner*, Four Winds Press, 1982.

Nonfiction: *Vast Domain of Blood*, Westernlore, 1968; *The "Citizen": A Century of Arizona Journalism*, Citizen Publishing Co., 1970. Contributor of occasional articles to *Arizona Highways*.

WORK IN PROGRESS: Two novels.

SIDELIGHTS: "Certainly it wasn't the sort of thing you know at the time, but my growing-up years in Chicago spanned three dramatic events in the history of our country—the Great Depression in its dying days, the whole of World War II and, what some had begun calling the 'dawn of the Atomic Age.'

"The block we lived on was one of thousands of such blocks in sprawling lower-middle-class Chicago, as remote from the city's truly deprived neighborhoods as from affluent suburbia. At times it seemed to be isolated, almost, from the turmoil that was happening 'out there' in the rest of the world. From the vantage point now of many years, that place, those times, seem to have been strangely innocent.

"They were times of listening to 'Jack Armstrong' and 'Captain Midnight' and all the other afternoon radio serials, of boys playing softball in the streets while the girls jumped rope to singsong chants on the sidewalk. They were times of going to the Saturday matinees at the neighborhood movie house, where nine cents bought three feature films, a cavalcade of comedies, cartoons and newsreels and always the cliff-hanging serial to be 'Continued Next Week.' (Another nickle would buy a chewy all-day sucker that you could count on lasting through at least the Western or maybe even the horror picture. They tasted awful, but in the matter of long-term investment, were a far better buy than a nickel sack of hot buttered popcorn.)

"Easily my most vivid childhood memories, though, are of the wartime years when grown-ups talked of rationing and shortages and spoke quietly the names of distant places where our boys were dying to save the world for democracy. Of course all of us were caught up in the patriotism of it all and we were forever collecting scrap newspaper, going through air raid drills at school, selling Defense Stamps to neighbors and wishing we were old enough to be in uniform so we could march off to war ourselves and 'lick those Japs and Nazis.'

"Somehow that war got won without those of us of my age. . . . "

SCHREIBER, Georges   1904-1977

BRIEF ENTRY: Born April 25, 1904, in Brussels, Belgium; died in 1977. Schreiber studied art in Berlin, London, Florence, and Paris before coming to the United States at the age of twenty-four. A prolific cartoonist and painter, he became known as one of the best interpreters of the American scene, noted for the lifelike realism of his portraits. Early in his career, he traveled to each American state to paint regional studies which in 1939 toured museums nationwide in an exhibition called "Panorama of America." The exhibition received wide critical acclaim and included such portraits as "Young American Girl," considered by many to be the typical portrait of America's young women, the "Night Haul in Maine," a fishing scene familiar to almost any "Down-Easterner."

Schreiber established a reputation as an illustrator, contributing drawings to such periodicals as *Fortune, Nation,* and *Saturday Review,* and in 1948 he received the Randolph J. Caldecott Medal for his book *Bambino the Clown.* Other awards include a gold medal from the Art Director's Club, 1943, and a silver medal from the U.S. Department of the Treasury for a series of official War Loan posters. Schreiber taught art at the New School for Social Research in New York City and exhibited his work in numerous shows, including the New York World's Fair in 1939 and "Artists for Victory" held at the Metropolitan Museum of Art. His work is represented in the permanent collections of many museums, including the Whitney Museum of American Art, New York City, Bibliotheque Nationale, Paris, and Museum of Tel Aviv, Israel. Among the books he illustrated for children are Claire Bishop's *Pancake-Paris,* Alice Dalgliesh's *Ride on the Wind,* and Elpseth Bragdon's *That Jud!.* Other books written and illustrated by Schreiber include *Portraits and Self Portraits* and *Professor Bull's Umbrella,* written with William Lipkind. *For More Information See: New York Herald Tribune Books,* December 13, 1936; *New York Times Book Review,* December 13, 1936; *Nation,* February 12, 1938; *Saturday Review of Literature,* October 19, 1940; *Amer-*

ican Artist, April, 1943; *Newsweek,* June 26, 1944; *Publishers Weekly,* October 26, 1946; *Illustrators of Children's Books, 1946-1956,* Horn Book, 1958; *Who's Who in America,* 39th edition, Marquis, 1976.

SCHWARTZ, Daniel (Bennet) 1929-

BRIEF ENTRY: Born February 16, 1929, in New York, N.Y. An artist and illustrator of children's books, Daniel Schwartz has studied at the Art Students League in New York and the Rhode Island School of Design. His work has been included in numerous one-man and group shows, including those at the Davis Galleries, New York City, Maxwell Galleries, San Francisco, H. B. Clossen Galleries, Cincinnati, Babcock Galleries, New York City, Art Directors Club of New York, and the Boston Museum of Fine Art. Schwartz is the recipient of the Louis Comfort Tiffany Grant in Painting, 1956 and 1960, seven gold medals from the Society of Illustrators, between 1958 and 1972, and the purchase prize from Childe Hassam Fund of the American Academy of Arts and Letters, 1964. Schwartz illustrated Betsy Byars's book for children, *The House of Wings* (Viking, 1972). *Home:* 46 Remsen St., Brooklyn, N.Y. 11201. *For More Information See: Who's Who in America,* 38th edition, Marquis, 1974; *Who's Who in American Art,* Bowker, 1976.

SCHWENINGER, Ann 1951-

PERSONAL: Born August 1, 1951, in Boulder, Colo.; daughter of Ivan F. (a teacher) and Alice M. (a teacher; maiden name, Hill). *Education:* Attended the University of Colorado, 1969-72; California Institute of the Arts, B.F.A., 1975. *Home:* 319 E. 24th St., Apt. 15D, New York, N.Y. 10010.

CAREER: Author and illustrator of children's books, 1973—.

WRITINGS—For children: *The Hunt for Rabbit's Galosh* (illustrated by Kay Chorao), Doubleday, 1976; (self-illustrated) *A Dance for Three,* Dial Press, 1979; (compiler and editor) *The Man in the Moon as He Sails the Sky, and Other Moon Verse* (self-illustrated), Dodd, 1979; (self-illustrated) *On My Way to Grandpa's,* Dial Press, 1981.

Illustrator: Jean Marzollo, *Amy Goes Fishing,* Dial Press, 1981; Janice M. Udry, *Thump and Plunk,* Harper, 1981; Jim Erskine, *Bedtime Story,* Crown, 1982; Jean Van Leeuwen, *Amanda Pig and Her Big Brother Oliver,* Dial Press, 1982; Mary Caldwell, *Morning, Rabbit, Morning,* Harper, 1982; Dewitt Conyers (compiler), *Animal Poems for Children,* Western, 1982; Alan Benjamin, *Ribtickle Town,* Crown, 1983.

**As I shut the front gate
I felt the first drop of rain.**

■ (From *On My Way to Grandpa's* by Ann Schweninger. Illustrated by the author.)

ANN SCHWENINGER

SCOTT, Ann Herbert   1926-

BRIEF ENTRY: Born November 19, 1926, in Germantown, Philadelphia, Pa. Scott has taught English at Rider College and New Haven State Teachers College, both in New Jersey. Since 1966 has served as a member of the American Friends Service Committee. Also an author, she has written several books for children, including *Let's Catch a Monster* (Lothrop, 1967), *Sam* (McGraw, 1967), and *On Mother's Lap* (McGraw, 1972). For young adults, she wrote *Census U.S.A.: Fact Finding for the American People, 1790-1970* (Seabury, 1968). *Home:* 570 Cranleigh Dr., Reno, Nev. 89502. *For More Information See: Library Journal,* February 15, 1968; *Christian Century,* December 18, 1968; *Contemporary Authors,* Volumes 21-24, revised, Gale, 1977; *Authors of Books for Young People,* 2nd edition supplement, Scarecrow Press, 1979.

SELSAM, Millicent E(llis)   1912-

PERSONAL: Born May 30, 1912; daughter of Israel and Ida (Abrams) Ellis; married Howard B. Selsam (an author), September 1, 1936; children: Robert. *Education:* Brooklyn College, B.A., 1932; Columbia University, M.A., 1934. *Home:* 100 W. 94th St., New York, N.Y. 10025.

CAREER: Author of books for young people. *Member:* American Association for the Advancement of Science (fellow), American Nature Study Society, Authors Guild, National Audubon Society. *Awards, honors:* Boys' Club of America Gold

Medal Award, 1962, for *Stars, Mosquitoes, and Crocodiles: The American Travels of Alexander Von Humbolt;* Eva L. Gordon Award of the American Nature Study Society, 1964, for "many contributions to the literature of natural history"; Thomas A. Edison Award, 1965, for best juvenile science book, *Biography of an Atom;* Boys' Club of America Junior Book Award, 1967, for *Benny's Animals and How He Put Them in Order;* Washington Children's Book Guild nonfiction award, 1977, "for a total body of creative writing"; Garden State Children's Book award, 1978, for *How Kittens Grow;* nominee for Laura Ingalls Wilder award, 1980.

WRITINGS: Egg to Chick, International Publishers, 1946, revised edition, illustrated by Barbara Wolff, Harper, 1970; *Hidden Animals,* International Publishers, 1947, revised edition, Harper, 1969; *Play with Plants,* Morrow, 1948, revised edition, illustrated by Jerome Wexler, 1978; *Play with Trees* (illustrated by Fred F. Scherer), Morrow, 1950; *Play with Vines,* Morrow, 1951; *Play with Leaves and Flowers,* Morrow, 1952; *All about Eggs,* W. R. Scott, 1952, revised edition, Addison-Wesley, 1980; *Microbes at Work* (illustrated by Helen Ludwig), Morrow, 1953; *All Kinds of Babies,* W. R. Scott, 1953, revised edition, illustrated by Symeon Shimin, Scholastic, 1967; *A Time for Sleep,* W. R. Scott, 1953; *How the Animals Eat,* W. R. Scott, 1955; *Plants We Eat* (illustrated by H. Ludwig), Morrow, 1955; *See Through the Sea,* Harper, 1955; *See Through the Forest,* Harper, 1956; *Exploring the Animal Kingdom,* Doubleday, 1957; *Play with Seeds* (illustrated by H. Ludwig), Morrow, 1957; *See Through the Jungle,* Harper, 1957; *See Through the Lake,* Harper, 1958; *How to Be a Nature Detec-*

MILLICENT E. SELSAM

tive, W. R. Scott, 1958, revised edition entitled *Nature Detective* (illustrated by Ezra Jack Keats), Harper, 1966; *Plants That Heal,* Morrow, 1959; *Seeds and More Seeds* (illustrated by Tomi Ungerer), Harper, 1959; (editor) Charles Darwin, *Voyage of the Beagle,* Harper, 1959; *Birth of an Island,* Harper, 1959.

How to Grow House Plants (illustrated by Kathleen Elgin), Morrow, 1960; *Plenty of Fish* (illustrated by Erik Blegvad), Harper, 1960; *Around the World with Darwin,* Harper, 1961; *Tony's Birds* (illustrated by Kurt Werth), Harper, 1961; *See along the Shore,* Harper, 1961; *Underwater Zoos,* Morrow, 1961; *Language of Animals,* Morrow, 1962; (editor) *Stars, Mosquitoes and Crocodiles: The American Travels of Alexander Von Humboldt* (*Horn Book* honor list), Harper, 1962; *Terry and the Caterpillers,* Harper, 1962; *The Quest of Captain Cook,* Doubleday, 1962; *Plants That Move* (contains *Play with Vines,* and *Play with Leaves and Flowers*), Morrow, 1962; *How Animals Sleep,* Scholastic, 1962; *How Animals Live Together,* Morrow, 1963, 1979; *Greg's Microscope* (illustrated by Arnold Lobel), Harper, 1963; *You and the World Around You,* Doubleday, 1963; *First Guide to Wildflowers,* Doubleday, 1964; *Courtship of Animals,* Morrow, 1964; *Birth of a Forest* (illustrated by B. Wolff), Harper, 1964; *Let's Get Turtles* (illustrated by A. Lobel), Harper, 1965; (with J. Bronowski) *Biography of an Atom,* Harper, 1965; *Animals as Parents,* Morrow, 1965; *Benny's Animals and How He Put Them in Order* (illustrated by A. Lobel), Harper, 1966; *When an Animal Grows* (illustrated by John Kaufman), Harper, 1966; *The Bug That Laid the Golden Eggs* (photographs by Harold Krieger), Harper, 1967; *Questions and Answers about Ants* (illustrated by Arabelle Wheatley), Scholastic, 1967; *How Animals Tell Time* (illustrated by J. Kaufman), Morrow, 1967; *Milkweed* (photographs by J. Wexler), Morrow, 1967; *Maple Tree* (illustrated by J. Wexler), Morrow, 1968; (with George Schaller) *The Tiger: Its Life in the Wild,* Harper, 1969; *Peanut* (illustrated by J. Wexler), Morrow, 1969.

The Tomato and Other Fruit Vegetables (photographs by J. Wexler), Morrow, 1970; *How Puppies Grow,* Scholastic, 1971, revised edition, illustrated by Esther Bubley, Four Winds, 1972; *Is This a Baby Dinosaur?,* Scholastic, 1971; *The Carrot and Other Root Vegetables,* Morrow, 1971; *Vegetables from Stems and Leaves* (illustrated by J. Wexler), Morrow, 1972; *More Potatoes!* (illustrated by Ben Shecter), Harper, 1972; *Is This a Baby Dinosaur? and Other Science Picture-Puzzles,* Harper, 1972; (editor with Joyce Hunt) *A First Look at Leaves* (illustrated by Harriett Springer), Walker, 1972; *A First Look at Fish* (illustrated by H. Springer), Walker, 1973; *A First Look at Mammals,* Walker, 1973; *The Apple and Other Fruits* (photographs by J. Wexler), Morrow, 1973; *Questions and Answers About Horses* (illustrated by Robert J. Lee), Four Winds, 1973; *A First Look at Birds* (illustrated by H. Springer), Walker, 1974; *Bulbs, Corms, and Such* (illustrated by J. Wexler), Morrow, 1974; *A First Look at Insects* (illustrated by H. Springer), Walker, 1975; *How Kittens Grow* (illustrated by E. Bubley), Four Winds, 1975; *The Harlequin Moth: Its Life Story* (illustrated by J. Wexler), Morrow, 1975; *Animals of the Sea* (illustrated by John Hamberger), Scholastic, 1975; *A First Look at Snakes, Lizards and Other Reptiles* (illustrated by H. Springer), Walker, 1975.

A First Look at Frogs, Toads, & Salamanders (illustrated by H. Springer), Walker, 1976; *Popcorn* (illustrated by J. Wexler), Morrow, 1976; (with J. Hunt) *A First Look at Animals Without Backbones* (illustrated by H. Springer), Walker, 1976; *Sea Monsters of Long Ago,* Scholastic, 1977; (with J. Wexler) *The Amazing Dandelion* (illustrated by J. Wexler), Morrow, 1977; (with Kenneth Dewey) *Up Down and Around: The Force of Gravity,* Doubleday, 1977; (with Deborah Peterson) *Don't Throw It Grow It Book of Houseplants,* Random House, 1977; (with J. Hunt) *A First Look at Flowers* (illustrated by H. Springer), Walker, 1977; *Land of the Giant Tortoise: The Story of the Galapagos* (self-illustrated with Les Line), Scholastic, 1977; *Sea Monsters of Long Ago* (illustrated by J. Hamberger), Four Winds, 1978; *Mimosa: The Sensitive Plant* (illustrated by J. Wexler), Morrow, 1978; *A First Look at the World of Plants* (illustrated by H. Springer), Walker, 1978; (with J. Hunt) *A First Look at Animals with Backbones* (illustrated by H. Springer), Walker, 1978; *Tyrannosaurus Rex,* Harper, 1978; *A First Look at Monkeys and Apes* (illustrated by H. Springer), Walker, 1979; (with others) *A First Look at Sharks,* Walker, 1979; *A First Look at Whales,* Walker, 1980; *Eat the Fruit, Plant the Seed* (illustrated by J. Wexler), Morrow, 1980; *Night Animals,* Scholastic, 1980; *First Look at Cats* (illustrated by H. Springer), Walker, 1981; *First Look at Days* (illustrated by H. Springer), Walker, 1981. Also cooperating editor of *See Up The Mountain* by Betty Morrow, Harper, 1958.

SIDELIGHTS: Selsam was born May 30, 1912, in Brooklyn, New York, the youngest of eight children of Israel and Ida Ellis. She attended New York schools and was graduated magna cum laude with a B.A. degree in biology from Brooklyn College. She received a M.A. in botany and a M.Ph. at Columbia University. On September 1, 1936, she married author Howard B. Selsam.

"When I go into the water, does my blood get as cold as the water?" asked Billy. ■ (From *Let's Get Turtles* by Millicent E. Selsam. Illustrated by Arnold Lobel.)

He made a picture of an orange
He made a picture of a lemon.
He put the pictures on the pots.
"Now when they grow," said Benny,
"I'll know which is which."

■ (From *Seeds and More Seeds* by Millicent E. Selsam. Illustrated by Tomi Ungerer.)

Selsam's career is closely connected with biology and botany. She taught science at Brooklyn College and in New York City high schools until her son, Robert, was born.

With her background in biology and botany, Selsam began writing science books for children. "I got tired of teaching but still enjoyed the idea of communicating with young people regarding science."[Lee Bennett Hopkins, *Books Are by People,* Citation Press, 1969.[1]]

She published her first book, *Egg to Chick,* in 1946 and is now an award-winning author of more than ninety-four children's science books communicating her love and knowledge of science. "I have certain childlike qualities. I love to investigate everything and get great pleasure from growing plants indoors and out. I have always loved to know the *why* of everything. Science is dynamic and exciting, and it has changed the world.

"A good science book leads to an appreciation of the methods of science. Scientists find the answers to their questions by observing and experimenting. Children are excellent observers, and if they are given a chance to look at things themselves, they will begin to appreciate the kind of patience and effort that goes into careful observations. Science books should encourage this habit of careful observations. A good book on the seashore should move the reader to go out and examine for himself the wonderful life at the edge of the sea. A good astronomy book should turn the reader's eye to the sky and make him want to buy a small telescope. A good nature book should stimulate a young person to hear, see, smell, and taste things—to use all of his senses to observe."[1]

In 1959, Selsam edited Darwin's *The Voyage of the Beagle.* "There are several reasons for this volume. One is that considerable additional material on the voyage of the *Beagle* has been made available only in the last twenty-five years. Most of this was written by Darwin himself but never previously published. Another is that no analysis of the voyage and its scientific meaning has ever been published alongside the text itself, as in this edition. Finally, the original text runs to about five hundred pages. Much of it is tedious and uninteresting to the general reader, as Darwin himself feared, either because of its technical details or because it is unrelated to the main purpose and meaning of the voyage. The present text, although less than one-half the length of the original, still keeps the continuity of Darwin's trip and virtually everything significant for his later development of the theory of evolution. At the same time, it includes most of the observations and episodes that have made Darwin's account a warm and revealing record of the travels of a unique and sensitive person at a particular stage in world history.

"The editor feels strongly that anyone reading the journal will be moved by this example of an inquiring mind devoted to the truth. Here one can see the process of creative science at work. It is not enough to know the end results of Darwin's life and thought. A fuller, richer, and more human understanding comes from acquaintance with Darwin's own account of his experiences. As the story of the voyage unfolds, we see how he steadily advances in knowledge and develops his imagination and ability to theorize. We see the growth of the man capable of making the historic discovery of evolution." [Millicent E. Selsam, "Editors Note" in *The Voyage of the Beagle* by Charles Darwin, Harper, 1959.[2]]

Selsam is presently an editor of Walker and Company in New York. She lives in Manhattan and summers on Fire Island, New York. ". . . I spend a lot of time with children in my cottage at Fire Island. I've gotten several ideas from contacts with them."[1]

FOR MORE INFORMATION SEE: Horn Book, October, 1962, June, 1963, August, 1964, June, 1965, June, 1977, August, 1977, June, 1978, October, 1978, February, 1979; Muriel Fuller, *More Junior Authors,* H. W. Wilson, 1963; *Fire Island News,* May 28, 1966; *Young Readers' Review,* October, 1966, May, 1967, November, 1967; *New York Times Book Review,* November 5, 1967; *Christian Science Monitor,* December 21, 1967; Lee Bennett Hopkins, *Books Are by People,* Citation Press, 1969.

MARGERY SHARP

SHARP, Margery 1905-

PERSONAL: Born 1905; daughter of J. H. Sharp; married Geoffrey L. Castle (a major in the Royal Army), 1938. *Education:* Streatham Hill High School; Bedford College, London University, B.A. (French honours). *Address:* c/o The Westminster Bank Ltd., St. James Square, London, S.W.1, England.

CAREER: Worked for the Armed Forces Education Program during World War II. Full-time professional writer.

*WRITINGS—*For children; all published by Little, Brown, except as noted: *The Rescuers* (illustrated by Garth Williams; ALA Notable Book), 1959; *Melisande* (illustrated by Roy McKie), 1960; *Something Light* (*Horn Book* honor list), Collins, 1960, Little, Brown, 1961; *Miss Bianca* (illustrated by Williams), 1962; *The Turret* (illustrated by Williams), 1963; *Lost at the Fair* (illustrated by Rosalind Fry), 1965; *Miss Bianca in the Salt Mines* (illustrated by Williams), 1966; *Miss Bianca in the Orient* (illustrated by Erik Blegvad), 1970, Dell, 1978; *Miss Bianca in the Antarctic* (illustrated by Blegvad), 1971; *Miss Bianca and the Bridesmaid* (illustrated by Blegvad), 1972; *The Children Next Door* (illustrated by Hilary Abrahams), Heinemann, 1974; *The Magical Cockatoo* (illustrated by Faith Jaques), Heinemann, 1974; *Bernard the Brave* (illustrated by Jaques), Heinemann, 1976, American edition (illustrated by Leslie Morrill), Little, Brown, 1977; *Bernard into Battle: A Miss Bianca Story* (illustrated by Morrill), 1979.

For adults; all published by Little, Brown, except as noted: *Rhododendron Pie*, Appleton, 1930; *Fanfare for Tin Trumpets*, Barker, 1932, Putnam, 1933; *The Nymph and the Nobleman*, Barker, 1932; *Flowering Thorn*, Putnam, 1934, reprinted, Hutchinson Library Service, 1972; *Sophie Cassmajor*, Putnam, 1934; *Four Gardens*, Putnam, 1935; *Nutmeg Tree*, 1937; *Harlequin House*, 1939; *Stone of Chastity*, 1940, reprinted, AMS Press, 1976; *Three Companion Pieces* (contains *The Nymph and the Nobleman, Sophie Cassmajor,* and *The Tigress on the Hearth*), 1941; *Cluny Brown* (serialized in *Ladies' Home Journal*), 1944; *Britannia Mews*, 1946; *Lise Lillywhite*, 1951; *The Gipsy in the Parlour*, 1954; *The Tigress on the Hearth*, Collins, 1955; *Eye of Love*, 1957, reprinted, Severn House, 1957; *Martha in Paris*, Collins, 1962, Little, Brown, 1963; *Martha, Eric and George*, 1964; *The Sun in Scorpio*, 1965; *In Pious Memory*, 1967; *Rosa*, 1970; *The Innocents*, Heinemann, 1971, Little, Brown, 1972; *The Last Chapel Picnic, and Other Stories*, 1973; *The Faithful Servants*, 1975; *Summer Visits*, Heinemann, 1977, Little, Brown, 1978.

Plays: "Meeting at Night," produced in London, 1934; *Lady in Waiting* (produced in New York, 1940), Samuel French, 1941; *The Foolish Gentlewoman* (produced in London, 1949), Samuel French, 1950; "The Birdcage Room," for television, 1954.

Frequent contributor to magazines in England and the United States, including *Ladies' Home Journal, Harper's Bazaar, Saturday Evening Post, Strand, Fiction Parade, Punch,* and *Collier's.* Contributor to *Encyclopaedia Britannica.*

*ADAPTATIONS—*Movies: "Cluny Brown," Twentieth Century-Fox, 1946; "Julia Misbehaves," adaptation of *The Nutmeg Tree,* Metro-Goldwyn-Mayer, 1948; "The Forbidden Street," adaptation of *Britannia Mews,* Twentieth Century-Fox, 1949; "The Notorious Landlady," adaptation from the short story "The Tenant," Columbia, 1962; "The Rescuers," Walt Disney Productions, 1977.

SIDELIGHTS: **1905.** Born to British parents and raised on the island of Malta. Graduated from Streatham Hill High School in England. "I started writing in the classic way—poetry, or rather verse—and I can remember that my first published poem was on that extremely classic subject, 'The Moon.' I was in the sixth form in high school (that is . . . the top form). I used to write these verses to fill up magazines. You know, a short story very rarely ends exactly at the bottom of a page. There's a gap of three or four inches, and the editors at that time were always willing to buy a poem to fill in. I was paid ten and sixpence, half a guinea, for each. For a high school student this is a very rewarding sum, at least it was when I was doing it.

"I had no idea of becoming anything except a writer—oh, possibly a painter. . . . I have had a certain training in painting, but I never really got serious about it because if you paint you must do so full time and I couldn't afford that. But I wanted to write, and the fact that I had to earn a living probably turned me into a writer rather than a painter. I think I obtain something of the tactile pleasure a painter gets from slamming paint on canvas. I write everything in longhand two or three times, and I quite enjoy the physical sensations of dealing with pen and ink and paper." [Roy Newquist, *Counterpoint*, Rand McNally, 1964.[1]]

Sharp received a B.A. degree in French from London University. In 1929 she made her first visit to the United States as a member of the British University Debating Team.

The funeral ceremonies for those slain in battle were impressive to a degree. ■(From *Bernard into Battle: A Miss Bianca Story* by Margery Sharp. Illustrated by Leslie Morrill.)

From a front seat up spoke a mouse almost as old and rheumatic as the Secretary himself.
■ (From *The Rescuers* by Margery Sharp. Illustrated by Garth Williams.)

1930. Began writing after graduation, "by design." "The very first [published novel] was called *Rhododendron Pie*. It's been out of print for decades, but I read it again the other day. It's not bad, not bad at all, but I do have the proportions wrong. I started out as though it were going to be a big book and it turned into a short one. I wouldn't make that mistake today.

"The first book which met with any success at all was the second, *Fanfare for Tin Trumpets*. I was going in for rather *chichi* titles at the time. Now I call them things like *Martha in Paris* and *Martha, Eric and George*. Very *terre-á-terre*. But *Fanfare* had a nice little success, did me a lot of good, and I simply went on from there."[1]

For three decades Sharp concentrated on the writing of adult fiction. Several of her novels were serialized in magazines. ". . . The basic idea [for her novel, *The Nutmeg Tree*] was a theory that people often aren't bad but circumstances sometimes make them so. I think of Julia, particularly, a warm-hearted and completely amoral person who was perfectly good in her way, but if placed in a completely conventional society she looked bad. In fact, she *was* bad for them because she broke up all their patterns.

"I know how *Britannia Mews* started. I was walking through a semislum stable that was being converted into these elegant little town-cottages, and I thought, 'What a history that place has had from the day it was built!'—carriages and horses, then desolation, now cocktail parties and theater clubs.

"Of course, it's remarkably easy to define where *Martha, Eric and George* sprang from, because it's a sequel to *Martha in Paris*. If you remember, Martha was a very headstrong, determined young woman who was going to paint and that was that. She was very annoyed at the prospect of having a baby; she didn't want the husband to go with it, didn't want the baby, and actually went out of her way and spent extra francs in taxi fare to leave the infant on its father's doorstep. Martha wondered why it should always be the woman who is saddled with a little illegitimate, so she reversed things. This reversal—beginning, of course, with the wonderful moment of discovery when Eric is handed his baby—made a natural springboard into the book.

"But I sometimes feel that we had better not dig too deeply into the roots of novels to figure out where they come from. If it has come, wonderful, but let's not pull up the roots to examine them."[1]

1938. Married Geoffrey Lloyd Castle.

1959. First of many juveniles was published. Several of her novels have become movies. "I enjoy writing [children's books] immensely because they are a complete release of the imagination. The first of the Miss Bianca series was called *The Rescuers*. It was about the Prisoners Aid Association of Mice—mice are traditionally the prisoner's friend, you know—so I describe how the organization works with all its branches in various countries, the basic idea being the cheering of prisoners in their cells. You might say that it's national service stuff all mice go through. But then there are adventures when they feel prisoners have been wrongly imprisoned and should be released. It's fascinating to me, and I hope to the people who read the books.

"I think a great deal of the success has been due to Garth Williams' illustrations. His technique is marvelous, but he shows the most wonderfully sympathetic imagination. For ex-

...Miss Bianca for the last time sang Patience to sleep. She didn't sing the lullaby about the doves, but a variation composed on the spur of the moment. ■ (From *Miss Bianca* by Margery Sharp. Illustrated by Garth Williams.)

ample, in one place I describe the chairman's chair as being made from walnut shells, so Garth Williams carpentered a walnut shell into a chair and then drew it.

". . . The foreign companies have told me that the stories are written in such good English they are a pleasure to translate. Then it's fascinating to see the questionnaires at the end of chapters, like the Dutch edition, for schools, where one question reads, 'Why did they put Nils in the pocket closest to the poet's heart?' Answer: 'Because they were both Norwegians.' It's all very fascinating."[1]

When asked to give advice to the new writer, Sharp responded: "First of all I'd tell them never to think about the results. You must learn to write rather than be a writer. Write as well as you can. Don't think of what is wanted, what is popular, what will sell. Write what you want, and write as well as you can.

"I think it's not only useful but almost essential for a writer to have other experiences. I think it would be terrible for a person of sixteen or seventeen to leave school and go home and say, 'I'm going to be a writer' and sit down and write all

(From the animated movie "The Rescuers," featuring the voices of Bob Newhart, Eva Gabor, and Geraldine Page. Copyright © 1977 by Walt Disney Productions.)

day. Far better to have a job, or as many jobs as possible. Do all sorts of things because you must first have actual experience to work with. Otherwise the things you write will be derived only from books, already processed through someone else's mind. Don't get on a magazine staff—get a job in a grocery store, a lumber camp. Fish, be a secretary, a switchboard operator, go on the stage. But don't just confine yourself to writing.

"Of course, when you actually are writing, you must regard time as a sacred thing. Writing time, your treasured hours, dare not be violated.

"I feel that I have an obligation to write good English and another to be interesting to the reader. I can't remember who said it, but someone stated that the cardinal quality of a novel is that it should be interesting.

"I think this really sums up its imperatives, because if it is to be truly interesting the characters cannot be falsified and it must be readable. If not stylistically pure, at least readable."[1]

HOBBIES AND OTHER INTERESTS: ". . . I'm particularly fond of embroidery—gros point, not petit point, which is too hard on the eyes. I find it relaxing and agreeable, and I love to create my own designs. . . . I also find it useful, when I'm traveling, to have a piece of embroidery with me because you can get held up at airports for two hours or two days, and when you embroider the time passes quickly. . . .

"I'm fond of gardening—I have a little garden in the country. And I swim and draw. But I haven't enough time. All I want is time—I would like to live two or three lives concurrently.

"I have always thought that a jobbing gardener must lead an interesting life, going from house to house, working for several people, visiting each family once per week and getting to know them. And I have always thought that it would be nice to be the lady in a troupe of adagio dancers—the one they fling through the air. I've always thought it would be delightful to be flung about like that, though probably it would be grueling—not able to eat for several hours beforehand, then only sole. Perhaps I should have been both a jobbing gardener *and* an adagio dancer. I might not have had time to write a word, but I'd have had a splendidly exciting life."[1]

FOR MORE INFORMATION SEE: Roy Newquist, *Counterpoint,* Rand McNally, 1964; *Who's Who of American Women,* 8th edition, Marquis, 1973; *Contemporary Novelists,* 2nd edition, St. Martin's, 1976; *Who's Who, 1981-1982,* St. Martin's, 1981; *The Writers Directory, 1982-1984,* Gale, 1981.

SHELLEY, Mary Wollstonecraft (Godwin) 1797-1851

PERSONAL: Born August 30, 1797, in London, England; died February 1, 1851, in Bournemouth, England; buried at Bournemouth; daughter of William (the philosopher and writer) and Mary (the writer; maiden name, Wollstonecraft) Godwin; married Percy Bysshe Shelley, December 30, 1816 (died, 1822); children: first child, a daughter, died in infancy; William (died, 1819), Clara (died, 1818), Percy Florence. *Education:* No formal schooling; influenced by the intellectual discussions of her philosopher father and his friends. *Home:* London, England.

CAREER: Novelist, essayist, critic, and editor; following the death of her husband, devoted herself to full-time writing in order to support herself and her surviving son. Although *Frankenstein*, her first novel, was an immediate success, none of her later work matched its appeal.

WRITINGS—Of special interest to young readers: *Frankenstein; or, The Modern Prometheus*, Lackington, Hughes, Harding, Mavor, & Jones (London), 1818, University of Chicago Press, 1982 [other editions include those illustrated by Lynd Ward, Smith & Haas, 1934; Everett Henry, Heritage Press, 1962; Robert Andrew Parker, Potter, 1976; Alice and Joel Schick, Delacorte, 1980; Gary Kelley, Raintree, 1981].

Other writings: *History of a Six Weeks' Tour*, Hookham, 1817; *Valperga: or, The Life and Adventures of Castruccio, Prince of Lucca*, Whittaker, 1823; *The Last Man* (novel), Colburn, 1826; *The Fortunes of Perkin Warbeck* (novel), Colburn & Bentley, 1830; *Lodore*, Wallis & Newell (New York), 1835; *Falkner* (novel), Harper & Brothers, 1837; *Rambles in Germany and Italy*, Moxon, 1844; *The Choice: A Poem on Shelley's Death*, edited by H. B. Forman, [London], 1876; *The Mortal Immortal* (short story), Mossant, Vallon, 1910; *Proserpine and Midas: Two Unpublished Mythological Dramas*, Milford, 1922.

Collections: *Tales and Stories*, edited by Richard Garnett, W. Paterson, 1891; *Letters of Mary W. Shelley (Mostly Unpublished)*, with an introduction and notes by Henry H. Harper, [Boston], 1918; *The Letters of Mary W. Shelley*, edited by Frederick L. Jones, University of Oklahoma Press, 1944; *Shelley at Oxford: The Early Correspondence of P. B. Shelley with His Friend T. J. Hogg*, edited by Walter Sidney Scott, Golden Cockerel Press, 1944, reprinted, Norwood, 1977; *Harriet & Mary: Being the Relations between Percy Bysshe Shelley, Harriet Shelley, Mary Shelley, and Thomas Jefferson Hogg*, edited by W. S. Scott, Golden Cockerel Press, 1944, reprinted, Norwood, 1978; *Mary Shelley's Journal*, edited by Frederick L. Jones, University of Oklahoma Press, 1947; *My Best Mary: The Selected Letters of Mary Wollstonecraft Shelley*, edited and with an introduction by Muriel Spark & Derek Stanford, Roy, 1953; *Collected Tales and Stories*, edited and with an introduction and notes by Charles E. Robinson, Johns Hopkins University Press, 1976; *The Letters of Mary Wollstonecraft Shelley*, edited by Betty T. Bennett, Johns Hopkins University Press, 1980.

Also editor of Percy Bysshe Shelley's *Posthumous Poems*, 1824; *Poetical Works*, 1839; and *Essays*, 1840.

ADAPTATIONS—All movies, except as noted: "Frankenstein," starring Colin Clive and Boris Karloff, Universal, 1931 (novel adaptation by Richard J. Anobile, Pan Books, 1974); "Bride of Frankenstein," starring Boris Karloff, Colin Clive,

Mary Shelley. Miniature by Reginald Easton.

and Elsa Lanchester, Universal, 1935; "Son of Frankenstein," starring Basil Rathbone, Boris Karloff and Bela Lugosi, Universal, 1939; "Frankenstein Meets the Wolf Man," starring Lon Chaney, Jr. and Bela Lugosi, Universal, 1943; "The Curse of Frankenstein," starring Peter Cushing and Christopher Lee, Warner Brothers, 1957; "Frankenstein, 1970," starring Boris Karloff and Tom Duggan, Allied Artists, 1958; "Frankenstein's Daughter," starring John Ashley and Sandra Knight, Astor, 1958.

"Frankenstein Meets the Space Monster," starring James Karen and Robert Reilly, Allied Artists, 1965; "Frankenstein Conquers the World," starring Nick Adams and Tadao Takashima, American International, 1966; "Frankenstein Created Woman," starring Peter Cushing and Susan Denberg, Twentieth Century-Fox, 1967; "Frankenstein's Bloody Terror," starring Paul Naschy and Dianik Zurakowska, Independent International, 1968; "Frankenstein Must Be Destroyed!," starring Peter Cushing, Simon Ward, and Freddie Jones, Warner Brothers, 1970; "Frankenstein: The True Story," starring Leonard Whiting, Michael Sarrazin, David McCallum, and James Mason, MCA-TV, 1973; "Frankenstein and the Monster from Hell," starring Peter Cushing, Shane Briant, and David Prowse, Paramount, 1974; "Young Frankenstein," starring Mel Brooks, Gene Wilder, Peter Boyle, and Marty Feldman, Twentieth Century-Fox, 1974; "Frankenstein" (filmstrip; sound version, with guide), Listening Library, 1979.

Plays: H. M. Milner, *Frankenstein: or, The Man and the Monster* (two-act), Lacy's Acting Edition (London), c.1850; David Campton, *Frankenstein: A Gothic Thriller* (two-act), Garnet Miller, 1973; Tim J. Kelly, *Frankenstein* (two-act), Samuel French, 1974; *Frankenstein: The Play*, Clarke, Irwin, 1976.

In the black, rainy night, he wandered along deserted alleys, groping with his hands along the walls as if to find his way out of a maze. ■ (From *Frankenstein* by Mary Wollstonecraft Shelley. Adapted by Dale Carlson. Cover illustrated by Tom Nachreiner.)

Recordings: "Frankenstein" (phonodisc), dramatization, with sound effects and music, with Derek Young, John Franklyn, Pamela Mant, Peter O'Connel, and Glynnis Casson, directed by Christopher Casson, Spoken Arts, 1970; "Frankenstein" (phonotape), dramatization, with sound effects and music, directed by Christopher Casson, Spoken Arts, 1974; "Frankenstein" (taken from a broadcast of the CBS program "Suspense," November 3, 1952), starring Herbert Marshall, American Forces Radio and Television Service, 1976; "Frankenstein," read by James Mason, Caedmon Records, 1977; "Weird Circle" (contains Edgar Allan Poe's *The Tell-tale Heart* and *Frankenstein;* recorded from original radio broadcasts), Golden Age, 1978.

SIDELIGHTS: **August 30, 1797.** Born in London, England, the daughter of Mary Wollstonecraft, a writer known for her feminist views, and William Godwin, a philosopher and noted author. From an early age Shelley enjoyed the conversations of the literary guests in her father's home and was exposed to her father's large library where she read constantly. "It is not singular that, as the daughter of two persons of distinguished literary celebrity, I should very early in life have thought of writing. As a child I scribbled; and my favourite pastime, during the hours given me for recreation, was to 'write stories.' Still I had a dearer pleasure than this, which was the formation of castles in the air—the indulging in waking dreams—the following up trains of thought, which had for their subject the formation of a succession of imaginary incidents. My dreams

were at once more fantastic and agreeable than my writings. In the latter I was a close imitator—rather doing as others had done, than putting down the suggestions of my own mind. What I wrote was intended at least for one other eye—my childhood's companion and friend; but my dreams were all my own; I accounted for them to nobody; they were my refuge when annoyed—my dearest pleasure when free. . . .

". . . It was beneath the trees of the grounds belonging to our house, or on the bleak sides of the woodless mountains near, that my true compositions, the airy flights of my imagination, were born and fostered. I did not make myself the heroine of my tales. Life appeared to me too common-place an affair as regarded myself. I could not figure to myself that romantic woes or wonderful events would ever be my lot; but I was not confined to my own identity, and I could people the hours with creations far more interesting to me at that age, than my own sensations." [R. Glynn Grylls, *Mary Shelley: A Biography,* Oxford University Press, 1938.[1]]

Mother died during childbirth. Father remarried when Shelley was four years old.

June, 1812-March, 1814. Stayed with family friends in Scotland for health reasons. Met Percy Bysshe Shelley on one of her visits back to London.

July 28, 1814. Eloped with Percy Bysshe Shelley to France, where they began their life together without society's approval, because he was still legally married.

September 13, 1814. Returned to England, where they lived in poverty. When her husband went into hiding to avoid arrest from unsettled debts, Shelley wrote to him: "I am so out of spirits. I feel so lonely but we shall meet tomorrow so I will try to be happy— Grays Inn Gardens is I fear a dangerous place yet can you think of any other.

"I received your letter tonight. I wanted one for I had not received one for almost two days but do not think I mean anything by this my love—I know you took a long long walk yesterday so you could not write but I who am at home who do not walk out I could write to you all day love—

"How you reason and philosophize about love—do you know if I had been asked I could not have given one reason in its favour—yet I have as great an opinion as you concerning its exaltedness and love very tenderly to prove my theory—adieu for the present it has struck eight & in an hour or two I will wish you goodnight." [Frederick L. Jones, editor, *The Letters of Mary W. Shelley,* Volume I, University of Oklahoma Press, 1944.[2]]

The couple were avid readers, spending each day reading and studying. ". . . Read 'Madoc' all morning, Shelley out on business. He reads the 'Curse of Kehama' to us in the evening. . . ." [Mary Wollstonecraft (Godwin) Shelley, *Mary Shelley's Journal,* edited by Frederick L. Jones, University of Oklahoma Press, 1947.[3]]

February 22, 1815. Daughter born prematurely and died in March. ". . . Read and talk. Still think about my little baby—'tis hard, indeed, for a mother to lose a child. . . ."[3]

Settled in Bishopgate, where her second child, William, was born.

1816. Began writing *Frankenstein*. "In the summer . . . we visited Switzerland, and became the neighbours of Lord Byron. At first we spent our pleasant hours on the lake, or wandering on its shores; and Lord Byron . . . was the only one among us who put his thoughts upon paper. . . .

"But it proved a wet, ungenial [sic] summer, and incessant rain often confined us for days to the house. Some volumes of ghost stories, translated from the German into French, fell into our hands. . . .

"'We will each write a ghost story,' said Lord Byron; and his proposition was acceded to. . . .

"I busied myself *to think of a story*,—a story to rival those which had excited us to this task. One which would speak to the mysterious fears of our nature, and awaken thrilling horror—one to make the reader dread to look around, to curdle the blood, and quicken the beating of the heart. If I did not accomplish these things, my ghost story would be unworthy of its name. I thought and pondered—vainly. I felt that blank incapability of invention which is the greatest misery of authorship, when dull Nothing replies to our anxious invocations. *Have you thought of a story?* I was asked each morning, and each morning I was forced to reply with a mortifying negative.

"Many and long were the conversations between Lord Byron and Shelley, to which I was a devout but nearly silent listener. During one of these, various philosophical doctrines were discussed, and among others the nature of the principle of life, and whether there was any probability of its ever being discovered and communicated. They talked of the experiments of Dr. Darwin . . . who preserved a piece of vermicelli in a glass case, till by some extraordinary means it began to move with voluntary motion. Not thus, after all, would life be given. Perhaps a corpse would be re-animated; galvanism had given token of such things: perhaps the component parts of a creature might be manufactured, brought together, and enbued with vital warmth.

"Night waned upon this talk, and even the witching hour had gone by, before we retired to rest. When I placed my head on my pillow, I did not sleep, nor could I be said to think. My imagination, unbidden, possessed and guided me, gifting the successive images that arose in my mind with a vividness far beyond the usual bounds of reverie. I saw—with shut eyes, but acute mental vision,—I saw the pale student of unhallowed arts kneeling beside the thing he had put together. I saw the hideous phantasm of a man stretched out, and then, on the working of some powerful engine, show signs of life, and stir with an uneasy, half vital motion. Frightful must it be; for supremely frightful would be the effect of any human endeavour to mock the stupendous mechanism of the Creator of the world. His success would terrify the artist; he would rush away from his odious handwork, horror-stricken. He would hope that, left to itself, the slight spark of life which he had communicated would fade; that this thing, which had received such imperfect animation, would subside into dead matter; and he might sleep in the belief that the silence of the grave would quench for ever the transient existence of the hideous corpse which he had looked upon as the cradle of life. He sleeps; but he is awakened; he opens his eyes; behold the horrid thing stands at his bedside, opening his curtains, and looking on him with yellow, watery, but speculative eyes.

"I opened mine in terror. The idea so possessed my mind, that a thrill of fear ran through me, and I wished to exchange the ghastly image of my fancy for the realities around. I see them

(From *Frankenstein* by Mary Wollstonecraft Shelley. Illustrated by Nino Carbe.)

still; the very room, the dark *parquet,* the closed shutters, with the moonlight struggling through, and the sense I had that the glassy lake and white high Alps were beyond. I could not so easily get rid of my hideous phantom; still it haunted me. I must try to think of something else. I recurred to my ghost story,—my tiresome unlucky ghost story! O! if I could only contrive one which would frighten my reader as I myself had been frightened that night!

"Swift as light and as cheering was the idea that broke in upon me. 'I have found it! What terrified me will terrify others; and I need only describe the spectre which had haunted my midnight pillow.' On the morrow I announced that I had *thought of a story*. I began that day with the words, *It was on a dreary night of November,* making only a transcript of the grim terrors of my waking dream.

"At first I thought but of a few pages—of a short tale; but Shelley urged me to develope the idea at greater length. I certainly did not owe the suggestion of one incident, nor scarcely of one train of feeling, to my husband, and yet but for his incitement, it would never have taken the form in which it was presented to the world. . . ."[1]

December 10, 1816. Shelley's first wife died. Less than two weeks later, they legalized their marriage at St. Mildred's Church in London. ". . . A marriage takes place on the 30th of December, 1816. . . ."[3]

(From the movie "Young Frankenstein," starring Gene Wilder, Teri Garr, Marty Feldman and Cloris Leachman, a satire based on characters in the novel *Frankenstein.* Copyright © 1974 by Twentieth Century-Fox Film Corp.)

(From the movie "Bride of Frankenstein," starring Elsa Lanchester and Boris Karloff, based on the novel *Frankenstein.* Copyright 1935 by Universal Pictures Corp.)

(From the movie "Frankenstein Meets the Wolf Man," starring Lon Chaney, Jr. and Bela Lugosi. Copyright 1943 by Universal Pictures Co., Inc.)

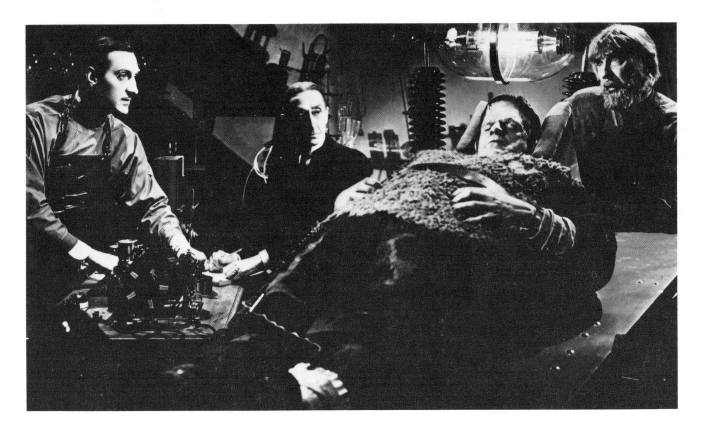

(From the movie "Son of Frankenstein," starring Basil Rathbone, Boris Karloff and Bela Lugosi, derived from the novel *Frankenstein.* Copyright 1939 by Universal Pictures Co., Inc.)

"A great fall of snow had taken place the night before, and the fields were of one uniform white."
■ (From *Frankenstein* by Mary Wollstonecraft Shelley. Edited and illustrated by Robert Andrew Parker.)

(From *Frankenstein* by Mary Wollstonecraft Shelley. Illustrated by Lynd Ward.)

"I THOUGHT THAT I HELD THE CORPSE OF MY DEAD MOTHER IN MY ARMS."

(From *The Annotated Frankenstein,* with an introduction and notes by Leonard Wolf. Illustrated by Marcia Huyette.)

1817. Moved to Marlow, where her third child, Clara Everina, was born. ". . . Our house is very political as well as poetical. . . . It is indeed a delightful place very fit for the luxurious literati who enjoy a good library—a beautiful garden and a delightful country surrounding it—"[2]

March, 1818. Moved to Italy for her husband's health. "We have at length arrived in Italy. After winding for several days through vallies & crossing mountains and passing [Mt.] Cenis we have arrived in this land of blue skies & pleasant fields. The fruit trees [are] all in bloom and the fields green with the growing corn—. . . .

". . . We live in our studious way. . . ."[2]

Daughter Clara died in September and son William died the following June [1819]. "You see by our hap how blind we mortals are when we go seeking after what we think our good— We came to Italy thinking to do Shelley's health good—but the Climate is not [by] any means warm enough to be of benefit to him & yet it is that that has destroyed my two children— We went from England comparatively prosperous & happy— I should return broken hearted & miserable— I never know one moments ease from the wretchedness and despair that possesses me— May you . . . never know what it is to lose two only & lovely children in one year—to watch their dying moments—& then at last to be left childless & for ever miserable. . . .

"I can assure you I am much changed—the world will never be to me again as it was—there was a life & freshness in it that is lost to me—on my last birthday when I was 21—I repined that time should fly so quickly and that I should grow older so quickly—this birthday—now I am 22—although the time since the last seems to have flown with speed of lightning—yet I rejoiced at that & only repined that I was not older—in fact I ought to have died on the 7th of June last—"[2]

November 12, 1819. Son, Percy Florence, born. ". . . I am very well—& the little boy also—he was born a small child but has grown so during this first fortnight that if his little face were not always the same one might almost think him a changed child—he takes after me—. . . .[2]

"I now begin a new year—may it be a happier one than the last unhappy one."[3]

"You cannot guess how busy & I may almost say now it is over uselessly busy I have been these last days . . . for 3 days we were without a servant for the child (chi è bello e grasso) now we have a German-Swiss who speaks Italian perfectly . . . so we are fortunate so far & now I think of beginning to read again. Study I cannot for I have no books & I may not call simple reading study for Papa is continually saying & writing that to read one book without others beside you to which you may refer is mere childs work—but still I hope now to get on with Latin & Spanish—. . . .

"I am well and so is the little boy who thrives surprisingly. . . . As it is for the first time in our lives we get on easily—our minds undisturbed by weekly bills & daily expenses & with a little care we expect to get the things into better order than they are.

"Shelley is tolerably well. The sunshine, however cold the air may be, agrees with me. . . . Do you not envy my luck, that, having begun Greek, an amiable, young, agreeable, and learned

Greek Prince comes every morning to give me a lesson of an hour and a-half?. . .

"I have finished the two 'Œdipi' with my Greek and am now half way through the 'Antigone.' He is also my pupil in English, though not very regular. . . ."[2]

Continued writing and working on a new novel, *Valperga.* "I get on with my occupation & hope to finish the rough transcript this month— I shall then give about a month to corrections & then I shall transcribe it— It has indeed been a child of mighty slow growth, since I first thought of it in our library at Marlow. I then wanted the body in which I might embody my spirit— The materials for this I found at Naples—but I wanted other books—nor did I begin it until a year afterwards at Pisa—it was again suspended during our stay at your house & continued again in the Baths— All the winter I did not touch it—but now it is in a state of great forwardness since I am at page 71 of the 3rd vol. It has indeed been a work of some labor since I have read & consulted a great many books—."[2]

July 8, 1822. Husband drowned in a boating accident. "Well here is my story—the last story I shall have to tell—all that might have been bright in my life is not despoiled— I shall live to improve myself, to take care of my child, & render myself worthy to join him. Soon my weary pilgrimage will begin—I rest now—but soon I must leave Italy—& then— there is an end of all but despair. . . . People used to call me lucky in my star. You see now how true such a prophecy is— I was fortunate in having fearlessly placed my destiny in the hands of one, who a superior being among men, a bright planetary spirit enshrined in an earthly temple, raised me to the height of happiness—so far am I now happy that I would not change my situation as His widow with that of the most prosperous woman in the world—. . . ."[2]

". . . For eight years I communicated, with unlimited freedom, with one whose genius, far transending mine, awakened and guided my thoughts. I conversed with him; rectified my errors of judgment; obtained new lights from him; and my mind was satisfied. Now I am alone—oh, how alone!. . . Well, I shall commence my task, commemorate the virtues of the only creature worth loving or living for. . . .

"I shall write his life, and thus occupy myself in the only manner from which I can derive consolation. . . . I must collect my materials, and then, in the commemoration of the divine virtues of [Shelley] I shall fulfil the only act of pleasure there remains for me. . . ."[3]

August, 1823. Returned to England. Novel *Valperga* and a dramatic adaptation of *Frankenstein* were well received. "I arrived Monday the 25th of August . . . I had an excellent passage of 11½ hours—a glassy sea and a contrary wind—the smoke of our fire was wafted right aft and streamed out behind us—but wind was of little consequence—the tide was with us—and though the engine gave a 'short uneasy motion' to the vessel, the water was so smooth that no one on board was sick and Persino played about the deck in high glee. . . .

"But lo and behold! I found myself famous!—'Frankenstein' had prodigious success as a drama and was about to be repeated for the 23rd night at the English Opera House. . . ."[2]

1824. Edited *Posthumous Poems,* a volume of unpublished poems of Percy Bysshe Shelley. "After all I spent a great deal of my time in solitude. I have been hitherto fully occupied in preparing Shelley's MS.—it is now complete, and the poetry alone will make a large volume. . . . A negociation is begun between Sir T. S.[helley; her father-in-law] and myself by which, on sacrificing a small part of my future expectations on the will, I shall ensure myself a sufficiency, for the present. . . . I have been obliged however as an indispensable preliminary, to suppress the—*Post*[*humous*] *Poems*—More than 300 copies had been sold so this is the less provoking, and I have been obliged to promise not to bring dear S.'s name before the public again during Sir. T.'s life. . . .''[2]

''I have just completed my 27th year; at such a time hope and youth are still in their prime, and the pains I feel, therefore, are ever alive and vivid within me. What shall I do? Nothing! I study, that passes the time. I write, at times that pleases me; though double sorrow comes when I feel that Shelley no longer reads and approves of what I write; besides, I have no great faith in my success. Composition is delightful, but if you do not expect the sympathy of your fellow creatures in what you write, the pleasure of writing is of short duration.''[3]

''I have not been . . . either in good health or good spirits lately—nor can I tell why, except that being early inoculated with a love of wandering and adventure, my monotonous present existence grows insurportably tedious. There is no hope nor any help, which ought to make me contented they say; yet I cannot be so;—I am told I might be worse off—that reflection redoubled my melancholy—I have been happy—I might have continued as I was, had I not been destined to experience every reverse of unkind fortune. These thoughts will not leave me— I detest England. . . .''[2]

''. . . What has my life been? What is it since I lost Shelley?— I have been alone—and worse— I had my father's fate for many a year a burthen pressing me to the earth—and I had Percy's [her son] education and welfare to guard over—and in all this I had no one friendly hand stretched out to support me. Shut out from even the possibility of making such an impression as my personal merits might occasion—without a human being to aid, or encourage or even to advise me, I toiled on my weary solitary way. . . .'' [Frederick L. Jones, editor, *The Letters of Mary W. Shelley*, Volume II, University of Oklahoma Press, 1944.[4]]

1829. Shelley's writing included articles and stories for *Westminster Review, The Keepsake* and other periodicals as well as her novels and editing her husband's works. ''. . . Routine occupation is the medicine of my mind. I write the 'Lives' in

(From the movie "Frankenstein," starring Mae Clarke and Boris Karloff. Copyright 1931 by Universal Pictures Corp.)

the morning. I read novels and memoirs of an evening—such is the variety of my days and time flies so swift, that days form weeks and weeks form months, before I am aware. . . .

"My heart and soul is bound up in Percy. My race is run. I hope absolutely nothing except that when he shall be older and I a little richer to leave a solitude, very unnatural to anyone and peculiarly disagreeable to me. . . ."[3]

1839. ". . . I almost think that my present occupation will end in a fit of illness. I am editing Shelley's Poems, and writing notes for them. I desire to do Shelley honour in the notes to the best of my knowledge and ability; for the rest, they are or are not well written; it little matters to me which. Would that I had more literary vanity. . . ."[2]

February, 1841. Son graduated from Trinity College. He asked his mother to travel abroad with him. ". . . It seems as if I were never to be stationary—I, who long so for a home. I am going for a few months abroad with Percy—perhaps as far as Milan. . . ."[4]

In Sorrento, Italy, Shelley wrote: "This place is quite adorable. It has but one drawback . . . shared by every other—that we have no money for excursions & that therefore Percy finds life very monotonous—& longs to be away. When once I have a home in England & feel settled I shall be content—& I trust all our journeying has done Percy good— It seemed to me very necessary to get him out of England when we left it. Things have not gone as I hoped & thought I had a right to expect— but still he has seen various scenes—& mingled in society— & might much more but for his distaste to the same. . . ."[4] Returned to England.

1844. Accounts of her Continental travels appeared in two volumes.

1848. Son married. Shelley lived with her son and daughter-in-law.

February 1, 1851. Died in London. Buried in Bournemouth, England. "God and good angels guard us! surely this world, stored outwardly with shapes and influences of beauty and good, is peopled in its intellectual life by myriads of loving spirits that mould our thoughts to good, influence beneficially the course of events, and minister to the destiny of man. Whether the beloved dead make a portion of this company I dare not guess, but that such exist I feel—far off, when we are worldly, evil, selfish; drawing near and imparting joy and sympathy when we rise to noble thoughts and disinterested action. Such surely gather round one on such an evening, and make part of that atmosphere of love, so hushed, so soft, on which the soul reposes and is blest."[3]

FOR MORE INFORMATION SEE: Lucy M. Rossetti, *Mrs. Shelley,* "Eminent Women Series," edited by J. H. Ingram, Allen, 1890, reprinted, Norwood, 1975; *The Romance of Mary W. Shelley, John Howard Payne and Washington Irving,* [Boston], 1907, reprinted, Norwood, 1978; William Godwin, *The Elopement of Percy Bysshe Shelley and Mary Wollstonecraft Godwin,* [Boston?], 1911, reprinted, Folcroft, 1977; *Letters of Mary W. Shelley (Mostly Unpublished),* (introduction and notes by Henry H. Harper), [Boston], 1918, reprinted, Norwood, 1976; Richard Church, *Mary Shelley,* Gerald Howe, 1928, reprinted, Alden, 1978; Glynn R. Grylls, *Mary Shelley: A Biography,* Oxford University Press, 1938, reprinted, Folcroft,

(From *Frankenstein* by Mary Wollstonecraft Shelley. Illustrated by Everett Henry.)

1973; Walter Sidney Scott, editor, *Shelley at Oxford: Early Correspondence of P. B. Shelley with His Friend, T. J. Hogg,* Golden Cockerel Press, 1944, reprinted, Norwood, 1977; W. S. Scott, editor, *Harriet & Mary: Being the Relations between Percy Bysshe Shelley, Harriet Shelley, Mary Shelley, and Thomas Jefferson Hogg,* Golden Cockerel Press, 1944, reprinted, Norwood, 1978.

(For children) Bridget MacCarthy, *The Later Women Novelists, 1744-1818,* Cork University, 1947; Muriel Spark, *Child of Light; A Reassessment of Mary Wollstonecraft Shelley,* Tower Bridge, 1951, reprinted, Folcroft, 1976; M. Spark and Derek Stanford, editors, *My Best Mary; The Selected Letters of Mary Wollstonecraft Shelley,* Roy, 1953, reprinted Folcroft, 1976; William A. Walling, *Mary Shelley,* Twayne, 1972; (for children) Margaret Leighton, *Shelley's Mary: A Life of Mary Godwin Shelley,* Farrar, 1973; Noel B. Gerson, *Daughter of Earth and Water: A Biography of Mary Wollstonecraft Shelley,* Morrow, 1973; George B. Smith, *Shelley: A Critical Biography,* Haskell, 1974; "Mary Shelley: In the Shadow of Frankenstein," *Ms.,* February, 1975; Jane Dunn, *Moon in Eclipse: A Life of Mary Shelley,* St. Martin's, 1978; (for children) Janet Harris, *The Woman Who Created Frankenstein: A Portrait of Mary Shelley,* Harper, 1979; Bonnie R. Nuemann, *The Lonely Muse: A Critical Biography of Mary Wollstonecraft Shelley,* Humanities, 1979.

SHERMAN, D(enis) R(onald)   1934-

BRIEF ENTRY: Born December 20, 1934, in Calcutta, India. Sherman, a certified telegraph operator began his career as a radio officer with Marconi Marine in England, and since 1956, has been station foreman for Rhodesia Railways in Africa. Also an author, Sherman has written adult books like *Old Mali and the Boy* (Little, Brown, 1964) and *Into the Noonday Sun* (Little, Brown, 1966). His first book for young people was *Brothers of the Sea* (Little, Brown, 1966), the story of a young boy who befriends a dolphin. Sherman's later books include a fast-paced Western novel, *Ryan* (Ace Books, 1973) and *The Lion's Paw* (Doubleday, 1975), the story of a young African boy who frees a lion from a trap and must face the difficulties of loving and losing a wild thing. *Address:* Box 22, Palapye, Bechuanaland, Africa. *For More Information See: New York Times Book Review,* September 25, 1966; *Times Literary Supplement,* October 6, 1966; *Publishers Weekly,* April 9, 1973; *Kirkus Reviews,* May 1, 1975; *Contemporary Authors,* Volumes 13-16, revised, Gale, 1975.

SIBERELL, Anne

PERSONAL: Born in Los Angeles, Calif.; daughter of Estill Brown (in business) and Bernice (a writer and musician; maiden name, Cornell) Hicks; married G. Peter Siberell; children: Peter, Brian, Justin. *Education:* Attended University of California, Los Angeles, 1948-50; Chouinard Art Institute, B.F.A., 1953; attended Silvermine College of Art, 1960-62, and College of San Mateo, 1968. *Home and office:* 1041 La Cuesta Rd., Hillsborough, Calif. 94010.

CAREER: Victor Gruen Architects, Los Angeles, Calif., 1954; Walt Disney Productions, Burbank, Calif., assistant art editor of publications, 1955-59; Publication Services, art director, 1960-64; free-lance artist, 1964-66. Member of faculty at Silvermine College of Art, 1966-68, Martin Luther King, Jr. Center, San Mateo, 1969-70; guest lecturer at California State College, Bakersfield, and San Jose State University, 1977; adult education teacher, 1969-75. *Member:* Los Angeles Printmaking Society, California Society of Printmakers, Pacific Center for the Book Arts, California Society of Printmakers. *Awards, honors: Our Friend the Atom* was a selection of American Institute of Graphic Arts, 1955-57; award from Los Angeles Rounce and Coffin Club, 1972, for *Lamb, Said the Lion, I Am Here.*

EXHIBITIONS—One woman shows: Garden Cafe Gallery, Burlingame, Calif., 1969, 1980; College of Notre Dame, Belmont, Calif., 1970; Nong Gallery, San Francisco, Calif., 1971; John Bolles Gallery Print Room, San Francisco, Calif., 1972; Marquoit Galleries, San Francisco, Calif., 1974; Tyson Gallery, San Francisco, Calif., 1976; Palo Alto Cultural Center, Calif., 1977; Zara Gallery, San Francisco, Calif., 1977; Bakersfield College Gallery, Bakersfield, Calif., 1977; Stuart Gallery, Berkeley, Calif., 1978; Art Institute of Chicago, Ill., 1981; Montalvo Center for the Arts, Saratoga, 1981; San Francisco Conservatory Gallery, 1982.

ANNE SIBERELL

(From *Feast of Thanksgiving* by June Behrens. Illustrated by Anne Siberell.)

Group shows: Everson Museum, Syracuse, N.Y., 1967; National Arts Clubs, New York, N.Y., 1968; Palace of the Legion of Honor, San Francisco, Calif., 1969; De Saisset Art Gallery, Santa Clara, Calif., 1971; Albany Institute of History and Art, N.Y., 1973; Los Angeles Municipal Gallery, Calif., 1973; Tusculum College, Greenville, Tenn., 1975; La Mamelle Art Center, San Francisco, Calif., 1975, 1976; Council of Ely House, London, England, 1975; Municipal Gallery, Tronheim and Oslo, Norway, 1975; ADI Gallery, San Francisco, Calif., 1975; Royal College of Art, London, England, 1976; Art in Embassies, Washington, D.C., 1976; Union Gallery, San Jose State University, Calif., 1976; Mandeville Art Gallery, University of California, San Diego, Calif., 1977; California State University, Los Angeles, Calif., 1977; Marshall-Myers Gallery, San Francisco, Calif., 1978; World Print Gallery, San Francisco, Calif., 1980; Cal State University, Hayward, Calif., 1980.

Permanent collections: Oakland Museum, Calif.; Arthur Andersen & Co., San Francisco, Calif.; Banker's Trust, San Francisco, Calif.; Bankamericard, San Francisco, Calif.; Republic Bank of New York and other collections.

WRITINGS—Self-illustrated children's books: (With Eastwick) *Rainbow over All*, McKay, 1967; (with Mark Taylor) *Lamb, Said the Lion, I Am Here*, Golden Gate Junior Books, 1971; (with Johanna Johnston) *Who Found America?*, Childrens Press, 1973; (with June Behrens) *Feast of Thanksgiving*, Childrens Press, 1974; (with Behrens) *Martin Luther King, Jr.: The Story of a Dream*, Childrens Press, 1979; *Houses: Shelters from Prehistoric Times to Today*, Holt, 1979.

Illustrator: Walt Disney and Heinz Haber, *Our Friend the Atom*, Simon & Schuster, 1956; John and Patricia Beatty, *A Donkey for the King (Horn Book* honor list), Macmillan, 1966; Jean Montgomery, *The Wrath of the Coyote*, Morrow, 1968; Montgomery, *Passage to Drake's Bay*, Morrow, 1972; Marjorie Thayer and Elizabeth Emanuel, *Climbing Sun: The Story of a Hopi Indian Boy*, Dodd, 1980; *Whale in the Sky*, Dutton, 1982.

WORK IN PROGRESS: A picture book.

SIDELIGHTS: ''I began making my own books at about age six. My very short stories were typed, then I drew pictures to go along with the words. I made end papers and sewed book covers from discarded wallpaper sample books. I sewed pages into signatures and glued the parts together.

"My involvement with books may have come from my mother's writing. She interviewed published authors for *Writers Markets & Methods* magazine in Los Angeles.

"In art school I concentrated on illustration and design, later worked for an architectural firm.

"When I went to Walt Disney Productions as assistant art editor I learned about magazine and book production, and co-illustrated *Our Friend the Atom.*

"When I moved to the East Coast I illustrated books for various publishers, usually in woodcut. Then back on the West Coast I worked with an editor at Golden Gate Junior Books who encouraged me to write *Houses: Shelters from Prehistoric Times to Today*—a subject our youngest son was interested in. I wrote the story [*Whale in the Sky*] based on tales from the Pacific Northwest, illustrated with woodcuts.

"I use printmaking in making paper construction and have exhibited in the United States and abroad. I make one of a kind works that are usually shown in university and art school libraries.

"I am interested in the communication of ideas through books, and enjoy seeing children enjoying books. And it is always nice to hear when children have seen books I have had a part in, not only in local libraries but also in a midwestern town, or a city in Australia. I enjoy talking with children, and encouraging them to read, write and draw."

It is Siberell's goal "to combine all of her experiences in different mediums and communicate these in book form. But, not necessarily in published books." [*Boutique & Villager,* Hillsborough & Burlingame, August 6, 1981.[1]]

In discussing her technique, Siberell noted: "I've always been mastering new materials since I'm pretty much self-taught. And it's fun to use new tools, exciting tools. Now I can go to a hardware store and really get involved. Right now I'm getting into lighting, a whole new direction, to make the light a part of the work, too.

". . . The needs of the piece determine the tools. It all starts from the work. For example, I'm using an oven in San Francisco—think of your kitchen oven magnified twenty times—to do things with plexiglass, throwing it around, wearing asbestos gloves, all of that—a situation I'd never be involved in except that the work I'm doing requires it. These pieces started with that need to make the piece a unified whole. . . . It's a very exciting process because I somehow know what it's going to be as I'm working and it gradually becomes that. It's exhilarating, like being on top of a mountain.

". . . I'm fascinated with changing one material to another, like burning or sand-blasting, creating new surfaces. Getting from one thing into something totally different, a progression . . . Hemingway said he felt most alive when he was in danger, and that's the way I feel about materials, pushing the materials. I'm most excited when I'm at the edge of strain a material will take, when I'm in danger of losing it. I like pushing the stuff to the breaking point, tearing paper, stressing it, pressing through it, melting the plastic. . . . And then putting it back together. That's another one of the important themes in my work, pulling things back together, tearing the paper and bringing it back, using staples, chains, laces, ropes, a lot of things that pull back together, making a piece whole. There's something about seeing a thing outside its normal context, something about the

artist's ability to bring things back together in a surprising way, not in a prescribed way." [*Currant* (art magazine), Volume I, #6, February, March, April, 1976.[2]]

When asked what the purpose of her work was, Siberell responded: "Art is enough in itself. I'm the most satisfied when I do something for myself. When I was younger I used to understand how a painter painted something, but that wasn't enough. I wanted to get into the painting, to be a part of it, escape into it. Now, the art is enough.

". . . I've always considered myself an artist. I've worked at it eight hours a day ever since I can remember. And I've always experimented. . . . You never know until you try. I'm happy with my work. My art is all over the world, in museums. I'd like a New York show, of course.

"And now I'm thinking about some performance pieces, trying to get some action into the work. Something like the beauty in boiling oatmeal, getting the audience to see that . . . that sort of thing. I want to keep working, keep forcing the materials."[2]

Siberell is best known for the woodcuts that illustrate her books, but uses other media as well, including pen and ink. Her studio contains a book press, an etching press, and a proof press and she prefers to make her own paper by hand, a durable paper that will stand the test of time.

She enjoys teaching, both adults and children, and has presented slide programs. Siberell's work is included in the Kerlan Collection at the University of Minnesota and the De Grummond Collection at the University of Southern Mississippi.

FOR MORE INFORMATION SEE: Currant art magazine, Volume I, #6, February, March, April, 1976; *San Mateo Times,* December 15, 1980.

SMUCKER, Barbara (Claassen) 1915-

PERSONAL: Born September 1, 1915, in Newton, Kan.; daughter of Cornelius W. (a banker) and Addie (Lander) Claassen; married Donovan E. Smucker (a minister and professor of religion), January 21, 1939; children: Timothy, Thomas, Rebecca. *Education:* Kansas State University, B.S., 1936; further study at Rosary College, 1963-65, and University of Waterloo, 1975-77. *Politics:* Democrat. *Religion:* Mennonite. *Home:* 57 McDougall Rd., Waterloo, Ontario, Canada N2L 2W4. *Office:* Renison College, University of Waterloo, Waterloo, Ontario, Canada N2L 3G2.

CAREER: Harper, Kan., public schools, high school teacher of English and journalism, 1937-38; *Evening Kansas Republican,* Newton, Kan., reporter, 1939-41; Ferry Hall School, Lake Forest, Ill., teacher, 1960-63; Lake Forest Bookstore, Lake Forest, bookseller, 1963-67; Kitchener Public Library, Kitchener, Ontario, children's librarian, 1969-77; Renison College, Waterloo, Ontario, head librarian, 1977—. Has also worked as an interviewer for Gallup Poll. *Member:* Children's Reading Roundtable, American Association of University Women, Canadian Association of University Women, Canadian Society of Children's Authors, Illustrators and Performers, Canadian Writers Union. *Awards, honors:* Brotherhood Award, National Conference of Christians and Jews, 1980, for *Underground to Canada,* which was also selected by the Children's Book Centre in 1978 as one of the fifty best books of all time in Canada;

BARBARA SMUCKER

children's literary award, Canada Council, 1980, Ruth Schwartz Foundation Award, 1980, both for *Days of Terror;* distinguished service award for children's literature, Kansas State University, 1980, Senior Honorary Fellow, Renison College, 1982.

WRITINGS—All for children: *Henry's Red Sea,* Herald Press, 1955; *Cherokee Run,* Herald Press, 1957; *Wigwam in the City,* Dutton, 1966, published as *Susan,* Scholastic Book Services, 1978; *Underground to Canada,* Clarke, Irwin, 1977, published as *Runaway to Freedom: A Story of the Underground Railway,* Harper, 1978; *Days of Terror,* Clarke, Irwin, 1979. Contributor of articles to *American Educator Encyclopedia.*

WORK IN PROGRESS: A children's book with an Amish theme.

SIDELIGHTS: Smucker's writing career began during grade school in Kansas: "My first novel was written with a girl friend. We decided to bury it so it would always be a secret. I was in grade eight at the time." [Taken from an article entitled "Barbara Smucker," by *The Children's Book Centre* (Toronto, Canada), 1977.[1]]

After college, she worked briefly as a high school teacher until she joined the staff of a small Kansas newspaper, where she met her husband, a Mennonite minister and professor of religion during an interview.

Her first two books for children, historical accounts of the Mennonites, were written to help Mennonite children understand their heritage. Her book, *Days of Terror,* about a Mennonite family forced to leave Russia because of religious persecution, combined history with her personal interests. "I felt closer to the characters in *Days of Terror* than in any of the other books I wrote, because some of my relatives experienced the same thing."[1]

While working as a librarian at the Kitchener Public Library in Canada, Smucker became aware of a lack of historical books about slavery. "Kids used to come into the library to do research on slavery, but there weren't many good books, and none which told about the blacks in Canada."[1]

A trip to the Dresden Museum in Canada cemented her intention to write about the "underground railroad." "Slaves who had escaped to Canada had built a house, a saw mill and a chapel for other black slaves who would follow. For the first time in their lives, they knew they'd be free."[1] *Underground to Canada* has been published in various languages in Tokyo, Vienna, Copenhagen, and Montreal.

About her writing, which she now combines with her work as head librarian of Renison College in Ontario, she says: "I really get involved in writing. Sometimes I write steadily for an entire weekend, stopping only for sleep and food. Then there are the stretches between books. Such times make me uneasy."[1]

Smucker tries to produce a complete draft before she rewrites. "If you stop to rewrite, you never get through the story. Some chapters read very well, some have to be rewritten, and others are thrown out altogether."[1]

FOR MORE INFORMATION SEE: In Review, Fall, 1977; *New York Times Book Review,* April 30, 1978; *Canadian Children's Literature,* No.22, 1981; *Who's Who in America,* 42nd edition, 1982-83.

JUDIT STANG

She looked so woe begone that the men could not help but feel sorry for her. ■ (From *Once-a-Year Witch* by Judy Varga. Illustrated by the author.)

STANG, Judit   1921-1977
(Judy Stang, Judy Varga)

PERSONAL: Born August 14, 1921, in Hungary; died August 28, 1977; daughter of Varga and Cecilia (Valdmari) Jeno; married Soren Stang (now an executive), June 27, 1947; children: Erik. *Education:* Studied at Hungarian Royal School of Commercial Art, 1939, and Alma College, St. Thomas, Ontario, Canada, 1942. *Religion:* High Episcopalian. *Residence:* Montego Bay, Jamaica, West Indies. *Agent:* Mary Gerard, 8 Jane St., New York, N.Y. 10014.

CAREER: National Film Board of Canada, Ottawa, Ontario, artist, 1942-45; free-lance author and artist, beginning 1945.

WRITINGS—All under name Judy Varga; all for children; all self-illustrated: *Gremlins on the Job,* [Canada], 1942; *The Dragon Who Liked to Spit Fire,* Morrow, 1961; *Miss Lollipop's Lion,* Morrow, 1963; *Pig in the Parlor,* Morrow, 1963; *The Sociable Seal,* Morrow, 1965; *The Crow Who Came to Stay,* Morrow, 1967; *The Puppy Who Liked to Chew Things,* Morrow, 1968; *Janko's Wish,* Morrow, 1969; *Let's Think about Time,* Holt, 1969; *Magic Wall,* Morrow, 1970; *The Monster behind Black Rock,* Morrow, 1971; *The Mare's Egg,* Morrow, 1972; *Once-*a-Year Witch, Morrow, 1973; *Battle of the Wind Gods,* Morrow, 1974; *Circus Cannonball,* Morrow, 1975. Also author of *Who Lives Here* for Wonder Books.

Under name Judy Stang: *The Pet in the Jar* (juvenile; self-illustrated), Western Publishing, 1975.

Illustrator; under name Judy Stang: Peter Stillman, *That Happy Feeling of Thank You,* C. R. Gibson, 1964; (with Leslie Gray) *The Magic Realm of Fairy Tales,* Western Publishing, 1968; Mary E. Boyd, *What Is Home,* C. R. Gibson, 1969; Betty R. Wright, *This Room Is Mine: A Story about Sharing,* Western Publishing, 1979. Also illustrator of *Mother Goose* for Wonder Books.

Books, like proverbs, receive their chief value from the stamp and esteem of ages through which they have passed.

—Sir William Temple

STEPP, Ann   1935-

PERSONAL: Born July 20, 1935, in Headrick, Okla; daughter of William W. (a postmaster) and Anna Juanita (a postmistress; maiden name, Ragon) Stepp. *Education:* University of Oklahoma, B.S., 1957; Chapman College, M.A., 1971; also attended Texas Christian University, 1956, University of California, Los Angeles, 1969, California State University, Long Beach, 1969, California State University, Fullerton, 1974-77, and University of Southern California. *Home:* 12758 Ascot Dr., Garden Grove, Calif. 92640. *Office:* Lampson Junior High School, 10851 East Lampson, Garden Grove, Calif. 92640.

CAREER: Lampson Junior High, Garden Grove, Calif., teacher of life science, 1957—. Member of the board of directors, Aquanga Wildlife Reserve Society, 1979—. *Member:* American Cetacean Society, Authors Guild, National Science Teacher's Association, Parent-Teacher Association (honorary member).

WRITINGS—All for children: *Setting Up a Science Project* (illustrated by Polly Bolian), Prentice-Hall, 1966; *The Story of Radioactivity* (illustrated by James E. Barry), Harvey House, 1971; *Grunion: Fish out of Water* (illustrated by Anne Lewis), Harvey House, 1971; *A Silkworm Is Born,* Sterling, 1972.

(From *Setting Up a Science Project* by Ann Stepp. Illustrated by Polly Bolian.)

ANN STEPP

WORK IN PROGRESS: Life with Rhoda, Gigi: The California Gray Whale, The Pundits, The Elm Tree, and *Bill Cosby: A Comedian Who Educates.*

STILL, James   1906-

PERSONAL: Born July 16, 1906, in LaFayette, Ala.; son of J. Alex (a veterinarian) and Lonie (Lindsey) Still. *Education:* Lincoln Memorial University, A.B., 1929; Vanderbilt University, M.A., 1930; University of Illinois, B.S., 1931. *Home address:* Wolfpen Creek, Mallie, Ky. 41836. *Agent:* International Creative Management, 40 West 57th St., New York, N.Y. 10019. *Office address:* Drawer T, Hindman, Ky. 41822.

CAREER: Hindman Settlement School, Hindman, Ky., librarian, 1932-39, 1952-62; free-lance writer, 1939-41, 1946-51, 1971—; Morehead State University, Morehead, Ky., associate professor of English, 1962-70. *Military service:* U.S. Army Air Forces, 1941-45; served in Africa and the Middle East.

MEMBER: Kentucky Humanities Council. *Awards, honors:* MacDowell Colony fellowship, 1938; O. Henry Memorial Prize, 1939, for short story, "Bat Flight"; Southern Authors Award from Southern Women's National Democratic Organization, 1940, for *River of Earth;* Guggenheim fellowships, 1941-42,

1946-47; fiction award from American Academy of Arts and Letters, 1947; Litt.D. from Berea College, 1973; L.H.D. from Lincoln Memorial University, 1974; Litt.D. from Morehead State University, 1978; Litt.D. from University of Kentucky, 1979; Weatherford Award for Appalachian Writing, 1978; Marjorie Peabody Waite Award from the American Academy of Arts and Letters, 1979; James Still fellowships for Advanced Study in Humanities and Social Sciences established by the University of Kentucky, 1980; James Still scholarships established by Morehead State University, 1981; Milne Award from Kentucky Arts Council, 1981; Phi Beta Kappa.

WRITINGS: Hounds on the Mountain (poems), Viking, 1937, 1965; *River of Earth* (novel), Viking, 1940, University Press of Kentucky, 1977; *On Troublesome Creek* (stories), Viking, 1941; *Way Down Yonder on Troublesome Creek* (juvenile; illustrated by Janet McCaffery), Putnam, 1974; *The Wolfpen Rusties: Appalachian Riddles and Gee-Haw Whimmy-Diddles* (juvenile; illustrated by J. McCaffery), Putnam, 1975; *Pattern of a Man* (stories), Gnomon Press, 1976; *Jack and the Wonder Beans* (juvenile; illustrated by Margot Tomes), Putnam, 1976; *Sporty Creek: A Novel about an Appalachian Boyhood,* Putnam, 1977; *The Run for the Elbertas* (stories), University Press of Kentucky, 1980.

Work represented in anthologies, including *O. Henry Memorial Prize Stories,* edited by Harry Hanson, Doubleday, 1939; *O. Henry Memorial Prize Stories,* edited by Hershall Brickell,

Doubleday, 1937, 1938, 1939, 1941; *The Yale Review Anthology,* edited by Wilbur Cross and Helen MacAfee, Yale University Press, 1942; *The Best American Short Stories,* edited by Martha Foley, Houghton, 1946, 1950, 1952; *Twenty-Three Modern Stories,* edited by Barbara Howes, Random House, 1963; *The World of Psychoanalysis,* edited by C. B. Levitas, Braziller, 1966; and *From the Mountain,* edited by Helen White and Redding S. Sugg, Jr., Memphis State University Press, 1972. Contributor of stories and poems to popular magazines and literary journals, including *Atlantic, Esquire, Nation, New Republic, Saturday Evening Post, Yale Review, Poetry, Virginia Quarterly Review,* and *Sewanee Review.*

WORK IN PROGRESS: Journeys to the Sun, a travel book based on his ten winters in Yucatan, Guatamala, Belize, El Salvador and Honduras.

SIDELIGHTS: ''There were ten children in our family, five boys and five girls. Our father was both farmer and 'horse doctor.' A horse doctor is a veterinarian with little formal training. We attended the school at LaFayette, walking the two miles in all weathers, and we cultivated our fields during the growing seasons. Large families were the rule among us and my uncles and aunts and many cousins on my mother's side of the family lived on nearby farms. The Stills, fully as numerous, were not much farther away. I recall great Sunday dinners, barbecues on the fourth of July, picnics on Hootlocka Creek, the frequent visiting among us. We were blessed with

JAMES STILL

And the high tall woman said, "He hain't come in yet, and woe when he does. He eats tadwhackers the likes of you. Boiled, fried, or baked in a pie. Any which way when he's hungry."

Now, Jack wasn't easily frightened, and he said, "Old Sister, I'm hungry myself. What's a-cooking?"

(From *Jack and the Wonder Beans* by James Still. Illustrated by Margot Tomes.)

loving grandparents, three of whom lived until I was of age. They gave us a sense of the past we might not have gained otherwise. My maternal grandmother's first husband was killed in the Civil War. My grandfather on my father's side lost a finger in the conflict.

"There were three books in our home: *The Holy Bible, Anatomy of the Horse,* and *Cyclopedia of Universal Knowledge.* The *Cyclopedia* opened up a world of wonders to me as soon as I learned to read. I mastered fifty Arabic words, and a like number of several other languages. It introduced me to the great poets. And there I learned how to prune an apple tree, dehorn a cow, parse a sentence, and tell fortunes. By the age of nine I had a smattering of knowledge of many arcane subjects. In my eleventh year we moved into the Chattahoochee Valley, on the Alabama side of the river, into the village of Shawmut. In the town's small library I encountered Honore Balzac's *Father Goriot* and became aware I could experience more lives than one through the world of books.

"After high school, I attended a college for Appalachian youth near Cumberland Gap, Tennessee, working out my expenses in a rock quarry while not in class, and as a janitor by night. Following other schooling on scholarships, I joined the staff of the Hindman Settlement School on Troublesome Creek in the mountains of Kentucky. Among my duties was the operation of the library. Once, visiting in a primitive home, a small child brought the single book they owned to me and said, 'Teach me to read.' It was a golden request, one not to be denied. I was soon spending one day a week delivering books

on foot to schools in remote hollows. Approaching the play yard I would usually hear the cry, 'Here comes the book boy!' Teachers called me the 'foot mobile.'

"These were the years of economic depression in the 1930s and the Hindman Settlement had little money. I had none. Only during the last three years of a six-year stint could they pay me a small amount. My average income for six years was six cents a day.

"In 1939 I moved into a log house built during pioneer days on a farm between the waters of Dead Mare Branch and Wolfpen Creek on Little Carr Creek. I grew most of my food, tramped the wooded mountains and high fields, and took part in the life of the isolated neighborhood. And there I wrote poems and short stories and a novel. When necessity compelled, I went away and taught school for a while. In time my interest in primitive peoples took me to Central America for ten winters to study the Mayan Indians and their mysteriously abandoned cities.

"When I moved into the ancient log house on Little Carr Creek I had expected to stay a single summer. I have remained forty-two years, being away only for periods of teaching, travel abroad, and overseas duty in Africa with the U.S. Army during World War II. I am still here.

"I shall not leave these prisoning hills
Though they topple their barren heads to level earth
And the forests slide uprooted out of the sky.
Though the waters of Troublesome, of Trace Fork,
Of Sand Lick rise in a single body to glean the valleys,
To drown lush pennyroyal, to unravel rail fences;
Though the sun-ball breaks the ridges into dust
And burns its strength into the blistered rock
I cannot leave. I cannot go away.

"Being of these hills, being one with the fox
Stealing into the shadows, one with the new-born foal,
The lumbering ox drawing green beech logs to mill,
One with the destined feet of man climbing and
   descending,
And one with death rising to bloom again, I cannot go.
Being of these hills I cannot pass beyond."

FOR MORE INFORMATION SEE: Stanley J. Kunitz and Howard Haycraft, editors, *Twentieth Century Authors,* H. W. Wilson, 1942, first supplement, 1955; Thomas S. Ford, editor, *Southern Appalachian Region,* University of Kentucky Press, 1962; Frank N. Magill, editor, *Cyclopedia of Literary Characters,* Harper, 1963; Dean Cadle, "Man on Troublesome," *Yale Review,* Winter, 1968; "An Interview with James Still," *Appalachian Journal,* Winter, 1979; Fred Chappell, "The Seamless Vision of James Still," *Appalachian Journal,* Spring, 1981; Rebecca L. Briley, "River of Earth: Myth Consciousness in the Works of James Still," *Appalachian Heritage,* Fall, 1981.

Child of the pure, unclouded brow
And dreaming eyes of wonder!
Though time be fleet and I and thou
Are half a life asunder,
Thy loving smile will surely hail
The love-gift of a fairy tale.

—Lewis Carroll
(pseudonym of Charles Lutwidge Dodgson)

FRANK STILLEY

STILLEY, Frank 1918-

PERSONAL: Born April 18, 1918, in Wardville, Okla.; son of William Frank (a railroad agent) and Mabel (Watson) Stilley; married Joy Turner (a writer and editor for Associated Press), September 3, 1943; children: Brenn, Gay. *Education:* University of Oklahoma, A.B., 1942. *Home:* 254-13 75th Ave., Glen Oaks, N.Y. 11004.

CAREER: Shawnee News-Star, Shawnee, Okla., managing editor, 1942-43; Associated Press, New York, N.Y., reporter, writer, editor, 1943-65; media relations director for New York firms, Dudley-Anderson-Yutzy, 1965-69, Partners for Growth, Inc., 1969-71; independent public relations consultant in New York, 1971-72; media relations director for American Can Co., New York, 1972-74; writer and independent public relations consultant, 1974—. *Member:* Society of Professional Journalists, New York. *Awards, honors:* The Child Study Association named the following as Children's Books of the Year: *The $100,000 Rat: And Other Animal Heroes for Human Health,* 1975, and *Here Is Your Career: Veterinarian,* 1976.

WRITINGS—Of interest to young people; all published by Putnam: *The $100,000 Rat: And Other Animal Heroes for Human Health,* 1975; *Here Is Your Career: Veterinarian,* 1976; *The Search: Our Quest for Intelligent Life in Outer Space,* 1977; *Here Is Your Career: Airline Pilot,* 1978. Contributor to popular magazines. Reviewer of books and contributor to the Associated Press.

WORK IN PROGRESS: A book for young people on careers in the food service and restaurant business for Putnam.

SIDELIGHTS: "I strive my best to make my books exciting, informative and entertaining—even downright fun—to read. Learning *can* be made enjoyable. My hope is to capture the attention and fancy of readers, young or adult, in such a way that they are eager to see what comes next. And when they've finished a book, I'd like for them to wish there had been still more of it, from the sheer pleasure of reading and learning.

"This earth and the great universe around it are full of wondrous, exciting, enchanting and even awesome things and events. Nature is a stunning and never-ceasing provider of mysteries and puzzles. The more we study nature the more its grandeur and majesty are perceived. At the same time we glimpse that there is still far more to know. Will mankind ever know all?

"Likewise, the works of men and women can be marvels to behold, even in routine occupations or professions. To me it is most fulfilling to convey to others as fully as I can, especially to young people yet undecided on careers, both the pleasures and problems relating to what people *do* in this world, *what* they've learned, *how* they learned it and what they *hope* to learn or do in the future.

"It seems especially important to me that young men and women, from grade school on up, have available books which will help them in making a choice as to their life's work. I want them to know precisely what the rewards can be, as well as what aspects of a given career may make it undesirable to them.

"I still seek to make the book enjoyable reading and a simultaneous *learning* process—covering everything from a knowledge of everyday work functions to the astounding depths of science—whether the books are about biomedical research with animals, the work of a veterinarian, astronomers seeking evidence of intelligent life elsewhere in the universe, or how one gets to be an airline pilot.

"I do my best to make my books lively and delightful to the reader. No lecturing whatsoever. I want to have the subject matter tell its own story, with, of course, the help of experts involved in the particular field. I've been blessed with the assistance of hundreds of truly remarkable people. In every case, they seemed to get as excited about the book underway as I have and have taken great pleasure in recounting their own experiences. That, I feel, is the way to put the story on the human level—just where it ought to be for a person wishing to know about the work of other persons.

"One other goal I have is a bit more difficult to explain. But it goes like this: Before a reader has gone very far I hope he or she will begin to think, consciously or subconciously: 'The person who wrote this book makes me feel that he is right here with me, and is having a lot of enjoyment in telling me these things. . . . I can tell that he had a lot of excitement in learning all this himself, too.'

"I started writing books because of a magazine article I turned out some years ago. The substance of the article was that, while nearly everyone thinks the guinea pig is the prime animal used in biomedical research, it might surprise people to learn that a far greater laboratory star for years has been none other than the old despicable character, the rat. Actually, the rat is now one of the most valuable animal research tools of all. An editor friend at G. P. Putnam's Sons of New York read the article and then asked if I'd like to write a book on the biomedical research done with all kinds of animals. The result was *The $100,000 Rat: And Other Animal Heroes for Human Health.*

"The people at Putnam then had the idea that maybe I ought to do a book for young people on what a career in veterinary medicine is like. There didn't seem to be any really good ones available. So I set to work. Before I got the book finished, Putnam decided to use it to start a series of career books for its young adult line. All the titles would begin with *Here Is Your Career.*

"So, one way and another, I've been at it ever since, although *The Search: Our Quest for Intelligent Life in Outer Space* was not designed as a career book, but was written for anyone interested in what science knows and doesn't know about the possibility of life on other planets beyond our own solar system.

"When I was a boy, growing up back in Tecumseh, Oklahoma, there were a few authors whose writings intrigued me. In particular there was Paul de Kruif, who wrote *Microbe Hunters.* He was the first I found who could explain the infinite complexities of great scientific achievements in understandable and compelling fashion. He kept me spellbound.

"In a way I think I've been trying to emulate de Kruif in my own books—and beat him at his own game if I can. I don't think he'd mind."

A golden Lakeview hamster with its cheek pouches stuffed after a tasty and filling repast.
■ (From *The $100,000 Rat: And Other Animal Heroes for Human Health* by Frank Stilley. Photograph courtesy of Charles River Breeding Laboratories.)

Signed portrait of Bram Stoker as a young man.

STOKER, Abraham   1847-1912
   (Bram Stoker)

PERSONAL: Born about November 8, 1847, in Dublin, Ireland; died April 20, 1912, in London, England; son of Abraham (a civil servant) and Charlotte Matilda Blake (Thornley) Stoker; married Florence Ann Lemon Balcombe; children: one son. *Education:* Trinity College, Dublin, M.A. (honors in science), 1870. *Home:* London, England.

CAREER: Novelist, journalist, and creator of the literary vampire, Dracula. Following graduation from Trinity College, spent ten years as an Irish civil servant; served as an unpaid drama critic for the Dublin *Evening Mail*, 1871-76; literary, art, and drama critic for various newspapers; barrister of the Inner Temple; business manager for the actor, Henry Irving, 1878-1905; later served on the literary staff of the London *Telegraph*. *Member:* National Liberal Club. *Awards, honors:* Medallist, Royal Humane Society.

*WRITINGS—*Fiction; of interest to young readers: *Under the Sunset* (stories for children; illustrated by W. Fitzgerald and W. V. Cookburn), Sampson Low (London), 1881; *The Snake's Pass*, Harper, 1890; *Crooken Sands*, T. L. De Vinne (New York), 1894; *The Watter's Mou'*, T. L. De Vinne, 1894; *Dracula*, Modern Library, 1897, reprinted, 1970 [other editions include that illustrated by Felix Hoffman, with an introduction

by Anthony Boucher, Heritage Press, 1965; *The Illustrated Dracula* (illustrated with stills from the 1930 film version), Drake Publishers, 1975; *The Annotated Dracula,* edited by Leonard Wolf, C. N. Potter, 1975; *The Essential Dracula,* edited by Raymond McNally and Radu Florescu, Mayflower Books, 1979; *Bram Stoker's Dracula* (illustrated and adapted by Alice and Joel Schick), Delacorte, 1980]; *The Jewel of the Seven Stars,* Heinemann, 1903, reprinted, Arrow Books, 1975; *Dracula's Guest and Other Weird Stories,* George Routledge & Sons, 1914, reprinted, Arrow Books, 1974; *The Bram Stoker Bedside Companion: Ten Stories by the Author of Dracula* (edited and introduced by Charles Osborne), Taplinger, 1973 (contains *Dracula's Guest, Crooken Sands, The Watter's Mou'*).

Other principal writings: *The Man from Shorrox's,* T. L. De Vinne, 1894; *The Shoulder of Shasta,* Constable, 1895; *Miss Betty,* C. A. Pearson, 1898; *The Mystery of the Sea* (novel), Doubleday, 1902; *The Man* (novel), Heinemann, 1905; *Personal Reminiscences of Henry Irving,* Heinemann, 1906; *The Gates of Life,* Cupple & Leon, 1908; *Lady Athlyne,* P. R. Reynolds, 1908; *The Lady of the Shroud,* Heinemann, 1909; *Famous Imposters,* Sturgis & Walton, 1910; *The Lair of the White Worm,* W. Rider & Son, 1911.

*ADAPTATIONS—*All movies, except as noted: "Nosferatu," starring Max Schreck and Alexander Granach, Film Arts Guild, 1922; "Dracula," starring Bela Lugosi and Edward Van Sloan, Universal Pictures, 1931, starring Jack Palance and Simon Ward, Dan Curtis Productions, 1974, starring Frank Langella and Laurence Olivier, Universal Pictures, 1979; "Dracula's Daughter," starring Gloria Holden and Otto Kruger, Universal Pictures, 1936; "The Return of the Vampire," starring Bela Lugosi and Frieda Inescort, Columbia Pictures, 1943; "Son of Dracula," starring Lon Chaney and Robert Paige, Universal Pictures, 1943; "House of Dracula," starring Lon Chaney, Jr. and John Carradine, Universal Pictures, 1945; "Horror of Dracula," starring Peter Cushing and Christopher Lee, Hammer Film Productions, 1958; "The Brides of Dracula," starring Peter Cushing and David Peel, Universal Pictures, 1960; "Kiss of the Vampire," starring Clifford Evans and Noel Willman, Universal Pictures, 1963; "Dracula, Prince of Darkness," starring Christopher Lee and Barbara Shelley, Twentieth Century-Fox, 1965; "Dracula Has Risen from the Grave," starring Christopher Lee and Veronica Carlson, Warner Brothers, 1968; "Taste of Blood of Dracula," starring Christopher Lee and Geoffrey Keen, Warner Brothers, 1970; "Scars of Dracula," starring Christopher Lee and Dennis Waterman, Levitt-Pickman, 1970; "Countess Dracula," starring Ingrid Pitt and Nigel Green, Twentieth Century-Fox, 1971; "Dracula, A.D.," starring Christopher Lee and Peter Cushing, Warner Brothers, 1972; "Count Dracula" (three-part television series), starring Louis Jourdan, presented on WNET-TV, beginning March 1, 1978; "Horror Classics" (filmstrip, sound accompaniment and teacher's guide), Spoken Arts, 1979; "Love at First Bite," starring George Hamilton, American International Pictures, 1979; "Dracula," starring Frank Langella, Universal City Studios, 1979.

Plays: Hamilton Deane and John Lloyd Balderston, *Dracula* (three-act), Samuel French, 1960; Ronald Bruce, *Dracula, Baby* (musical comedy; music by Claire Strauch, lyrics by John Jakes), Dramatic Publishing, 1970; Leon Katz, *Dracula: Sabbat,* Studio Duplicating Service, 1970; Ted Tiller, *Count Dracula* (three-act), Samuel French, 1972; Crane Johnson, *Dracula,* Dramatist Play Service, 1976; Bob Hall, *The Passion of Dracula* (three-act), Samuel French, 1979.

Recordings: "Dracula," dramatized by Charles Curran, Robert Somerset, Barbara McCaughey, and Ivan de Burca, directed by Curran, Spoken Arts, 1974; "Four Scenes from Dracula," read by David McCallum and Carole Shelley, Caedmon, 1975; "Dracula," dramatized by Orson Welles, Martin Gabel, George Couloris, and Agnes Moorehead, adapted by Welles for the CBS radio program "Mercury Theatre on the Air," July 11, 1938, Mark 56 Records, 1976; "Chicago Radio Theatre's Production of Bram Stoker's Dracula," dramatized by D. Nicholas Ruddall, Nicholas Simon, and Shari Narens, adapted and directed by Yuri Rasovsky, All Media Dramatic Workshop, 1976.

SIDELIGHTS: **November 8, 1847.** Born in Dublin, Ireland, son of Abraham, a civil servant and Charlotte Stoker. ". . . In my babyhood I used, I understand, to be often at the point of death. Certainly till I was about seven years old I never knew what it was to stand upright. I was naturally thoughtful and the leisure of long illness gave opportunity for many thoughts which were fruitful according to their kind in later years.

"This early weakness, however, passed away in time and I grew into a strong boy and in time enlarged to the biggest member of my family." [Bram Stoker, *Personal Reminiscences of Henry Irving,* Volume I, Macmillan, 1906.[1]]

November, 1864. Entered Trinity College. "In my College days I had been Auditor of the Historical Society—a post which corresponds to the Presidency of the Union in Oxford or Cambridge—and had got medals, or certificates, for History, Composition and Oratory. I had been President of the Philosophical Society; and got Honours in pure Mathematics. I had won numerous silver cups for races of various kinds. I had played for years in the University football team, where I had received the honour of a 'cap!' I was physically immensely strong. In fact I feel justified in saying I represented in my own person something of that aim of university education *mens sana in corpore sano.* . . . "[1]

Upon graduation from Trinity, Stoker worked in Civil Service. "I had been for ten years in the Civil Service and was then engaged on a dry-as-dust book on *The Duties of Clerks of Petty Sessions.* I had edited a newspaper, and had exercised my spare time in many ways. As a journalist; as a writer of short and serial stories; as a teacher."[1]

Stoker was attracted to the theater, where he met Henry Irving, an actor. ". . . I was a playgoer very early in life. . . .

"...A long leiter-waggon which swept from side to side, like a dog's tail wagging...." ■(From *The Annotated Dracula,* with an introduction, notes and bibliography by Leonard Wolf. Illustrated by Sätty.)

(From "The Invisible Giant," in *Under the Sunset* by Bram Stoker. Illustrated by W.V. Cookburn.)

"SHE'S A RUSSIAN, BY THE LOOK OF HER; BUT SHE'S KNOCKING ABOUT
IN THE QUEEREST WAY."

(From *The Annotated Dracula,* with an introduction, notes and bibliography by Leonard Wolf.
Illustrated by Sätty.)

(From the movie "Son of Dracula," starring Lon Chaney, Jr., developed from the novel *Dracula.* Copyright 1943 by Universal Pictures Co., Inc.)

(From the German silent film "Nosferatu," starring Max Schreck and Alexander Granach. Released by Film Arts Guild, 1922.)

(From the three-part PBS-TV series "Count Dracula," starring Louis Jourdan. Presented on Great Performances, WNET-TV, beginning March 1, 1978.)

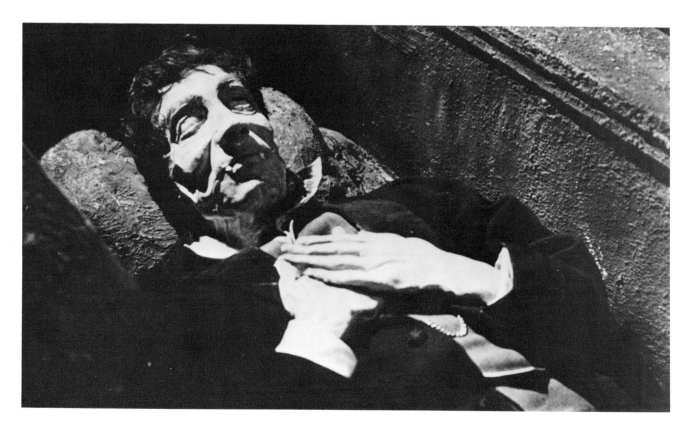

(From the movie "Horror of Dracula," starring Christopher Lee and Peter Cushing. Copyright 1957 by Hammer Film Productions.)

(From the movie "Dracula," starring Bela Lugosi. Copyright 1931 by Universal Pictures Corp.)

(From the movie "Dracula," starring Frank Langella. Copyright © 1979 by Universal City Studios.)

Bram Castle in Roumania, where Vlad Dracula stayed.

"The first time I ever saw Henry Irving was at the Theatre Royal, Dublin, on the evening of Wednesday, August 28, 1867. . . .

". . . Being then in the Civil Service, I could only get away in the 'prime of summer time' as my seniors preferred to take their holidays in the early summer or the late autumn. I had, when we next met, been for five years a dramatic critic. In 1871 my growing discontent with the attention accorded to the stage in the local newspaper had culminated with the neglect of *Two Roses*. I asked the proprietor of one of the Dublin newspapers whom I happened to know . . . to allow me to write on the subject in the *Mail*. He told me frankly that the paper could not afford to pay for such special work, as it was in accordance with the local custom of the time done by the regular staff who wrote on all subjects as required. I replied that I would gladly do it without fee or reward. This he allowed me to carry out.

"From my beginning the work in November 1871 I had an absolutely free hand. I was thus able to direct public attention, so far as my paper could effect it, where in my mind such was required. In those five years I think I learned a good deal. As Bacon says, 'Writing maketh an exact man,' and as I have always held that in matters critical the critic's personal honour is involved in every word he writes I could always feel that the duty I had undertaken was a grave one. I did not shirk work in any way; indeed, I helped largely to effect a needed reform as to the time when criticism should appear. In those days of single printings from slow presses 'copy' had to be handed in very early. The paper went to press not long after

midnight, and there were few men who could see a play and write criticism in time for the morning's issue. . . . This was very hard upon the actors and companies making short visits. The public *en bloc* is a slow-moving force; and when possibility of results is cut short of effluxion of time it is a sad handicap to enterprise and to exceptional work.

"I do not wish to be egotistical and I trust that no reader may take it that I am so, in that I have spoken of my first experience of Henry Irving and how, mainly because of his influence on me, I undertook critical work with regard to his own art. My purpose in doing so is not selfish. I merely wish that those who honour me by reading what I have written should understand something which went before our personal meeting; and why it was that when we did meet we came together with a loving and understanding friendship which lasted unbroken till my dear friend passed away.

". . . My wish to get to London where as a writer I should have a larger scope and better chance of success than at home. One morning . . . [at] the office of the *Nineteenth Century* . . . I saw the Editor and owner, Sir (then Mr.) James Knowles, who received me most kindly and asked me all sorts of questions as to work and prospects. . . .

"Are you not dissuading me from venturing to come to London as a writer?

"I was smiling to think that if I had not known the accuracy and wisdom of all you have said I should have been here long ago!"[1]

1878. Became acting manager of Lyceum Theatre for Irving. Stoker held the post for twenty-seven years. "We had now been close friends for over two years. We understood each other's nature, needs and ambitions, and had a mutual confidence, each towards the other in his own way, rare amongst men. . . .

". . . He told me that he had arranged to take the management of the Lyceum into his own hands. He asked me if I would give up the Civil Service and join him; I to take charge of his business as Acting Manager.

"I accepted at once. I had then had some thirteen years in the public service . . . but I was content to throw in my lot with his. In the morning I sent in my resignation and made by telegram certain domestic and other arrangements for supreme importance to me at that time—and ever since. . . .

"I left Glasgow on November 25, and took up my work with Irving at Birmingham on December 9, having in the meantime altered my whole business life, arranged for the completion of my book on *The Duties of Petty Sessions Clerks,* and last, not least, having got married—an event which had already been arranged for a year later.

"This 'Lyceum audience,' whose qualities endeared them to me from that first night, December 30, 1878, became a quantity to be counted on for twenty-four years of my own experiences. . . .

". . . It was the first time that I had had the privilege of seeing a play 'produced.' I had already seen rehearsals, but these except of pantomime had generally been to keep the actors, supers and working staff up to the mark of excellence already arrived at. But now I began to understand *why* everything was as it was. With regard to stagecraft it was a liberal education."[1]

(From the movie "Love at First Bite," with George Hamilton as the Count, a comic spoof based on the novel *Dracula.* Copyright © 1979 by American International Pictures.)

October, 1883-March, 1904. Toured with theater company in America each year after the London season. ". . . The club in America, is indeed, to the masculine wayfarer the shadow of a great rock in a lone and thirsty land. I often felt chagrin at the thought that we English can never repay in any similar way this expression of American hospitality." [Daniel Farson, *The Man Who Wrote Dracula: A Biography of Bram Stoker,* St. Martin's Press, 1975.[2]]

"When we had gone to America in 1883 I had found myself so absolutely ignorant of everything regarding that great country that I took some pains to post myself up in things exclusively and characteristically American. Our tour of 1883-4 was followed by another in 1884-5, so that in the space of a year which the two visits covered I had fine opportunities of study. . . .

". . . Before we left at the conclusion of our second visit I had accumulated a lot of books—histories, works on the constitution, statistics, census, school books, books of etiquette for a number of years back, Congressional reports on various subjects—in fact all the means of reference and of more elaborate study. When I had studied sufficiently—having all through the tour consulted all sorts of persons—professors, statesmen, bankers, &c.—I wrote a lecture, which I gave at the Birkbeck Institution in 1885 and elsewhere. This I published as a pamphlet in 1886, as *A Glimpse of America.* . . ."[1]

1890. ". . . I had . . . written an Irish novel, *The Snake's Pass,* which after running as a serial through the London *People* and several provincial papers had now been published in book form. . . .

". . . The cares and responsibilities of a theatre are always exacting, and the demands on the time of any one concerned in management are so endless that the few hours of leisure . . . are rare." [Bram Stoker, *Personal Reminiscences of Henry Irving,* Volume II, Macmillan, 1906.[3]]

1897. *Dracula* published after many hours of research at the British Museum. "I read that every known superstition in the world is gathered into the horseshoe of the Carpathians, as if it were the centre of some sort of imaginative whirlpool."[2]

1905. After Irving's death Stoker continued his writing. He completed eighteen books in his lifetime but he received little in reward.

April 20, 1912. Died in London, England, at the age of sixty-four still planning more publications.

FOR MORE INFORMATION SEE: Harry Ludlam, *A Biography of Dracula: The Life Story of Bram Stoker,* Foulsham, 1962; (for children) Brian Doyle, editor, *Who's Who of Children's Literature,* Schocken, 1968; Daniel Farson, *Man Who Wrote Dracula: A Biography of Bram Stoker,* St. Martin's, 1975; J. Stewart-Gordon, "Durable Dracula: Beloved Fiend of the Horror Circuit," *Readers Digest,* November, 1975; D. F. Glut, *The Dracula Book,* Scarecrow, 1975; W. J. McCormack, "Bram Stoker," *The Novel to 1900,* St. Martin's, 1980.

Bram Stoker. Sketch by W.W. Denslow.

JOZEF SUMICHRAST

SUMICHRAST, Jözef 1948-

PERSONAL: Surname is pronounced "Sum-mer-krast"; born July 26, 1948, in Hobart, Ind.; son of Joseph (retired) and Stela (Ozug) Sumichrast; married Susan (maiden name, Snyder; a book designer and fabric illustrator), May 22, 1971; children: Kristin, Lindsay. *Education:* American Academy of Art, Chicago, Ill., diploma, 1970. *Religion:* Christian. *Home:* 860 N. Northwoods, Deerfield, Ill. 60015.

CAREER: Illustrator. *Exhibitions:* New York Historical Society, 1981; Society of Illustrators, New York, N.Y., 1981; Chicago Historical Society; Library of Congress. Permanent collections: Poster Biennale of Warsaw, Los Angeles County Museum of Art, Society of Illustrators, Chicago Historical Society, Milwaukee Art Directors Club, New York History Museum. *Member:* Chicago Artist Guild. *Awards, honors:* Award for excellence, 1978, Society of Illustrators, 1980, Chicago Artist Guild and American Institute for Graphic Arts.

ILLUSTRATOR: Mildred W. Willard, *The Ice Cream Cone,* Follett, 1973; May Garelick, *Runaway Plane,* O'Hara, 1973; Marci Carafoli, *The Strange Hotel: Five Ghost Stories,* Follett, 1975; Ed Leander, *Q Is for Crazy,* Harlin Quist, 1977; Margaret Hillert, *The Funny Ride,* Follett, 1981; Jean Zelasney, *Do Pigs Sit in Trees?,* Follett, 1981.

WORK IN PROGRESS: Illustrating *Russian Dressing* and *Onomatopoeia.*

SIDELIGHTS: Sumichrast is probably best known for his ingenious alphabets, playfully distorting objects, animals and people into letterforms. The poster prints of his "English" and "Cyrillic" alphabets have won awards in the United States and Europe and are also in the permanent collections of the Poster Biennale of Warsaw, the Los Angeles County Museum of Art and the New York History Museum. "The idea started with a concept I thought of for K&S Photolab. It was going to be 'K&S presents the rest of the alphabet.' They weren't interested so I figured I'd do it for myself.

"The alphabets are based on color. The Cyrillic alphabet, for instance, is based on red, the Russian color, and the opposite of red would be green so that was my second color and then I used black and brown as neutral tones to pull everything together.

"In the Hebrew alphabet, I've got ideas for all their characters, but they could change because I could like an idea for one letter, an animal say, but that would effect the letter next to it. I wouldn't want to have two animals together, so by changing that one letter and considering the color, I might change half a dozen letters throughout the alphabet. I see something inside something else, one thing evolves into another and I constantly refine it.

"Everything is drawn out and I think in terms of color before I start to paint.

"My work may be very realistic or graphic depending on the job and age of my audience. I work with transparent watercolor.

"I might use a pencil for a highlight or something like that, but an eye, for instance, is just white paper and that's why I have to know exactly what I'm going to do before I do it. If I make a mistake, there's no way I can correct it. If you start re-working dyes they'll become muddy or the surface of the paper will fall apart."

From a small town in Indiana, Sumichrast attended the American Academy of Art in Chicago off and on over several years.

"The first year, I finished about two years of work, because it was based on a system of having monthly assignments and you filled all the requirements and then moved on. I had to work for half a year in the steel mills to raise the tuition. Sometimes I could go all year and then work between classes."

After leaving school, Sumichrast did the typical things; went to work in a Chicago studio as an apprentice, stayed there about six months, decided to freelance, rented space from a studio and then, atypically, went to Europe.

"The studio I rented space from folded and I couldn't decide if I was going to go on with illustration or not so we decided to take some time and think it over. We lived in the back of a car we bought in Paris and found that camp sites were quite inexpensive. Our time was spent in museums, bookstores and galleries. After six months, our minds made up, we came back to Chicago and rented a studio apartment on Michigan Boulevard."

About half of Sumichrast's commercial work comes to him over the telephone, clients requesting his sample case or giving him assignments, and he has a long standing relationship with his Chicago rep, Jim Berntsen. Sometimes there is a layout, but for editorial illustrations or for a book he frequently works from a thumbnail.

He likes to have tight scrap or the three dimensional object in front of him and finds it very helpful to have his wife and daughter handy as models.

Sumichrast has no desire to change the pattern of long hours. ''As long as it's fun, it's not really like work. There are times when one particular job becomes frustrating if there are changes to be made, then it all catches up with me and I feel tired and I don't really want to work so hard, but most of the time it's very enjoyable. It's like getting paid to do something you really want to do. It's a hobby as well as a business.

''For the past few years both editorial and advertising illustration have consisted of decorative hard edge and possibly 'cartooney' explosions of color. Today we have reached a stylistic turning point. Two dimensional drawing with an illusionary three dimensional rendering. Sculptural techniques such as pencil shading, air brush, and a combination of mediums have expanded and replaced the outline. The new illustrations seem to be looking back to the past to primitive art. Frequently, the subject matter is made prominent by enlarging its size in relation to other elements of the illustration. In Rousseau's 'Landscape with Cow,' the importance of the cow is felt by its

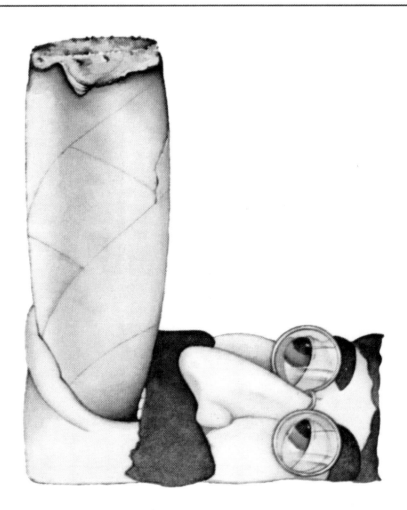

L is for Laughter and Looking real Loony

And Lying around upside down.

It's L-oquent, L-egant, and L-emental –

It's anything L-se but a frown.

(From *Q Is for Crazy* by Ed Leander. Illustrated by Jözef Sumichrast.)

abnormal size in relation to man. The subject is obvious; its style of manner of rendering is not. In the past, only in children's books, certain editorial work and a few good studios such as Chicago's Graphique was an illustrator called upon to interpret the work. The illustrator has been treated as a decorator or graphic designer rather than a free individual. Today's art is freer. It's dreamy and magical. The illustration not only has to convey the message, but given to a more demanding audience, it has to entertain.''

FOR MORE INFORMATION SEE: Graphis, The Graphis Press (Zurich), 1973; *Communication Arts,* January/February, 1981.

SUTTON, Larry M(atthew)   1931-

PERSONAL: Born February 24, 1931, in Winter Haven, Fla.; son of Clarence F. (a businessman) and Irma L. (Ashley) Sutton; married Margalo Ann Roller (a teacher), October 18, 1952; children: Debra, Jeffrey, Hollee, Jodi. *Education:* Florida Southern College, B.S., 1954; University of Florida, M.Ed., 1965. *Home:* 1000 West Lake Martha Dr., Winter Haven, Fla. 33880. *Office:* Department of English, Polk Community College, Winter Haven, Fla. 33880.

CAREER: Ward's Nursery, Avon Park, Fla., production manager, 1959-64; Polk Community College, Winter Haven, Fla., professor of English, 1965—. Director, American Red Cross, Winter Haven chapter, 1972. *Military service:* U.S. Army, 1949-51; became sergeant; received three battle stars. *Member:* Modern Language Association of America, Florida Association of Junior Colleges, Florida Council of Teachers of English.

WRITINGS—Of interest to young people, except as noted: (With Maurice Sutton and R. W. Puckett) *College English: A Beginning* (adult), Holbrook, 1969; (with M. Sutton and R. W. Puckett) *A Simple Rhetoric,* Holbrook, 1969; (with R. W. Puckett and Dion Brown) *Journeys: An Introduction to Literature,* Holbrook, 1970; *The Mystery of the Late News Report* (illustrated by Pat Blumer), Carolrhoda Books, 1981; *The Mys-*

tery of the Blue Champ (illustrated by P. Blumer), Carolrhoda Books, 1981; *Ghost Plane over Hartley Field* (illustrated by P. Blumer), Carolrhoda Books, 1981; *The Case of the Trick Note* (illustrated by P. Blumer), Carolrhoda Books, 1981; *The Case of the Smiley Faces,* Carolrhoda Books, 1981. Contributor to *Walt Whitman Journal, Real West, Far West, Pets, Reflector,* and other publications.

WORK IN PROGRESS: A novel for young readers entitled *Champ Redhawk,* a story about a young girl who lives with her grandfather on a small orange grove in central Florida—a story about flying, survival, and growing up.

SIDELIGHTS: ''For a long time after getting out of the army, my main writing interest lay in writing serious adult novels depicting the drama of people affected by war. These stories weren't all 'war' stories. Most were stories intended to show how absurdly war affects people and how our new, young heroes tended to mock the lingering romantic tradition associated with war. But most of these long works, except for spinoff stories or articles, never saw the light of publication. My attic grew heavy.

''Lately I've become interested in writing for and about children; this seems to give me a new zest for writing and I have stories and books going into print.

''For settings, I'm interested in the wilderness or other adventurous places such as airports. This apparently stems from my childhood spent mostly alone in the backwoods of Florida. Above all I want these stories to be interesting, with swift rising action, a good climax. If they also happen to say something 'uplifting,' that's for the better; and I hope they do. . . .

''About writing in general, I have this comment: It's hard for many readers to understand how something which appears so simple after it's written—such as a good, exciting story—could be so hard to write. But the writer's job isn't over when he visualizes interesting settings and begins to feel the emotions of his characters; he must then 'show' these items to his readers

"A whole week of camping at Disney World!" said Hollee. "I can't believe it!" ■ (From *The Case of the Smiley Faces* by Larry Sutton. Illustrated by Patt Blumer.)

LARRY M. SUTTON

so that they can judge if character X is lazy or heroic or caught in a bad situation. It would be much easier for a writer to 'explain.' But explaining is not the writer's job; he must *show* or *dramatize* (and it's much easier to *explain* than it is to *show*). This showing, so that readers can make their own inferences, is what good writing is all about. It calls for hours of work, of revision, in order to find the right words that evoke the proper impression in the reader.

"From the standpoint of fiction, I'm very much interested in the absurd. Writers such as Kurt Vonnegut, Joseph Heller and Norman Mailer influence me. The matter of choice—or lack of it—as influenced by tradition, seems to be central to my thinking. I plan to continue trying to write novels, short stories, and articles."

TOMALIN, Ruth

PERSONAL: Born in County Kilkenny, Ireland; daughter of Thomas Edward (a professional gardener and writer) and Elspeth Rutherford (Mitchell) Tomalin; divorced; married William N. Ross (a journalist), 1971; children: (first marriage) Nicholas Leaver. *Education:* King's College, London, Diploma in Journalism. *Address:* c/o Barclay's Bank, 15 Langham Pl., London W.1, England.

CAREER: Journalist and author. Began newspaper work in 1942 with *Portsmouth Evening News,* Portsmouth, Hampshire, England, and has since been a staff reporter, at various times, for other newspapers in England, and a press agency reporter in London law courts. *Member:* Society of Authors.

WRITINGS: Threnody for Dormice (poems), Fortune Press, 1947; *The Day of the Rose* (essays and portraits), Fortune Press, 1947; *Deer's Cry* (poem), Fortune Press, 1952; *All Souls* (novel), Faber, 1952; *W. H. Hudson* (biography), Witherby & Philosophical Library, 1954; *The Daffodil Bird* (juvenile novel), Faber, 1959, A. S. Barnes, 1960; *The Sea Mice* (juvenile novel), Faber, 1962; *The Garden House* (novel), Faber, 1964; *The Spring House* (novel), Faber, 1968; (editor) *Best Country Stories,* Faber, 1969; *Away to the West* (juvenile novellas), Faber, 1972; *A Green Wishbone* (juvenile novel), Faber, 1975; *A Stranger Thing* (juvenile novel), Faber, 1975; *The Snake Crook* (juvenile novel), Faber, 1976; *Gone Away* (juvenile novel), Faber, 1979; (contributor) *Henry Williamson, the Man, the Writings: A Symposium,* Tabb House, 1980; *W. H. Hudson, Field Naturalist,* Faber, 1982.

WORK IN PROGRESS: A novel about country homes in England and Ireland (*The Garden House* was the first of the series); a juvenile textbook on ecology, for Faber.

HOBBIES AND OTHER INTERESTS: Country life and wildlife preservation.

SIDELIGHTS: Though born in Kilkenny, Ireland, the daughter of the late T. E. Tomalin, writer, gardener and lecturer, Tomalin was brought up in the Forest of Bere on the Hampshire-Sussex border. After working on the land and in a stable she spent some years as a staff reporter on papers in Hampshire, Sussex, Dorset and Hertfordshire, and now works as a crime reporter, spending two days a week in the London courts. Married with one son, she lives in Highgate, but spends all her spare time in the country sitting under trees, always peaceful and rewarding for a naturalist, and watching water voles

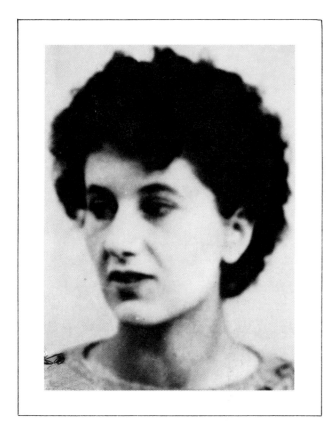

RUTH TOMALIN

in Oxfordshire, red squirrels in Scotland and the Lake District, and red deer and seals in the Western Highlands.

Tomalin's first book, the verse collection *Threnody for Dormice,* was published in 1947, to be followed by a biography of W. H. Hudson and other books of verse, novels and children's stories. Her books reflect her love for and knowledge of the countryside and its inhabitants, human and animal.

TREVIÑO, Elizabeth B(orton) de 1904-

PERSONAL: Born September 2, 1904, in Bakersfield, Calif.; daughter of Fred Ellsworth (a lawyer) and Carrie (Christensen) Borton; married Luis Treviño Gómez (dealer in insurance and real estate), August 10, 1935; children: Luis Federico (deceased), Enrique Ricardo. *Education:* Stanford University, B.A. in Latin American history, 1925; studied violin Boston Conservatory of Music. *Religion:* Roman Catholic. *Residence:* Cuernavaca, Morelos, Mexico. *Agent:* McIntosh and Otis, 475 Fifth Ave., New York, N.Y. 10017.

CAREER: Formerly reviewer of performing arts for *Boston Herald,* Boston, Mass.; now professional writer and journalist, American Institute for Foreign Trade, honorary lecturer. *Awards, honors:* Honorary citizen of Texas; medal of Kansas City Woman's Organization; Newbery medal, 1966, for *I, Juan de Pareja.*

WRITINGS—All of interest to young people, except as noted: *Pollyanna in Hollywood,* L. C. Page, 1931; *Our Little Aztec Cousin,* L. C. Page, 1934; *Pollyanna's Castle in Mexico,* L.

C. Page, 1934; *Our Little Ethiopian Cousin,* L. C. Page, 1935; *Pollyanna's Door to Happiness,* L. C. Page, 1936; *Pollyanna's Golden Horseshoe,* L. C. Page, 1939; *About Bellamy,* Harper, 1940; *My Heart Lies South* (memoirs), Crowell, 1953, reissued, 1972; *A Carpet of Flowers,* Crowell, 1955; *Even As You Love* (novel), Crowell, 1957; *The Greek of Toledo* (novel about El Greco), Crowell, 1959; *Where the Heart Is* (memoirs), Doubleday, 1962; *Nacar, the White Deer,* Farrar, Straus, 1963; *I, Juan de Pareja,* Farrar, Straus, 1965; *The Fourth Gift* (novel), Doubleday, 1966; *Casilda of the Rising Moon,* Farrar, Straus, 1967; *Turi's Poppa,* Farrar, Straus, 1968; *House on Bitterness Street* (novel), Doubleday, 1970; *Here Is Mexico,* Farrar, Straus, 1970; *Beyond the Gates of Hercules: A Tale of the Lost Atlantis,* Farrar, Straus, 1971; *The Music Within* (novel), Doubleday, 1973; *Juarez, Man of Law,* Farrar, Straus, 1974; *The Hearthstone of My Heart* (memoirs), Doubleday, 1977; *Among the Innocent* (adult), Doubleday, 1981.

SIDELIGHTS: **September 2, 1904.** Born in Bakersfield, California. ''My earliest memories are of the little house in Bakersfield. . . . I remember the little house. It was a small wooden frame cottage with four rooms—a 'front room,' bedroom, dining room and kitchen. Shaded in front by umbrella trees, it had a large back yard where Papa grew alfalfa for the horse and Mama raised chickens and planted vegetables. I soon learned that one put seeds into the ground and afterward plants came up and reproduced themselves. Accordingly, I once buried my mother's rings, in the hope of getting a good crop. I must have been about two. Somehow I was persuaded to dig them up before they sprouted.

ELIZABETH B. de TREVIÑO

The illustration on the front of the jacket depicts Diego Velasquez sketching the self-portrait which appears in his painting "Las Meninas." On the back of the jacket, the finished self-portrait is being embellished with the Cross of Santiago. ■ (From *I, Juan de Pareja* by Elizabeth Borton de Treviño. Jacket design by Enrico Arno.)

"By the time I was five, we had moved from our little house to the other side of the city, because I would soon be in school and had to be near enough to walk. In our new house we were only five blocks from Papa's office in the Producer's Bank Building, and he came home for lunch every day. Our house was on Twentieth Street on the block between C and D streets, a street full of children. (By then I had a little Sister, Barbara, and when I was eight and a half, my baby brother Dick arrived.) These friends of my childhood, and of my sister's and brother's, were a whole world to us, and those of us who survive are fast friends to this day.

"The block was a small community in itself. . . . We children all played together in the evenings during the hot summer months, and I recall Crack the Whip, Statues, Prisoner's Base (which our dogs played with us), Tag and many other games. The girls (who predominated) also played jacks and jumprope and hopscotch on the sidewalks, and once in a while we played with dolls. . . .

"The day came when I was to enter school. I was to go to what was called 'the receiving grade,' which antedated the kindergarten. . . .

"My teacher was Miss Timmons. I will never forget her, because through her I had the greatest thrill of my life, and

something happened which has enriched all my days, and will until I die.

"She had a big chart, with leaves that flopped over, and a long-handled pointer. With this she showed us a letter of the alphabet (which we all knew and recognized) and taught us to make appropriate sounds. *Aaaaaa* for A. A stuttering *bbbbbb*, then a sound like K, or *kkkkkk* for C, and so on. This went on for some time, and seemed to have no reason. It was just something teachers made you do.

"But one day she showed three letters and we sounded each one. C*(kkkkkk)* A *(aaaaaa)* T *(tttttt)*. And there, on the chart, was a picture of a cat. And we had said it! CAT! The wonderful, radiant light broke over me. This was reading! I never got over it.

"Reading has always been the chief joy, a never-ending topic of conversation, and often a lifesaver, in my family.

"So it was not strange that one of us should try to write, as well. . . .

"I was moved to write poetry when I was about eight, producing a work of three verses, three lines each, based on the beauty of a frost-covered lawn. I took my poem to my father at once for approbation. He put down his book, read it carefully, and then gave me a lesson on meter and rhyme, found some great collections of poetry for me to browse in, and started me on a love of poetry that has grown with the years." [Elizabeth Borton de Treviño, *The Hearthstone of My Heart,* Doubleday, 1977.[1]]

Besides reading and writing, de Treviño also loved music. "One day, as I was listlessly practicing, making mistakes and not correcting them, watching the clock diligently, my father came home early. He listened a while, then said, 'Stop that. Now tell me why you have lost interest in your music lessons.'

"'Papa, I don't want to play the piano! I want to learn to play the violin and work in orchestras!'

"'We will stop the piano lessons at once,' he answered quietly.

"Within two days he came home with a violin. . . . He had found a man who would start me out on the open strings and show me how to use the bow, and I began a devotion to the instrument I have loved ever since."[1]

1912. First poem published. ". . . While I was staying in Monterey with my grandmother, the blue sea, sparkling with white caps, the cypresses, and the pine-clad hills inspired me again. I labored mightily and brought forth a small mouse of a poem, which, due to Papa's instructions, well-remembered, had rhyme and rhythm. I was deeply pleased with my poem, and I intended it to burst upon a waiting world like a new star. I therefore made a clean copy, in secret, and when sent on an errand into town, I found the office of the *Peninsula Herald* and demanded to see the Editor. I suppose he must have had a slack afternoon, for he received me.

"I handed him my poem. So determined was I on publication that I told him he might have it for nothing. I hadn't said a word about this to Grandma, and I still kept my secret. There followed six days of agony, while I waited for my poem to appear in print.

'At last! It did, boxed in a fine position, and underneath there was a short explanation. 'This poem was written by little Beth Borton, aged eight.' I saw nothing odd in that, no hint of apology on the Editor's part. I was eight, and I was little Beth Borton. I sat back and allowed myself to be admired.

"Thus vaccinated with printer's ink. I never got over it, and I continued producing works of poetry and prose with regularity.

"All through high school I worked at short stories. . . .

"While I was in high school I wrote another poem, which was accepted and published by the *Literary Digest* and was later set to music by a composer whose name I have forgotten. So again, there arose in me that hope which is a basic ingredient in the making of a professional writer.

"In my last year in high school, as editor of our year book, it fell to me to deal with printers. This was salutary too, for I learned something about the mechanics of turning manuscript into print. . . .

"Therefore, when I went away to college at Stanford University I looked for courses in literature and in writing."[1]

1925. Graduated from Stanford University with a B.A. in Latin American history. Treviño went to Boston to study violin and later was a reporter for the Boston *Herald*. "I spent a year learning solfeggio, harmony, and music history . . . at the Boston Conservatory. . . .

"I loved the concerts, to begin with, and I liked bustling down to the *Herald* office to type out my review and hand it in. It gave me a heady feeling of being a professional newspaperwoman, a dream I still nourished with hope.

"So, little by little, what with studying background, interviewing, and gaining experience of various orders, I began to find out that although I had considered myself educated when I graduated from college, my education was just beginning.

"My life as a reporter carried me into places and situations I would never have known as an ordinary young woman merely passing time until 'the right man' came long. I visited prisons, I attended murder trials, I studied mental hospitals, I called on people in all sorts of trouble.

"The result was that I soon got channeled into the slot where I belonged: interviews. Here I had to develop a technique and depend on intuition, and I began to garner the most delightful assignments, interviews with people like Tallulah Bankhead, Jane Cowl, Eva Le Gallienne, and many others."[1]

August 10, 1935. Married Luis Treviño Gómez. "I had come to Mexico . . . as a reporter, and the very first Mexican I met was young Luis Treviño Gómez. The Monterrey Chamber of Commerce had sent him to escort the visiting woman journalist across the border; he was to serve as her public relations manager and interpreter during her stay. The most Mexican of his family, the most traditional, the most conservative and the least impetuous, he was the last one they might have expected to get mixed up with a self-supporting, opinionated, independent American girl. . . . But . . . before I returned to my native country with a sheaf of articles on prominent Mexicans, I was an engaged woman. A year later we were married and I came with my husband to live in Monterrey and to begin a painful course in how to change a hard-headed career girl into a gentle, soft, and clinging Mexican señora." [Elizabeth Borton de Treviño, *Where the Heart Is,* Doubleday, 1962.[2]]

The couple had two sons. ". . . My first son .. baptized Luis Federico, for his father and my father, was called Guicho for short. . . . My second child . . . Enrique (Kique, or Wicky). . . .

"Just how does a place at first new and strange, come to take on a beloved familiarity? Living in another country, with people of another upbringing, under new sets of traditions, speaking another language, at what moment does one suddenly feel that he has fallen into place and is no longer alien?

"It happens imperceptibly.

"There comes a time when unconsciously one slips into thinking in the language so painfully learned from books, when the pattern of one's thoughts grown naturally from the first strange but dutiful accepted premise, into a new design. There is a moment when suddenly all that was outlandish, quaint, and exotic, is restored to strangeness only by the amazed comments of visitors from afar." [Elizabeth Borton de Treviño, *My Heart Lies South,* Crowell, 1953.[3]]

Family moved from Monterrey to San Angel, near Mexico City. "This then was the town I had chosen for my home, and where my little boys would grow to manhood. This town was to be my town, with its society as flamboyant and varied as the society of Monterrey had been simple and candid.

"Long before I had made friends with other mothers in San Angel, I had become a sort of older sister to the young women who worked in the office where I was employed mornings. My little boys were in kindergarten and then in primary school during the morning hours only, and I hung onto the little job I had rounded up. . . .

"I wrote publicity releases in English for a group of private persons and companies who dedicated themselves to promoting travel to Mexico. This was long before the organization of a government tourist department, and the whole travel business was in its infancy in Mexico. Publicity releases about the beauties of Mexico were really a sort of pioneering. . . .

"I collected many small items of news that could be expressed in a few lines and began sending them out to editors. Because of their brevity, they were given consideration. (I well remembered when I was a reporter, being passed quantities of 'publicity releases' with the order, 'Cut these down to a stick each.') So our releases began to be picked up and used with some regularity. I developed a fine incandescent missionary feeling, for I wanted Mexico to be known and loved for what she really is, and not for qualities alien to her integrity."[2]

1966. Won the Newbery Medal for *I, Juan de Pareja.* "When I was a child, I really suffered when I had to lay down my book in order to set the table or dust the parlor for my mother. My greatest reward for tasks well done was to be allowed to go to the library and browse among the shelves so laden with treasure. My father and mother peppered their conversation with quotations from Shakespeare, the Bible, Byron, and Bobbie Burns. My maternal grandmother loved poetry and could recite it, pages and pages of it, by heart; my paternal grandmother passed her last illness reading and died with a copy of my first published book in her hand. My Danish grandfather sang me to sleep with his own translations of Norse sagas.

"I am recounting all this in order to make it clear that this literary award, the Newbery Medal, had been given to a person conditioned from birth and by education and taste to feel that it is the most wonderful thing that could possibly happen to her. It is a platform of achievement which will make the continuing road both easier and harder. Easier, because I will have with me the feeling of pride in the trust and confidence shown me and my work; harder, because now self-criticism must be less indulgent, for there is a higher ideal to keep in view. One cannot, one dare not, do less than his best, always, after such an award as the Newbery.

"But it would be presumptuous and untrue to accept this award as if it were something earned entirely without help or cooperation. When an accolade such as the Newbery is awarded, surely it recognizes, in its implications, more than one book written in a given year. The recipient, it seems to me, accepts in the name of all the people and things, all that life has presented in its multiple experiences, which made the book possible. "I am glad, I am honored, to remember and to mention many of the influences which helped me, and which to this day sustain and encourage me in my work.

"First, my parents, who taught me to love books and reading. After I had begun writing, my father did many wonderful things for me. Before I had achieved any publication, he took an office for me, equipped it with table, typewriter, and chair,

A middle-aged man with a big black mustache, his head tied up in a red scarf, golden earrings flashing in the morning sun, stepped forward. ■ (From *Turi's Poppa* by Elizabeth Borton de Treviño. Illustrated by Enrico Arno.)

and paid me a small salary. 'Now,' he said, 'you will write every day from nine to twelve and from one to five. Writing is work. You may have Saturdays off.' When I reported to him one day that I had started a novel, he commented, 'Probably 5649 other persons started novels today. Chances are that 5640 have more talent than you. But honey, you can do what 5000 won't do. You can finish yours.' Splendid advice; never forgotten.

"Time has robbed me of my remarkable father, but I am fortunate to have still an equally remarkable and wonderful mother. She is a sensitive and stern critic, and all my work is colored by a promise I made her long ago. 'Promise me,' she asked, 'that you will never write anything that you know would be offensive to me.' With perfect confidence in her taste and judgment, I promised, and I will not.

"While I was in high school and in college, several teachers took time from their busy days to draw me to one side, to help and advise me. . . .

"At the university I was taught another invaluable lesson by Professor David Grey, who taught the writing of drama. He read my efforts aloud to his classes, with malicious amusement; and since my plays were tragic and he made the class laugh at them, he sent me back to my dormitory in tears after every session. By his own words, he had been at pains to teach us all that the climate of writing is frustration and disappointment, that there will always be some people along our way who will not like what we have written. 'You might just possibly,' he said in his dry English way,' have the makings of a writer in you. For I couldn't make you stop writing, and essentially that is what writing boils down to. People who allow themselves to be discouraged are not for this trade.'

"Now I must list two newspapermen who helped form me as a writer, and I mention them with enduring gratitude. The first was the late, great Philip Hale, well-known music and drama critic of *The Boston Herald*. When he first hired me as an assistant music reviewer, he made gentle fun of me for writing poetry and dubbed me 'Elizabeth Barrett Borton.' But one day he summoned me by telegram, as was his custom, and told me in his tired old voice, 'Continue writing poetry, please. Poetry, in its essence, reflects and awakens wonder, and the world, which I must leave all too soon, is a wonderful place. A wonderful place.' Then, shouldering his green baize bag full of books and adjusting his derby, he shuffled out. . . .

"I give honor to George Minot, city editor of *The Boston Herald* when I went there as a reporter. . . . He taught me the inestimable value of the blue pencil. I used to tremble when he crossed out my beautiful words; now, remembering his advice, I rejoice in each work I can cut. 'Make it accurate,' he told me, 'but rip out anything that has no right to be there.'

"My friend Dr. Isaac Goldberg was the next person to give me counsel that has made my life as a writer possible. I was asked to write a book to continue the Pollyanna series, the original author having died. Though I was longing to see my name on a published book, I was young and arrogant and I chanted all the sophisticated clichés of my day. I was appalled at the idea of writing a *Pollyanna!* I asked Dr. Goldberg what to do.

"'If you want to be a professional writer,' he advised me, 'take every commission that you can get and do the best possible job with it. And write all the time, besides. The world is bursting with material, and no material is too high or too low for a writer. *Transfigure* it; that's what writing means.'

"Editors, too, have been my teachers, each one showing me some valuable lesson of technique, point of view, or attitude. . . .

"I cannot leave out my family, which endures me through the vagaries and struggles of my writing life and which makes excuses for me when I neglect my household duties, or when, in the heat of composition, I forget even my name.

"*I, Juan de Pareja* tells a story I learned, loved, and researched many years before it was written. The Newbery Medal really goes to the two protagonists who lived the lives I told about. If there had not been a noble and generous Velázquez and a loyal and loving Juan de Pareja in real life, there would have been no book to tell of their friendship.

"And so, because 'no man is an island' but we are all 'part of the main'—and this applies to the writer of books especially—I have told about the many people, living and dead, present or far away, who have helped me write *I, Juan de Pareja*. . . . [Elizabeth Borton de Treviño, "Newbery Award Acceptance," *Horn Book,* August, 1966.[4]]

A resident of Mexico since 1935, Treviño retained her American citizenship, and made frequent trips back to America. "My trips home, besides providing me with much refreshment of the spirit, gave me opportunity to think over the home and family left behind in Mexico, and get a perspective on their specially endearing qualities, as well. It was a knitting together of two lives. I have never wanted these two lives to be cut off from each other, and I have never wanted to be a stranger in my childhood home and my home town, nor yet a foreigner in the home and within the family I hold so dear in Mexico. It has taken a bit of doing, but I thank God for the chance to travel back and forth very often.

". . . When Mexico decided no longer to allow dual citizenship in 1944, I chose American, although Mexicans insist that I list myself as a *norte-americana*.

Settled in Cuernavaca. ". . . From the beginning of my life in California I felt inclined toward Mexico. I have lived in Mexico . . . and although I have never given up my American citizenship, I am in some ways more Mexican than the Mexicans. Yet there is a little undying core of gringa in me too. . . ."[2]

"I live in a very simple Mexican ranch-style home in the midst of a large garden with tall trees, only two blocks from the big city market. I hear footsteps all day long, passing on the sidewalk outside my high stone walls. Cuernavaca is a small enough town so that every trip to the post office means I will see two or three friends. This is delightful. My social life is rich in friends who love the same things I do. We exchange books; we play bridge occasionally, I play violin and piano sonatas every week and quartets a few times a year. The whole town joins in much charitable work. Cuernavaca is beautifully ecumenical, which makes me proud to live here. I love my friends, and I love making chamber music. I adore all sorts of animals and birds. I do some handiwork. I read all the time.

"My favorite possessions are my violins, my carved Spanish furniture, and many hand-knitted and hand-made articles, especially needlepoint, made for me by my mother, and knitted garments made by my sisters. I also treasure an antique Chinese cloisonné teapot and an assortment of other tea pots. I drink lots of tea, you see.

"I am a typical American in appearance—fair, somewhat plump, graying blond hair. Thank God I am reasonably active and have not lost any of my faculties." [Lee Bennett Hopkins, *More Books by More People,* Citation, 1974.[5]]

About her writing, Treviño commented: "I generally get story ideas from some true event or moment in history that fires my imagination. All of my books contain a little kernel of truth, something that really happened. . . .

"At the same time, each of my stories tries to show some phase of love, that powerful emotion that makes the world go round. I rewrite only after the first draft is down on paper. I try out my ideas on friends, especially friends with children.

"Many children write to me. Mostly they want to know how I get my ideas for stories. But one practical child wrote to ask how long it took me to write a book and how much money I made. I am always delighted to hear from my readers and to answer any questons if I can. I hope that my stories may be read over often and read aloud and shared.[5]

"It has been a great source of pride for me that every juvenile short story I have ever published in magazines has been incorporated into a collection or anthology for children."

FOR MORE INFORMATION SEE: Elizabeth Borton de Treviño, *My Heart Lies South,* Crowell, 1953; E. B. de Treviño, *Where the Heart Is,* Doubleday, 1962; *Horn Book,* August, 1966; Doris de Montreville and Donna Hill, editors, *Third Book of Junior Authors,* H. W. Wilson, 1972; Lee Bennett Hopkins, *More Books by More People,* Citation, 1974; E. B. de Treviño, *The Hearthstone of My Heart,* Doubleday, 1977.

VANCE, Marguerite 1889-1965

PERSONAL: Born November 27, 1889, in Chicago, Ill.; died May 22, 1965, in Camden, Me.; daughter of Joseph H. and Ida Anna (Kramer) Schlund; married William Little Vance in 1910 (died, 1931); children: one son (died in infancy). *Education:* Attended the Villa Dupont School, Paris, 1907-1910; studied acting under Emile Vilemain of the Comédie Francaise.

MARGUERITE VANCE

CAREER: Editor and author of books for young people. Eastman Bolton Gallery, Cleveland, Ohio, head of children's department, 1931; Dutton's Book Store, New York City, head of children's book department, 1933-40; E. P. Dutton & Co., New York City, children's book editor, 1940-55. *Awards, honors:* Thomas Alva Edison Award, 1960, for *Willie Joe and His Small Change.*

WRITINGS—All for children; all published by Dutton, except as indicated: *A Star for Hansi* (illustrated by Grace Paull), Harper & Brothers, 1936; *Marta* (illustrated by Mildred Boyle), Harper & Brothers, 1937; *Capitals of the World,* Crowell, 1938; *Paula* (illustrated by Valenti Angelo), Dodd, 1939; *Paula Goes Away to School* (illustrated by Maginel W. Barney), Dodd, 1940; *While Shepherds Watched* (illustrated by Nedda Walker), 1946; *Martha, Daughter of Virginia: The Story of Martha Washington* (Junior Literary Guild selection), 1947, reissued, 1967; *Patsy Jefferson of Monticello* (Junior Literary Guild selection), 1948; *The Lees of Arlington: The Story of Mary and Robert E. Lee* (Junior Literary Guild selection), 1949.

Marie Antoinette, Daughter of an Empress (Junior Literary Guild selection), 1950; *Lady Jane Grey, Reluctant Queen* (illustrated by Walker), 1952, reissued, 1969; *The Jacksons of Tennessee* (illustrated by Walker), 1953; *Elizabeth Tudor, Sovereign Lady* (illustrated by Walker), 1954, reissued, 1967; *The Boy on the Road: A Christmas Story* (illustrated by Walker), 1955; *On Wings of Fire: The Story of Nathaniel Hawthorne's Daughter, Rose* (illustrated by Walker), 1955; *The Empress Josephine: From Martinique to Malmaison* (illustrated by Walker), 1956; *Windows for Rosemary* (illustrated by Robert Doares), 1956; *Flight of the Wildling: Elisabeth of Austria* (illustrated by J. L. Pellicer), 1957; *Secret for a Star,* 1957; *Leave It to Linda* (illustrated by Dorothy Bayley Morse), 1958; *Song for a Lute* (illustrated by Pellicer), 1958; *Ashes of Empire:*

When I had finished, everyone clapped—that is, everyone but Daddy. He came and put his arms around me.... ■ (From *A Rainbow for Robin* by Marguerite Vance. Illustrated by Kenneth Longtemps.)

I can still hear the shuffle and crunch of gravel in the garden as we girls played *Diabolo* to the laughing shout of 'Prenez!' and 'Vite!' Vite! Vite!' and the lazy clop-clop-clop of *fiacre* horses on the *Avenue du Bois,* only a block away. On warm summer days Mimi, the big tortoise-shell Persian, would jump up into one of the tubs of oleander and coil herself around the thick stem at its base to sleep on the cool black earth under the flowering branches, looking for all the world like a fur doily.

"They were wonderfully carefree, happy days, filled with all the things young girls love: the *Opéra Comique,* and *Comédie Francaise,* the *Odéon,* the fencing lessons over on the Avenue Kleber, horseback riding in the *Bois,* skating at the *Palais de Glace,* tea at Rumpelmayer's and the Ritz, chocolate at Gage's— these for the winter months. In the midst of it, when Christmas came, we filled wooden *sabots* with gifts for one another before leaving for midnight mass at Notre Dame or St. Eustace or the Madeleine. On Christmas Day there was always the big Christmas dinner with American friends as our guests, and then following day off to Switzerland or Holland or North Africa for the winter vacation.

"I remember what fun it was, in the spring and summer, to drive out to that stranger-than-strange garden—Robinson—for supper up in the treetops while your little platform dining room swayed pleasantly in the breeze. Food came up in baskets, and here and there a saucy thrush scolded you from a near-by branch and hopped very close for crumbs.

"But two of my closest friends and I loved more than anything else to get our favorite chaperone, Madame Piétri, to take us out to *Versailles* for the day. Over a long period we had made Marie Antoinette our favorite, our idol. We wrote themes about her. We read everything we could find about her. We adored her. So we never were so happy as when, notebooks and sketchbooks in our bags, we four would pile into a car and go whizzing out through the *Bois,* into the country, and presently to the great gates of *Versailles.* With what speed we skirted the palace and tore off into the park! And so at last to *Petit Trianon* and the *hameau,* the little fairytale world where I'm sure even today the ghosts of beautiful ladies and their handsome cavaliers walk through the shadows. How we loved it! To three romantic girls it was actually living in a dream, and that dream actually history!

"If you walk beside the winding waterways at *Trianon,* where Marie Antoinette so often walked; if you go into the exquisite little palace and look at the things she loved and touched—the delicately shaped bed in which she slept, the dainty little desk at which she sat to write the many notes she was constantly writing to invite this or that friend to come and share the fun at *Trianon;* and then if you think of the shrieking mobs that came storming out from the Paris underworld to take her and her children to one of the most dreaded prisons in all Europe, the *Conciergerie*—then you can understand how almost anyone to whom she had been a favorite heroine for many years would count it a privilege to write about her. For Marie Antoinette was accused of many crimes about which she knew nothing and died a martyr to senseless class hatred. I hope every girl who reads her story may one day go to see for herself the beautiful place where Marie Antoinette lived, a place still full of her radiant personality."

You liked the way she held you, tucked under her chin, for one thing, and called you "Dinah Baby" which was almost as pleasant as having your chin and ears scratched. ■ (From *A Flower from Dinah* by Marguerite Vance. Illustrated by Susanne Suba.)

Carlota and Maximilian of Mexico (illustrated by Pellicer), 1959; *Willie Joe and His Small Change* (illustrated by Robert MacLean), 1959, reissued, 1965.

Jeptha and the New People (illustrated by MacLean), 1960; *The Lamp Lighters: Women in the Hall of Fame* (illustrated by Pellicer), 1960; *Dark Eminence: Catherine de Medici and Her Children* (illustrated by Pellicer), 1961; *The World for Jason* (illustrated by MacLean), 1961; *A Flower from Dinah* (illustrated by Susanne Suba), 1962; *Scotland's Queen: The Story of Mary Stuart* (illustrated by Pellicer), 1962; *The Beloved Friend* (illustrated by Leonard Weisgard), Holt, 1963; *Courage at Sea* (illustrated by Lorence F. Bjorklund), 1963; *Hear the Distant Applause: Six Great Ladies of the American Theatre,* 1963; *Esther Wheelwright, Indian Captive* (illustrated by Bjorklund), 1964; *Jared's Gift: A Christmas Story* (illustrated by Reisie Lonette), 1965; *Six Queens: The Wives of Henry VIII* (illustrated by Pellicer), 1965; *A Rainbow for Robin* (illustrated by Kenneth Longtemps), 1966.

SIDELIGHTS: "Long ago when I was a young girl, I lived in Paris and went to school there in a red brick-and-stone house set in a garden between high brick walls. It was a lovely spot, shaded by plane trees. Even today—many, many years later—

OBITUARIES: Current Biography, Wilson, 1965; *New York Times,* May 25, 1965; *Publishers Weekly,* May 31, 1965; *Library Journal,* September 15, 1965.

VON HAGEN, Victor Wolfgang   1908-

PERSONAL: Born February 29, 1908 in St. Louis, Mo.; son of Henry (a chemist) and Eleanor Josephine (Stippe-Hornbach) Von Hagen; married Christine Brown, May 28, 1933 (divorced); married Silvia Hofmann-Edzard, 1951 (divorced, 1962); children: (first marriage) Victoria (Mrs. Jacques Bordaz); (second marriage) Adriana and Bettina. *Education:* Attended Morgan Park Military Academy, New York University, University of Quito, and University of Gottingen. *Home:* Trevignano Romano, Rome, Italy, 00069. *Agent:* John McLaughlin, c/o Campbell, Thompson, McLaughlin Ltd., 31 Newington Green, London N16 9PU, England.

CAREER: Author, explorer, naturalist. Embarked upon exploratory expedition to Africa, 1927; completed expeditions to Mexico, and to Galapagos Islands, 1931-33, 1957, Ecuador, the Upper Amazon, and Peru, 1934-36; conducted additional research in the regions of the Mosquito Coast of Honduras and Guatemala to find and capture the quetzal bird, 1937-38; explored Panama and Costa Rica, 1940; toured Colombia and Peru, 1947-48; resided in the British West Indies, 1949-50; director of the Inca Highway Expedition to Peru, Bolivia, and Ecuador for the American Geographic Society, 1953-55; studied Roman roads from the Rhine to Africa, 1955; further exploration of the Yucatan Peninsula, 1958-59; organizer and leader of the Roman Road expeditions throughout Europe and North Africa, 1961-70; organizer and leader of the American Geographic Society Expedition through Iran, Iraq, and Turkey mapping the Royal Persian Road, 1973-75. Research associate at Museum of the American Indian, New York, N.Y.; advisor on Latin America to *Encyclopedia Americana;* consultant to the United Nations; founder and organizer of a project to establish a Charles Darwin Residence Station in the Galapagos Islands, 1936-63. *Military service:* U.S. Army, 13th Infantry, served in World War II.

MEMBER: American Geographical Society (director), Royal Geographic Society, Academia de Historia de Bogota (Columbia), Centro de Historia de Pasto (Columbia), Instituto Investigaciones Historicas del Puna (Peru), Zoological Society of London. *Awards, honors:* Orden de Merito (Ecuador); Commander, Orden de Merito (Peru); Guggenheim fellowship for creative writing, 1949, 1950; American Philosophical Society research fellow.

*WRITINGS—*For children: (With Quail Hawkins) *Treasure of the Tortoise Islands* (illustrated by Antonio Sotomayor), Harcourt, 1940; *Miskito Boy* (illustrated by A. Sotomayor), Collins, 1943; *The Sun Kingdom of the Aztecs* (illustrated by Alberto Beltran), World Publishing, 1958; *Maya: Land of the Turkey and the Deer,* Collins-World, 1960; *The Incas: People of the Sun* (ALA Notable Book), Collins-World, 1961; *Roman Roads,* World Publishing, 1966.

"A Guide to" series: *A Guide to Cusco,* Guide Books, 1949; *. . . Lima, the Capital of Peru,* Farnam, 1949; *. . . Machu Picchu,* Farnam, 1949; *. . . Sacsahuaman, the Fortress of Cusco,* Guide Books, 1949; *. . . Guayaquil,* Farnam, 1950.

Other: *Off with Their Heads,* Macmillan, 1937; (with Q. Hawkins) *Quetzal Quest: The Story of the Capture of the Quetzal, the Sacred Bird of the Aztecs and the Mayas* (illustrated by A. Sotomayor), Harcourt, 1939; *The Tsatchela Indians of Western Ecuador,* Museum of the American Indian, 1939; (author of preface) M. Maeterlinck, *Life of the White Ant,* McClelland, 1939; *Ecuador the Unknown: Two and a Half Years Travels*

Von Hagen examines Achiote seeds.

in the Republic of Ecuador and Galapagos Islands, Jarrolds, 1939, Oxford University Press, 1940.

Jungle in the Clouds, Duell, Sloan, 1940; (author of epilogue and bibliographic notes) Herman Melville, *Las Encantadas,* W. P. Wreden, 1940; *Riches of South America* (illustrated by Paul Kinnear), Heath, 1941; *Riches of Central America* (illustrated by P. Kinnear), Heath, 1942; *The Aztec and Maya Papermakers,* J. J. Augustin, 1943, reprinted, Hacker Art Books, 1977; *The Jicaque (Torrupan) Indians of Honduras,* Museum of the American Indian, 1943, reprinted, AMS Press, 1980; *South America Called Them: Exploration of the Great Naturalists, La Condamine, Humboldt, Darwin, Spruce,* Knopf, 1945; *South American Zoo* (illustrated by Francis Lee Jaques), Messner, 1946; *Maya Explorer: John Lloyd Stephens and the Lost Cities,* University of Oklahoma Press, 1947; (editor) *The Green World of the Naturalists: A Treasury of Five Centuries of Natural History in South America,* Greenberg, 1948; *Ecuador and the Galapagos Islands,* University of Oklahoma Press, 1949.

Frederick Catherwood, Architect, introduction by Aldous Huxley, Oxford University Press, 1950, published as *Frederick Catherwood, Architect-Explorer of Two Worlds,* Barre Publishers, 1968; (with Christine Von Hagen) *The Four Seasons of Manuela, a Biography: The Love Story of Manuela Saenz and Simon Bolivar,* Duell, Sloan, 1952 (published in England as *The Love Story of Manuela Saenz and Simon Bolivar,* Dent, 1952); *Highway of the Sun,* Little, Brown, 1955; *Realm of the Incas,* New American Library, 1957, revised edition illustrated by A. Beltran, 1961; *The Aztec: Man and Tribe* (illustrated by A. Beltran), New American Library, 1958, revised edition, 1962; (editor) Pedro de Cieza de Leon, *The Incas,* University of Oklahoma Press, 1959.

The puma knows how to use his concealment. Soon it is close enough to make its lunge. ■ (From *South American Zoo* by Victor W. von Hagen. Illustrated by Francis Lee Jaques.)

World of the Maya (illustrated by A. Beltran), New American Library, 1960; *The Ancient Sun Kingdoms of the Americas: Aztec, Maya, Inca* (illustrated by A. Beltran), World Publishing, 1961; (editor) William H. Prescott, *History of the Conquest of Peru*, Muller, 1961; (editor) John Lloyd Stephens, *Incidents of Travel in Yucatan*, University of Oklahoma Press, 1962; *The Desert Kingdoms of Peru*, New American Library, 1964; *The Roads That Led to Rome* (photographs by Adolfo Tomeucci), World Publishing, 1967.

(Editor) John Lloyd Stephens, *Incident of Travel in Egypt, Arabia Petraea, and the Holy Land*, University of Oklahoma Press, 1970; *Der Ruf der Neuen Welt: Deutsche Bauen Amerika*, Droemer Knaur, 1970, translation published as *The Germanic People in America*, University of Oklahoma Press, 1976; *Search for the Maya: The Story of Stephens and Catherwood*, Saxon House, 1973; *The Golden Man: A Quest for El Dorado*, Saxon House, 1974; *Ecuador: A Journey in Time*, Plata Verlag (Switzerland), 1976; *The Royal Road of the Inca*, Gordon & Cremonesi, 1976; *Alexander Von Humboldt's America*, Plata Verlag, 1977; *The Persian Realms*, New American Library, 1977.

Also author of *El Dorado: The Golden Kingdoms of Colombia*, 1951; *The Life of E. George Squier*, 1951; *The High Voyage*, 1956; (translator) *The Journals of J. B. Boussingault*, 1957; *People's War, People's Army*, 1962; *The Mochicas and the Chimus*, 1963; *The Road Runner* (autobiography), 1970; *I, Bernal Diaz, Conus Conquistador* (for children), 1977.

Contributor to the *Encyclopaedia Britannica* as well as various periodicals including *Travel, Science Digest, Nature Magazine, Natural History,* and *Scientific Monthly.*

SIDELIGHTS: Born in 1908 in St. Louis, Missouri. As the son of a paper-chemist, Von Hagen was reared in a "paper" world.

During his years in private schools in both America and England, he found himself torn between literature and science; between the active life of an explorer and the solitary life of a writer. It was during an early expedition to Mexico at the age of twenty-three that he decided to devote his energy to writing and exploring.

On expedition to Ecuador, Von Hagen and first wife lived for about eight months with the Jivaros Indians, a tribe of headhunters, observing their culture and publishing those findings in *Off with Their Heads*. Von Hagen became so engrossed in his study that he accompanied some of the war parties on their excursions to witness the ancient art and ritual of head shrinking.

On exhibition to Honduras and Guatemala, Von Hagen located and captured specimens of the quetzal, a bird revered by the Aztecs and Mayas. With the aid of a twelve-year-old boy, Dr. Von Hagen was able to overcome the superstitions of the natives and secure quetzals to be shipped to the London and Bronx Zoos. During this same expedition Von Hagen discovered a tribe of Jicaque Indians, descendants of the Mayas, formerly believed to be extinct.

The explorer-naturalist is credited with compiling the first complete study of the Great Tortoise of the Galapagos Islands and is also regarded as an authority on the ecology of plant life in the archipelago. Von Hagen was instrumental in the erection of a monument to Charles Darwin and for the establishment of the Charles Darwin Residence Station in the Galapagos.

His interest in papermaking is reflected in his work, *The Aztec and Maya Papermakers*, in which he corrected the misconception that Mexican paper was made from the agave plant. He found, in fact, that the Aztecs and Mayas made paper by preparing the inner bark of the fig tree and of trees in the mulberry family.

In 1961 the American Broadcasting Corporation televised the documentary motion picture, "Weavers of Death," which filmed one of Von Hagen's Peruvian expeditions searching through the ruins of the ancient Nazca, Ica, and Inca civilizations.

Collections of Von Hagen's artifacts are on display at the British Museum and the American Museum of Natural History.

FOR MORE INFORMATION SEE: Horn Book, January-December, 1947, August, 1966; *New Yorker,* January 3, 1953; *Cosmopolitan,* January, 1960.

Matilda told such dreadful lies,
It made one gasp and stretch one's eyes;
Her aunt, who, from her earliest youth,
Had kept a strict regard for truth,
Attempted to believe Matilda:
The effort very nearly killed her.

—Hilaire Belloc

WAIDE, Jan 1952-

PERSONAL: Born June 7, 1952, in Wichita Falls, Tex.; daughter of Elmer A. (a petroleum engineer) and Margaret (an artist; maiden name, Jones) Milz; married John Waide (a professor of philosophy), January 5, 1974. *Education:* Attended University of Texas, Austin, 1970-72; Harris School of Art, Franklin, Tenn., certificate in illustration, 1975. *Home and office:* 1750 Crump Ave., Memphis, Tenn. 38107.

CAREER: Free-lance artist and illustrator, 1975—; United Methodist Publishing House, Nashville, Tenn., artist and designer, 1978-79. Has given illustration and writing demonstrations and has taught art at elementary schools. Has had one-woman shows in Georgetown, Tex., and Austin, Tex., both in 1977; work included in group exhibitions at the Watercolor Art Society, Houston, Tex., 1976, and the Southwestern Wa-

JAN WAIDE

tercolor Society, 1977. *Member:* Society of Children's Book Writers, Gray Panthers, Watercolor Art Society (Houston), Germantown Art League (Memphis).

WRITINGS—All juveniles: *Jennifer* (self-illustrated), Shoal Creek Publishers, 1978; *Weed* (self-illustrated), Shoal Creek Publishers, 1980.

Illustrator: Vivian Montgomery, *Mr. Jellybean,* Shoal Creek Publishers, 1980.

WORK IN PROGRESS: Four picture books—two based on childhood memories, and one fantasy and one folktale; a nonfiction book about blackbirds.

SIDELIGHTS: "Having grown up with an artistic mother, painting and drawing have been my companions for most of my life. Writing is newer to me. I first became interested in writing as well as illustrating books for children when I heard an interview with Leo Lionni in 1975. He described the joy and the challenge of creating a book whose design, words, and pictures work together as a whole.

"Since then, *Jennifer* and *Weed* have been published. I've read what many illustrators and writers have written about picture books and have experimented with their advice. I do aspire to making books that adults consider well-designed works of art. My fondest hope, though, is someday to take a book I've written and illustrated from a library shelf and find its pages scribbled on, smudged, and dog-eared. Then I'd know that children loved it."

"I do like plants," she said, "but this is a dandelion...."
■ (From *Weed* by Jan Waide. Illustrated by the author.)

WARNER, Oliver 1903-1976

PERSONAL: Born February 28, 1903, in London, England; died August 14, 1976; son of Richard Cromwell and Grace (Wilson) Warner; married Elizabeth Strahan, 1937; children: Charles, Olivia. *Education:* Attended Denstone College; Gonville and Caius College, University of Cambridge, B.A., 1925, M.A., 1946. *Religion:* Church of England. *Home:* Old Manor Cottage, Haslemere, Surrey, England.

CAREER: Chatto and Windus Ltd., London, England, reader, 1926-41; British Admiralty, London, civilian officer, 1941-47; British Council, London, deputy director of publications, 1947-63. Writer. *Member:* Royal Society of Literature (fellow), Society for Nautical Research (council, 1955-63), Navy Records Society (council, 1960-64), Royal Automobile Club (London), Three Counties Club (Haselmere).

WRITINGS: Victory: The Life of Lord Nelson (U.S. History Book Club selection), Little, 1958; *Trafalgar* (British Battle Series), Macmillan, 1959; *The Battle of the Nile,* Macmillan, 1960; *The Glorious First of June,* Macmillan, 1961; *Great Sea Battles,* Macmillan, 1963; (with Chester W. Nimitz) *Nelson and the Age of Fighting Sail,* American Heritage, 1963; (with J. C. Beaglehole) *Captain Cook and the South Pacific,* Harper, 1963; *The Sea and the Sword: The Baltic, 1630-1945,* Morrow, 1965.

SIDELIGHTS: Warner is a descendant of Oliver Cromwell.

HOBBIES AND OTHER INTERESTS: Coins, marine painting, Venice.

WESTERBERG, Christine 1950-

PERSONAL: Born September 26, 1950, in Glen Cove, N.Y.; daughter of Arthur R. (a personnel manager) and Jane (an artist; maiden name, McCaffrey) Westerberg; married Richard J. de Monda (a biomedical engineer), October 5, 1974. *Education:* Philadelphia College of Art, B.F.A., 1972; also studied at C. W. Post College of Long Island University.

CAREER: American Institute of Physics, New York, N.Y., member of art staff, 1972; children's book illustrator, 1972—; World-Book-Childcraft International, Inc., member of art staff, 1980-81.

WRITINGS—Juvenile; all self-illustrated: *A Little Lion,* Prentice-Hall, 1975; *The Cap That Mother Made,* Prentice-Hall, 1977.

Illustrator—Juvenile: *Tom Thumb,* retold by Mercy Yates, Prentice-Hall, 1973; Eleanor J. Lapp, *Duane the Collector,*

The gleaming crown was coming closer and closer, and he knew that he could *not* say no to a King.

Then he remembered something. He bowed deeply, swept the cap off his head....

■ (From *The Cap That Mother Made,* adapted and illustrated by Christine Westerberg.)

Addison Wesley, 1975; Mark Taylor, *The Hiding Place*, Allyn & Bacon, 1975.

SIDELIGHTS: ''My interest in illustrating children's stories and writing them is partly because I enjoy it, and partly because I feel a child's interest in reading must be stimulated early and be cultivated, as a basis for his whole attitude toward reading and learning as an adult.''

WHITE, E(lwyn) B(rooks)   1899-

PERSONAL: Born July 11, 1899 in Mount Vernon, N.Y.; son of Samuel Tilly (a piano manufacturer) and Jessie (Hart) White; married Katharine Sergeant Angell (a *New Yorker* editor), November 13, 1929; children: Joel McCoun. *Education:* Cornell University, A.B., 1921. *Residence:* North Brooklin, Me. *Office: New Yorker,* 25 West 43rd St., New York, N.Y. 10036.

CAREER: Reporter with *Seattle Times,* Seattle Wash., 1922-23; worked two years in advertising agency as production assistant and copywriter; writer, contributing editor, *New Yorker,* 1927—. Regular contributor of column, ''One Man's Meat,'' to *Harper's,* 1938-43. *Military service:* U.S. Army, 1918. *Member:* National Institute of Arts and Letters, American Academy of Arts and Sciences (fellow), Phi Beta Kappa, Phi Gamma Delta.

AWARDS, HONORS—For children's books: *Charlotte's Web* was named a Newbery Honor Book, 1953, and received the Lewis Carroll Shelf Award, 1958, the George G. Stone Center for Children's Books Recognition of Merit Award, 1970, and the New England Round Table of Children's Libraries Award, 1973; *The Trumpet of the Swan* was nominated for a National Book Award, 1971, was included on the International Board on Books for Young People Honor List, 1972, and received the Children's Book Award from the William Allen White Library at Emporia State University, 1973, the Sequoyah Children's Book Award from the Oklahoma Library Association, 1973, the Sue Hefley Award from the Louisiana Association of School Librarians, 1974, and the Young Hoosier Award from the Indian School Librarians Association, 1975; Laura Ingalls Wilder Medal, 1970, for ''a lasting contribution to children's literature.''

Other awards: Gold Medal Award, Limited Editions Club, 1944, for *One Man's Meat;* National Association of Independent Schools Award, 1955, for *The Second Tree from the Corner;* Gold Medal, Institute of Arts and Letters, 1960; Presidential Medal of Freedom, 1963; National Medal for Literature, National Institute of Arts and Letters, 1971; Pulitzer Prize Committee special citation, 1978, for the full body of his work. Numerous honorary degrees include Litt.D., Dartmouth, 1948, University of Maine, 1948, Yale University, 1948, Bowdoin

E.B. WHITE

College, 1950, Hamilton College, 1952, Harvard University, 1954; L.H.D., Colby College, 1954.

WRITINGS—For children: *Stuart Little* (illustrated by Garth Williams), Harper, 1945, reprinted, 1973; *Charlotte's Web* (illustrated by Williams), Harper, 1952, reprinted 1973; *The Trumpet of the Swan* (illustrated by Edward Frascino), Harper, 1970.

Other: *The Lady Is Cold* (poetry), Harper, 1929; (with James Thurber) *Is Sex Necessary?* (essays), Harper, 1929, reprinted, 1973; *Ho Hum,* Farrar & Rinehart, 1931; *Another Ho Hum,* Farrar & Rinehart, 1932; *Alice through the Cellophane,* John Day, 1933; *Every Day Is Saturday* (commentary), Harper, 1934; (with R. L. Stout) *Farewell to Model T,* Putnam, 1936; *The Fox of Peapack* (poetry), Harper, 1938; *Quo Vadimus?* (essays), Harper, 1939; (editor, with K. S. White) *A Subtreasury of American Humor,* Coward, McCann, 1941; *One Man's Meat,* Harper, 1942, enlarged edition, Harper, 1944; *The Wild Flag,* Houghton, 1946; *Here Is New York,* Harper, 1949; *The Second Tree from the Corner,* Harper, 1954, reprinted, 1965; (editorial supervisor and contributor) *The Elements of Style,* by William Strunk, Jr., 3rd edition, Macmillan, 1979; *The Points of My Compass,* Harper, 1962; *An E. B. White Reader,* edited by William W. Watt and Robert W. Bradford, Harper, 1966; *The Letters of E. B. White,* edited by Dorothy L. Guth, Harper, 1976; *Essays of E. B. White,* Harper, 1977; (editor) Katharine S. White, *Onward and Upward in the Garden,* Farrar, Straus, 1979; *Poems and Sketches of E. B. White,* Harper, 1981.

Manuscript collection is held at Cornell University Library.

ADAPTATIONS—Movies and filmstrips: ''Charlotte's Web'' (motion picture), Paramount, 1972; ''Charlotte's Web'' (filmstrip), narrated by E. B. White, Stephen Bosustow Productions, 1974, Films Incorporated, 1976. ''Stuart Little'' has been televised by NBC.

Recordings: ''Stuart Little'' (phonotape), Dell, 1973; ''Charlotte's Web,'' read by the author, RCA, 1976.

SIDELIGHTS: **July 11, 1899.** Born in Mount Vernon, New York. ''On the summer morning when I arrived in this world, there was a breakdown in communications. Dr. Archibald Campbell was supposed to come to the house and deliver me, but he couldn't be reached. At the last minute, some member of the family looked out of a front window, saw Dr. Campbell driving by in his buggy, flagged him down, and hustled him up to Mother's bedroom, where he took over. My numbers were lucky ones: July is the seventh month, and I appeared on the eleventh day. Seven, eleven, I've been lucky ever since and have always counted heavily on luck.

''If an unhappy childhood is indispensable for a writer, I am ill-equipped: I missed out on all that and was neither deprived nor unloved. It would be inaccurate, however, to say that my childhood was untroubled. The normal fears and worries of each child were in me developed to a high degree; every day was an awesome prospect. I was uneasy about practically everything: the uncertainty of the future, the dark of the attic, the panoply and discipline of school, the transitoriness of life, the mystery of the church and of God, the frailty of the body, the sadness of afternoon, the shadow of sex, the distant challenge of love and marriage, the far-off problem of a livelihood. I brooded about them all, lived with them day by day. Being the youngest in a large family, I was usually in a crowd but often felt lonely and removed. I took to writing early, to assuage

my uneasiness and collect my thoughts, and I was a busy writer long before I went into long pants.

''Our big house at 101 Summit Avenue was my castle. From it I emerged to do battle, and into it I retreated when I was frightened or in trouble. The house even had the appearance of a fortress, with its octagonal tower room for sighting the enemy and its second-story porches for gun emplacements. Just inside the massive front door was the oak hatrack, next to the umbrella stand. On the left the parlor, where the action was; on the right the 'reception room,' where no one was ever received but where I found my mother one day stretched out on the settee, recovering from an accident with a runaway horse. I thought she was dead.

''I remember the cellar, its darkness and dampness, its set tubs, its Early American water closet for the help, its coal furnace that often tried to asphyxiate us all, and the early sound of the Italian furnace man who crept in at dawn and shook the thing down. As a very small boy, I used to repair to the cellar, where I would pee in the coal bin—for variety. Out back was the stable, where I spent countless hours hobnobbing with James Bridges, the coachman, watching him polish harness and wash carriages.

''My father, Samuel Tilly White, was born in Brooklyn, the son of a carpenter and the grandson of a contractor. I don't know a great deal about my father's upbringing and home life. I don't think there was much money there, and there may have been some rough times. My father was, all his life, a sober and abstemious man, but I'm not sure his father was. . . . At any rate, young Samuel, my father . . . felt obliged to quit school at thirteen and go to work. He found a job as 'bundle boy' (wrapping packages) with the piano firm of Horace Waters & Company, at 134 Fifth Avenue, Manhattan. . . .

''Sam White not only wrapped bundles for his employer, he began pulling at his own bootstraps. He informed himself about every aspect of the business, learned bookkeeping, learned to play the piano, kept his eyes and ears open, and was soon climbing life's ladder. . . . When I was a child, I used to watch parades from a front-row seat next to the big plate glass window on the second floor of 134 Fifth Avenue—a splendid vantage point. I was 'Mr. White's boy,' marked for the special treatment. I made many visits to 134 and remember particularly the wonderful sad sound of a piano being tuned somewhere in the building.

''One of the fringe benefits of being the son of a piano man was that our parlor at 101 Summit Avenue was well supplied with musical instruments: a Waters grand, a reed organ with phony pipes, and, at one period, a Waters player piano called an 'Autola.' There were six of us children, and we were practically a ready-made band. All we lacked was talent. We had violins, cellos, mandolins, guitars, banjos, and drums, and there was always a lot of music filling the air in our home, none of it good. We sang, composed, harmonized, drummed, and some of us took lessons for brief spells in an attempt to raise the general tone of the commotion. My brother Stanley was a fiddler. I played piano, picked at the mandolin, and at one point acquired a three-quarter-size cello and took lessons. But I failed to develop musical curiosity, learned nothing about the works of the great, and was content to make a noise, whether ragtime or schmalz or Czerny. Like my father, I liked the sound of music but was too lazy to follow it to its source.

''In the order of our arrival, we were Marion Robertson White, Clara Frances White, Albert Hunt White, Stanley Hart White,

"I have news for you,"she said. "Your son Louis is in love, and the swan of his choice, the female of his desiring, pays no attention to him." ■ (From *The Trumpet of the Swan* by E.B. White. Illustrated by Edward Frascino.)

Lillian White, and Elwyn Brooks White. There was a seventh child—Mother's second—who died in infancy. Father and Mother almost never mentioned her, and it was as though she had never existed.'' [Dorothy Lobrano Guth, editor and compiler, *Letters of E. B. White*, Harper, 1976.[1]]

1904. ''When the time came for me to enter kindergarten, I fought my parents with every ounce of my puny strength. I screamed and carried on. The idea of school terrified me—I wanted to stay home and live peacefully in familiar surroundings. My parents, of course, won, after a showdown, and I was bundled off to P.S. 2 on Lincoln Avenue. The name of my kindergarten teacher was Miss Greene. We sat in little chairs in a circle. There was a pudgy girl who thought I was cute and wanted to hold my hand. I hated her with all my heart and would pull my hand away in revulsion.

''I spent the next nine years in P.S. 2. I covered the distance on foot or on a bicycle. There were no school buses, and there was no nonsense in the classroom, either. Nothing was called 'language arts' or 'social studies.' Everything went by its simple name: reading, writing, spelling, arithmetic, grammar, geography, history, music. I was a diligent scholar—more from fear of falling behind than from intellectual curiosity—and got good marks. School opened with an assembly, in a big room where we saluted the flag, listened to the principal read a passage from the Bible, heard one student recite a piece from the platform, and then marched out to piano music by Mrs. Schuyler, with whom I was in love. It was in P.S. 2 that I contracted the fear of platforms that had dogged me all my life and caused me to decline every invitation to speak in public. For the assembly performances, pupils were picked in alphabetical order, and since there were a great many pupils and my name began with W, I spent the entire term dreading the ordeal of making a public appearance. I suffered from a severe anticipatory sickness. Usually the term ended before my name came up, and then the new term started again at the top of the alphabet. I mounted the platform only once in my whole career, but I suffered tortures every day of the school year, thinking about the awesome—if improbable—event.''[1]

1913. ''From P.S. 2, I went on to the Mount Vernon High School. I liked Latin pretty well but never was able to get a modern language and am still monolingual. Some of the girls were beginning to wear silk stockings, and this got my thoughts moving. I didn't care for athletics, being skinny and small, but I liked ice ponds and skating, and on winter afternoons and evenings I would visit a pond (a fifteen-minute ride on a trolly car) and skate with a girl named Mildred Hesse. Her eyes were blue and her ankles were strong. Together we must have covered hundreds of miles, sometimes leaving the pond proper and gliding into the woods on narrow fingers of ice. We didn't talk much, never embraced, we just skated for the ecstasy of skating—a magical glide. After one of these sessions, I would go home and play 'Liebestraum' on the Autola, bathed in the splendor of perfect love and natural fatigue. This brief interlude on ice, in the days of my youth, had a dreamlike quality, a purity, that has stayed with me all my life; and when nowadays I see a winter sky and feel the wind dropping with the sun and the naked trees against a reddening west, I remember what it was like to be in love before any of love's complexities or realities or disturbances had entered in, to dilute its splendor and challenge its perfection.''[1]

1917. Graduated from high school, where he had won two scholarships totaling $1000—a large sum, considering that the tuition at Cornell, which he planned to attend, was $100 a year. ''When I landed in Ithaca, I was a green boy if ever there was one.''[1]

While at Cornell, White worked on the Cornell *Daily Sun*. At the end of his junior year he was elected editor-in-chief. He became president of his fraternity and was elected to the senior honorary society, Quill and Dagger. ''. . . I majored in English partly because I didn't know what else to do, but mostly because I did have a strong tendency to write. (I was a writing fool when I was eleven years old and have been tapering off ever since.) Because of this desire to write, I was one of the lucky ones. It ought to cheer you up, though, to know that my interest in the world's great literature was woefully anemic; I got very little out of my courses, didn't understand half of what I read, skimped wherever I could, did rather badly, and came away from Cornell without a solid education and have never got round to correcting this deficiency. Primarily, my interest was in journalism, and most of my life has been spent in that arena, tilting at the dragons and clowning with the clowns. Even at Cornell, most of my time was spent getting out the daily newspaper."[1]

1921. Following graduation from Cornell, White went to New York City to find work. "The job I took . . . is with the United Press—an organization similar to and rivalling the Associated Press. I start feeding wires in the New York bureau Saturday morning. Doubtless I'll drive right into the middle of the Arbuckle case. The officers are in the Pulitzer building on Park Row—right in the newspaper district so I'll be within lunching distance of my friends.

"I could have had a job with the N.Y. Edison Company editing their house organ, if I had wanted to. I was seriously tempted, too, but my conscience (damn it) troubled me. It was almost too soft—all I would have had to do would have been to sit in a beautifully upholstered private office with a stenographer who reads the *Saturday Evening Post* all day, and edit a small paper once a week. They actually wanted to pay me to do that. I'll probably wish I were doing it, along about Saturday morning at 11:30 when I am dizzy from the wheels going round."[1]

December, 1921. Left the United Press and went to work for a public relations man. "I am now a dirty publicity person: I am the person at whom the city editors shy their paper weights and other missiles. I sneak into their office when the desk-boy isn't looking and hand them stories that they don't like. I don't blame them for not liking them. I am the person who furnishes the material that keeps the janitors employed. If it wasn't for me there would be thousands of janitors out of work in New York City. I write the stories, the city editors brush 'em onto the floor, and the janitors sweep 'em up. So you see I am actually doing a very valuable work—the janitors *must* live. The reason I haven't been fired is because my boss hasn't got round to it yet. It's one of the things he has on his desk calendar, to be done when he finds the time. I am convinced that my boss is a rascal—and I've only seen him three times since I've had the job. Such perception!"[1]

January, 1922. Joined the American Legion News Service. ". . . My job with the News Service of the Legion is very good in many respects. It gives me the opportunity to learn publicity by practising it on a very large scale—the Legion covers an awful lot of ground and the stuff I turn out reaches in the neighborhood of 15,000 papers—and there is the chance, in the spring, of my being handed the boss's job, inasmuch as he contemplates moving west. He doesn't like New York City. The result is it has a black eye in journalistic circles. Take this for instance . . . I had a talk with the editor of *Editor and Publisher*, whom I know. He offered me a job, first of all, with his publication—which I didn't take for certain reasons. Then he asked me what I was doing—he thought I was still with the United Press—and when I told him that I was in publicity he gave me a beautiful calling down—'a man of your ideals in a tainted profession.' All that kind of stuff. That was at ten minutes to nine—nice pleasant way to start the day having a person like that inform you that you're tainted. I had a mental picture of Mother sniffing me when I came home at night, the way she does butter to see if it is all right. . . .

"Sold a story to the N.Y. *Sun* last week, so I'm not entirely rancid yet. . . ."[1]

Spring, 1922. Quit his job and travelled cross country with a friend. In Seattle, White worked on the Seattle *Times*. "The *Times* is very highbrow, very conservative, very rich, and entirely unreadable. It is one of the most splendidly equipped newspaper organizations in the country—wonderful big new building occupying an entire block in the center of the city; and five enormous rotary presses. When you are sent out to get a story, you go in as much style as the Prince of Wales. It's like this: You are sitting at your typewriter, simulating work. The city editor approaches rapidly. He speaks a name and a location, turns on his heel, and is gone. You press the elevator button and land downstairs, where a staff photographer and a staff automobile await you at the door.—Can you beat that for service?

"I work from 7:30 a.m. until I'm through—which is anywhere from 2:30 to 11:30 p.m., according to what my assignments have been. At present I have no regular beat, but am on general assignment and rewrite, which means that one minute I am reporting a drowning at the waterfront, and the next minute interviewing a member of the Japanese Embassy.

"This is a very peculiar city. It rains here every day all winter long—and it has begun already. I find it a trifle depressing. . . . But I guess I'll stay here, for I've at last got a job on a newspaper. . . ."[1]

1923. When White was let go by the Seattle *Times,* he boarded a ship, the *S.S. Buford,* bound for Alaska and Siberia. "My trip to Alaska, like practically everything else that happened to me in those busy years, was pure accident. I was living in Seattle; I was unemployed, my job on a newspaper having blown up in mid-June; and although I had no reason for going to Alaska, I had no reason for staying away, either. The entries in my journal covering the four-week period between the loss of my job and the start of my trip to the north reveal a young man living a life of exalted footlessness. I was a literary man in the highest sense of the term, a poet who met every train. No splendor appeared in the sky without my celebrating it, nothing mean or unjust took place but felt the harmless edge of my wildly swinging sword. I walked in the paths of righteousness, studying girls. In particular, I studied a waitress in a restaurant called the Chantecler. I subscribed to two New York dailies, the *World* and the *Evening Post.* I swam alone at night in the canal that connects Lake Union and Lake Washington. I seldom went to bed before two or three o'clock in the morning, on the theory that if anything of interest were to happen to a young man it would almost certainly happen late at night. Daytimes, I hung around my room in Mrs. Donohue's boarding house, reading the 'Bowling Green' and the 'Conning Tower,' wondering what to do next, and writing.

"My entry for June 15, 1923, begins, 'A man must have something to cling to. Without that he is as a pea vine sprawling in search of a trellis.' Obviously, I was all asprawl, clinging to Beauty, which is a very restless trellis. My prose style at this time was a stomach-twisting blend of the Bible, Carl Sandburg, H. L. Mencken, Jeffrey Farnol, Christopher Morley, Samuel Pepys, and Franklin Pierce Adams imitating Samuel Pepys. I was quite apt to throw in a 'bless the mark' at any spot, and to begin a sentence with 'Lord' comma.

"On June 19, I recorded my discharge from the *Times* and noted that the city editor said it was 'no reflection on my ability.' I didn't believe then, and do not believe now, that it was no reflection on my ability. As a newspaper reporter, I was almost useless, and it came as no surprise when one more trellis collapsed on me. When I left the *Times* office with my

(From the one-hour television special "Stuart Little," narrated by Johnny Carson. Presented on NBC-TV March 6, 1966. Photograph courtesy of National Broadcasting Co., Inc.)

final pay check in my pocket, I 'sauntered' down Pine Street. I can still recall experiencing an inner relief—the feeling of again being adrift on life's sea, an element I felt more at home in than in a city room. On June 25, I clipped a sonnet sequence by Morley from the 'Bowling Green' and pasted it in the journal. The second sonnet began, 'So put your trust in poets.' As though I needed to be told that!

''For one week I worked on Hearst's *Post-Intelligencer,* commonly called the *P.I.,* substituting for a reporter on vacation. My entry for July 18 (1:30 A.M.) begins, 'A man scarce realizes what a terrible thing scorn is until he begins to despise himself.' I doubt that I found myself despicable; I simply found life perplexing. I did not know where to go. On Friday, July 20 (3 A.M.), appears the abrupt entry. 'I sail Monday on *S.S. Buford* for Skagway.' No explanation or amplification follows, only an account of an evening spent with a girl who lived on Lake Union. (She fed me bread and apple jelly.)

''Working in a ship is a far better life than sailing in one as a passenger. Alaska, the sea, and the ship herself became real to me as soon as I was employed; before that, all three had suffered from a sort of insubstantiality. Passengers never really come to know a ship; too much is hidden from their sight, too little is demanded of them. They may love their ship, but without their participating in her operation the identification is not established. As saloonsman, I was a participant—at first a slightly sick participant. I worked from eight in the evening till six in the morning. I set tables, prepared late supper for thirty, served it (sometimes carrying a full tray in a beam sea), cleaned the tables, washed the dishes, stropped the glasses, swept down the companionway leading to the social hall, and shined brass. This was hard work, dull work, and, until my stomach adjusted to the ripe smell of the pantry, touchy work. But when, at around three o'clock, I stepped out onto the

forward deck for a smoke, with the sky showing bright in the north and the mate pacing the bridge and the throaty snores of the passengers issuing from the staterooms, the ship would throb and tremble under me and she was *my* ship, all mine and right on course, alive and purposeful and exciting. . . .

''. . . On September 4, we docked at Seattle. I collected my pay and went ashore. My next entry is dated September 6, from a room in the Frye Hotel—a poem called 'Chantecler.'

'How many orders of beef have you passed over the
     counter,
Girl with white arms, since I've been gone?
How many times have you said.
''Gravy?''

'Your arms are still white,
And you're still the thing in all the room
That transcends foodstuffs.

'By standing there
You make the restaurant part of September,
And September, girl, is part of the world—
A sad-voiced, beautiful part.

'How many orders of beef have you passed over the
     counter,
Girl with white arms, since I've been gone?'

''Like so many other questions that stirred in me in those years of wonder and of wandering, this one was to go forever unanswered.'' [E. B. White, ''The Years of Wonder,'' *The Points of My Compass: Essays,* Harper, 1962.[2]]

Fall, 1923. Returned to parents' home in Mount Vernon. Worked in the advertising business for the next two years.

November, 1925. Moved to Manhattan. "Everything was great, everything was exciting, except that for much of the time I didn't have a job, having drifted out of advertising, which I hated. . . . I acquired a caged bird to keep me company and tried my hand at free lancing—nothing new for me, as I had been submitting poems and sketches to newspapers and magazines for years. . . . Christopher Morley had published a sonnet to a bantam rooster—for which I won a prize, competing with other sonneteers. To appear in the Conning Tower gave a young poet a great lift to the spirit: it did not give him any money. The arrival on the scene of Harold Ross's *New Yorker* . . . was a turning point in my life, although I did not know it at the time. I bought a copy of the first issue at a newsstand in Grand Central, examined Eustace Tilley and his butterfly on the cover, and was attracted to the newborn magazine not because it had any great merit but because the items were short, relaxed, and sometimes funny. I was a 'short' writer, and I lost no time in submitting squibs and poems. In return I received a few small checks and the satisfaction of seeing myself in print as a pro."[1]

January, 1927. Agreed to work part time for the *New Yorker,* gradually increasing his work at the magazine to a full-time job. "The cast of characters in those early days was as shifty as the characters in a floating poker game. People drifted in and drifted out. Every week the magazine teetered on the edge of financial ruin. Katharine Angell arrived in 1925. Fillmore Hyde, from the Peapack hunting set, arrived. . . . Then Ralph McAllister Ingersoll arrived, right out of the social register. Lois Long, Peter Arno, Rogers Whittaker arrived, right out of

the subway. Rea Irvin, the art editor, arrived before anybody else. He was the one person around the place who seemed to know what he was doing. . . . It was chaos, but it was enjoyable. I dropped the name James Thurber, and Ross [editor of the *New Yorker*] hired him immediately. 'I hire anybody,' he remarked, gloomily. Thurber and I shared a sort of elongated closet, just big enough to hold two desks, two typewriters, and a mountainous stack of yellow copy paper, which the two of us set about covering with words and pictures. Raoul Fleischmann poured money in, Ross fought with Fleischmann and erected an impenetrable barrier between the advertising department and the editorial department. It was known as the Ross Barrier."[1]

1929. First two books were published.

November 13, 1929. Married a young divorcee and editor of the *New Yorker,* Katharine Angell. Angell had two children from her first marriage. "I soon realized I had made no mistake in my choice of a wife. I was helping her pack an overnight bag one afternoon when she said, 'Put in some tooth twine.' I knew then that a girl who called dental floss tooth twine was the girl for me. It had been a long search, but it was worth it."[1]

December 21, 1930. Son born. "Sex is male, color white, and a dandy son all right all right. First name Joel, then McCoun, and all in all he's such a boon. Now I'll slip into prose, naturally and easily. . . . I can now mix his formula—no harder than mixing a good Martini—and am in complete charge of his life and character; he has plenty of both. He weighs, at this writing,

He wondered whether Harriet would notice that his paddle was really just an ice cream spoon.
■ (From *Stuart Little* by E.B. White. Illustrated by Garth Williams.)

Wilbur jumped as high as he could ■ (From *Charlotte's Web* by E.B. White. Illustrated by Garth Williams.)

eleven pounds no ounces. Much of the time he spends in Washington Square, with the rest of the unemployed. When, after a cry, he stares at me with a critical and resentful gaze, just out of focus, I feel the mixed pride and oppression of fatherhood in the very base of my spine.''[1]

1936. Offered the editorship of the *Saturday Review of Literature*, but declined. ''I can't edit the *Sat. Review*, & this is the more painful for me because I like it. . . . I am, furthermore, hot for change (for myself)—which doesn't mean disloyalty to the *N.Y.'er* but more of a kind of super-loyalty to myself. I often feel out on a limb, doing what I'm doing. . . . The trouble with me is I am no editor even with a small E. Understanding this has saved me, & my beloved magazine, much woe. I can't edit the side of a barn. . . . At the *NYer* I am an office boy de-luxe—a happy & profitable arrangement. My function is solely contributive except for one or two perfunctory chores which I can now do with my left hind foot. I am appalled when I think of taking over the *Review*. . . . My health is always whimsical, and I turn out shockingly little work in the course of a week—much less than I wish I did & far less, I'm sure, than you imagine. Being the head of anything would bust me up in no time. What I do hope for myself is

that before long I can rearrange my affairs so that I can devote my limited energy & curious talents to the sort of writing nearest to my heart & pen. If this should turn out to be interesting to the *Sat. Review*, that might be another story.''[1]

1938. Moved to a farm in North Brooklin, Maine. Maintained close ties with the *New Yorker* and contributed a monthly column, ''One Man's Meat'' to *Harper's* magazine. A book of poems was published. ''The copies of *The Fox of Peapack* have arrived and I think they look fine. Now that the dove hangs over Middle Europe, America ought to be right in the mood for a little book of topical ballads, nicely rhymed and essentially cheerful in tone. Throwing modesty to the winds I sat down and wrote the . . . suggestion for an advertisement which I would like . . . to insert in all morning and evening papers in the United States at a cost of only three million dollars. I think it will whet people's curiosity in great shape. . . . I used to be in the advertising business and was doing very well when something snapped and I began writing ballads. Naturally I don't believe all those nice things I have said about myself in the ad, but we poets have to get along somehow. I really wrote it because I have always wanted to put William Randolph Hearst next to a concrete septic tank.

". . . I finally quit thinking about book titles when I arrived at one called 'The Pop-Up Book for Sit-Down People.' "[1]

1939. Began writing his first children's book, *Stuart Little.* ". . . The principal character in the story has somewhat the attributes and appearance of a mouse. This does not mean that I am either challenging or denying Mr. Disney's genius. At the risk of seeming a very whimsical fellow indeed, I will have to break down and confess to you that Stuart Little appeared to me in dream, all complete, with his hat, his cane, and his brisk manner. Since he was the only fractional figure ever to honor and disturb my sleep, I was deeply touched, and felt that I was not free to change him into a grasshopper or a wallaby. Luckily he bears no resemblance, either physically or temperamentally, to Mickey. I guess that's a break for all of us."[1]

1941. During World War II the Whites returned to New York from Maine to the *New Yorker,* whose editorial staff had been drastically reduced.

1943. Returned to Maine. "For some months I have been trying to figure out what I had better do about my life, since it is apparent that I am trying to do too many things. I have talked this over with myself, back and forth, and am reluctantly reporting that I must quit 'One Man's Meat' [his monthly column for *Harper's*]. This must seem rather odd and sudden . . . but the truth is I have had great difficulty, all along, writing essays of this sort, as they do not seem to come naturally to me and I have to go through the devil to get them written. Several times I have sent off a department which did not satisfy me and which I sent only because it was to fulfill a promise, or continuing obligation, or whatever you call a monthly deadline. So the only thing for me to do is to quit.

"I feel a peculiar disappointment, almost a defeat, in this, and hope *Harper's* will feel mildly disappointed too. It ought to be the most congenial job in the world for me, and the fault is entirely mine if it isn't. . . .

". . . I haven't figured out just what I will use for money from now on, and I trust I may occasionally be able to sell *Harper's* something or other. For the present, I have farm work and editorial work enough to keep me busy if not solvent, and I am hoping that my health (which has been rather sketchy lately) will improve by my cutting out this regular chore."[1]

1945. Published his first children's book, *Stuart Little,* which was illustrated by Garth Williams. "Quite a number of children have written me to ask about Stuart. They want to know whether he got back home and whether he found Margalo. They are good questions but I did not answer them in the book because, in a way, Stuart's journey symbolizes the continuing journey that everybody takes—in search of what is perfect and unattainable. This is perhaps too elusive an idea to put into a book for children, but I put it in anyway."[1]

1946. Declined an invitation to join the National Institute of Letters. ". . . I do not decline invitations for the sheer fun of declining them, or because it seems a brisk and cocky thing to do. The fact is, I have no membership in any society or organization, and this non-joining comes naturally to me. I sometimes suspect that I go a little out of my way to stay clear, and that this has the look of attitudinizing.

"I am extremely grateful for [the] invitation to become a member of the National Insitute. But I realized, when I got thinking about it, that the only legitimate reason for joining anything at all is an intention of participating in the work of it. And I long ago discovered that I had neither the energy nor the inclination nor the special talents that belong to membership in a group, whether literary or social."[1]

1948. Received an honorary Doctor of Letters from Dartmouth College. ". . . The President cited me for literary bravery (he little knew), the hood was slipped over my head, the diploma was slipped into my hand, there was some clapping and a couple of boos, and I walked back to sit down. I guess it must have been when I reached over to pick the program off the chair that my hood got hung up on Ben Ames Williams. Anyway, when I got seated the thing was up over my face, as in falconry. I truly lived up to the *New Yorker's* reputation for waggishness and clowning, as I sat there feebly pulling at the hood—a fully masked Doctor of Letters, a headless poet. I gave the boys their money's worth and I didn't mind it, particularly, as I wasn't really sure that anything much was wrong. Some learned man in the row behind me finally reached forward and rearranged me into some semblance of academic dignity.

"Hoods have a tiny loop that you are supposed to pass around a button on your vest, to give them a downhaul. But I forgot to do it. I guess I am the type that would forget to pull the ripcord."[1]

1952. *Charlotte's Web,* illustrated by Garth Williams, was published. All of White's juvenile books were written on his Maine farm. "I like animals and my barn is a very pleasant place to be, at all hours. One day when I was on my way to feed the pig, I began feeling sorry for the pig because, like most pigs, he was doomed to die. This made me sad. So I started thinking of ways to save a pig's life. I had been watching a big, grey spider at her work and was impressed by how clever she was at weaving. Gradually I worked the spider into the story . . . a story of friendship and salvation on a farm. Three years after I started writing it, it was published. (I am not a fast worker, as you can see.)" [Lee Bennett Hopkins, *More Books by More People,* Citation, 1974.[3]]

". . . When Garth Williams tried to dream up a spider that had human characteristics, the results were awful. He tried and tried, but we ended up with a Charlotte that was practically right out of a natural history book, or, more precisely, out of my own brain. And I pulled no punches in the story: the spider in the books is not prettified in any way, she is merely endowed with more talent than usual. This natural Charlotte was accepted at face value, and I came out ahead because of not trying to patronize an arachnid. I think a film maker might have the same good results by sticking with nature and with the barn. . . . I saw a spider spin the egg sac described in the story, and I wouldn't trade the sight for all the animated chipmunks in filmland. I watched the goslings hatch every spring, and I feel the same about that."[1]

When asked the difference between writing for children and writing for adults, White responded: ". . . In my experience, the only difference (save for a very slight modification of vocabulary) is in one's state of mind. Children are a wonderful audience—they are so eager, so receptive, so quick. I have great respect for their powers of observation and reasoning. But like any good writer, I write to amuse myself, not some imaginary audience, and I rather suspect that it is a great help if one has managed never really to grow up. Some writers, I have noticed, have a tendency to write *down* to children. That way lies disaster. Other writers feel they must use only the easy words, the familiar words. I use any word I feel like using, on the theory that children enjoy new encounters and that I don't gain anything by depriving myself of the full scope of the language. When I mentioned a 'very slight modification of vocabulary,' I was really alluding to the state of one's mind—which has an effect on the state of one's vocabulary.'' [Justin Wintle and Emma Fisher, *The Pied Pipers,* Paddington Press, 1974.[4]]

October, 1952. ''. . . My first fan mail on Charlotte was a long letter from a California vegetarian, who feels that my book shows that I am ripe to take the veil and live on grain, fruit, and nuts. I guess I'll never lack for nuts, anyway.

''So far, *Charlotte's Web* seems to have been read largely by adults with a literary turn of mind. I have had only a sprinkling of childhood reaction to the book—those vital and difficult precincts—and will not know for a little while how it sits with the young. I have a step grandchild named Caroline Angell who is a quiet little girl of about five. She listened attentively to the reading of the book by her father, and said: 'I think there was an easier way to save Wilbur, without all that trouble. Charlotte should have told him not to eat, then he wouldn't have been killed because he would have been too thin.''

''Trust an author to go to a lot of unnecessary trouble.''[1]

1958. *Charlotte's Web* received a Lewis Carroll Shelf Award as a book ''worthy enough to sit on the shelf with *Alice in Wonderland.*'' ''Margaret Mitchell once remarked: 'It is a full-time job to be the author of *Gone With the Wind.*' This remark greatly impressed me, as being an admission of defeat, American style. (Miss Mitchell, incidentally, was not overstating the matter—she never produced another book.) I don't want being the author of *Charlotte's Web* to be a full-time job or ever a part-time job. It seems to me that *being an author* is a silly way to spend one's day.''[1]

1963. Named by President John F. Kennedy as one of thirty-eight Americans to receive the Presidential Medal of Freedom—the highest honor a civilian can receive in time of peace. ''I know President Kennedy must have approached the freedom award list as he approached everything else—with personal concern, lively interest, and knowledge. To find myself on his list was the most gratifying thing that ever happened to me, as well as a matter of pride and sober resolve. . . .''[1]

1966. *Stuart Little* was adapted for television. ''. . . I wasn't satisfied with 'Stuart Little' on TV, but I didn't expect to be. It came out about the way I figured it would. By the terms of my contract with NBC, I was entitled to see and approve the

(From the animated film "The Family That Dwelt Apart," narrated by E.B. White, based on his *New Yorker* magazine story. Produced by Learning Corporation of America, 1974.)

script. A year ago, they sent me a script; I edited it (very slightly, but with a few good fixes) and returned it to them with my approval. Weeks later, I was told that they lost or misplaced *my* copy of the script, with my revisions. Then, months later, a brand new script arrived, and the glad tidings that the whole thing was wrapped up anyway, so I never bothered to read it.

"It is the fixed purpose of television and motion pictures to scrap the author, sink him without a trace, on the theory that he is incompetent, has never read his own stuff, is not responsible for anything he ever wrote, and wouldn't know what to do about it even if he were. I believe this has something to do with the urge to create, and the only way a TV person or a movie person can become a creator is to sink the guy who did it to begin with. I'm not really complaining about NBC, because by and large they set out to be fairly faithful to the general theme of Stuart, and they did not try to corrupt or demolish it. But there were a hundred places that, if they had wanted to take me into their confidence, I could have bettered for them. It was their choice not mine. The Johnny Carson narration was straight-forward, but muffed several spots that need not have been muffed. The music was good but in many places overpowering and over-riding. It fought with the words just when it should have been peaceable. I am fairly familiar with the text of *Stuart Little,* but when Stuart asked Margalo where she came from, and she replied, 'I came from fields once tall with wheat, from pastures deep in fern and thistle' I couldn't hear a damn thing against the musical background. At that particular moment, there shouldn't have been any music anyway, if I may rudely suggest such a departure.

"But the filming was ingenious throughout, and it certainly took a lot of dedication and a lot of doing. The sailboat race was pulled off despite great physical difficulties, and the schoolroom scene was effective because of the good faces, even though the script was not right, to my mind. . . .''[1]

1969. Worked on his children's book, *Trumpet of the Swan.* ''. . . I work three or four hours every morning, trying to finish a storybook for children. The first draft is done, but I'm now engaged in the more difficult job of regurgitating it and swallowing it again. I am also greatly handicapped by being unfamiliar with some of the terrain the story unhappily takes me into. I think it was extremely inconsiderate of my characters to lead me, an old man, into unfamiliar territory. At my age I deserve better.''[1]

December, 1969. With the manuscript of *Trumpet of the Swan* in the hands of his publishers, White was greatly disappointed that Garth Williams had been turned down as the illustrator and wrote to him: "I had always hoped that Williams and White would be as indestructible as ham and eggs, Scotch and soda, Gilbert and Sullivan.

"When I turned in my book manuscript, just before Thanksgiving, I asked . . . to . . . get the book out in the spring—not wait till fall, which would have been more to Harper's liking. . . . I got a letter back asking about 'illustration.' I replied, saying that . . . I felt deeply indebted to you. . . . An author is not in a position to make a deal with an artist.

"The impression I got, after a couple of phone calls, was that, although everybody wanted you to do the book, distance was a controlling factor, and they didn't think—since it is a long book requiring thirty or forty pictures—that spring publication would be possible with you working from Mexico. This is the impression I got, and I held out for spring publication; so the

blame, if any blame is to be attached to anybody, belongs with me.

"Anyway, I am very sad tonight, the last night of a disturbing year. I'm not entirely happy about the text of the book—I am old and wordy, and this book seems to show it. . . .

"Although you and I have had very little communication and contact over the years, I have always felt immensely in your debt—particularly for your characterization of Stuart, which really blew life into him and was the start of the whole business. Without your contribution, I don't think Stuart would have traveled very far. Whether my cygnet ever gets off the ground remains to be seen. Whether he does or not, I am unhappy about being separated from you after these many fine and rewarding years. I never expected it to happen, and I never wanted it to happen.''[1]

1970. Received the Laura Ingalls Wilder Award for *Charlotte's Web* and *Stuart Little*. "I have two or three strong beliefs about the business of writing for children. I feel I must never kid them about anything. I feel I must be on solid ground myself. I also feel that a writer has an obligation to transmit, as best he can, his love of life, his appreciation for the world. I am not averse to departing from reality, but I am against departing from the truth.''[3]

1971. Received the National Medal for Literature. ". . . I fell in love with the sound of an early typewriter and have been stuck with it ever since. I believed then, as I do now, in the goodness of the published word; it seemed to contain an essential goodness, like the smell of leaf mold. Being a medalist at last, I can now speak of the 'corpus' of my work—the word has a splendid sound. But glancing at the skimpy accomplishment of recent years, I find the 'cadaver of my work' a more fitting phrase.

"I have always felt that the first duty of a writer was to ascend—to make flights, carrying others along if he could manage it. To do this takes courage, even a certain conceit. My favorite aeronaut was not a writer at all, he was Dr. Piccard, the balloonist, who once, in an experimental moment, made an ascension borne aloft by two thousand small balloons, hoping that the Law of Probability would serve him well and that when he reached the rarified air of the stratosphere some (but not all) of the balloons would burst and thus lower him gently to earth. But when the Doctor reached the heights to which he had aspired, he whipped out a pistol and killed about a dozen of the balloons. He descended in flames, and the papers reported that when he jumped from the basket he was choked with laughter. Flights of this sort are the dream of every good writer: the ascent, the surrender to Probability, finally the flaming denouement, wracked with laughter—or with tears.

"Today, with so much of earth damaged and endangered, with so much of life dispiriting or joyless, a writer's courage can easily fail him. I feel this daily. In the face of so much bad news, how does one sustain one's belief? Jacques Cousteau tells us that the sea is dying; he had been down there and seen its agony. If the sea dies, so will Man die. Many tell us that the cities are dying; and if the cities die, it will be the same as Man's own death. Seemingly, the ultimate triumph of our chemistry is to produce a bird's egg with a shell so thin it collapses under the weight of incubation, and there is no hatch, no young birds to carry on the tradition of flight and of son. 'Egg is all,' quoth Dr. Alexis Romanoff, the embryologist, who spent his life examining the egg. Can this truly be the triumph of our chemistry—to destroy all by destroying the egg?

(From the animated movie "Charlotte's Web," featuring the voices of Debbie Reynolds, Paul Lynde, and Henry Gibson. Produced by Paramount Pictures. Copyright © 1972 by Hanna-Barbera Productions, Inc. [Sagittarius Productions, Inc.])

"But despair is not good—for the writer, for anyone. Only hope can carry us aloft, can keep us afloat. Only hope, and a certain faith that the incredible structure that has been fashioned by this most strange and ingenious of all the mammals cannot end in ruin and disaster. This faith is a writer's faith, for writing itself is an act of faith, nothing else. And it must be the writer, above all others, who keeps it alive—choked with laughter, or with pain." [E. B. White, "The Faith of a Writer: Remarks by E. B. White Upon Receiving the 1971 National Medal for Literature," *Publishers Weekly,* December 6, 1971.[4]]

1975. After his wife recovered from heart failure, White wrote her: ". . . This made me realize more than anything else ever has how much I love you and how little life would mean to me were you not here. Welcome back, and do not ever leave me."[1]

1976. The publication of *The Letters of E. B. White* made White's birthday a well-known date.

1979. A bibliographic catalogue of E. B. White's printed materials in the Department of Rare Books at Cornell University, White's alma mater, was published. "A copy of the manuscript

of this implausible book was delivered to my house one day by its author, Katherine Romans Hall. It was embalmed in three stiff hardcover binders in unrelieved black—a funereal sight, a forbidding trilogy. After thanking the author, about whom there is nothing implausible except her choice of project, I took the three volumes to the kitchen and weighed them. They went two ounces short of nine pounds, an impossible burden. Could this horrid, heavy, dismal thing be the record of my life as a writer? I looked into one of the volumes, saw that it was written in librarian's language, which I have never tried to master, and set the thing to one side, to await the day when I could give it the attention it deserved.

". . . The record is too revealing for comfort. It appears to be the account of a trigger-happy young man (who eventually grew old) for whom the slightest event, the most trivial occurrance, the most inconsequential thought sent him to his typewriter and, with luck, into the nearest magazine or newspaper. . . . It lists two thousand one hundred and ninety items. What possessed me, anyway, that I behaved so badly? Do I have a nervous tic?. . ." [Taken from the Preface of *E. B. White: A Bibliographic Catalogue of Printed Materials in the Depart-*

ment of Rare Books, Cornell University Library, compiled by Katherine Romans Hall, Garland Publishing, 1979.⁵]

FOR MORE INFORMATION SEE: New York Times, January 17, 1954, July 11, 1969, January 23, 1970, November 17, 1976; Muriel Fuller, editor, *More Junior Authors,* H. W. Wilson, 1963; *The Children's Bookshelf,* Child Study Association of America, Bantam, 1965; Nancy Larrick, *A Teacher's Guide to Children's Books,* Merrill, 1966; Brian Doyle, editor, *Who's Who of Children's Literature,* Schocken, 1968; (for children) Norah Smaridge, *Famous Modern Storytellers for Young People,* Dodd, 1969; Eleanor Cameron, *The Green and Burning Tree,* Atlantic-Little, Brown, 1969; *Library Journal,* March 15, 1970; *New York Times Book Review,* May 24, 1970; *Horn Book,* August, 1970; Selma G. Lanes, *Down the Rabbit Hole,*

Atheneum, 1971; Miriam Hoffman and Eva Samuels, editors, *Authors and Illustrators of Children's Books,* R. R. Bowker, 1972; Lee Bennett Hopkins, *More Books by More People,* Citation Press, 1974; Leonard Unger, editor, *American Writers,* Scribner, 1974; Edward C. Sampson, *E. B. White,* Twayne, 1974; Nancy Larrick, *A Parent's Guide to Children's Reading,* 4th revised edition, Doubleday, 1975; Justin Wintle and Emma Fisher, *The Pied Pipers,* Paddington Press, 1975; *Authors in the News,* Volume 2, Gale, 1976; *Children's Literature Review,* Gale, 1976; ''E. B. White: A Man of Letters'' (photographs by Jill Krementz), *Publishers Weekly,* December 13, 1976; *Twentieth Century Children's Writers,* St. Martin's, 1978; Charlotte Huck and Doris Young, *Children's Literature in the Elementary School,* 3rd revised edition, Holt, 1979; Zena Sutherland, *Children and Books,* 6th edition, Scott, Foresman, 1981.

I have a sister.
My sister is deaf.

■ (From *I Have a Sister—My Sister Is Deaf* by Jeanne Whitehouse Peterson. Illustrated by Deborah Ray.)

JEANNE WHITEHOUSE

WHITEHOUSE, Jeanne   1939-
(Jeanne Whitehouse Peterson)

PERSONAL: Born May 8, 1939, in Walla Walla, Wash.; daughter of Earl Austin (a pharmacist) and Lillian Dell (a teacher; maiden name, Von Pinnon) Whitehouse; married; children: Frances Elizabeth Peterson, Ellen Louise Peterson, Catherine Dell Peterson. *Education:* Washington State University, B.A., 1961; Columbia University, M.A. 1965. *Home:* 207 Aliso Dr. N.E., Albuquerque, N.M. 87108.

CAREER: Teacher at Pullman, Wash., public schools, 1961-62; U.S. Peace Corps., Sabah, Malaysia, teacher of English as a foreign language, 1962-64; University of New Mexico, Albuquerque, educational advisor to teacher aides, 1971-75, lecturer in children's literature, 1975—.

WRITINGS—All under name Jeanne Whitehouse Peterson: *I Have a Sister—My Sister Is Deaf* (juvenile; illustrated by Deborah Ray), Harper, 1977; *That Is That* (juvenile; illustrated by Ray), Harper, 1979; *While the Moon Shines Bright*, Harper, 1981.

WORK IN PROGRESS: A biography of Ann Nolan Clark; more picture-story books that deal with family relationships.

SIDELIGHTS: "I guess I have always wanted to write. I started writing stories in the hayloft of my uncle's barn when I was twelve. I would fold up the little sheets of notebook paper into tiny squares and leave them for the cows to eat (I thought), always wondering if the music of my words would be transferred to the milk my aunt gave me to drink. My mother tells me, though, that there were other times I stood by the window

and sang little songs to myself. I ɔoked out of windows a lot, I think, because my first three manuscripts for children all have windows in them. And, when my father died, I remember standing before a mirror and singing, making up words in praise of my father. Everyone else was sitting in the room and crying, but I was singing and feeling so much better.

"I began composing *I Have a Sister—My Sister is Deaf* early on, I am sure, for in college I wrote a short story about a girl going deaf. Always I thought I would keep working on it, to make it bigger and better, but later I realized that I really wanted to write about how it feels to have a sister who is deaf. That was what I knew best, because I do have a deaf sister, and I wanted to share the joys and sorrows, and especially the strengths, of the deaf child. Because of these experiences, the sounds of children's books mean a lot to me. I still like to hear someone reading aloud, and like to be the one doing the reading. I hope my work reflects this oral quality."

WHITNEY, David C(harles)   1921-

BRIEF ENTRY: Born March 8, 1921, in Salina, Kan. A publisher and editor, Whitney began his career as feature writer and news editor for United Press Associations in New York City and was editor in chief of *Encyclopedia Americana* from 1964 to 1965. Since 1972 he has been president and editor of David C. Whitney Assciates, Inc. Whitney has written many books for both adults and young people which cover American history from revolutionary to modern times. His works for adults include *The American Presidents* (Doubleday, 1967), *The Trials and Triumphs of Two Dynamic Decades* (J. G. Ferguson, 1968), and *The American Legacy* (J. G. Ferguson, 1975). Whitney has also published over twenty children's books, including *The First Book of Facts and How to Find Them* (F. Watts, 1966), *The Picture Life of Lyndon Baines Johnson* (F. Watts, 1966), *Limpy the Lion* (F. Watts, 1969), and several books on mathematics. Editor of the *Reader's Digest Almanac* since 1974, Whitney is also the inventor of the Cycloteacher teaching machine and creator of several educational curriculum systems. *Address:* 291 Roaring Brook Rd., Chappaqua, N.Y. 10514. *For More Information See: New York Times Book Review*, November 6 1966; *Contemporary Authors*, Volumes 9-12, revised, Gale, 1974; *Library Journal*, October 1, 1975; *Directory of American Scholars*, Volume 1, 7th edition, R. R. Bowker, 1978; *Who's Who in America*, 41st edition, Marquis, 1980.

WILDER, Laura Ingalls   1867-1957

PERSONAL: Born February 7, 1867, at Pepin, Wisconsin; died February 10, 1957, in Mansfield, Missouri; buried in Mansfield Cemetery; daughter of Charles Philip and Caroline Lake (Quiner) Ingalls; married Almanzo J. Wilder, August 25, 1885 (died October 23, 1949); children: Rose Wilder Lane (an author). *Education:* Attended schools in Wisconsin, Iowa, Minnesota and the Dakota territory. *Home:* Rocky Ridge Farm, Mansfield, Missouri.

CAREER: Teacher, 1882-85, in schools near De Smet; household editor and contributor of articles to *Missouri Ruralist*, 1911-24; Mansfield Farm Loan Association, secretary-treasurer, 1919-27; author, 1932-43. *Member:* Athenian Club, Justamere Club, Interesting Hour Club, Wednesday Study Club, and Eastern Star. *Awards, honors:* Runner-up for the Newbery Medal, 1938, for *On the Banks of Plum Creek*, and 1941, for *The Long Winter;* Pacific Northwest Library Association Young

Photograph of Laura Ingalls Wilder, about two years after her stay in San Francisco.

Readers' Choice Award, 1942, for *By the Shores of Silver Lake; Book World* Children's Spring Book Festival Award, 1943, for *These Happy Golden Years;* Laura Ingalls Wilder Award presented by the American Library Association, 1954, for the "Little House" books (since 1960 this award in her honor is made every five years to an outstanding author or illustrator of children's books); elected to the Ozark Hall of Fame, 1977; inducted into the South Dakota Cowboy and Western Hall of Fame, 1978.

WRITINGS—All novels based on her life; all published by Harper, except as noted: *Little House in the Big Woods* (illustrated by Helen Sewell), 1932; *Farmer Boy* (illustrated by Sewell), 1933; *Little House on the Prairie* (illustrated by Sewell), 1935; *On the Banks of Plum Creek* (illustrated by Helen Sewell and Mildred Boyle), 1937; *By the Shores of Silver Lake* (illustrated by Sewell and Boyle), 1939, special edition, E. M. Hale, 1956; *The Long Winter* (illustrated by Sewell and Boyle), 1940; *Little Town on the Prairie* (illustrated by Sewell and Boyle), 1941; *These Happy Golden Years* (illustrated by Sewell and Boyle), 1943. Each of the above titles was published by Harper in a new edition, illustrated by Garth Williams, in 1953.

On the Way Home: The Diary of a Trip from South Dakota to Mansfield, Missouri, in 1894, edited by Rose Wilder Lane, Harper, 1962; Roger Lea MacBride, editor, *The First Four Years* (illustrated by Garth Williams), Harper, 1971; *West from Home: Letters of Laura Ingalls Wilder, San Francisco, 1915*, edited by R. L. MacBride, Harper, 1974.

Contributor of articles and poetry to various magazines and newspapers including *Country Gentleman, McCall's, Youth's Companion, St. Nicholas, Child Life, San Francisco Bulletin, St. Louis Star, Missouri Ruralist, De Smet News,* and *Christian Science Monitor.*

ADAPTATIONS: "Little House on the Prairie," NBC-TV series starring Michael Landon, 1974—; a Broadway musical, "Prairie," 1982.

Recordings: "Little House in the Big Woods" was recorded by Julie Harris for Pathways of Sound, 1976.

SIDELIGHTS: "I was born in the 'Little House in the Big Woods' of Wisconsin on **February 7** in the year **1867.** I lived everything that happened in my books. It is a long story, filled with sunshine and shadow. . . .

"Father's ancestors arrived in America on the *Mayflower* and he was born in New York state. But he was also raised on the frontier. He was always jolly, inclined to be reckless and loved his violin. . . . I remember seeing deer that Father had killed hanging in the trees around our forest home.

"Mother was descended from an old Scotch family and inherited the Scotch thriftiness which held with the livelihood. Although born and raised on the frontier, she was an educated, cultured woman. She was very quiet and gentle, but proud and particular in all matters of good breeding.

"So Ma taught us books and trained us in our manners, while Pa taught us other things and entertained us. In the depression following the Civil War [Pa and Ma were married in 1860] my parents, as so many others, lost all their savings in a bank failure. They farmed the rough land on the edge of the Big Woods of Wisconsin, within four miles of legend-haunted Lake Pepin." [Laura Ingalls Wilder, speech at Detroit, Michigan, 1937, taken from the collection in the Herbert Hoover Presidential Library.[1]]

1870s. Family journeyed west through Kansas, Minnesota, and Iowa to the Dakota Territory, homesteading. "I know that we were three miles over the line into Indian Territory. . . ."

Because the Ingalls family had mistakenly settled on land belonging to the Osage Indians, they were forced to leave in 1871. Years later, her daughter, Rose Wilder Lane, described the historical background: "The Indians in Missouri in 1545 when De Soto and his men went there were the Missouris, Ioways, Kansas, Osages, and Arkansas (Quawpaws), all the latter being offshoots of the Missouris, who told De Soto that their ancestors had come down the Ohio River from the east six centuries earlier. These tribes continued to live in French and Spanish Missouri with no troubles until the American occupation of 1803-4. There were no serious troubles then, but the Indians were greatly disturbed by the bad influence of the Americans on the young Indians. So in 1810 the chiefs of all the tribes went to William Clark (of the Lewis and Clark expedition of the mouth of the Columbia, earlier) who was then governor of the Territory, and offered to leave the green hills and streams of Missouri and move out to the Great American Desert if Washington would agree never to disturb them, never to invade their grounds in the desert. The agreement was made; and that was the cause of the war-dancing that Laura heard all night in *Little House on the Prairie.* The settlers were breaking the agreement that the Indians had taken as the price of their ancestral homes and hunting grounds in the rich and beautiful Missouri." [Letter from Rose Wilder Lane to William T. Anderson, 1966, taken from the personal collection of William T. Anderson.[2]]

1874-1876. The Ingalls family lived first in a dugout and then in a frame house near Plum Creek, a mile from Walnut Grove, Minnesota. ''. . . There were runaways and fires and storms—such terrible storms—and the grasshoppers—the grasshopper plague of 1874, the worst ever known since the plagues of Egypt. . . . I saw them destroy every green thing on the face of the earth, so far as a child would know. . . . I have lived among uncounted millions of them. There are unforgetable pictures of these grasshoppers in my mind that I have tried to draw plainly in [my book] *On the Banks of Plum Creek.*''[1]

''My education has been what a girl would get on the frontier. I went to 'little red school houses all over the west' and was never graduated from anything.'' [William T. Anderson, ''Stories That Had to be Told,'' *American Ideals,* 1981.[3]]

Wilder credited her parents with her talent in expression. ''The only reason I can think of being able to write at all was that father and mother were great readers and I read a lot at home with them.''[3]

1876. Family moved to Burr Oak, Iowa to work as inn-keepers. ''My family did live in Burr Oak for nearly two years, but I fear my memories of that time . . . are more of the place than of the people. At first we lived in the old Masters Hotel. My parents were partners in business with the new owners. . . . Pa used to play his fiddle in the hotel office, and one of the boarders, a Mr. Bisbee, taught me to sing the notes of the musical scale.

''Mary [Wilder's sister] and I were going to school. It seemed to us a big school but as I remember there were only two rooms. One began in the downstairs room and when advanced enough was promoted upstairs. Next term we went upstairs to the principal. . . . He was an elocutionist and I have always been grateful to him for the training I was given in reading. . . .

''In the spring we moved to a little brick house at the edge of town. It was a happy summer. I loved to go after the cows in the pasture by the creek where the rushes and blue flags grew and the grass was so fresh and smelled so sweet. . . .

''I spent a great deal of time that summer [1877] caring for Baby Grace [her sister], with the big blue eyes and soft fair hair. That fall we left Burr Oak and drove our covered wagon back to Walnut Grove, Minnesota and the banks of Plum Creek.'' [Laura Ingalls Wilder, taken from a letter to the *Decorah Public Opinion,* 1947.[4]]

1879. From Walnut Grove, Minnesota, the Ingalls moved to Dakota Territory to homestead. At first, her father worked for the Chicago and Northwestern Railroad. Her sister, Carrie, recalled: ''Father and mother, Mr. and Mrs. C. P. Ingalls, with their family, Mary, Laura, Grace and myself, came to the C. & N.W.R.R. construction camp on the banks of Silver Lake in 1879 where father was timekeeper, bookkeeper and paymaster. This was the stretch of the R.R. grading from Brookings to De Smet, South Dakota. . . . It was an ideal place for a camp for Silver Lake was a beautiful lake full of water. This was probably why the Surveyor's House was built on its banks.

''In the fall of 1879 when . . . the grading work broke up and the surveyors went away . . . they persuaded father and mother to stay and move into their house for the winter where they could leave the surveying outfit.'' [The Surveyors' House, where the family lived, is now restored for visitors in De Smet, S.D.] [William T. Anderson, *The Story of the Ingalls,* Laura Ingalls Wilder Memorial Society (De Smet, S.D.), 1971.[5]]

1880. Town of De Smet built. Laura and Carrie Ingalls attended the first school.

1880-1881. ''That winter, known still . . . as 'the hard winter,' we demonstrated that wheat could be ground in an ordinary coffee mill and used for bread making. Prepared in that way it was the staff of life for the whole community.

One game they loved was called mad dog. ■ (From *Little House in the Big Woods* by Laura Ingalls Wilder. Illustrated by Garth Williams.)

The wind was rising and wildly screaming. Thousands of birds flew before the fire, thousands of rabbits were running. ■ (From *Little House on the Prairie* by Laura Ingalls Wilder. Illustrated by Garth Williams.)

"De Smet was built as the railroad went through, out in the midst of the great Dakota prairies far ahead of the farming settlements, and this was the winter it was isolated from the rest of the world from December 1 until May 10 by the fearful blizzards that piled the snow 40 feet deep on the railroad tracks. The trains could not get through. . . .

"The houses were not overheated . . . for the fuel gave out early in the winter and all there was left with which to cook and keep warm was the long prairie hay. A handfull of hay was twisted into a rope, then doubled and allowed to twist back on itself and the two ends came together in a knot, making what we called 'a stick of hay.'" [Laura Ingalls Wilder, "According to Experts," *Laura Ingalls Wilder Lore,* Fall-Winter, 1980.[6]]

1882-1885. Taught three terms of country school near De Smet.

August 25, 1885. Married Almanzo Wilder ("Manly"). "And so on Thursday, the twenty-fifth of August, at ten o'clock in the morning the quick-stepping brown horses and the buggy with the shining top flashed around the corner of Pierson's livery barn, came swiftly over and half mile, and drew up at the door of the little claim house in its hollow square of young cottonwoods.

"The preacher lived on his homestead two miles away and it seemed to Laura the longest drive she had ever taken, and yet it was over all too soon. Once in the front room, the ceremony was quickly performed. Mr. Brown came hurriedly in, slipping on his coat. His wife and daughter, Ida, [my] dearest friend, with her betrothed, were the witnesses and those present.

"Laura and Manly were married for better or worse, for richer or poorer.

"Then back to the old home for a noon dinner, and in the midst of good wishes and cheerful good-bys, once more into the buggy and away for the new home on the other side of town. The first year was begun." [Laura Ingalls Wilder, *The First Four Years,* edited by Roger L. MacBride, Harper, 1971.[7]]

December 5, 1886. Daughter born. "Christmas was at hand and Rose was a grand present.

"Rose was such a good baby, so strong and healthy that Ma stayed only a few days. Then Hattie Johnson came. 'To wash baby this time, instead of windows,' she said.

"A hundred precious dollars had gone for doctor bills and medicine and help through the summer and winter so far; but after all, a Rose in December was much rarer than a rose in June, and must be paid for accordingly.'"[7]

August, 1889. Birth and death of infant son. Destruction of the house by fire.

1890. Wilder, her husband and daughter spent a year living with Almanzo's parents in Spring Valley, Minnesota. From there, they went by train to Westville, Florida, to live, hoping that the climate would aid Almanzo's health, which had deteriorated after a diptheria attack.

1892. Returned to De Smet for two more years. Rose attended school, while Wilder and her husband worked to save money for a new start in the "land of the big red apple" in the Ozark Mountains of Missouri.

July 17, 1894. Left De Smet for Missouri because of severe droughts and the Panic of 1893. Kept a diary of the journey that covered 650 miles and lasted nearly six months.

"The long, hot, dusty journey was made in a two-seated hack which Almanzo had converted to a covered wagon. Almanzo brought along a supply of the new and unbelievable 'fire mats' which he planned to sell at ten cents, but no one had ten cents. Often the mats were traded for eggs or milk instead. The Wilders were not the only family dislodged from their land and traveling in search of new farms. . . ." [William T. Anderson, *The Story of the Wilders,* Laura Ingalls Wilder Memorial Society, 1973.[8]]

August 23, 1894. After driving through South Dakota, Nebraska, Kansas and reaching Lamar, Missouri, Wilder wrote an account of the trip thus far for the readers of the *De Smet News* (which was her first published writing): "Editor, News and Leader: Thinking our friends in De Smet might like to hear how we are progressing on our journey, I will send you a short account of it so far.

"We reached Yankton in just a week from the time we started, crossed the Missouri river on the ferry and bade good-by to Dakota. The crops that far were about the same as they were around De Smet.

"The next town of importance we saw was Schuyler, Nebraska, where we stayed a few hours for Mr. Cooley's people [the family with whom the Wilders were traveling] to visit friends. We went through Lincoln and saw the capital buildings, the court house and a great deal of the city; then to Beatrice, which is a nice city. The crops of wheat and oats through eastern Nebraska were good. Corn was damaged by the drouth [sic].

"We saw the capital in Topeka famous for the legislative war. It is a grand building. From Topeka we went to Ottawa and from there to Fort Scott, which is a lovely place. Coal crops out of the ground all through the country around Fort Scott, and at the mines it is only two feet below the surface. It is worth $1.00 per ton at the mines or $1.25 delivered. Crops through eastern Kansas are fair. It is a grand sight to see hundreds of acres of corn in one field.

"We have had a very pleasant trip so far, no bad weather to delay us, having had only a few light showers, and those in the night. Our camping places have been delightful. We camped on the Jim river in Dakota, and on the Missouri and the Platte in Nebraska and the Blue in Kansas and nearly every night beside, we have camped on creeks among the trees. It is a continual picnic for the children to wade in the creeks and play in the woods, and sometimes we all think we are children and do alike.

"We have eaten apples, grapes, plums, and melons until we actually do not care for any more, and to satisfy a Dakota appetite for such things is truly something wonderful.

"There are hazelnuts, hickory nuts and walnuts along the road, but they are green yet.

"The country is full of emigrants traveling in every direction.

"Our horses are in good condition and our wagons are whole yet, having no accidents. We are near Lamar, Missouri now and expect to be on the road a week longer before we reach the land of promise." [Taken from an 1894 letter to the editor, *De Smet News*. Reprinted by permission of Sherwood Publishing Co.[9]]

August 30, 1894. Arrived in Mansfield, Missouri. Bought land, which they named Rocky Ridge Farm. "The only building on the land was a one-room log cabin with a rock fireplace, one door but no windows. When the door was closed light came in between the logs of the walls where the mud chinking had fallen out. We lived there a year.

"Almanzo had recovered from the stroke but was not strong. He changed work with neighbors to build a log barn for his horses and a henhouse for a few hens." [Laura Ingalls Wilder, "A Letter from Laura Ingalls Wilder," *Horn Book* magazine, December, 1953.[10]]

Spring, 1895. "In the Spring we planted a garden and together we cleared land of timber. I never could use an ax but I could handle one end of a cross-cut saw and pile brush ready to burn. Almanzo made rails and stove wood out of the trees we cut down. With the rails he fenced the land we cleared. . . . I hoed in the garden and tended my hens. We sold eggs and potatoes from our new-ground planting besides the wood and when we were able to buy a cow and a little pig we thought we were rich."[10]

1895-1900. ". . . We worked and saved from year to year, adding to our land until we owned 200 acres well improved; a fine herd of cows; good hogs and the best laying flock of hens in the country.

"These years were not all filled with work. Rose walked three-quarters of a mile to school the second year and after and her schoolmates visited her on Saturdays. She and I played along the little creek near the house. We tamed the wild birds and squirrels; picked wild flowers and berries. Almanzo and I often

(From *By the Shores of Silver Lake* by Laura Ingalls Wilder. Illustrated by Garth Williams.)

went horseback riding over the hills and through the woods. And always we had our papers and books from the school library for reading in the evenings and on Sunday afternoon."[10]

Content in the peaceful vistas of Rocky Ridge, Wilder found purpose in her role as farmwife. "We who lived in quiet places have the opportunity to become acquainted with ourselves, to think our own thoughts and live our own lives."[3] She questioned women who rallied against the lives of housewives. "Farm women have always been wage earners and partners in their husbands' business. It is rather amusing to read flaring headlines announcing the fact that women are at last coming into their own. Farm women have always been business women, but no one has even noticed it."[3]

Working together, the Wilders started to build their permanent home on Rocky Ridge. It started as a one-room frame house at the top of a wooded ridge—and finally consisted of ten rooms. All the materials—lumber and rock for fireplace and chimney—came from their farm. "We cut and planed and fitted every stick of it."

Early 1900s. Moved into the town of Mansfield, where Almanzo worked as a drayman, while Wilder boarded the bank and railroad workers.

1910. Officer of the Missouri Home Development Association. Developed an interest in improving conditions for farm women in Missouri. Began appearing as a speaker at farmer's institutes and meetings, discussing her poultry methods and improvements for country living.

Laura and Almanzo, shortly after their marriage.

February, 1911. Published her first article in the Missouri *Ruralist*, titled "Favors the Small Farm." Her articles appeared regularly in the *Ruralist* for many years while she served as household editor. She also wrote articles on farm and country life for other newspapers and magazines.

1912. Home on Rocky Ridge Farm completed.

1915. Visited San Francisco to see the Panama-Pacific Exposition and spend time with daughter, Rose, and her husband. Rose was a star reporter for the San Francisco *Bulletin* and coached her mother in writing styles and methods.

September 13, 1915. Wrote to Almanzo: "Then I do want to do a little writing with Rose to get the hang of it a little better so I can write something that perhaps I can sell.

"I am going to do the things I absolutely must do before I come home. There are a few, you know, such as going over some of my copy with Rose and going out to the Fair a couple more times, and then I am coming home. Rose is very busy with her copy and the house and all, so we do not accomplish much in a day. I am doing what she will let me help me and to go play at the Fair with me. I am anxious to get back and take charge of the hens again. Believe me, there is no place like the country to live and I have not heard of anything so far that would lead me to give up Rocky Ridge for any other place."]*West from Home: Letters of Laura Ingalls Wilder to Almanzo,* edited by R. L. MacBride, Harper, 1974.[11]]

1916. Joined the Athenian Club, which had the goal of establishing a county library.

1919. Founder of the Mansfield Farm Loan Association, a branch of the Federal Loan Bank, which offered low-interest loans of Ozark farmers. Served as secretary-treasurer for the company for eight years, giving out nearly a million dollars in federal loans. She conducted the business from her small study off the living room at Rocky Ridge.

1925. "We are not doing much farming now . . . Rose is still here and working on a new book. I don't know what the title is nor how soon it will be finished. It is a story of the Ozarks. Her friend Helen Boylston from New Hampshire is still here with her.

"I am very busy these days with my writing, though I do not pretend to write anything like Rose. Still I have no trouble in having the things I do write published. Keeping house does not leave much time for other things. . . ." [Letter of Laura Ingalls Wilder to her aunt. Taken from the personal collection of William T. Anderson.[12]]

1928. Moved to a newly built, modern house on Rocky Ridge, which Rose gave as a gift to her parents. Rose occupied the old farmhouse, wrote books and articles and entertained visiting authors from the east. The Wilders lived in the new house for about eight years.

Late 1920s. Wrote *Pioneer Girl* (never published), an autobiography that was the first step in writing her "Little House" stories.

The train stopped. It was really there, a train at last.

"Oh, I do hope that Harthorn and Wilmarth both get all the groceries they ordered last fall," said Ma. ■
(From *The Long Winter* by Laura Ingalls Wilder. Illustrated by Garth Williams.)

April 6, 1932. Publication of *Little House in the Big Woods,* when Wilder was sixty-five. "These were family stories and I believed they should be preserved. When to my surprise the book made such a success and children all over the U.S. wrote to me begging for more stories, I began to think what a wonderful childhood I had had. How I had seen the whole frontier, the woods, the Indian country of the great plains, the frontier towns, the building of railroads in wild, unsettled country, homesteading and farmers coming in to take possession. I realized that I had seen and lived it all. . . . I wanted children now to understand more about the beginning of things, to know what is behind the things they see—what it is that made America as they know it . . . I thought of writing the story of my childhood in several volumes—an eight volume historical novel for children covering every aspect of the American frontier.

"Every story . . . all the circumstances, each incident are true."[1]

1932-1943. Set of eight "Little House" books written. All were written on Rocky Ridge Farm. "I have learned in this work that when I went as far back in my memory as I could and left my mind there a while it would go farther back and still farther, bringing out of the dimness of past things that were beyond my ordinary remembrance."[1]

1935. Celebrated fiftieth wedding anniversary.

1937. Moved back into the farmhouse at Rocky Ridge. Trip to Detroit, where Wilder spoke at a book fair, sponsored by J. L. Hudson Department Store.

1938. Trip to California and Oregon by car. A stop was made at De Smet for Old Settler's day and visiting with Wilder's sisters, Carrie and Grace.

1939. Return trip to De Smet. ". . . One morning when the blue haze hung over the Ozark hills Almanzo said, 'Let's go

LAURA INGALLS WILDER

back to De Smet for the Old Settler's Day celebration. I would like to see the old place and the folks we used to know.'

"'Let's do,' I agreed eagerly, for I had just finished writing *By the Shores of Silver Lake.* We could see the homestead Pa took so long ago. . . .

"Almanzo said, 'I have driven horses all over that country and the roads to it and I can drive a car there.'

"'I rode behind those horses with you and I can still ride wherever you can drive.'

"Then early one morning, we packed our bags, put them in the trunk of the Chrysler, said goodby to our pet bulldog and started to South Dakota and the 'land of used to be.'" [*Laura Comes Home,* Laura Ingalls Wilder Memorial Society, 1975.[13]]

1943. At seventy-six, Wilder finished her series. "The day is always full, for I do all my own work, and to care for a ten-room house is no small job. Besides the cooking and baking there is the churning to do. I make all our own butter from cream off the goat milk." [Rose Wilder Lane, "Laura Ingalls Wilder and the Little House Books," *Horn Book,* October-November, 1943.[14]]

1947. "It is surprising how many people are interested in my account of early times. I have letters from all over the country and Canada. One came from Holland this week.

"I am glad if I have made them all interested in De Smet for we have always been proud of the town.

"A great many people traveling through stop to see me and I am glad not all come this way for I have never gotten over my timidity with perfect strangers.

So, patiently she began again, dipping her fingers for the calf to suck, trying to keep the milk in the pail and to teach the calf to drink it. ■ (From *Little Town on the Prairie* by Laura Ingalls Wilder. Illustrated by Garth Williams.)

(The 1974 cast of the television series "Little House on the Prairie," starring Michael Landon, Melissa Sue Anderson, and Melissa Gilbert. Produced by NBC-TV.)

"Mr. Wilder and I are very well for persons ninety and eighty years old. Still caring for ourselves and our home." [Laura Ingalls Wilder, letter to Aubrey Sherwood of the *De Smet News*. Reprinted by permission of Aubrey Sherwood.[15]]

". . . I am the only one of the Ingalls family living now. Pa and Ma lived on at De Smet until their deaths years ago. Mary never recovered her sight. She lived at home with Pa and Ma and then with Carrie. Grace married a farmer and lived only seven miles from De Smet. Carrie married a mine owner and made her home in the Black Hills near Mt. Rushmore.

"Almanzo and I have retired from farming . . . have sold part of the land so now we have only 70 acres instead of 200, and no stock except two milk goats and a pet bulldog." [Letter of Laura Ingalls Wilder. Taken from the personal collection of William T. Anderson.[16]]

1949. Dedication of Laura Ingalls Wilder Branch Library in Detroit. "The Branch being named for me is such a wonderful thing that at times it has seemed incredible. . . ." [William T. Anderson, *Laura Wilder of Mansfield,* Laura Ingalls Wilder Memorial Society, 1974.[17]]

October 23, 1949. Death of Almanzo at ninety-two. "It is very lonely without my husband, but there is nothing left but to go on from here alone. Our daughter, Rose Wilder Lane, was here for awhile, but has returned to her home in Connecticut."[17]

1950. Dedication of Laura Ingalls Wilder Room in the Ponoma Public Library. "There are neighbors just across the road and a short distance at the side. Groceries are delivered at the door; mail every morning by the box at the road; my fuel tank is kept filled with no trouble to me and electricity and telephone ready at my touch. The house is warm and comfortable, two boys from the neighbors on the East come every day to see if there is anything I want and a taxi from town is on call to take me wherever I wish to go. Friends from town, only ¼ mile away come often to see me.

". . . There were forty-nine letters in my mail box yesterday morning. Most of them must be answered. I do all my own work and it is now house-cleaning time for this ten-room house."

February 7, 1951. Nine hundred birthday cards arrived on her eighty-fourth birthday.

September 28, 1951. Dedication of the Laura Ingalls Wilder Library in Mansfield, Missouri.

October 14, 1953. Publication of the new edition of the "Little House" books with illustrations by Garth Williams.

1954. Establishment of the Laura Ingalls Wilder Medal of the American Library Association. Given every five years to an author or illustrator who has contributed to children's literature over a period of years.

1955. "My 88-year-old hand grows tired. . . .

"It seems impossible to me that I have seen so many changes in living, some good, some very wrong in my opinion. The

(In this two-part episode of "Little House on the Prairie," the grown-up Laura [Melissa Gilbert] marries Almanzo [Dean Butler]. Presented on NBC-TV, September 22, 1980, and September 29, 1980. Photograph courtesy of National Broadcasting Co., Inc.)

old spirit of sturdy independence seems to be vanishing. We all depend too much on others. As modern life is lived, we have to do so, and more and more the individual alone is helpless. A conflict with nature and the elements is a clean fight, but a struggle against man and his contrivances is something very different. At times I have a homesick longing for the old days and the old ways. However, I know there is no turning back. We must go on.

"The 'Little House' books are stories of long ago. Today our way of living and our schools are much different; so many things have made living and learning easier. But the real things haven't changed. It is still best to be honest and truthful; to make the most of what we have; to be happy with simple pleasures and have courage when things go wrong. Great improvements in living have been made because every American has always been free to pursue his happiness and so long as Americans are free they will continue to make our country ever more wonderful."[3]

February 10, 1957. Died at the age of ninety at Rocky Ridge Farm in Mansfield, Missouri. "There is a purple haze over the hill tops and a hint of sadness in the sunshine because of summer's departure: on the low ground down by the spring the walnuts are dropping from the trees and squirrels are busy hiding away their winter supply. Here and there the leaves are beginning to change color and a little, vagrant, autumn breeze goes wandering over the hills and down the valleys whispering to 'follow, follow,' until it is almost impossible to resist.

"Right seems to be obscured and truth is difficult to find. But if the difficulty of finding the truth has increased our appreciation of its value, if the beauty of truth is plainer to us and more desired, then we have gathered treasure for the future.

"We lay away the gleanings of our years in the edifice of our character, where nothing is ever lost. What have we stored away in this safe place during the season that is past? Is it something that will keep sound and pure and sweet or something that is faulty and not worth storing?" [Donald Zochert, *Laura: The Life of Laura Ingalls Wilder,* Henry Regency Co., 1966.[18]]

So he stepped into the water. ◼(From *Farmer Boy* by Laura Ingalls Wilder. Illustrated by Garth Williams.)

Laura Ingalls Wilder in her later years.

As a re-education process, the U.S. State Department ordered the "Little House" books translated and published for readers in Japan and Germany after World War II. Since then, they have been translated into dozens of other languages, including French, Italian, Spanish, Chinese, Arabic, Bengali, Burmese, Danish, Dutch, Finnish, Hindi, Indonesian, Norwegian, Portuguese, Swedish, and Tamil.

For visiting information and material on the real little houses, write: Laura Ingalls Wilder Memorial Society, Pepin, Wis. 54759; Little House on the Prairie, Inc., Independence, Kan. 67301; Franklin County Historical Society, Malone, N.Y. 12953; Laura Ingalls Wilder Tourist Center, Walnut Grove, Minn. 56180; Laura Ingalls Wilder Park and Museum, Burr Oak, Iowa 52131; Laura Ingalls Wilder Memorial Society, De Smet, S.D. 57231; Laura Ingalls Wilder Home and Museum, Mansfield, Mo. 65704.

FOR MORE INFORMATION SEE: M. Cimino, "Laura Ingalls Wilder," *Wilson Library Bulletin,* April, 1948; Elizabeth Rider Montgomery, *Story behind Modern Books,* Dodd, 1949; V. Kirkus, "Discovery of Laura Ingalls Wilder," *Horn Book,* December, 1953; "Letter from Laura Ingalls Wilder," *Horn Book,* December, 1953; "Letters to Laura Ingalls Wilder," *Horn Book,* December, 1953; J. D. Lindquist, "Tribute to Laura Ingalls Wilder," *Horn Book,* December, 1953; Garth Williams, "Illustrating the Little House Books," *Horn Book,* December, 1953; F. Flanagan, "Tribute to Laura Ingalls Wilder," *Elementary English,* April, 1957; Jane Muir, *Famous Modern American Women Writers,* Dodd, 1959; D. N. Anderson, "A Little More about Laura: Her Relatives in Wisconsin," *Elementary English,* May, 1964; W. J. Jacobs, "Frontier Faith Revisited," *Horn Book,* October, 1965.

C. Kies, "Laura and Mary and the 3 R's" *Peabody Journal of Education*, September, 1966; Doris Kerns Eddins, *Teacher's Tribute to Laura Ingalls Wilder*, National Education Association, 1967; A. B. Potter, "Visit at Rocky Ridge Farm," *Instructor*, November, 1967, February, 1975; L. H. Mortensen, "Little Houses and Magnificent Mansions," *Elementary English*, May, 1968; Eugenia Garso, *The Laura Ingalls Wilder Songbook*, Harper, 1968; Norah Smaridge, *Famous Modern Storytellers for Young People*, Dodd, 1969; C. Elliott, "Little Houses," *Time*, March 15, 1971; Betty Coody, "Introduce Children to Books Through Laura Ingalls Wilder's 'Little House' Series," *Instructor*, November, 1971; M. Ward, "Laura Ingalls Wilder: An Appreciation," *Elementary English*, October, 1973; Susan Bagg, "Now Is Now," *The Atlantic*, February, 1975; Donald Zochert, *Laura: The Life of Laura Ingalls Wilder*, Henry Regnery, 1976; Mary D. Wade, "Home Is Where the Hearth Is," *Top of the News*, Winter, 1977; Barbara Walker, *The Little House Cookbook*, Harper, 1979; *Jack and Jill*, March 1981; William T. Anderson, "How the Little House Books Found a Publishing Home," *Language Arts*, April, 1981; *Christian Science Monitor*, June 23, 1981; *Modern Maturity*, April, 1982; *Treasures from Laura Wilder*, Sherwood Publishing, 1982.

Obituaries: *New York Times*, February 12, 1957; *Publishers Weekly*, February 25, 1957; *Wilson Library Bulletin*, April, 1957; *Current Biography Yearbook 1957*.

WILLIAMS-ELLIS, (Mary) Amabel (Nassau) 1894-

PERSONAL: Born in 1894 in Newlands Corner, near Guildford, England; daughter of John St. Loe Strachey (a journalist and editor); married Bertram Clough Williams-Ellis (an architect), 1915; children: Christopher, Susan Charlotte. *Education:* Educated at home. *Home:* Plas Brondanw, Llanfrothen, North Wales.

CAREER: Writer. Literary editor of *Spectator* magazine, 1922-23.

WRITINGS—Juveniles: But We Know Better (illustrated by husband, [Bertram] Clough Williams-Ellis), J. Cape, 1929; *How You Began: A Child's Introduction to Biology*, Gerald Howe, 1928, revised edition, Coward, 1929, reprinted, Transworld, 1975; *Men Who Found Out: Stories of Great Scientific Discoverers*, Gerald Howe, 1929, Coward, 1930, reprinted, Bodley Head, 1952; *How You Are Made*, A. & C. Black, 1932; *What Shall I Be?*, Heinemann, 1933; *Ottik's Book of Stories*, Methuen, 1939; *The Puzzle of Food and People: A Geography Reader*, Manhattan Publishing, 1951; *Engines, Atoms, and Power*, Putnam, 1958; *They Wanted the Real Answers* (includes "They Dared to Ask Questions," "Magic, Science, and Invention," and "You, Yourself"), Putnam, 1958, revised, 1959, published as *Seekers and Finders*, Blackie & Son, 1958; *The Unknown Ocean*, Putnam, 1959; *Princesses and Witches*, Blackie & Son, 1966; (contributor) *Monkeys and Magicians: A Collection of Modern and Traditional Stories*, Blackie & Son, 1967; (with William Stobbs) *Life in England: A Pictorial History*, Blackie & Son, Volume 1: *Early and Medieval Times*, 1968, Volume 2: *Tudor England*, 1968, Volume 3: *Seventeenth-Century England*, 1968, Volume 4: *Georgian England*, 1969, Volume 5: *Victorian England*, 1969, Volume 6: *Modern Times*, 1970; *Wonder Why Book of Your Body: What You Eat and Where it Goes* (illustrated by Rowan Barnes Murphy), Transworld, 1978.

Fairy tales and folk tales retold: *Fairies and Enchanters*, T. Nelson, 1933; *Princesses and Trolls*, Barrie & Rockliff, 1950; *The Arabian Nights*, Blackie & Son, 1957, Criterion, 1958, published in two volumes as *Ali Babba and the Forty Thieves from the Thousand and One Nights* and *Aladdin and Other Stories from the Thousand and One Nights*, Carousel, 1973; Brothers Grimm, *Fairy Tales*, Blackie & Son, 1959, revised edition published as *Fairy Tales from Grimm*, 1968, published as *Grimm's Fairy Tales*, Pan Books, 1964; (editor) *Fairy Tales from the British Isles*, Blackie & Son, 1960, Warner, 1964, published in two volumes as *British Fairy Tales* and *More British Fairy Tales*, Blackie & Son, 1965; *Round the World Fairy Tales*, Blackie & Son, 1963, Warner, 1966; (compiler and translator with Moura Budberg) *Russian Fairy Tales*, Blackie & Son, 1965; *Dragons and Princes: Fairy Tales from Round the World*, Blackie & Son, 1966; *Old World and New World Fairy Tales*, Warner, 1966; (editor) Brothers Grimm, *More Fairy Tales*, Blackie & Son, 1968, published as *More Fairy Tales from Grimm*, 1978; *Gypsy Folk Tales*, Pan Books, 1971; *Fairy Tales from East and West*, Blackie & Son, 1977; *Fairy Tales from Everywhere* (illustrated by William Stobbs), Blackie & Son, 1977; *Fairy Tales from Here and There* (illustrated by W. Stobbs), Blackie & Son, 1977; *Fairy Tales from Near and Far* (illustrated by W. Stobbs), Blackie & Son, 1977; (reteller) *The Rain-God's Daughter, and Other African Fairy Tales* (illustrated by T. Brooks), Blackie & Son, 1977; *The Story Spirits* (illustrated by D. Woods), Heinemann, 1981.

Science fiction: (Editor with Mably Owen) *Out of This World: An Anthology of Science Fiction*, Blackie & Son, 1960; (compiler with M. Owen) *Worlds Apart: An Anthology of Science Fiction*, Blackie & Son, 1966; (editor with Michael Pearson) *Tales from the Galaxies*, Pan Books, 1973, White Lion Publishers, 1976; (compiler with M. Pearson) *Strange Universe: An Anthology of Science Fiction*, Blackie & Son, 1974; (editor with M. Pearson) *Strange Orbits: An Anthology of Science Fiction*, Blackie & Son, 1976; *Strange Planets: An Anthology of Science Fiction*, Blackie & Son, 1977.

Novels: *Noah's Ark; or, The Love Story of a Respectable Young Couple*, J. Cape, 1925, George H. Doran, c. 1926; *The Wall of Glass*, George H. Doran, 1927; *To Tell the Truth*, J. Cape, 1933; *The Big Firm*, Houghton, 1938; *Learn to Love First*, Gollancz, 1939.

Other: *The Sea-Power of England* (play), Humphrey Milford, England, 1913; (with Clough Williams-Ellis) *The Tank Corps*, George Newnes, London, 1919; *An Anatomy of Poetry*, Basil Blackwell, 1922, reprinted, Folcroft, 1973; (with C. Williams-Ellis) *The Pleasures of Architecture*, J. Cape, 1924, revised edition, 1954; *Good Citizens* (short stories), Gerald Howe, 1928, published as *Courageous Lives: Stories of Nine Good Citizens*, Coward, 1939; *The Tragedy of John Ruskin* (critical biography), J. Cape, 1928, published as *The Exquisite Tragedy: An Intimate Life of John Ruskin*, Doubleday, 1929, reprinted under both titles, Richard West, 1973; (with L. A. Plummer) *Why Should I Vote?: A Handbook for Voters*, Gerald Howe, 1929.

H.M.S. Beagle in South America (adapted from the narratives and letters of Charles Darwin and Captain Fitz Roy), C. A. Watts, 1939, published as *The Voyage of the Beagle*, Lippincott, 1931; (author of introduction) *The Modern Schools Handbook* (edited by Trevor Eaton Blewitt), Gollancz, 1934; (translator, editor, author of introduction) *The White Sea Canal*, John Lane, 1935; (with Frederick Jack Fisher) *The Story of English Life*, Coward, 1936, revised edition, 1947, published

As for the little men, they were all round him, laughing and skipping about. ■(From "Saturday, Sunday, Monday" in *Fairy Tales from Everywhere,* retold by Amabel Williams-Ellis. Illustrated by William Stobbs.)

in England as *A History of English Life, Political and Social,* Methuen, 1936, third edition, 1953.

Women in War Factories, Gollancz, 1943; (editor with C. Williams-Ellis) *Vision of England,* Elek, 1946; (with Susan, Charlotte, Christopher and C. Williams-Ellis) *In and Out of Doors,* Routledge & Kegan Paul, 1937; (editor with C. Williams-Ellis) *Vision of Wales,* Elek, 1949.

The Art of Being a Woman, Longmans, Green, 1951; (with C. Williams-Ellis) *Headlong Down the Years: A Tale of Today,* University of Liverpool Press, 1951; (with Euan Stewart Cooper Willis) *Laughing Gas and Safety Lamp: The Story of Sir Humphry Davy,* Methuen, 1951, revised edition, Abelard, 1954; *The Art of Being a Parent,* Bodley Head, 1952; *Changing the World: Further Stories of Great Scientific Discoveries,* Bodley Head, 1956; *Darwin's Moon: A Biography of Alfred Russel Wallace,* Blackie & Son, 1966.

Contributor to periodicals, including *Saturday Review of Literature, Fortune,* and *Living Age.*

SIDELIGHTS: Williams-Ellis was born in Newlands Corner near Guildford, England. Although she was educated at home, she received a varied cultural and literal education. Her career began in 1911 as a writer for *The Spectator,* a magazine of which her father, John Strachey, was editor. In 1915 she married Bertram Clough Williams-Ellis, a well-known Welsh architect and town planner. They have collaborated on many books.

Williams-Ellis has had various interests in literature, including writing for children. Many of her children's books were written for her own three children with specific ideas about what good writing should convey. ". . . It is the job of a writer to convey as sharp an impression of what is described as possible. . . . The reader should, when reading a description generally be made to use at least four out of his five senses, smell, hearing, taste, sight and touch." [Amabel Williams-Ellis, "Our Readers Get to Work," *Left Review,* December, 1934.[1]]

"A work of art is one of those things for which so far no satisfactory definition has been found. . . . In the first place, it is not complete until it has been received, i.e., not necessarily understood, not necessarily enjoyed, but either understood or enjoyed, or in some way has struck a spark from somebody else. Herein a work of art differs from a dream or a fantasy— the visions of sleep or the long rigmaroles that we tell ourselves as children or when we are sick. These are only one sided works of art, incomplete because they mean something only to the creator. The poem or picture differs from them in meaning something both to the creator and to somebody else.

"Now one thing has been fairly well established about the deeper layers of the mind (that is, the layers from the unconscious to those purely practical, purely intellectual layers with which we catch trains or solve arithmetical problems), and that is that these deeper layers are more primitive and respond more slowly to change. They are, in fact, more old fashioned. Therefore, if you want to convey a new idea in a way which will affect not only the upper but also the deeper layers—that is, produce emotions of one sort or another—it often pays to use a form to which the deeper layers are accustomed. They—the emotional layers—will then catch the writer's meaning at the same time as the top layers. This is the technique practised by nearly all poets and very markedly by prose writers such as James Joyce. . . ." [Amabel Williams-Ellis, "Not so Easy," *Left Review,* February, 1934.[2]]

Williams-Ellis has traveled extensively, enjoys walking and sailing and is fluent in French, German and Russian.

HOBBIES AND OTHER INTERESTS: Sailing, walking.

FOR MORE INFORMATION SEE: Amabel Williams-Ellis, "Not so Easy," *Left Review,* February, 1934; Amabel Williams-Ellis, "Our Readers Get to Work," *Left Review,* December, 1934; *Spectator,* April 13, 1951; Charles Richard Sanders, *The Strachey Family, 1588-1932: Their Writings and Literary Associations,* Duke University Press, 1953; *Horn Book,* June, 1966.

WOSMEK, Frances 1917-

PERSONAL: Born December 16, 1917, in Popple, Minn.; daughter of Frank J. (a farmer) and R. Mabel (Fenton) Wosmek; married Paul Brailsford, November 18, 1949 (divorced); children: Brian, Robin. *Education:* Attended Wadena Teacher's Training College, Wadena, Minn., and Meinzinger's Art School, Detroit, Mich. *Religion:* "Life and the pursuit of its meaning." *Home:* 90 West St., Beverly Farms, Mass. 01915.

CAREER: Rural school teacher in Minnesota; designer of greeting cards for American Greetings, Cleveland, Ohio, and Rustcraft, Boston, Mass.; also has done layout and advertising art; presently free-lance designer and writer.

WRITINGS: (Self-illustrated) *Sky High,* Sam Lowe, 1949; (self-illustrated) *Twinkle Tot Tales,* Sam Lowe, 1949; (self-illustrated) *Cuddles and His Friends,* Sam Lowe, 1949; *Little Dog, Little Dog,* Rand McNally, 1963; *In the Space of a Wink* (juvenile), Follett, 1969; (self-illustrated) *A Bowl of Sun,* Childrens Press, 1976; *Never Mind Murder,* Westminster, 1977; *Mystery of the Eagle's Claw,* Westminster, 1979; *Let's Make Music,* Houghton, 1980; *The ABC of Ecology,* M. Davenport, 1981. Contributor of poems to *Christian Science Monitor.*

Illustrator: Josephine van Dolzen Pease, *One, Two, Cock-a-Doodle-Do,* Rand McNally, 1959; Helen Earle Gilbert, *Go to Sleep Book,* Rand McNally, 1969.

WORK IN PROGRESS: Designing products and toys for young children; a mystery for children with its background based on experiences in Ireland.

FRANCES WOSMEK

SIDELIGHTS: "I began writing and drawing as a child, winning a lot of prizes in a children's newspaper club. (The Fair Play Club in the *Duluth Herald* [Minn.]).

"I have never gotten over being stunned by the fact that I exist at all. I feel that everything we know is hardly a beginning of what is yet to be known. I have always thought that I, as much as anyone, could discover something new, any time . . . any minute. That because of me there could be some slipping into place of a tiny piece of the puzzle mankind is gradually putting together.

"I love to experiment, try things a new way. Creativity is letting the mind wander through the little known space that belongs to all of us . . . from which anyone can bring back clues of what is truth.

"I am only one in a multitude, but I feel a responsibility to offer my small contribution as a miniscule, partial payment for all that others have given to me.

"I have won more than fifty prizes for creative endeavors."

She kept the shop tidy, sweeping up the scraps of leather that fell to the floor. ■ (From *A Bowl of Sun* by Frances Wosmek. Illustrated by the author.)

Give a little love to a child, and you get a great deal back.

—John Ruskin

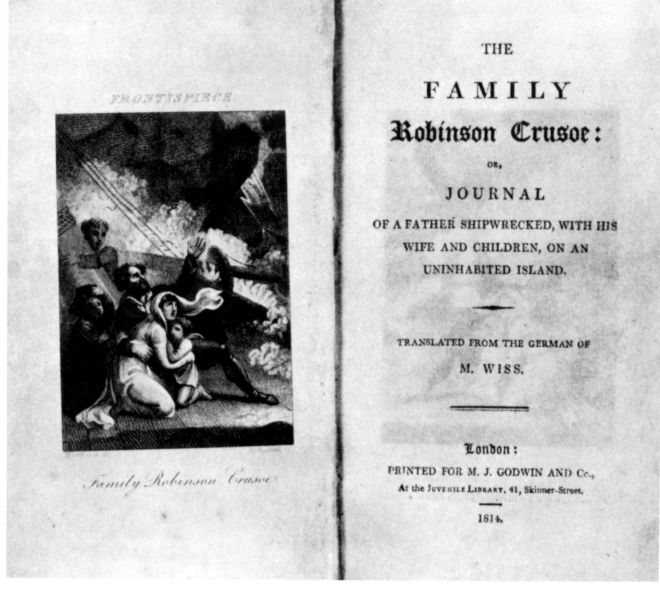

FRONTISPIECE.

Family Robinson Crusoe.

THE

FAMILY

Robinson Crusoe:

OR,

JOURNAL

OF A FATHER SHIPWRECKED, WITH HIS

WIFE AND CHILDREN, ON AN

UNINHABITED ISLAND.

TRANSLATED FROM THE GERMAN OF

M. WISS.

London:

PRINTED FOR M. J. GODWIN AND Co.,

At the Juvenile Library, 41, Skinner-Street.

1814.

Inspired by Daniel Defoe's *Robinson Crusoe* many eighteenth century writers began to use the theme of shipwreck and survival. Imitations of the original became so widespread that a special word, "Robinsonnades," was created to describe them. The most famous of the Robinsonnades, written by Johann David Wyss, is now known as *The Swiss Family Robinson*. The book, initially published in German, had 'its first' English translation published in 1814 by M.J. Godwin and was then entitled *The Family Robinson Crusoe, or, Journal of a Father Shipwrecked, with His Wife and Children, on an Uninhabited Island.* ■ (From *The Family Robinson Crusoe, or, Journal of a Father Shipwrecked, with His Wife and Children on an Uninhabited Island,* translated by M. Wiss.)

WYSS, Johann David Von   1743-1818

PERSONAL: Born in 1743, in Berne, Switzerland; died in 1818; married; children: four sons, including Johann Rudolph (1781-1830), his second son, and Johann Emanuel.

CAREER: Little is known of the life of Johann David Wyss. He served in Italy as chaplain in the Swiss Army and as pastor of the Reformed Protestant Cathedral in Berne, Switzerland. He is best known for the story *Der Schweizerische Robinson*

(The Swiss Family Robinson), which he composed for the entertainment of his four young sons. Although he wrote out the story for reading aloud to his family, he never tried to publish it. Later his son, Johann Rudolph, edited the manuscript and had it published. Johann Rudolph was given as the author on the title page of the first edition, but would not take credit as the author, explaining in the preface that he only adapted his father's original work. A noted scholar and professor of philosophy at the University of Berne, Johann Rudolph also published writings on Swiss folklore, travel, history, and philosophy, as well as writing the lyrics of the Swiss national anthem.

WRITINGS: Der Schweizerische Robinson, edited and adapted by son, Johann Rudolph Wyss (illustrated by son, Johann Emanuel Wyss), [Zurich], 1812-1813, the first edition of the first translation into English [a book of great rarity] was published as *The Family Robinson Crusoe; or, Journal of a Father Shipwrecked, with His Wife and Children on an Uninhabited Island,* M. J. Godwin & Co. [London], 1814, the second English edition was translated by William Godwin and published as *The Swiss Family Robinson,* M. J. Godwin & Co. [London], 1818, French translation, revised and enlarged edition by the Baroness de Montolieu published as *Le Robinson Suisse, ou Journal d'un père de famille naufragé avec ses enfants,* [Paris], 1816. The French edition has served as the basis for most of the 200 subsequent editions of *The Swiss Family Robinson.* Later editions include those edited by: Mrs. H. B. Paull, Chandos Classics, 1868; William H. Kingston, Routledge & Sons, 1882, reprinted (illustrated by Don Irwin), Classic Press, 1968; William Dean Howells (illustrated by Louis Rhead), Harper & Brothers, 1909; John Henry Groth, Macmillan, 1929; Mabel Dodge Holmes (illustrated by Frank Godwin), John C. Winston, 1929; John Maddison (illustrated with photographs from the 1940 film), Pilot Press, 1945; Robert Cushman Murphy (illustrated by David Gentleman), Heritage Press, 1963; Allen R. Bosworth, Harper, 1966; Naunerle Farr, Pendulum Press, 1978.

Illustrated editions include those illustrated by: Charles Folkard, Dutton, 1910, reprinted, 1958; Elenore Plaisted Abbott, G. W. Jacobs, 1914; Charles Copeland, Ginn, 1915; Milo Winter, Rand McNally, 1916; Harry Rountree, A. & C. Black, 1920; Frances Brundage, Saalfield Publishing, 1924; Harry Rountree, Macmillan, 1927; Juanita Bennett, World Publishing, 1947; Lynd Ward, Grosset, 1949; Fritz Kredel, Doubleday, 1954; Leon Gregori, Grosset, 1963; Jeanne Edwards, World Publishing, 1972.

Adaptations for children include those edited by: Felix Sutton, Grosset, 1960; Audrey Butler (illustrated by Gay Galsworthy), American Education Publications, 1970; Ann Carmichael (illustrated by Hutchings), Robert Tyndall, 1972; Ronald D. K. Storer (illustrated by Joseph Acheson), Oxford University Press, 1974; Jimmy Corinis (adaptation of the Walt Disney motion picture), New English Library, 1976; Michael West (revised by D. K. Swan; illustrated by Mary Dinsdale), Longman, 1977; Jane Carruth (published as *Johann Wyss's 'Swiss Family Robinson'*; illustrated by Gordon King), Purnell, 1977; Joan Marlow Rodd (published as *A Child's Swiss Family Robinson*; illustrated by Violette Diserens), Hart Publishing, 1978; Georgina Hargreaves (self-illustrated), Dean, 1979; Harry Stanton (illustrated by Brian Price Thomas), Ladybird Books, 1979.

ADAPTATIONS—Movies and filmstrips: "Swiss Family Robinson" (motion picture), starring Thomas Mitchell, Edna Best,

Poor Jack was in a terrible fright; kick as he would, his enemy still clung on.... ■ (From *The Swiss Family Robinson* by Johann Wyss. Illustrated by Lynd Ward.)

"I proceeded more cautiously in my pursuit of the wounded bird." ■ (From *The Swiss Family Robinson* by Johann Wyss. Illustrated by T.H. Robinson.)

...Though my nautical knowledge was not great, I succeeded in steering the boat into the favorable stream, which carried us nearly three-fourths of our passage with little or no trouble to ourselves. ■ (From *The Swiss Family Robinson* by Johann Wyss. Illustrated by Lynd Ward.)

(From the movie "Swiss Family Robinson," starring Thomas Mitchell, Freddie Bartholomew, and Tim Holt. Copyright 1940 by RKO Radio Pictures Inc.)

(From the movie "The Swiss Family Robinson," starring John Mills and Dorothy McGuire. Copyright © 1960 by Walt Disney Productions.)

Freddie Bartholomew, and Terry Kilburn, Towne and Baker Productions, 1940; "Swiss Family Robinson" (filmstrip; captioned and with teacher's guide), Eye Gate House, 1958; "Swiss Family Robinson" (motion picture), starring John Mills, Dorothy McGuire, James MacArthur, and Tommy Kirk, Walt Disney Productions, 1960; "Swiss Family Shipwrecked" (filmstrip), Encyclopaedia Britannica Films, 1964; "Swiss Family Rescued" (filmstrip), Encyclopaedia Britannica Films, 1964; "Swiss Family Robinson" (television film), starring Martin Milner, Pat Delaney, Eric Olsen, and Cindy Fisher, Twentieth Century-Fox, 1974.

Recordings: "The Swiss Family Robinson," with sound effects by Bill Golding, Barbara McCaughey, Paul Tully, and Simon Tully, Spoken Arts, 1970; "Swiss Family Robinson," narrated by Anthony Quayle, Caedmon, 1975.

SIDELIGHTS: **1743.** Born in Berne, Switzerland. Little is known about the author of *The Swiss Family Robinson* except that in 1766 he became a military chaplain, and later rector of the Reformed Protestant cathedral in Berne. He was reputed to be an accomplished linguist, speaking and writing four languages. Wyss was married and had four sons.

To my amazement, I perceived that he really had struck the tortoise with a harpoon; a rope was attached to it, and the creature was running away with us. ■ (From *The Swiss Family Robinson* by Johann Wyss. Edited by William H.G. Kingston. Illustrated by Jeanne Edwards.)

We dragged the whole herd towards land. ■ (From *The Swiss Family Robinson* by Johann Wyss. Illustrated by Charles Folkard.)

On the origin of the famous book, *The Swiss Family Robinson,* Robert Wyss, a descendant, wrote: *"The Swiss Family Robinson* was never meant to be published. At least that was never the intention of my great-great-great grandfather during all those months some 150 years ago when he painstakingly set down the story in 841 pages of manuscript. Johann David Wyss was only playing the role of a devoted father, recording the adventures which he and his sons made up as they went along and which they decided to keep in handwritten form for their own pleasure.

"This kind of group activity was characteristic of the Wyss family. Johann David Wyss . . . spent all his spare time with his four sons, going with them on long hikes and hunting trips and inspiring them with his own love of nature. Together at home they liked to read and discuss travel and adventure stories like *Robinson Crusoe* which had been published in 1719 by the Englishman Daniel Defoe. This practice led to the family's imagining itself on some faraway island, leading a life like that of Crusoe and thinking of all the possible things that could happen to a family shipwrecked upon a deserted shore.

". . . At the time, adventure books motivated by the Robinson Crusoe theme were known as Robinsoniads, and so he titled the Wyss tale *Der Schweizerische Robinson (The Swiss Robinson),* hoping thereby to help sales.

In a fit of mischief they seized little Francis, tossed him into the basket, and began to run about with him inside. ■ (From *Swiss Family Robinson* by Johann Wyss. Illustrated by Charles Folkard.)

"The Swiss family of the book is the same as the Wyss family of real life. The shipwrecked parents are a pedantic parson and his wife, while their four young sons experience parental instruction and family relationships just like those of the four Wyss children themselves.

"It is the setting for the story that is purest fabrication, conceived with a wildly imaginative disregard for the facts of nature. Plants and animals from every climate in the world abound on the tropical island, which the manuscript locates 'in the neighborhood of New Guinea.' But no single place on earth has—or could have—such a conglomeration of exotic plants and animals as Wyss managed to bring together." [Robert L. Wyss, "The Real Swiss Wysses," *Life* magazine, Volume 37, December, 1954.[1]]

The Swiss Family Robinson was translated into French by the Baroness Isabelle de Montolieu in 1816. Encouraged by its success, she asked Wyss's son, Johann Rudolf to extend the original manuscript. Not having the time to do it himself, he gave her permission to complete it. This new version came out in 1824, but apparently did not satisfy Johann Rudolf, so in 1827, he published his own two-volume addition to the original two volumes. In it's preface, Rudolf Wyss noted: "It will be understood that the ending of the book as here given owes nothing to the work of Mme. de Montolieu. I follow my father's original manuscript just as before; but always with the same freedom that I used in the earlier volumes. Many things are not suitable for publication, which, in the author's family circle where the manuscript up to this time had alone been read, were entirely in place. Also the end of the story appears (in the original manuscript) rather sketched than carefully worked out." [Francis H. Allen, "News for Bibliophiles," *The Nation*, Volume 95, September, 1912.[2]]

There have been many editions and translations of *The Swiss Family Robinson*, but some doubt remains as to whose ending

is the definitive one. One critic claimed that Johann Rudolf's ending was almost entirely copied from Mme. de Montolieu's version. The first English translation of the extended version was executed by Mrs. H. B. Paull in 1868.

Wyss's great-great-grandson Robert revealed an interesting and little known fact about the original manuscript: "To illustrate the story as it was being set down, Wyss's third son, Johann Emanuel, did a series of 60 remarkably detailed drawings, gouaches and water colors. Bound into the volumes of hand-written manuscript . . . they portray the adventures with childish gusto. They also show an impressive variety of animals which are surprisingly accurate considering that the artist, a boy at the time, knew most of them only secondhand from descriptions and illustrations in zoological books.

"But the illustrations of Johann Emanuel Wyss were never included in any one of the countless published editions. Considered only curious family possessions, they were handed down from one generation of Wysses to another but never shown to the public."[1]

1818. Wyss, almost entirely forgotten as the author of the original manuscript of *The Swiss Family Robinson*, died in Berne, Switzerland.

FOR MORE INFORMATION SEE: William Dean Howells, editor and author of introduction, *The Swiss Family Robinson*, Harper & Brothers, 1909; *Bookman*, Volume XXXIV, 1911; Solomon Eagle, *Essays at Large*, George H. Doran, 1922; James O'Donnell Bennett, *Much Loved Books*, Boni & Liveright, 1927; Vincent Starrett, *Books Alive*, Random House, 1940; Elizabeth Rider Montgomery, *The Story behind Great Books* (juvenile; illustrated by Friedebald Dzubas), McBride, 1946; *Life*, December 27, 1954; *Encyclopedia of World Authors*, Magill, 1958; William Gerald Golding, *The Hot Gates and Other Occasional Pieces*, Harcourt, 1961; Brian Doyle, editor, *Who's Who of Children's Literature*, Schocken, 1968.

CUMULATIVE INDEX TO ILLUSTRATIONS AND AUTHORS

Illustrations Index

(In the following index, the number of the volume in which an illustrator's work appears is given *before* the colon, and the page on which it appears is given *after* the colon. For example, a drawing by Adams, Adrienne appears in Volume 2 on page 6, another drawing by her appears in Volume 3 on page 80, another drawing in Volume 8 on page 1, and another drawing in Volume 15 on page 107.)

YABC

Index citations including this abbreviation refer to listings appearing in *Yesterday's Authors of Books for Children,* also published by the Gale Research Company, which covers authors who died prior to 1960.

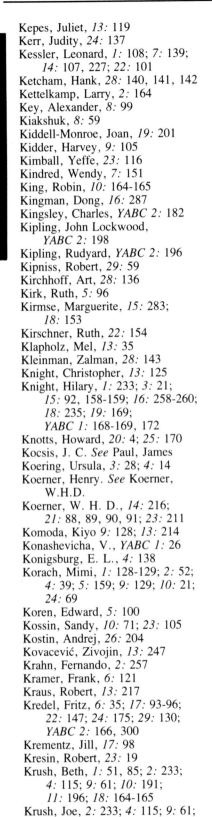

Author Index

(In the following index, the number of the volume in which an author's sketch appears is given *before* the colon, and the page on which it appears is given *after* the colon. For example, the sketch of Aardema, Verna, appears in Volume 4 on page 1).

YABC

Index citations including this abbreviation refer to listings appearing in *Yesterday's Authors of Books for Children*, also published by the Gale Research Company, which covers authors who died prior to 1960.

Alexander, Rae Pace. *See*
Alexander, Raymond Pace,
22: 10
Alexander, Raymond Pace
1898-1974, *22:* 10
Alexander, Sue   1933- , *12:* 5
Alexander, Vincent Arthur
1925-1980, *23:* 1 (Obituary)
Alexeieff, Alexandre A.   1901- ,
14: 5
Alger, Horatio, Jr.   1832-1899,
16: 3
Alger, Leclaire (Gowans)
1898-1969, *15:* 1
Aliki. *See* Brandenberg, Aliki,
2: 36
Alkema, Chester Jay   1932- ,
12: 7
Allamand, Pascale   1942- , *12:* 8
Allan, Mabel Esther   1915- , *5:* 2
Allee, Marjorie Hill   1890-1945,
17: 11
Allen, Adam [Joint pseudonym].
See Epstein, Beryl and Samuel,
1: 85
Allen, Allyn. *See* Eberle,
Irmengarde, *2:* 97; *23:* 68
(Obituary)
Allen, Betsy. *See* Cavanna, Betty,
1: 54
Allen, Gertrude E(lizabeth)
1888- , *9:* 5
Allen, Jack   1899- , *29:* 32 (Brief
Entry)
Allen, Leroy   1912- , *11:* 7
Allen, Marjorie   1931- , *22:* 11
Allen, Maury   1932- , *26:* 23
Allen, Merritt Parmelee
1892-1954, *22:* 12
Allen, Nina (Strömgren)   1935- ,
22: 13
Allen, Rodney F.   1938- , *27:* 22
Allen, Samuel (Washington)
1917- , *9:* 6
Allerton, Mary. *See* Govan,
Christine Noble, *9:* 80
Alleyn, Ellen. *See* Rossetti,
Christina (Georgina), *20:* 147
Allison, Bob, *14:* 7
Allred, Gordon T.   1930- , *10:* 3
Allsop, Kenneth   1920-1973,
17: 13
Almedingen, E. M.   1898-1971,
3: 9
Almedingen, Martha Edith von. *See*
Almedingen, E. M., *3:* 9
Almquist, Don   1929- , *11:* 8
Alsop, Mary O'Hara   1885-1980,
2: 4; *24:* 26 (Obituary)
Alter, Robert Edmond   1925-1965,
9: 8
Althea. *See* Braithwaite, Althea,
23: 11
Altsheler, Joseph A(lexander)
1862-1919, YABC *1:* 20
Alvarez, Joseph A.   1930- , *18:* 2

Ambler, C(hristopher) Gifford
1886- , *29:* 33 (Brief Entry)
Ambrus, Victor G(tozo)   1935- ,
1: 6
Amerman, Lockhart   1911-1969,
3: 11
Ames, Evelyn   1908- , *13:* 1
Ames, Gerald   1906- , *11:* 9
Ames, Lee J.   1921- , *3:* 11
Ames, Mildred   1919- , *22:* 14
Amon, Aline   1928- , *9:* 8
Amoss, Berthe   1925- , *5:* 4
Anckarsvärd, Karin   1915-1969,
6: 2
Ancona, George   1929- , *12:* 10
Andersen, Hans Christian
1805-1875, YABC *1:* 23
Andersen, Ted. *See* Boyd, Waldo
T., *18:* 35
Andersen, Yvonne   1932- , *27:* 23
Anderson, C(larence) W(illiam)
1891-1971, *11:* 9
Anderson, Clifford [Joint
pseudonym]. *See* Gardner,
Richard, *24:* 119
Anderson, Ella. *See* MacLeod,
Ellen Jane (Anderson), *14:* 129
Anderson, Eloise Adell   1927- ,
9: 9
Anderson, George. *See* Groom,
Arthur William, *10:* 53
Anderson, J(ohn) R(ichard) L(ane)
1911-1981, *15:* 3; *27:* 24
(Obituary)
Anderson, Joy   1928- , *1:* 8
Anderson, LaVere (Francis
Shoenfelt)   1907- , *27:* 24
Anderson, (John) Lonzo   1905- ,
2: 6
Anderson, Lucia (Lewis)   1922- ,
10: 4
Anderson, Madelyn Klein, *28:* 24
Anderson, Margaret J(ean)
1931- , *27:* 26
Anderson, Mary   1939- , *7:* 4
Anderson, Norman D(ean)   1928- ,
22: 15
Andre, Evelyn M(arie)   1924- ,
27: 27
Andrews, F(rank) Emerson
1902-1978, *22:* 17
Andrews, J(ames) S(ydney)
1934- , *4:* 7
Andrews, Julie   1935- , *7:* 6
Andrews, Roy Chapman
1884-1960, *19:* 1
Angell, Judie   1937- , *22:* 18
Angell, Madeline   1919- , *18:* 3
Angelo, Valenti   1897- , *14:* 7
Angier, Bradford, *12:* 12
Angle, Paul M(cClelland)
1900-1975, *20:* 1 (Obituary)
Anglund, Joan Walsh   1926- , *2:* 7
Angrist, Stanley W(olff)   1933- ,
4: 9
Anita. *See* Daniel, Anita, *23:* 65

Annett, Cora. *See* Scott, Cora
Annett, *11:* 207
Annixter, Jane. *See* Sturtzel, Jane
Levington, *1:* 212
Annixter, Paul. *See* Sturtzel,
Howard A., *1:* 210
Anno, Mitsumasa   1920- , *5:* 6
Anrooy, Frans van. *See* Van
Anrooy, Francine, *2:* 252
Anthony, Barbara   1932- , *29:* 33
Anthony, C. L. *See* Smith, Dodie,
4: 194
Anthony, Edward   1895-1971,
21: 1
Anticaglia, Elizabeth   1939- ,
12: 13
Anton, Michael (James)   1940- ,
12: 13
Appel, Benjamin   1907-1977,
21: 5 (Obituary)
Appiah, Peggy   1921- , *15:* 3
Appleton, Victor [Collective
pseudonym], *1:* 9
Appleton, Victor II [Collective
pseudonym], *1:* 9; *29:* 26
(Obituary)
Apsler, Alfred   1907- , *10:* 4
Aquillo, Don. *See* Prince, J(ack)
H(arvey), *17:* 155
Arbuthnot, May Hill   1884-1969,
2: 9
Archer, Frank. *See* O'Connor,
Richard, *21:* 111
Archer, Jules   1915- , *4:* 9
Archer, Marion Fuller   1917- ,
11: 12
Archibald, Joseph S.   1898- ,
3: 12
Arden, Barbie. *See* Stoutenburg,
Adrien, *3:* 217
Ardizzone, Edward   1900-1979,
1: 10; *21:* 5 (Obituary); *28:* 25
Arehart-Treichel, Joan   1942- ,
22: 18
Arenella, Roy   1939- , *14:* 9
Armer, Alberta (Roller)   1904- ,
9: 11
Armer, Laura Adams   1874-1963,
13: 2
Armour, Richard   1906- , *14:* 10
Armstrong, George D.   1927- ,
10: 5
Armstrong, Gerry (Breen)   1929- ,
10: 6
Armstrong, Richard   1903- ,
11: 14
Armstrong, William H.   1914- ,
4: 11
Arnett, Carolyn. *See* Cole, Lois
Dwight, *10:* 26; *26:* 43
(Obituary)
Arno, Enrico   1913-1981, *28:* 38
(Obituary)
Arnold, Elliott   1912-1980, *5:* 7;
22: 19 (Obituary)
Arnold, Oren   1900- , *4:* 13

Brown, Irving. *See* Adams, William Taylor, *28:* 21

Brown, Ivor (John Carnegie) 1891-1974, *5:* 31; *26:* 38 (Obituary)

Brown, Judith Gwyn 1933- , *20:* 15

Brown, Marc Tolon 1946- , *10:* 17

Brown, Marcia 1918- , *7:* 29

Brown, Margaret Wise 1910-1952, *YABC 2:* 9

Brown, Margery, *5:* 31

Brown, Marion Marsh 1908- , *6:* 35

Brown, Myra Berry 1918- , *6:* 36

Brown, Pamela 1924- , *5:* 33

Brown, Robert Joseph 1907- , *14:* 48

Brown, Rosalie (Gertrude) Moore 1910- , *9:* 26

Brown, Vinson 1912- , *19:* 48

Brown, Walter R(eed) 1929- , *19:* 50

Brown, Will. *See* Ainsworth, William Harrison, *24:* 21

Brown, William L(ouis) 1910-1964, *5:* 34

Browne, Hablot Knight 1815-1882, *21:* 13

Browne, Matthew. *See* Rands, William Brighty, *17:* 156

Browning, Robert 1812-1889, *YABC 1:* 85

Brownjohn, Alan 1931- *6:* 38

Bruce, Dorita Fairlie 1885-1970, *27:* 36 (Obituary)

Bruce, Mary 1927- , *1:* 36

Brunhoff, Jean de 1899-1937, *24:* 56

Brunhoff, Laurent de 1925- , *24:* 59

Bryant, Bernice (Morgan) 1908- , *11:* 40

Brychta, Alex 1956- , *21:* 21

Bryson, Bernarda 1905- , *9:* 26

Buchan, John 1875-1940, *YABC 2:* 21

Buchwald, Art(hur) 1925- , *10:* 18

Buchwald, Emilie 1935- , *7:* 31

Buck, Lewis 1925- , *18:* 37

Buck, Margaret Waring 1910- , *3:* 29

Buck, Pearl S(ydenstricker) 1892-1973, *1:* 36; *25:* 63

Buckeridge, Anthony 1912- , *6:* 38

Buckley, Helen E(lizabeth) 1918- , *2:* 38

Buckmaster, Henrietta, *6:* 39

Budd, Lillian 1897- , *7:* 33

Buehr, Walter 1897-1971, *3:* 30

Buff, Conrad 1886-1975, *19:* 51

Buff, Mary Marsh 1890-1970, *19:* 54

Bugbee, Emma 1888(?)-1981, *29:* 51 (Obituary)

Bulla, Clyde Robert 1914- , *2:* 39

Bunting, A. E.. *See* Bunting, Anne Evelyn, *18:* 38

Bunting, Anne Evelyn 1928- , *18:* 38

Bunting, Eve. *See* Bunting, Anne Evelyn, *18:* 38

Bunting, Glenn (Davison) 1957- , *22:* 60

Burch, Robert J(oseph) 1925- , *1:* 38

Burchard, Peter D(uncan), *5:* 34

Burchard, Sue 1937- , *22:* 61

Burchardt, Nellie 1921- , *7:* 33

Burdick, Eugene (Leonard) 1918-1965, *22:* 61

Burford, Eleanor. *See* Hibbert, Eleanor, *2:* 134

Burger, Carl 1888-1967, *9:* 27

Burgess, Anne Marie. *See* Gerson, Noel B(ertram), *22:* 118

Burgess, Em. *See* Burgess, Mary Wyche, *18:* 39

Burgess, Mary Wyche 1916- , *18:* 39

Burgess, Michael. *See* Gerson, Noel B(ertram), *22:* 118

Burgess, Robert F(orrest) 1927- , *4:* 38

Burgess, Thornton W(aldo) 1874-1965, *17:* 19

Burgess, Trevor. *See* Trevor, Elleston, *28:* 207

Burgwyn, Mebane H. 1914- , *7:* 34

Burke, John. *See* O'Connor, Richard, *21:* 111

Burkert, Nancy Ekholm 1933- , *24:* 62

Burland, C. A. *See* Burland, Cottie A., *5:* 36

Burland, Cottie A. 1905- , *5:* 36

Burlingame, (William) Roger 1889-1967, *2:* 40

Burman, Alice Caddy 1896(?)-1977, *24:* 66 (Obituary)

Burman, Ben Lucien 1896- , *6:* 40

Burn, Doris 1923- , *1:* 39

Burnett, Frances (Eliza) Hodgson 1849-1924, *YABC 2:* 32

Burnford, S. D. *See* Burnford, Sheila, *3:* 32

Burnford, Sheila 1918- , *3:* 32

Burningham, John (Mackintosh) 1936- , *16:* 58

Burns, Paul C., *5:* 37

Burns, Raymond (Howard) 1924- , *9:* 28

Burns, William A. 1909- , *5:* 38

Burroughs, Jean Mitchell 1908- , *28:* 57

Burroughs, Polly 1925- , *2:* 41

Burroway, Janet (Gay) 1936- , *23:* 24

Burt, Jesse Clifton 1921-1976, *20:* 18 (Obituary)

Burt, Olive Woolley 1894- , *4:* 39

Burton, Hester 1913- , *7:* 35

Burton, Maurice 1898- , *23:* 27

Burton, Robert (Wellesley) 1941- , *22:* 62

Burton, Virginia Lee 1909-1968, *2:* 42

Burton, William H(enry) 1890-1964, *11:* 42

Busby, Edith (?)-1964, *29:* 51 (Obituary)

Busoni, Rafaello 1900-1962, *16:* 61

Butler, Beverly 1932- , *7:* 37

Butler, Suzanne. *See* Perreard, Suzanne Louise Butler, *29:* 162 (Brief Entry)

Butters, Dorothy Gilman 1923- , *5:* 39

Butterworth, Oliver 1915- , *1:* 40

Butterworth, W(illiam) E(dmund III) 1929- , *5:* 40

Byars, Betsy 1928- , *4:* 40

Byfield, Barbara Ninde 1930- , *8:* 19

C.3.3. *See* Wilde, Oscar (Fingal O'Flahertie Wills), *24:* 205

Cable, Mary 1920- , *9:* 29

Caddy, Alice. *See* Burman, Alice Caddy, *24:* 66 (Obituary)

Cadwallader, Sharon 1936- , *7:* 38

Cady, (Walter) Harrison 1877-1970, *19:* 56

Cain, Arthur H. 1913- , *3:* 33

Cain, Christopher. *See* Fleming, Thomas J(ames), *8:* 19

Cairns, Trevor 1922- , *14:* 50

Caldecott, Moyra 1927- , *22:* 63

Caldecott, Randolph (J.) 1846-1886, *17:* 31

Caldwell, John C(ope) 1913- , *7:* 38

Calhoun, Mary (Huiskamp) 1926- , *2:* 44

Calkins, Franklin. *See* Stratemeyer, Edward L., *1:* 208

Call, Hughie Florence 1890-1969, *1:* 41

Callahan, Philip S(erna) 1923- , *25:* 77

Callen, Larry. *See* Callen, Lawrence Willard, Jr., *19:* 59

Callen, Lawrence Willard, Jr. 1927- , *19:* 59

Calvert, John. *See* Leaf, (Wilbur) Munro, *20:* 99

Cameron, Ann 1943- , *27:* 37

Cameron, Edna M. 1905- , *3:* 34

Author Index

Author Index

Mulvihill, William Patrick 1923- ,
8: 140
Mun. *See* Leaf, (Wilbur) Munro,
20: 99
Munari, Bruno 1907- , *15:* 199
Munce, Ruth Hill 1898- , *12:* 156
Munowitz, Ken 1935-1977,
14: 149
Munro, Alice 1931- , *29:* 156
Munson(-Benson), Tunie 1946- ,
15: 201
Munzer, Martha E. 1899- , *4:* 157
Murphy, Barbara Beasley 1933- ,
5: 137
Murphy, E(mmett) Jefferson
1926- , *4:* 159
Murphy, Pat. *See* Murphy,
E(mmett) Jefferson, *4:* 159
Murphy, Robert (William)
1902-1971, *10:* 102
Murray, Marian, *5:* 138
Murray, Michele 1933-1974,
7: 170
Musgrave, Florence 1902- ,
3: 144
Musgrove, Margaret W(ynkoop)
1943- , *26:* 147
Mussey, Virginia T. H. *See* Ellison,
Virginia Howell, *4:* 74
Mutz. *See* Kunstler, Morton, *10:* 73
Myers, Bernice, *9:* 146
Myers, Caroline Elizabeth (Clark)
1887-1980, *28:* 158
Myers, Hortense (Powner) 1913- ,
10: 102
Myers, Walter Dean 1937- ,
27: 153 (Brief Entry)
Myller, Rolf 1926- , *27:* 153
Myrus, Donald (Richard) 1927- ,
23: 147

Namioka, Lensey 1929- , *27:* 154
Nash, Linell. *See* Smith, Linell
Nash, *2:* 227
Nash, (Frediric) Ogden
1902-1971, *2:* 194
Nast, Elsa Ruth. *See* Watson, Jane
Werner, *3:* 244
Nathan, Dorothy (Goldeen)
(?)-1966, *15:* 202
Nathan, Robert 1894- , *6:* 171
Navarra, John Gabriel 1927- ,
8: 141
Naylor, Penelope 1941- , *10:* 104
Naylor, Phyllis Reynolds 1933- ,
12: 156
Nazaroff, Alexander I. 1898- ,
4: 160
Neal, Harry Edward 1906- ,
5: 139
Nee, Kay Bonner, *10:* 104
Needleman, Jacob 1934- , *6:* 172
Negri, Rocco 1932- , *12:* 157
Neigoff, Anne, *13:* 165

Neigoff, Mike 1920- , *13:* 166
Neilson, Frances Fullerton (Jones)
1910- , *14:* 149
Neimark, Anne E. 1935- , *4:* 160
Nelson, Cordner (Bruce) 1918- ,
29: 156 (Brief Entry)
Nelson, Esther L. 1928- , *13:* 167
Nelson, Lawrence E(rnest)
1928-1977, *28:* 160 (Obituary)
Nelson, Mary Carroll 1929- ,
23: 147
Nesbit, E(dith) 1858-1924,
YABC 1: 193
Nesbit, Troy. *See* Folsom, Franklin,
5: 67
Nespojohn, Katherine V. 1912- ,
7: 170
Ness, Evaline (Michelow) 1911- ,
1: 165; *26:* 149
Neufeld, John 1938- , *6:* 173
Neumeyer, Peter F(lorian) 1929- ,
13: 168
Neurath, Marie (Reidemeister)
1898- , *1:* 166
Neville, Emily Cheney 1919- ,
1: 169
Neville, Mary. *See* Woodrich, Mary
Neville, *2:* 274
Nevins, Albert J. 1915- , *20:* 134
Newberry, Clare Turlay
1903-1970, *1:* 170; *26:* 153
(Obituary)
Newbery, John 1713-1767,
20: 135
Newcomb, Ellsworth. *See* Kenny,
Ellsworth Newcomb, *26:* 130
(Obituary)
Newell, Crosby. *See* Bonsall,
Crosby (Barbara Newell), *23:* 6
Newell, Edythe W. 1910- ,
11: 185
Newell, Hope (Hockenberry)
1896-1965, *24:* 154
Newfeld, Frank 1928- , *26:* 153
Newlon, Clarke, *6:* 174
Newman, Daisy 1904- , *27:* 154
Newman, Robert (Howard)
1909- , *4:* 161
Newman, Shirlee Petkin 1924- ,
10: 105
Newton, James R(obert) 1935- ,
23: 149
Newton, Suzanne 1936- , *5:* 140
Nic Leodhas, Sorche. *See* Alger,
Leclaire (Gowans), *15:* 1
Nichols, Cecilia Fawn 1906- ,
12: 159
Nichols, (Joanna) Ruth 1948- ,
15: 204
Nickelsburg, Janet 1893- ,
11: 185
Nickerson, Betty. *See* Nickerson,
Elizabeth, *14:* 150
Nickerson, Elizabeth 1922- ,
14: 150

Nicol, Ann. *See* Turnbull, Ann
(Christine), *18:* 281
Nicolas. *See* Mordvinoff, Nicolas,
17: 129
Nicolay, Helen 1866-1954,
YABC 1: 204
Nicole, Christopher Robin 1930- ,
5: 141
Nielsen, Kay (Rasmus)
1886-1957, *16:* 210
Nielsen, Virginia. *See* McCall,
Virginia Nielsen, *13:* 151
Niland, Deborah 1951- , *27:* 156
Nixon, Joan Lowery 1927- ,
8: 143
Nixon, K. *See* Nixon, Kathleen
Irene (Blundell), *14:* 152
Nixon, Kathleen Irene (Blundell),
14: 152
Noble, Iris 1922- , *5:* 142
Nodset, Joan M. *See* Lexau, Joan
M., *1:* 144
Nolan, Jeannette Covert
1897-1974, *2:* 196; *27:* 157
(Obituary)
Nolan, William F(rancis) 1928- ,
28: 160 (Brief Entry)
Noonan, Julia 1946- , *4:* 163
Norcross, John. *See* Conroy, Jack
(Wesley), *19:* 65
Nordhoff, Charles (Bernard)
1887-1947, *23:* 150
Nordlicht, Lillian, *29:* 157
Nordstrom, Ursula, *3:* 144
Norman, James. *See* Schmidt,
James Norman, *21:* 141
Norman, Steve. *See* Pashko,
Stanley, *29:* 159
Norris, Gunilla B(rodde) 1939- ,
20: 139
North, Andrew. *See* Norton, Alice
Mary, *1:* 173
North, Captain George. *See*
Stevenson, Robert Louis,
YABC 2: 307
North, Joan 1920- , *16:* 218
North, Robert. *See* Withers, Carl
A., *14:* 261
North, Sterling 1906-1974, *1:* 171;
26: 155 (Obituary)
Norton, Alice Mary 1912- ,
1: 173
Norton, Andre. *See* Norton, Alice
Mary, *1:* 173
Norton, Browning. *See* Norton,
Frank R(owland) B(rowning),
10: 107
Norton, Frank R(owland)
B(rowning) 1909- , *10:* 107
Norton, Mary 1903- , *18:* 236
Nowell, Elizabeth Cameron,
12: 160
Numeroff, Laura Joffe 1953- ,
28: 160
Nurnberg, Maxwell 1897- ,
27: 157

Nussbaumer, Paul (Edmond) 1934- , *16:* 218
Nyce, (Nellie) Helene von Strecker 1885-1969, *19:* 218
Nyce, Vera 1862-1925, *19:* 219
Nye, Robert 1939- , *6:* 174

Oakes, Vanya 1909- , *6:* 175
Oakley, Don(ald G.) 1927- , *8:* 144
Oakley, Helen 1906- , *10:* 107
Obrant, Susan 1946- , *11:* 186
O'Brien, Robert C. *See* Conly, Robert Leslie, *23:* 45
O'Brien, Thomas C(lement) 1938- , *29:* 158
O'Carroll, Ryan. *See* Markun, Patricia M(aloney), *15:* 189
O'Connell, Peg. *See* Ahern, Margaret McCrohan, *10:* 2
O'Connor, Patrick. *See* Wibberley, Leonard, *2:* 271
O'Connor, Richard 1915-1975, *21:* 111 (Obituary)
O'Daniel, Janet 1921- , *24:* 155
O'Dell, Scott 1903- , *12:* 161
Odenwald, Robert P(aul) 1899-1965, *11:* 187
Oechsli, Kelly 1918- , *5:* 143
Offit, Sidney 1928- , *10:* 108
Ofosu-Appiah, L(awrence) H(enry) 1920- , *13:* 170
Ogan, George F. 1912- , *13:* 171
Ogan, M. G. [Joint pseudonym]. *See* Ogan, George F. and Margaret E. (Nettles), *13:* 171
Ogan, Margaret E. (Nettles) 1923- , *13:* 171
Ogburn, Charlton, Jr. 1911- , *3:* 145
Ogilvie, Elisabeth 1917- , *29:* 158 (Brief Entry)
O'Hara, Mary. *See* Alsop, Mary O'Hara, *2:* 4; *24:* 26 (Obituary)
Ohlsson, Ib 1935- , *7:* 171
Olcott, Frances Jenkins 1872(?)-1963, *19:* 220
Old Fag. *See* Bell, Robert S(tanley) W(arren), *27:* 32 (Brief Entry)
Olds, Elizabeth 1896- , *3:* 146
Olds, Helen Diehl 1895-1981, *9:* 148; *25:* 186 (Obituary)
Oldstyle, Jonathan. *See* Irving, Washington, *YABC 2:* 164
O'Leary, Brian 1940- , *6:* 176
Oliver, John Edward 1933- , *21:* 112
Olmstead, Lorena Ann 1890- , *13:* 172
Olney, Ross R. 1929- , *13:* 173
Olschewski, Alfred 1920- , *7:* 172
Olsen, Ib Spang 1921- , *6:* 177
Olugebefola, Ademole 1941- , *15:* 204

Ommanney, F(rancis) D(ownes) 1903-1980, *23:* 159
O Mude. *See* Gorey, Edward St. John, *27:* 104 (Brief Entry)
O'Neill, Mary L(e Duc) 1908- , *2:* 197
Opie, Iona 1923- , *3:* 148
Opie, Peter (Mason) 1918-1982, *3:* 149; *28:* 162 (Obituary)
Oppenheim, Joanne 1934- , *5:* 146
Oppenheimer, Joan L(etson) 1925- , *28:* 162
Optic, Oliver. *See* Adams, William Taylor, *28:* 21
Orbach, Ruth Gary 1941- , *21:* 112
Orgel, Doris 1929- , *7:* 173
Orleans, Ilo 1897-1962, *10:* 110
Ormondroyd, Edward 1925- , *14:* 153
Ormsby, Virginia H(aire), *11:* 187
Orth, Richard. *See* Gardner, Richard, *24:* 119
Orwell, George. *See* Blair, Eric Arthur, *29:* 39
Osborne, Chester G. 1915- , *11:* 188
Osborne, David. *See* Silverberg, Robert, *13:* 206
Osborne, Leone Neal 1914- , *2:* 198
Osmond, Edward 1900- , *10:* 110
Ossoli, Sarah Margaret (Fuller) marchesa d' 1810-1850, *25:* 186
Otis, James. *See* Kaler, James Otis, *15:* 151
O'Trigger, Sir Lucius. *See* Horne, Richard Henry, *29:* 106
Ottley, Reginald (Leslie), *26:* 155
Ouida. *See* De La Ramée, (Marie) Louise, *20:* 26
Ousley, Odille 1896- , *10:* 111
Owen, Caroline Dale. *See* Snedecker, Caroline Dale (Parke), *YABC 2:* 296
Owen, Clifford. *See* Hamilton, Charles Harold St. John, *13:* 77
Oxenbury, Helen 1938- , *3:* 151

Pace, Mildred Mastin 1907- , *29:* 159 (Brief Entry)
Packer, Vin. *See* Meaker, Marijane, *20:* 124
Page, Eileen. *See* Heal, Edith, *7:* 123
Page, Eleanor. *See* Coerr, Eleanor, *1:* 64
Pahz, (Anne) Cheryl Suzanne 1949- , *11:* 189
Pahz, James Alon 1943- , *11:* 190
Paice, Margaret 1920- , *10:* 111

Paine, Roberta M. 1925- , *13:* 174
Paisley, Tom. *See* Bethancourt, T. Ernesto, *11:* 27
Palazzo, Anthony D. 1905-1970, *3:* 152
Palazzo, Tony. *See* Palazzo, Anthony D., *3:* 152
Palder, Edward L. 1922- , *5:* 146
Pallas, Norvin 1918- , *23:* 160
Pallister, John C(lare) 1891-1980, *26:* 157 (Obituary)
Palmer, Bernard 1914- , *26:* 157
Palmer, C(yril) Everard 1930- , *14:* 153
Palmer, (Ruth) Candida 1926- , *11:* 191
Palmer, Heidi 1948- , *15:* 206
Palmer, Helen Marion. *See* Geisel, Helen, *26:* 83
Palmer, Juliette 1930- , *15:* 208
Panetta, George 1915-1969, *15:* 210
Pansy. *See* Alden, Isabella (Macdonald), *YABC 2:* 1
Panter, Carol 1936- , *9:* 150
Papashvily, George 1898-1978, *17:* 135
Papashvily, Helen (Waite) 1906- , *17:* 141
Pape, D(onna) L(ugg) 1930- , *2:* 198
Paradis, Adrian A(lexis) 1912- , *1:* 175
Paradis, Marjorie (Bartholomew) 1886(?)-1970, *17:* 143
Parish, Peggy 1927- , *17:* 144
Park, Bill. *See* Park, W(illiam) B(ryan), *22:* 188
Park, Ruth, *25:* 190
Park, W(illiam) B(ryan) 1936- , *22:* 188
Parker, Elinor 1906- , *3:* 155
Parker, Nancy Winslow 1930- , *10:* 113
Parker, Richard 1915- , *14:* 156
Parker, Robert. *See* Boyd, Waldo T., *18:* 35
Parkinson, Ethelyn M(inerva) 1906- , *11:* 192
Parks, Edd Winfield 1906-1968, *10:* 114
Parks, Gordon (Alexander Buchanan) 1912- , *8:* 145
Parley, Peter. *See* Goodrich, Samuel Griswold, *23:* 82
Parlin, John. *See* Graves, Charles Parlin, *4:* 94
Parnall, Peter 1936- , *16:* 220
Parr, Lucy 1924- , *10:* 115
Parrish, Anne 1888-1957, *27:* 157
Parrish, Mary. *See* Cousins, Margaret, *2:* 79

Pizer, Vernon 1918- , *21:* 116
Place, Marian T. 1910- , *3:* 160
Plaidy, Jean. *See* Hibbert, Eleanor, *2:* 134
Plaine, Alfred R. 1898(?)-1981, *29:* 162 (Obituary)
Platt, Kin 1911- , *21:* 117
Plimpton, George (Ames) 1927- , *10:* 121
Plomer, William (Charles Franklin) 1903-1973, *24:* 163
Plowman, Stephanie 1922- , *6:* 184
Pluckrose, Henry (Arthur) 1931- , *13:* 183
Plum, J. *See* Wodehouse, P(elham) G(renville), *22:* 241
Plumb, Charles P. 1900(?)-1982, *29:* 162 (Obituary)
Plummer, Margaret 1911- , *2:* 206
Podendorf, Illa E., *18:* 247
Poe, Edgar Allan 1809-1849, *23:* 167
Pohl, Frederik 1919- , *24:* 165
Pohlmann, Lillian (Grenfell) 1902- , *11:* 196
Pointon, Robert. *See* Rooke, Daphne (Marie), *12:* 178
Pola. *See* Watson, Pauline, *14:* 235
Polatnick, Florence T. 1923- , *5:* 149
Polder, Markus. *See* Krüss, James, *8:* 104
Polhamus, Jean Burt 1928- , *21:* 118
Politi, Leo 1908- , *1:* 177
Polking, Kirk 1925- , *5:* 149
Polland, Madeleine A. 1918- , *6:* 185
Pollock, Mary. *See* Blyton, Enid (Mary), *25:* 48
Pollowitz, Melinda (Kilborn) 1944- , *26:* 160
Polseno, Jo, *17:* 153
Pomerantz, Charlotte, *20:* 146
Pomeroy, Pete. *See* Roth, Arthur J(oseph), *28:* 177 (Brief Entry)
Pond, Alonzo W(illiam) 1894- , *5:* 150
Poole, Gray Johnson 1906- , *1:* 179
Poole, Josephine 1933- , *5:* 152
Poole, Lynn 1910-1969, *1:* 179
Portal, Colette 1936- , *6:* 186
Porter, Katherine Anne 1890-1980, *23:* 192 (Obituary)
Porter, Sheena 1935- , *24:* 166
Porter, William Sydney 1862-1910, *YABC 2:* 259
Posell, Elsa Z., *3:* 160
Posten, Margaret L(ois) 1915- , *10:* 123
Potter, (Helen) Beatrix 1866-1943, *YABC 1:* 205

Potter, Margaret (Newman) 1926- , *21:* 119
Potter, Marian 1915- , *9:* 153
Potter, Miriam Clark 1886-1965, *3:* 161
Pournelle, Jerry (Eugene) 1933- , *26:* 161
Powell, Richard Stillman. *See* Barbour, Ralph Henry, *16:* 27
Powers, Anne. *See* Schwartz, Anne Powers, *10:* 142
Powers, Margaret. *See* Heal, Edith, *7:* 123
Poynter, Margaret 1927- , *27:* 165
Prelutsky, Jack, *22:* 195
Preussler, Otfried 1923- , *24:* 167
Price, Christine 1928-1980, *3:* 162; *23:* 192 (Obituary)
Price, Garrett 1896-1979, *22:* 197 (Obituary)
Price, Jennifer. *See* Hoover, Helen (Drusilla Blackburn), *12:* 100
Price, Lucie Locke. *See* Locke, Lucie, *10:* 81
Price, Margaret (Evans) 1888-1973, *28:* 166 (Brief Entry)
Price, Olive 1903- , *8:* 157
Price, Susan 1955- , *25:* 206
Priestley, Lee (Shore) 1904- , *27:* 166
Prieto, Mariana B(eeching) 1912- , *8:* 160
Prince, Alison 1931- , *28:* 166
Prince, J(ack) H(arvey) 1908- , *17:* 155
Pringle, Laurence 1935- , *4:* 171
Proctor, Everitt. *See* Montgomery, Rutherford, *3:* 134
Professor Zingara. *See* Leeming, Joseph, *26:* 132
Provensen, Alice 1918- , *9:* 154
Provensen, Martin 1916- , *9:* 155
Pryor, Helen Brenton 1897-1972, *4:* 172
Pudney, John (Sleigh) 1909-1977, *24:* 168
Pugh, Ellen T. 1920- , *7:* 176
Pullein-Thompson, Christine 1930- , *3:* 164
Pullein-Thompson, Diana, *3:* 165
Pullein-Thompson, Josephine, *3:* 166
Purdy, Susan Gold 1939- , *8:* 161
Purscell, Phyllis 1934- , *7:* 177
Putnam, Arthur Lee. *See* Alger, Horatio, Jr., *16:* 3
Pyle, Howard 1853-1911, *16:* 224
Pyne, Mable Mandeville 1903-1969, *9:* 155

Quackenbush, Robert M. 1929- , *7:* 177
Quammen, David 1948- , *7:* 179

Quarles, Benjamin 1904- , *12:* 166
Queen, Ellery, Jr. *See* Holding, James, *3:* 85
Quennell, Marjorie (Courtney) 1884-1972, *29:* 162
Quick, Annabelle 1922- , *2:* 207
Quin-Harkin, Janet 1941- , *18:* 247
Quinn, Elisabeth 1881-1962, *22:* 197
Quinn, Vernon. *See* Quinn, Elisabeth, *22:* 197

Rabe, Berniece 1928- , *7:* 179
Rabe, Olive H(anson) 1887-1968, *13:* 183
Rabinowich, Ellen 1946- , *29:* 165
Rackham, Arthur 1867-1939, *15:* 213
Radford, Ruby L(orraine) 1891-1971, *6:* 186
Radlauer, David 1952- , *28:* 167
Radlauer, Edward 1921- , *15:* 227
Radlauer, Ruth (Shaw) 1926- , *15:* 229
Radley, Gail 1951- , *25:* 206
Raebeck, Lois 1921- , *5:* 153
Raftery, Gerald (Bransfield) 1905- , *11:* 197
Rahn, Joan Elma 1929- , *27:* 167
Raiff, Stan 1930- , *11:* 197
Ralston, Jan. *See* Dunlop, Agnes M. R., *3:* 62
Ramal, Walter. *See* de la Mare, Walter, *16:* 73
Ranadive, Gail 1944- , *10:* 123
Rand, Paul 1914- , *6:* 188
Randall, Florence Engel 1917- , *5:* 154
Randall, Janet. *See* Young, Janet Randall and Young, Robert W., *3:* 268-269
Randall, Robert. *See* Silverberg, Robert, *13:* 206
Randall, Ruth Painter 1892-1971, *3:* 167
Randolph, Lieutenant J. H. *See* Ellis, Edward S(ylvester), *YABC 1:* 116
Rands, William Brighty 1823-1882, *17:* 156
Ranney, Agnes V. 1916- , *6:* 189
Ransome, Arthur (Michell) 1884-1967, *22:* 198
Rapaport, Stella F(read), *10:* 126
Raphael, Elaine (Chionchio) 1933- , *23:* 192
Rappaport, Eva 1924- , *6:* 189
Raskin, Edith (Lefkowitz) 1908- , *9:* 156
Raskin, Ellen 1928- , *2:* 209

Author Index